CONTENTS

HUMAN ENVIRONMENTS
AND
NATURAL SYSTEMS

A CONFLICT OF DOMINION

Ned H. Greenwood
Dept. of Geography
California State University
San Diego, California

and J.M.B. Edwards
Professional
Science Writer

DUXBURY PRESS
North Scituate, Massachusetts
A Division of Wadsworth Publishing Company, Inc.
Belmont, California

TO OUR WIVES
ALVERTA and PAT

Duxbury Press
A Division of Wadsworth Publishing Company, Inc.

ISBN-087872-014-6
L. C. Cat. Card No. 72-075107
Printed in the United States of America

2 3 4 5 6 7 8 9 10—76 75 74 73

PREFACE

Now that the word "environment" has become one of the most over-worked in the language, another book on environmental studies may seem neither necessary nor desirable. And yet this book grew out of a certain dissatisfaction with the existing environmental literature. On the one hand, there is an abundance of studies dealing with this or that particular environmental problem; on the other, there is at least an adequate supply of symposia and books of readings. But the textbook user, whether instructor or student, is not nearly as well served.

In part, of course, this is because the environmental movement is so new. For years there had been excellent textbooks on conservation, ecology, and population studies. Their use, however, had generally been confined to students of forestry, soil conservation, environmental biology, or demography—and rarely, except in the field of conservation, did these categories overlap. In the public arena, advocates of population control and wilderness preservation had long pleaded their respective causes without attempting to find out what they might have in common. Still less had any systematic attempt been made to connect hunger and poverty in the Third World with highways and pollution at home.

The environmental movement changed all that. It may be as well to remember the context in which the change occurred. Historians will differ, no doubt, over the movement's precise origins, but if any one person or organization deserves the credit it is surely Barry Commoner and the St. Louis Committee for Nuclear Informa-tion (C.N.I.). Dr. Commoner and his associates spearheaded the public information campaign against radioactive fallout that led eventually to the Limited Nuclear Test Ban Treaty of 1963. Another crucial event in the movement's history was the publication, in 1962, of Rachel Carson's *Silent Spring,* which aimed at educating both expert and layman on the dangers of pesticides. The dangers, alas, are still with us, but there is at least the beginning of a consensus that they should be minimized.

Both Dr. Commoner and Miss Carson were trained in biology. Ten years ago, it was hard to be an environmentalist without such training: most of the relevant literature was available only in professional journals. In addition, the types of environmental issue that seemed most pressing were ones that fell unambiguously in the biologist's sphere. Today, however, thanks to the environmentalist tradition of appealing to the public, there is a large body of environmentally relevant literature that is more or less easily accessible to the nonspecialist. If this very heterogeneous literature has one thing in common it is the growing realization that, as Barry Commoner has written in *Science and Survival,* "the separation of the laws of nature among the different sciences is a human conceit; nature itself is an integrated whole." At the same time, environmentalists have moved from preoccupation with this or that current environmental issue to systematic formulation of the ways in which industrial man's entire relationship with his environment must be considered problematic.

In this book we have attempted to provide not a synthesis of the environmentalist literature (would anyone be equal to such a task?), but a framework in which representative samples of it can meaningfully be displayed. A textbook, in our opinion, is first and foremost a pedagogical device, not a work of reference; still less is it a learned treatise. Nor should it aim at being self-sufficient, especially in a field so new and so loosely defined as environmental studies. The instructor should therefore prescribe his own supplementary readings, and not count on us to tell his students all they should know about each topic raised. That is why, throughout this book, we have done our best to stress materials that are easily and cheaply available. No doubt we could have given the book a more esoteric and even forbidding appearance by citing more articles from professional journals. But this would have been irrelevant to our general purpose, which was to provide a readable, nontechnical introduction to the field of environmental studies as it has gradually emerged from the total body of environmentalist literature.

The book's plan, which was arrived at not without debate between the authors, reflects our conviction that the most expeditious way to approach the environmental predicament is through the concept of land use. It may be a truism to say that everything man is and does depends on the land, or that every human project and institution involves a decision to use some particular piece of land in one way rather than another. But it is the business of textbook writers to confirm that truisms are true. In part 1, then, we introduce the habitat before the inhabitants. Then, with the land/population ratio firmly established, we show in chapter 3 that land is not just surface but part of the ecosphere. In so doing, we define the basic concepts in the ecological vocabulary. Part 2 examines the problems of energy shortage, world hunger, and depletion of raw materials as aspects of men's failure to sustain basic ecological processes in a manner consistent with ultimate environmental limits. Part 3 is where we have chosen to consider what might be called the basic environmentalist case: the breakdown of natural recycling processes under the impact of man-made pollutants, including highly persistent chemical agents such as DDT. In part 4 we consider the "climax ecology" of the modern urban environment and some of the institutional pressures responsible for its malfunctions and lack of equilibrium. By way of contrast, part 5 reviews our uses of the nonurban environment, or what is left of it, and with the positive values for the human environment of leaving at least some natural systems to function as free from human impact as possible. Part 6 is programmatic and contro-versial; it deals with possible remedies for the environmental predicament, including population control and regulation of land use. The last chapter sets forth an environ-mental agenda for the United States that includes an all-out attack on pollution, drastically reduced levels of consumption, and eventual zero population growth, all within a worldwide framework of resource allocation and control.

We are so far from claiming any objectivity in these matters that we hope our biases (we would rather call them values) will be glaringly obvious. In fact, we invite disagreement, in the firm belief that a society reluctant to invite the spirit of controversy into its classrooms is not a society with very much of a future. However, the instructor who wants to give some topics a different emphasis than we have given them should find our outline sufficiently flexible. Inevitably, we have dwelt longest on the topics that concern us most. Since the senior author happens to be a geographer while the junior author has a degree in philosophy, and since both live in California (though one of us likes to describe himself as an ecological refugee from Manhattan), the reader can expect to feel that we have slighted some topics while dwelling on others at inordinate length. This is as it should be: in the final analysis, everyone has to construct his or her own environmental program.

Finally, we should explain our policy on citations, since it caused some comment among reviewers of preliminary drafts. We decided against footnotes or numbered references, partly because we want the statements in this text to be read and evaluated for their own sake, not for the sake of some imagined "authority" that a clutter of scholarly apparatus is popularly supposed to bring, and partly because we believe that every point made could have been documented at least ten times over, and we had no intention of turning the work into a bibliographical exercise. However, a list of works directly cited will be found at the end of each chapter; the interested reader is urged to read these works in their entirety, not just the passages that we have chosen to mention. Occasionally, a statistic will be found without any reference; in this case, it has been drawn from either the *Statistical Abstract of the United States* or the *U.N. Demographic Yearbook,* both of which should be among every environ-mentalist's principal working tools. It is easy enough to check such statistics against these sources, and that is what we urge the reader to do.

To thank each and every one of the friends, colleagues, and students who have helped us in so many ways would be an impossible task, but special mention should be made here of Georg Borgstrom, Reid A. Bryson, Stephen C. Jett, Jared E. Hazleton, H.L. Harvey, Michael Eliot Hurst, Albert J. Larson, Martin Litton, Richard Morrill, and David L. Sills. The combined patience and enthusiasm of our publisher,

Alexander A. Kugushev, went quite beyond what we had any right to expect. Betty Ritter's superb typing of numerous handwritten drafts and corrections was a major contribution to the entire project. To all these, and to the highly professional staff of the brand-new Duxbury Press, we are deeply grateful.

N.H.G.
J.M.B.E.

Free Enterprise System: The present laws in our free enterprise system permit unrestricted pollution. They also permit a total disregard for conservation of commonly used resources. Thus, as long as a resident in America can pay the bill, he can turn on all the faucets in his house and keep the water running until he decides to turn them off. The same is true of reproduction, if a person can find a willing and able partner. In other words, in America it is almost impossible to either stop pollution in its many nefarious forms, or to abate it significantly with present laws.

Paul Sarnoff in *The New York Times Encyclopedic Dictionary of the Environment* *

"Not enough land for sheep."

Only comment of Louis Tewanima, Hopi priest and member of U.S. 1912 Olympic team, on surveying New York City for the first time, from the top of the Empire State Building, 1954.

*Published by permission of Quadrangle/New York Times Book Co. Copyright, Quadrangle Books, Inc.

PART ONE

MAN AND ENVIRONMENT –

A CONFRONTATION

1 THE USE OF LAND

There are 196.9 million square miles of surface area on our globe. About 70 percent of this area is covered with water, leaving 57.3 million square miles or 36.6 billion acres, of land. In 1900 the amount of land per person was estimated at 24.4 acres. In 1970, when world population reached 3.6 billion, it was slightly over 10 acres per person. Comparison between these two ratios dramatizes the ominous growth of the human population, but is otherwise meaningless. We need a more detailed understanding of how land can be and is being used, and by how many people.

THE ECUMENE

Of the 36.6 billion acres of dry land, about 70 percent are not suited for human use. L. Dudley Stamp calculated that 20 percent are too cold, 20 percent too dry, 20 percent too steep, and 10 percent have no soil. The remaining 30 percent, nearly 11 billion acres, make up the **ecumene***, or inhabitable earth (Greek **oikoumene**, "inhabited"). By contrast, lands that do not produce food are known to geographers as **restrictive environments**. The most obvious examples are high mountain areas, which occupy perhaps 5 percent of the earth's surface, arid zones (nearly 20 percent), and

*Terms printed in boldface type are defined in the glossary.

3

4   *Man and Environment—A Confrontation*

polar wastes (another 20 percent). About 2 percent of the arid land can be cultivated, and a rather smaller proportion of the mountain land is suitable for pasture. There are also vast uncultivated tropical areas that hold more promise than the other restrictive environments. The bulk of our demands, however, must be filled by the present areas of high utilization.

The ecumene includes all arable land, but is not restricted to it. Some land economists define the ecumene as all the land people use or can use for any purpose. Thus it can increase through technology, extending to previously uninhabitable portions of the earth. Conversely, the existing stock of usable land can be diminished by abuse. Nevertheless, the concept of the ecumene is a useful one because it draws attention to the fact that the supply of land is finite. If the ecumene were divided equally among the people of the world, the average individual share would be about 3 acres. Imagine: only 3 acres of land to produce the food and fiber, provide shelter, transportation, recreation, education, and cultural amenities for one person's lifetime. In the United States, the average acreage used per person is actually over 7.7. In 1969, the average resident of this country consumed food and fiber equivalent to that produced on 1.6 acres of cropland, 2.7 acres of high quality pasture, and 1.5 acres of woodland pasture. Besides this, an average of 1.9 acres per resident was devoted to urban-industrial, transportation, residential, recreational, and military use. In some societies, however, the ecumene per person is as low as a single acre—for all uses.

The world's supply of arable land is considerably less than the total ecumene. Estimates of this supply have ranged from 4 to 18 billion acres; probably the best, prepared by the U.S. Department of Agriculture and the U.N. Food and Agriculture Organization, is 6 billion acres, a figure that includes 3.5 billion acres already in intensive use (figure 1.1). As with the ecumene, there is some leeway—but not much—for technology to extend the boundaries. This has been done at the experimental level by irrigation, **hydroponics**, and other artificial means. There is also a good possibility that improved technology may enable us to "farm the sea" a great deal more efficiently than hitherto.

Nevertheless, technology will not stave off land shortage forever. Let us assume, for example, that world population increases at a constant rate equal to the present 2 percent. By the year 2000, if technology has evolved no major improvements in efficiency of land use, the average ecumene per person will be only 1.8 acres. If population grows at the same rate but technology (according to the best available estimates) scores the greatest successes that can be hoped for it, then by 2000 the ecumene will still provide only 6 acres per person. This would require the effective use of every acre on earth, and the elimination of all natural ecosystems in favor of man-made ones. Needless to say, such an outcome is unlikely in the extreme.

Efficiency of Land Use

In earlier times, efficiency of land use was relatively unimportant. So-called slash and burn agriculture, as we shall see in chapter 6, was the method preferred

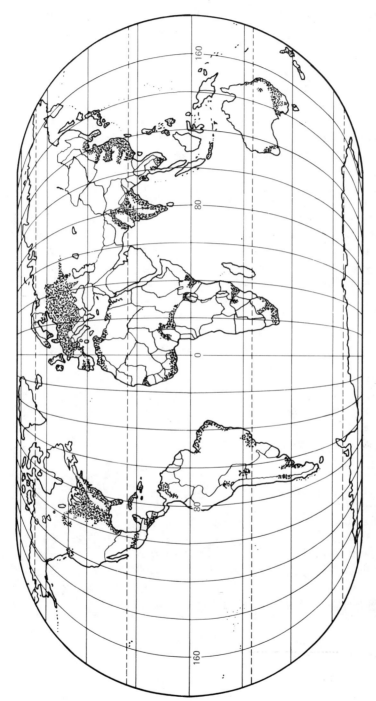

FIGURE 1.1.   The world's major areas of arable land, i.e., land of a productive quality sufficient to make row agriculture feasible. Some good land lies outside these areas, but there are compelling social and economic reasons why the basic supply depicted here is not likely to be much increased.

by peoples who could always move to another part of the forest. In the United States, the same mentality has shown itself, with considerably less excuse, under frontier conditions (figure 1.2). Land has been treated as expendable, and material commodities extracted from it by whatever means took the least labor and capital. Where populations are dense, however, the value of land often becomes greater than the worth of the commodities that can be taken from it.

      An ecologically sound resource management system conforms to the carrying capacity of the environment. In particular, two functions must be kept in balance: the provision of raw materials, and the reprocessing of wastes. Recycling wastes is as important as providing raw materials. Uneven distribution of population is a complicating factor. Nodes of dense concentration pose the most difficult problems of supply and reprocessing alike. And yet concentration of people can be a valuable conservation technique if managed skillfully enough. To return to our estimates of population density per acre of ecumene: if there are only 1.8 acres per person by the year 2000, the world population can expect, at best, only the basic elements for survival. The average experience of life would decrease in quality; at worst, the impact of such numbers of humans on the environment would be so injurious that the human population would decline and either stabilize at a low level or become mori-

FIGURE 1.2.   In 1868, when J.M. Ives made this lithograph, the Union Pacific – Central Pacific railroad was on the verge of completion and the possibilities seemed limitless. Although Hawaii was not annexed until thirty years later, Currier and Ives caught the nation's mood when they subtitled their picture: "Westward the course of Empire takes its way." (Library of Congress, Prints and Photographs Division)

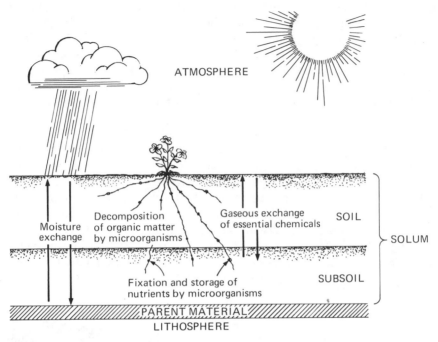

FIGURE 1.3.　Soil, an extension of the lithosphere, provides mineral nutrients and physical support for the growth of higher plants.

bund, exactly like a population of fruit flies multiplying in a limited environment. There are lands not presently in use because they have seemed virtually useless up until now; some of them look more tempting as world needs grow more desperate. If technological capabilities can grow faster than the population, such lands might be made to yield at least enough to afford a breathing space. Past experience, however, does not provide much justification for optimism.

Soil

We have been talking of land when in many instances we should have said soil (figure 1.3). Although soil is a renewable resource, the rate at which it is renewed is so slow that under present conditions we might as well treat it as nonrenewable. Produced first of all by the weathering of rocks and then by the organisms that live and die in it, soil is the vital intermediary between the earth's atmosphere (which it helped to create) and the mineral-laden rocks that form the **lithosphere,** that is, the earth's crust. The *topsoil,* often only a few inches and never more than a few feet thick, is the part of the *solum,* or true soil, in which plants take root and from which they gain most of their nourishment. Scientists have calculated that one inch of high-quality topsoil takes many hundreds of years to produce. Beneath the topsoil is the subsoil, conventionally defined as the soil below the normal depth of ploughing. Water is likely to collect here, as well as the sedimentary materials—mainly, organic wastes—that are worked on by microorganisms. The chemical recycling of these materials is described in chapter 3; here, it is enough to note that soil functions as a place of manufacture *and* storage for the chemical elements that make life possible. Beneath the solum lies the *parent rock* or *parent material* from which the soil was originally formed.

With proper care, soil can be used over and over again. But it is easily washed or blown away. This fact was well known to farmers in the ancient Middle East, who constructed cultivated terraces that have remained in use for thousands of years (figure 1.4). Such an attitude has not been transmitted to the United States. The Dust Bowl of the 1930s has been celebrated (if that is the right word) in song and story. Far less well known is the fact that the Great Plains continue to suffer major damage from wind erosion. In 1972 the Soil Conservation Service of the U.S. Department of Agriculture reported that over 2.2 million acres of Great Plains land had suffered damage from this source—admittedly a sharp decrease from the previous year's 4.8 million acres, but no particular cause for comfort. In addition, 3.3 million acres

FIGURE 1.4.   Rock-walled terraces protect this cultivated hillside in Lebanon from erosion after thousands of years of use. (Soil Conservation Service, U.S. Department of Agriculture)

were reported "in condition to blow," as compared with 2.8 million that had escaped damage because of emergency tillage. Among the factors contributing to wind erosion, the Soil Conservation Service drew special attention to the following:

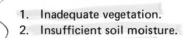

1.   Inadequate vegetation.
2.   Insufficient soil moisture.
3.   Poor tillage operations.
4.   Failure to perform emergency tillage.
5.   Overgrazing of crop residues.

The pattern of land damage in the Great Plains since 1934–35 is shown in figure 1.5.

Land and Population

The present uneven distribution of the world's population makes it even harder to use or develop resources efficiently. But spreading everybody out evenly would not help much. It is no accident that half the world's people are concentrated on 5 percent of its land surface. This 5 percent includes many of the world's richest river and coastal plains; on some of them, the population is as dense as 5,000 people per square mile. In other cases it is difficult to find a natural resource basis for such dense clusters of humanity; the concentration seems to be the result of sociological forces or historical accident even. But such cases are unusual. Normally, four factors combine to make a location desirable: low elevation, gentle topography, middle

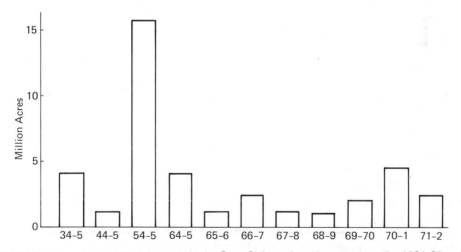

FIGURE 1.5.   Acres of land damaged in the Great Plains, selected seasons between 1934–35 and 1971–72. Although the number of counties reporting may vary from year to year, the index accurately reflects changes for the worse or better. (Soil Conservation Service, U.S. Department of Agriculture)

latitude or subtropical climate, and specific breaks in the natural landscape. Thus many people live below the altitude of 500 feet, and the majority below 1,500 feet. If society is to carry out its normal activities, especially agriculture, things could hardly be otherwise. It is true that man has shown great ingenuity in adapting himself to difficult terrain. But such terrain is not likely to encourage major population *growth.* The really dense population clusters tend to evolve around the natural "breaks" already mentioned—coastal harbors, lake heads, river terminals, and mountain passes.

Nodal settlement has obvious economic advantages, and some advantages for resource conservation as well. To benefit from the latter, however, requires more technical sophistication than is needed for a scattered population. Technology makes it possible for humans to live in close concentration, and to overcome bit by bit the obstacles to their activities. But social resistance to change also accumulates as civilization becomes more complex; economic affairs may continue to thrive, but pollution, congestion, and logistic problems may reach unmanageable proportions. In the United States, economic progress has reached this kind of blind alley in such massive conurbations as the so-called Megalopolis of the northeastern seaboard (p. 215). The dominant trend in land use, not only in the United States but in nearly all inhabited areas, is toward urbanization.

CHANGING LAND USE

Cultivated lands have comprised the bulk of the ecumene since the beginning of man's reliance on agriculture, perhaps about 10,000 years ago. The importance of the agricultural base is still obvious even in technologically advanced countries. In the United States, for example, all nonagricultural uses made of the land occupy less than 400 million acres, while 900 million acres regularly produce food and fiber. Forestry, which is essentially agricultural, accounts for another 500 to 590 million acres. There has been little change in the areal extent of U.S. agricultural land since 1920, although the price of land and the demand for it have risen steadily.

Land Hunger

The desire to own land, whether for its productive potential or for its own sake, is an old phenomenon. Frontier conditions intensify and encourage such an acquisitive attitude. When American colonists first penetrated the valleys of the Ohio, they regarded land as unlimited bounty. It appeared at the time that no demand could be too great for the new land to absorb, and that anyone could own as much land as he could use. In the newly emerging nations of the present, however, there is no comparable expanse of open land. In most cases, an already heavy population presses for more produce from an agricultural region that cannot be expanded. The typical experience of these countries is a chronic land shortage.

Land shortages also arise at a purely local level. Changes in the utility and availability of land occur, and land prices go up. Such changes may have more to do with current institutional arrangements (for instance, with how much of the land is privately owned) as with any absolute scarcity or pressure of population on resources. The situation is exploited for profit by real estate speculators, and the result is further exaggeration of demand and further inflation of prices. This applies today to the supply of open space around most American cities, as we shall see in chapter 13. If the tendency of our cities to expand outward into adjacent lands could be curbed, more open space would be available for aesthetic and recreational use at reasonable prices. This would make it a lot easier to put up with city life.

One method of protecting open space for rational development has been suggested by California Tomorrow, a private conservationist group. Briefly, what the group suggests is that land be taxed according to its optimum rather than its maximum use. In other words, they aim to take the profit out of exploiting a piece of land to its economic limit. Measures of this kind may well become necessary in our profit-oriented society.

Reform or Revolution?

Changing use of land in the United States brings the prospect of an absolute land shortage in the future, not just a relative or an artificially created one. Urban-industrial needs for space are expanding strongly. Even more significant, however, is the parallel growth of another type of space demand: the clamor for recreational lands. This is a consequence of our society's growing affluence. Our most scenic areas are being requisitioned for leisure-time use, along with any land that includes access to water, forests, or other features of quality recreation. Existing parks and resorts suffer from heavier use each year. There is no reason to expect a reversal or even a slowdown in this trend. This situation is discussed further in chapters 14 and 15.

Fortunately, landholding in the United States depends on economic rather than social factors. Accordingly, it is not necessary to institute a violent revolution in order to change land use practices; all that is necessary is for the government to supply the necessary economic incentives. In some less affluent countries, however, even though the need for changes in land use is far more pressing, especially where it concerns agricultural lands, social traditions stand in the way of efficient use. Peasant holdings are typically too scattered and tiny to be farmed with the efficiency needed to supply a rapidly growing population. In cases where it has been possible to reduce the number of parcels by one-fourth or one-half, production has increased 20 to 30 percent and production costs have been cut by as much as 15 percent. But if increases in productivity benefit only the richer peasants, the result is more social unrest than before. Equitable resource allocation is possible only when access to resources is controlled for the common good. Throughout much of the world, broadly based control of this kind does not exist and has never existed. Peasant land hunger has erupted in an estimated 1,622 revolts since medieval times, but few of them succeeded in correcting inequities or establishing adequate land reforms. Successful reform, as Clarence Senior has pointed out, must improve not only the land tenure system, but also related economic and political institutions. It must extend its benefits meaningfully to the masses or it will only serve to stimulate further decline in living standards and—eventually—further revolt.

The worldwide need for land reform has been analyzed in detail by Erich and Charlotte Jacoby, who point out the inadequacies of the purely technological approach to increasing food production. They argue that to consider all collective agriculture as unacceptably "revolutionary" and all individual farm ownership as compatible with "progress" on the Western model is to succumb to Cold War thinking of the most rigid and self-defeating type. Mere redistribution of land is of no use to peasants if everything else is allowed to go on as before.

> *It is a fallacy that the mere allocation of land to the peasants will alleviate rural misery as long as the powerful market forces that dominate economic life in the rural areas of underdeveloped countries are allowed to operate freely. Any redistribution of land or ownership rights which does not simultaneously check the market forces, cannot bring about any lasting improvement, since the latter will soon find ways and means to dictate the terms for the peasants' transactions and jeopardize their newly won position as owners. (Jacoby and Jacoby 1971, p. 81)*

For instance, as we shall see in chapter 5, the so-called Green Revolution is by no means an unmixed blessing (figure 1.6). Thus in India, where under 4 percent of the farmers held over 25 percent of the land in 1961 (table 1.1), introduction of the latest farming methods benefits mainly those who are already prosperous. The situation of the Philippine peasantry, despite numerous promises of land reform, is still worse.

INTENSIFICATION

At one time lack of technology limited human numbers. But now, although we have the technology to control human fertility, we seem to be applying our technological capacities to the opposite purpose. Advanced energy conversion—the basis of modern technology, as we shall see—is a tremendous stimulus to population growth. And this is only the beginning: this technology has so far touched most societies only superficially. The history of energy conversion is repeating itself worldwide in ever shorter cycles. Human cultural responses do not adapt to technical advances so swiftly.

Intensification of land use—essentially, greater exploitation of resources within the same territorial limits—is inevitable with the rapid increase of human numbers. If carefully planned, intensification can be mobilized to reduce the overall impact of humanity on the natural environment (figure 1.7). But if intensification of land use

FIGURE 1.6.   Training in progress at the International Rice Research Institute, Republic of the Philippines. Research at the Institute has been largely responsible for the high-yielding strains of rice that launched the Green Revolution. (Rockefeller Foundation)

continues unplanned, the opportunity to pit newer human knowledge against the consequences of earlier blundering will be lost. The concept of intensification is further discussed in chapter 3.

One of the principal forms taken by intensification is urbanization, the dominant cultural and economic response of the world's population to technological change. Over 70 percent of the U.S. population is urban, and there are attendant changes in economic patterns. As wealth becomes concentrated in the metropolitan

TABLE 1.1.   Agricultural holdings in India

Class of Farmer	Proportion of Operational Holdings (%)	Proportion of Area (%)
Poor farmers	81.81	38.83
Middle farmers	14.80	36.00
Well-off farmers	3.39	25.17

Source: Indian *National Sample Survey,* 1960–61, as reported in Erich H. Jacoby and Charlotte F. Jacoby, *Man and Land* (New York: Knops, 1971), p. 208 (by permission of the publisher).

FIGURE 1.7.   Rockefeller Center in midtown Manhattan, a virtual city-within-a-city covering 17 acres, is the classic example of intensification of urban land use. Designed for an earlier epoch, the Center now faces problems of adaptation. (Thomas Airviews)

areas, their future becomes a matter of overriding concern. Private wealth, however, is not necessarily a public benefit. City growth offers an excellent example of the need for planning as land use intensifies. Suburban development, especially in its U.S. form, is very wasteful of land and other resources; unplanned and uncontrolled, it is spreading. Eventually a kind of half-urban, half-rural environment may exist from coast to coast. The entire landscape would become an endless Los Angeles Basin; the sewage and transportation networks of the national community would become an incoherent tangle, riddled with conflict and breakdown; the taxation and zoning laws would be incomprehensible and unbearable; and the human values that attach people constructively to specific neighborhoods would be destroyed.

Modern cities at their best are struggling to provide economic and cultural amenities for their inhabitants as well as quiet, pleasant places to live. The bulk of all urbanized land is now occupied by residences, together with the extensive transportation networks needed for access to the city's economic functions. These two categories of land use usually occupy between 48 and 78 percent of city land. If more people were concentrated on each acre to create more compact cities, less space would be

FIGURE 1.8.   A country church in rural Nebraska, symbolizing a way of life that may soon vanish forever. (Nebraska Game Commission)

wasted on transportation functions and there would be less capital outlay for utility extension, as well as easier access to the integral functions.

The migration of people and wealth to urban areas has also caused much anxiety about the future of rural life in our society (figure 1.8). The shift of population from rural to urban has been too recent and too rapid for a full understanding of the situation to be achieved yet. Answers will have to be worked out carefully, with as many alternative choices as possible. Indeed, as we shall see in parts 4 and 5 of this book, flexibility becomes proportionately more important as the demands upon the land base grow heavier and more stringent. One thing is certain: we cannot afford to go on tolerating what Lewis Mumford has called the inner contradictions of the New World idea.

> *The most obvious contradiction is the fact that, in a finite world, expansion cannot continue indefinitely: there must come a moment when all the unknown lands have been explored, when all the arable soils have been put under cultivation, when even the largest city must cease to spread because it has coalesced with a dozen other large cities in a formless mass in which the very function of "city" has been lost. If every inhabitant on the planet owned a motor car, rapid movement, the rational reason for the motor car's use, would be almost as impossible in the open country as it is now in crowded urban areas. (Mumford 1962, p. 113)*

SYSTEMS OF LAND TENURE

Ownership of land, in most societies, involves complicated legal and social arrangements. It can be thought of as a bundle of legal rights that place the property owner under certain implicit social obligations. In societies with mainly economic concepts of land tenure, the obligations accompanying ownership are likely to be less comprehensive from a social point of view.

Land rights as we understand them in the United States have evolved gradually over the past four centuries. In the old feudal societies of Europe, the tenant had only the rights of tillage and **usufruct**; landlords retained legal possession. This arrangement caused innumerable revolts and was eventually replaced by **land franchise**. A system of widespread franchise was transplanted to the United States, and freedom to use the land at will increased until late in the nineteenth century. Then the owner's almost absolute control of land began to diminish under increasing population pressure, urbanization, and growing social consciousness.

The most common form of legal private controls is **fee simple**, which gives the owner the widest choice in the use and disposition of his land. *Less-than-fee-simple* forms of ownership are more restrictive; they can proscribe or control the use limit, define the use of the land in question, and even control the choice of purchaser if it is sold. One such form, *fee tail,* limits inheritance to particular heirs. These modified ownership patterns are coming into wider use as the pressure against private ownership grows. In urban and industrial areas, landholding is made less attractive by inflated land prices, high taxes, and strict zoning. The land is therefore held more for what it can realize than for any socially productive purpose. According to Marshall D. Harris, private land ownership enjoys at best a somewhat ambiguous status in this country because of the powers retained by government over the land. There are four sovereign or public controls limiting private authority: *escheat* allows public control of land in the absence of a competent heir, so that property rights cannot be carried to the grave; **eminent domain** gives government the right to condemn and acquire land, ostensibly for the public good; *police power* enables the authorities to insure the health, safety, and tenure of landholders and other members of society (this power gives rise to *zoning functions*); and *taxation,* perhaps the most important public power over land, creates a source of revenue and also acts as a use-control mechanism.

The growing costs, obligations, and limitations of owning land are leading to less individual ownership and more syndicated developments and condominium arrangements. Our land tenure system is moving away from traditional private ownership and toward increased public control. However, there is also a movement in the opposite direction: as the pressure of population on resources becomes greater, private business interests attempt more and more to gain control over public lands. At one time, as Ernest Swift has pointed out, U.S. public lands comprised over 1.8 *billion* acres; now they are down to some 40 percent of that amount. Public lands are owned in fee simple by the people of the United States, few of whom are aware of the fact. Private business interests, however, are only too well aware. An instructive case history is the Santa Barbara Channel oil spill of January, 1969, as recounted by former Secre-

tary of the Interior Walter J. Hickel. Offshore oil drilling licenses are granted by the Department of the Interior. And yet Secretary Hickel found that there was no clause in
the lease that permitted him to stop the drilling on the grounds that it was polluting
the environment. However, he was able to make use of a clause that gave him this authority if the oil was being wasted! It should be emphasized that this was almost a
year before the National Environmental Policy Act was signed into law by President
Nixon. Secretary Hickel was later to be sued under the provisions of the act by the
Wilderness Society, in an effort to prevent construction of the trans-Alaska oil pipeline (p. 81). National land use policy is further discussed in chapter 17.

OUR DWINDLING HABITAT

Despite technological advances that have made it possible to build major
cities, such as Murmansk on the Kola Peninsula, in areas previously considered inhospitable to man, the human habitat remains essentially the ecumene as defined earlier in
this chapter. A **habitat,** it should be emphasized, is not just an area where a species
happens to live; it is *the* area in which it is biologically suited to live. Most organisms, as
we shall see in chapter 3, are prevented from outgrowing their habitats by various natural checks and balances. The human species, for reasons that are not clearly understood
even today, is an exception. This tendency was first documented by the Reverend
Thomas Malthus (1766–1834), an English clergyman, who was able to make use of
American census figures, collected every ten years since 1790 (the British census did
not begin until the following decade). Despite the general perversity of Malthus' conclusions (he tended to view excess fertility as some sort of punishment visited by God
on the human race, especially the poor), he was quite correct in pointing out that
human population in his day was increasing faster than the capacity of the agricultural
base to support it.

> *If, setting out from a tolerably well-peopled country such as England,
> France, Italy, or Germany, we were to suppose that by great attention to
> agriculture, its produce could be permanently increased every twenty-five
> years by a quantity equal to that which it at present produces, it would be
> allowing a rate of increase decidedly beyond any probability of realiza-
> tion. . . . Yet this would be an arithmetical progression and would fall short,
> beyond all comparison, of the natural increase of population in a geomet-
> rical progression, according to which the inhabitants of any country in five
> hundred years, instead of increasing to twenty times, would increase to
> above a million times their present numbers. (Malthus 1960, p. 29)*

Today, we do as a matter of fact have the technology to feed the world's
growing population. But the melancholy truth is that, as we shall see in chapter 5,
this technology is not being effectively applied. Moreover, it is quite clear that world

population cannot be allowed to grow indefinitely without causing mass starvation and social chaos. Inhabitants of the United States have difficulty in grasping this because their country produces an enormous food surplus; indeed, the U.S. government pays farmers *not* to produce food, so that they will not depress prices. But it is already beyond the capacity of richer countries such as the United States to keep the poorer countries in food, even supposing the latter could pay for it. Meanwhile, the United States is becoming increasingly dependent on other countries, including some of the poorer ones, for minerals and other raw materials, which Americans are consuming at unprecedented rates (see chapter 6). If there is not a global land shortage now, there soon will be.

Over two decades ago, Aldo Leopold urged his fellow Americans to develop a new "land ethic" based on ecologically tested values. Such values are of course not primarily economic, but the irony of the present situation is that they may actually be the only means of insuring our economic survival. Coupled with the land ethic, however, we shall have to learn to respect what Erich Jacoby has called the Agrarian Creed—belief in the basic rights of those who work the land in countries that neither want nor need Western forms of development. Most of this book deals with conservation—or the lack of it—in the United States. We hope to make obvious, however, that the United States is at least as much of a conservation problem to the rest of the world as vice versa.

REFERENCES

California Tomorrow, *The California Tomorrow Plan,* revised edition (San Francisco: Cry California, 1972).

Harris, Marshall D., *Origin of the Land Tenure System in the United States* (Iowa State College Press, 1953).

Hickel, Walter J., *Who Owns America?* (New York: Paperback Library, 1972).

Jacoby, Erich H. and Charlotte F. Jacoby, *Man and Land: The Essential Revolution* (New York: Knopf, 1971).

Leopold, Aldo, *A Sand County Almanac,* enlarged edition (New York: Sierra Club and Ballantine, 1970).

Malthus, Thomas, "A Summary View of the Principle of Population," in Frank W. Notestein (ed.) *Three Essays on Population* (New York: Mentor, 1960). Reprint of an 1830 *Encyclopedia Britannica* article.

Mumford, Lewis, *The Transformations of Man* (New York: Collier, 1962).

Senior, Clarence, *Land Reform and Democracy* (University of Florida Press, 1958).

Stamp, L. Dudley, "World Land Utilization," *Land and Water,* winter 1959.

Swift, Ernest, "The Public's Land: Our Heritage and Opportunity," an illustrated pamphlet (Washington, D.C.: National Wildlife Federation, 1969).

U.S. Soil Conservation Service, "Wind Erosion Conditions—Great Plains" (Washington, D.C.: U.S. Department of Agriculture, 1972).

2 HUMAN POPULATION

Pressure of population on land is not new. At every stage of economic development, human societies have tended to increase their numbers to the limits of the territory available to them. But in the simple agrarian associations of earlier times imbalances between territory and population rarely lasted long. Population was limited by all the factors that Malthus called "misery"—famine, disease, war, and natural disasters. Today, however, these built-in environmental controls are being weakened by improved medicine and technology. Population growth has also been stimulated by other factors, many of them poorly understood. This chapter is an attempt to describe the world population problem and some of the standard approaches to it. A detailed discussion of population control will be found in chapter 16.

THE GROWTH OF POPULATION

Our knowledge of population trends before the sixteenth century is uncertain and spotty. Apparently population growth was very slow from prehistoric times until about three hundred years ago. It probably began to accelerate as early as the Neolithic period, but at nothing like the modern rate. About this time, plants were first cultivated and animals domesticated. The more plentiful and dependable food supply permitted further population increase, although it was still modest. Natural checks discouraged concentrations of people.

Figure 2.1 shows how populations continued their slow rate of expansion until increasing knowledge of the **environment** stimulated a wave of industrial and commercial activity. At first the acceleration came from declining mortality rather than from increased fertility. More people survived childhood to become parents, and people began to live longer. The hard conditions of life began to relax. One of the changes that contributed to easier, safer lives for Europeans was the opening of new continents as sources of food and other raw materials and as outlets for surplus population. The expansion of commerce, technological progress in agriculture and industry, and the accompanying revolution in housing, diet, and public health were all further encouragements to population growth.

By the middle of the nineteenth century, the Industrial Revolution had established both the incentive and the facilities for people to live in larger cities than ever before. After a while, urban birth rates began to drop. But even in the most advanced countries it was several generations before this drop began to compensate for the drop in death rates that had preceded it. The result was a permanent increase of vast proportions. The present world population, according to Edward S. Deevey, Jr., probably represents some 4 percent of all human births. Until very recently, over half of all babies born did not live to adulthood; women had to bear nearly as many children as was physically possible in their short lifetimes in order for the population to maintain itself or show a slight increase. The revolution in public health not only reduced infant mortality; it also extended the life expectancy and fertility span of mothers. The result has been the crisis that we face today.

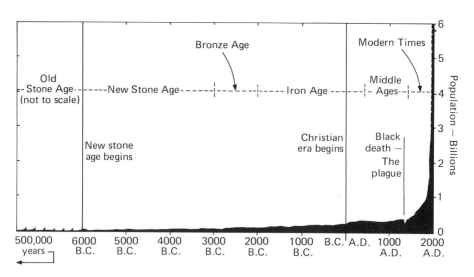

FIGURE 2.1.   The human population did not top 1 billion until modern times, but it seems likely to reach 6 billion by the year 2000. (*Population Bulletin,* February 1962; by permission of the publisher, Population Reference Bureau, Inc., Washington, D.C.)

The Population Explosion

Three major technological revolutions have influenced population growth: the *tool-using,* the *agricultural,* and the *scientific-industrial.* Each was followed by a surge in population growth that lasted several centuries. After each of the first two surges a long-lasting equilibrium was established. While these revolutions have not occurred at uniform intervals, there has been a surprising amount of uniformity in their effects. The scientific-industrial revolution, with which we are presently concerned, began in the middle of the seventeenth century, and is still going on. We can tell this because fairly precise world and continental population estimates are available from about 1650 onwards (table 2.1). From the beginning of the Christian era until 1650 world population growth was almost imperceptible—a matter of a few hundredths of a percent per year. It took the whole sixteen-and-one-half centuries for population to double. But the next doubling took only two centuries, and the next eighty years. The figures for 1970 indicate that it has doubled in the past fifty-five years. If projections hold it will double again in only thirty years.

The present phase of the population explosion, like much population growth since 1650, results from a birth rate that is declining far more slowly than the death rate. In medieval England, the average expectation of life at birth was 27 years. By 1700, it had crept up to 31 years—approximately the same level that had existed under the Roman Empire. Today, however, it is about 69 for males and 75 for females. Similar figures could be cited for the United States, Japan, and most of continental Europe. Elsewhere, the process has frequently been more rapid. It took the century from 1850 to 1950 to extend English longevity by 25 years, but the same thing was accomplished in India in a statistical generation. Medical advances achieved over three-and-one-half centuries of progress by the early industrial societies were handed on

TABLE 2.1. World population 1650–1970, by region (in millions)

Date	World	Asia	Europe and U.S.S.R.	Africa	Latin America	Anglo- America	Oceania
1650	545	327	103	100	12	1	2
1750	728	475	144	95	11	1	2
1800	906	597	192	90	19	6	2
1850	1,171	741	274	95	33	26	2
1900	1,608	915	423	120	63	81	6
1920	1,810	966	487	140	91	117	9
1930	2,013	1,072	532	155	109	135	10
1940	2,246	1,212	573	172	131	146	11
1950	2,495	1,376	576	200	163	167	13
1960	2,972	1,665	641	244	207	200	16
1965	3,295	1,830	676	311	246	214	18
1970	3,632	2,056	705	344	283	228	19

Source: Compiled from A.M. Carr-Saunders, *World Population: Past Growth and Present Trends* (Oxford: Clarendon Press, 1936), from issues of *U.N. Demographic Yearbook,* and from Population Reference Bureau data.

to the developing nations in a matter of years. In Ceylon, the death rate was cut 40 percent in a single year of intensive application of DDT and other antimalarial measures; deaths dropped from 22 to 12 per thousand in 7 years. A comparable drop took 70 years in England at an earlier time.

Another significant measure is the rate of infant mortality. For the United States in 1900 this stood at 16.2 percent. Fifty years later it had shrunk to 2.9 percent. Most of the developing nations had infant mortality rates close to 20 percent around mid-century, but these rates have declined rapidly in the last two decades. This has meant a great expansion of their population base. It is a dismaying paradox that the population explosion, with all its ugly prospects, is the direct result of mankind's proudest and most humane achievements. Figure 2.2 shows average declines in death rates for 21 countries over a 5-year period. Clearly, it is the birth rates that must now be altered before the situation can be controlled.

Theory of the Demographic Transition

Relying on the kinds of data just described, many social scientists (though not too many demographers in recent years) have gone on to conclude that the transition to a modern urban-industrial society is always accompanied first by a fall in death rates, and then (somewhat later) by a fall in birth rates and a general slowdown in population growth. This set of assumptions, in whatever form, is generally known as the *theory of the demographic transition* and occasionally as the *theory of the vital revolution.* Those who believe that it can be applied worldwide used to take comfort from the inference that worldwide industrialization and urbanization would in time reduce population growth in the less developed countries to more manageable levels—that, in other words, these countries were still in the first stage of the demographic transition. We say "used to" because the horrific consequences of worldwide industrialization, at least on the current Western model, are now becoming apparent (pp. 81, 169). Moreover, the theory itself does not look nearly as plausible now as it did thirty years ago. There was no reason then to believe that the pattern of decelerating population growth, which had taken hold in one (mainly Western) developed country after another, was anything but irreversible. But after the postwar "baby boom," which boosted the U.S. birth rate from a low of about 18 per 1,000 in 1933 to over 26 per 1,000 in 1947, it became clear that even the most advanced industrial societies could harbor forces making for rapid population growth, and that all future estimates would have to take volatile and unpredictable forces of this type into account.

As for the (mainly non-Western) less developed countries, the period since World War II has yielded no unambiguous evidence that they are in a state of demographic transition comparable to the Western one, just as there is little evidence that they will follow Western patterns of urbanization and industrialization.

Probably, despite the greater availability of population statistics through the United Nations, we are just too close to the events to project the long-term trend. Nevertheless, with a few notable exceptions such as Japan and Taiwan, the non-

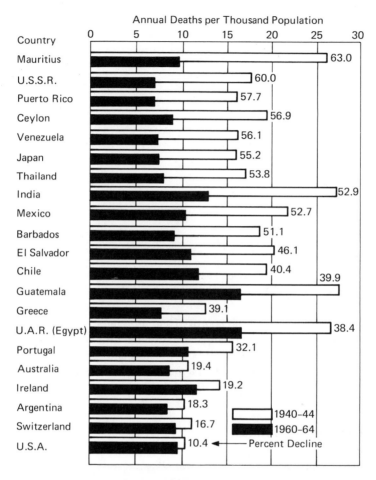

FIGURE 2.2.   Average death rates in 21 countries for the years 1940–44
and 1960–64. Ten of these countries show a decline of more than 50 percent. Decline is smaller in more industrialized countries, which achieved
their major public health advances before 1940. (*Population Bulletin,*
November 1968; by permission of the publisher, Population Reference Bureau,
Inc., Washington, D.C.)

Western countries, as we shall see, are not about to develop low-to-moderate birth rates.
This is not surprising. Most of these countries, as can be judged from the sample in
table 2.2 have only recently begun family-planning programs, and the beginning dates
have often preceded systematic and widespread action by many years. Japan, on the
other hand, has a tradition of birth control that goes back for centuries. This undoubtedly helped the Japanese to adopt the policies that we shall review in chapter 16. As for
Taiwan, according to Ronald Freedman surveys in the early 1960s showed that: (1)
most inhabitants of the island agreed that a moderate-sized family was desirable; (2) a

TABLE 2.2.   Year in which family-planning program was started:
selected developing countries

Country	Year Program Started
India	1951
Pakistan	1960
South Korea	1961
Taiwan	1964
Turkey	1965
Malaysia	1965
Ceylon	1965
Tunisia	1966
U.A.R.	1966
Morocco	1966
Singapore	1966

Source: Adapted from Oscar Harkavy, "Impact of Family-Planning Programs on the
Birth Rate," paper delivered at the Eighth International Conference of the International Planned Parenthood Federation, Santiago, Chile, April 9–15, 1967 (as
reprinted by the Ford Foundation, by permission).

"significant minority" of them both approved and used family planning; (3) most parents or prospective parents wanted sons (the traditional Chinese preference) and
favored social arrangements that made it both possible and desirable for sons to marry
relatively late. Of course, Taiwan was also a showcase for American foreign aid and a
target for investment by American industry.

Demographic Rates

The terms "birth rate," "death rate," and "rate of increase," as they are
popularly used, correspond to what demographers call *crude demographic rates,* or
rates per 1,000 of the general population per year. Thus a crude birth rate of 20 would
indicate that for each thousand members of the total population 20 births occurred.
Table 2.3 lists recent changes in crude demographic rates in selected countries.

Many demographic relationships, especially in the area of natality, are not
adequately reflected by crude rates. Moreover, no two populations are ever exactly
alike in their age structure or in any other demographically significant respect. Other
measures have therefore been devised. The most important are:

> *General fertility rate:*   this is the number of births for every one thou-
> sand women of childbearing age, usually set at either fifteen through
> forty-four or fifteen through forty-nine. The main disadvantage of this rate
> is that it takes no account of what proportion of these women are married.
> This in turn is likely to depend on the proportion of men in the population
> (which may be exceptionally low because of war or emigration) and their

TABLE 2.3.   Crude demographic rates (per 1,000 general population) for selected countries, 1935–70

Country	Demographic Rate	Average Annual Rate 1901–1910	Period					Highest Rate since 1930, and Year	Lowest Rate since 1930, and Year
			1935	1940	1948	1958	1970		
United States	Birth	31.5	16.9	17.9	24.2	24.3	19.4	25.7 (1947)	16.6 (1933)
	Death	15.5	10.9	10.7	9.9	9.5	9.6	11.6 (1936)	10.0 (1946)
	Increase	16.0	6.0	7.2	14.3	14.8	10.0	15.7 (1954)	5.1 (1936)
Mexico	Birth	—*	42.3	44.3	40.5	44.0	44.0	46.9 (1959)	35.6 (1943)
	Death	32.7	22.6	23.2	16.7	12.3	10.0	24.4 (1937)	10.3 (1964)
	Increase	—*	19.8	21.1	23.8	32.7	34.0	35.1 (1964)	13.2 (1943)
Japan	Birth	34.0	31.7	29.4	33.7	18.1	19.0	34.3 (1947)	16.9 (1961)
	Death	—*	16.8	16.4	11.9	7.5	7.0	29.2 (1945)	6.9 (1964)
	Increase	—*	14.9	13.0	21.8	10.6	11.0	20.6 (1949)	-6.0 (1945)
United Kingdom	Birth	27.2	15.2	14.6	18.1	16.9	17.1	20.7 (1947)	14.4 (1941)
	Death	15.4	12.0	14.4	10.9	11.7	11.9	14.4 (1940)	11.4 (1954)
	Increase	11.8	3.2	.2	7.2	5.2	5.0	17.6 (1947)	.2 (1940)

Source: *U.N Demographic Yearbook 1966*, and Population Reference Bureau, *1970 World Population Data Sheet*.
*Not available.

level of prosperity (which in most societies plays a large part in determining the age at which they marry). Moreover, since younger women in this age bracket tend to be more fertile than the older ones, the **general fertility rate** may obscure significant differences in the proportion of younger or older women. Fluctuations in the U.S. general fertility rates, with some of the factors associated with it, are shown in figure 2.3 for the period 1909–72.

Age-specific birth rates: this is the number of births for every one thousand women of a particular age or, more commonly, of a particular five-year age group, starting at ages fifteen through nineteen. The sum of each group's rates multiplied by five (because each woman spends five years in each age group) is known as the population's **total fertility**. Age-specific rates are essential for accurate comparison of birth rates in different populations, as well as for projection of future trends within populations.

Gross reproduction rate: this is a measure of a population's ability to

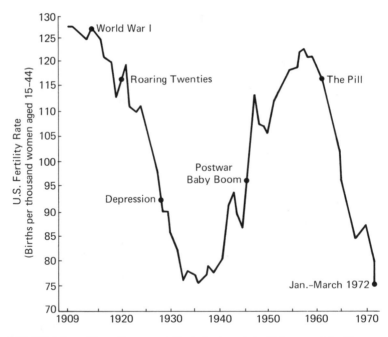

FIGURE 2.3.   The roller-coaster-like behavior of the U.S. general fertility rate since World War I well illustrates the unpredictability of birth rates in a society where children have become consumer goods. (National Center for Health Statistics; reprinted by permission from *The National Observer,* copyright Dow Jones & Company, Inc., 1972)

reproduce itself. It is obtained by projecting the number of females that will ever be born to all the women of childbearing age who are alive in a given year, provided that two assumptions hold good: (1) the age-specific birth rates for that year do not change; (2) none of the women die before they reach menopause. This sounds complicated, but a moment's reflection will show that the **gross reproduction rate** is only total fertility multiplied by whatever the percentage of female births happens to be (in the United States, according to a 1968 sample survey, it was 48.77).

Net reproduction rate: this, as its name implies, is an attempt at improving the gross reproduction rate. Unfortunately, it does so in only one respect: allowance is made, by means of a **life table**, for the women who die before reaching menopause. Thanks to the interest displayed in death rates by insurance companies, very accurate life tables are available for the United States and for most other developed countries, while U.N. demographers have worked out model **life tables** that can be applied to the less developed ones. No such tables, however, are available for age-specific birth rates, which in any case are inherently more unpredictable than death rates (just try taking out birth insurance!). Basically, what the net **net reproduction rate** tells us is whether a population's women are succeeding in replacing themselves. A monogamous society that does not produce at least one thousand girl babies for every one thousand women of childbearing age is obviously going to diminish if it keeps on that way. Comparison between gross and net reproduction rates is one measure of how many women of childbearing age are being lost to society before menopause. In 1968 the net reproduction rate for the United States was 1,166 and the gross reproduction rate 1,206. In the 1905–10 period the corresponding figures were respectively 1,336 and 1,793.

One of the problems that demographers have with fertility rates is lack of information, particularly with regard to age of mother in the less developed countries. Since, as we have seen, knowledge of age-specific birth rates is crucial in making projections of future population growth, some of the projections featured in today's newspaper headlines should be taken with a grain of salt. However, we can generally assume that a population with a large proportion of young women and girls is going to grow. Hasty conclusions, based on **crude rates**, as to the effectiveness of birth control programs often have to be revised after examination of age-specific rates, including rates of marriage. Oscar Harkavy relates the following example. Since 1951, the crude birth rate in Bombay, India has been about 30 percent below the estimated rate for the country as a whole. Does this mean that Bombay's family-planning programs, long a feature of the local scene, are succeeding? On the contrary: the general fertility rate for married women aged fifteen to forty-four in Bombay is 184.6, over 5 per cent *above* the national rate. The reason, according to Indian demographers, is that the population of Bombay includes an exceptionally high proportion of unmarried women aged fifteen to forty-four, as well as an exceptionally high proportion of men. Both circumstances seem due to economic factors: the extra men are immigrants who have left their families behind and come to the city in search of work. Analysis of the situation is further complicated, as so often in the less developed countries, by incomplete statistics—in this case, birth registrations, which are not one hundred percent reliable even when the birth takes place in a hospital. Indeed, there is reason to believe that the figures for registered births understate the actual number in the Greater Bombay area by over 20 percent. The United Nations has published a manual describing the methods demographers can use to overcome the limitations of faulty or incomplete data. Nevertheless, there are still a few populated areas of the world for which no reliable estimates of birth or death rates are available, even to the governments concerned, and a still greater number for which demographers have to make do with crude rates.

World Population Now and in the Future

All figures for world population must be considered approximate. In many countries, population censuses are difficult to undertake. In others, the figures reported cannot be considered reliable. Nevertheless, the overall picture is clear. In 1970 the population of the world stood at 3.63 billion. Projections based upon a 1.9 percent rate of increase (the 1960–69 average) indicate that at least 70 million hungry mouths are added to that total each year. Obviously, this cannot continue forever. But the maximum number of people the earth could support is a matter for speculation. Estimates range from 2.8 billion—which we have passed already— to over 157 billion. Wild as the latter figure sounds, our present rate of increase could take us to it in only 160 years. David L. Sills, director of the Population Council's demographic division, believes that a world population of between 12 and 15 billion is practically inevitable. The resulting food problems, he thinks, may eventually be solved—at the price of social changes so great that we in the developed countries can scarcely imagine them now.

When we think in terms of maximum population, we are overlooking what promises to be the gravest source of future misery. The world is not a single reservoir of goods and knowledge, available to everyone. There is no central granary, nor even any central exchange or regulator. What exists in reality is a large number of autonomous units, competing across social and political boundaries. While millions go hungry in one of these units, another one may actually be restricting food production in order to regulate its own internal economy. The question of whether it makes any sense to talk of an optimum, or ideal, population size is discussed in chapter 16. Meanwhile, it should be stressed that although there are international nutritional standards (p. 103), there is no such thing as an international standard of living.

Uneven population distribution further complicates the problems of rapid population growth. The bulk of world population is concentrated in middle-latitude lowland plains—two-thirds of the population on 7 percent of the land area. This represents in part an adjustment of population to natural resources that has evolved over thousands of years. The densest populations are in East and South Central Asia, Europe, and the northeastern United States. Asia, not counting the Soviet Union, is the most populous continent, with 55 percent of the total. If present growth rates continue, it will have 62 percent by the year 2000.

The most populous nation is China. We have little accurate knowledge of Chinese demographic trends, but everything indicates that China will stay in first place at least for a few decades. Estimates of the birth rate range from 21 to 37 per thousand (the U.N. estimate for 1965–70 was 33). Death rates may be from 15 (the U.N. estimate) to 21 per thousand. Net growth is probably 2 percent or higher, adding some 13 million to the population every year. These figures are consistent with other calculations that place the present Chinese population between 650 and 750 million. By the year 2000 it will reach 1.3 to 1.5 billion.

The subcontinent of India is expected to continue its rapid increase. The growth rate will probably be lower than that of most countries in Latin America or West Africa, but the increase in population density will be much higher. India's birth rate exceeds China's, as nearly as we can tell, by just enough to give them equal populations by the year 2000. However, India's land base is much smaller than China's. Table 2.4 shows that even if India succeeds in cutting its birth rate by half, it will have more than 900 million people by the end of the century. And it appears almost certain that this goal cannot be reached.

The other two countries with more than 200 million people, the Soviet Union and the United States, are much better off than China and India in terms of space, natural resources, and technological sophistication. Population pressure is therefore felt by both as a gradual undermining of the quality of life rather than as a lack of essentials. Demographic trends in the two countries show parallels, with growth increasing during economic prosperity and slowing in hard times. The surge and ebb in both cases seems to mirror the feelings of individual citizens about their chances in life.

TABLE 2.4. Population projections made in 1960 for India to the year 2000 (in millions)

| Year | Demographic Conditions | |
	Declining death rate, constant birth rate	Declining death rate, birth rate cut in half
1960	432.7	432.7
1970	542.7	541.0
1980	694.2	661.5
1990	914.2	782.9
2000	1,233.5	908.0

Source: U.S. Senate Subcommittee, Hearings on Foreign Aid Expenditures, *Population Crisis,* part 3, April 6, 1966, page 1008.

Note: The actual 1970 population for India was 555 million.

As Lincoln and Alice Day have argued, there is little evidence that the general good plays any considerable part in the ordinary American's thoughts about family size—a fact with important implications for birth control campaigns (p. 354).

Some Further Projections

The distinction between projection and prediction, an important one for science, is especially vital in the field of population statistics. A prediction, or forecast, is an assertion that such-and-such an event will occur. Some events occur with such regularity, or are governed by forces so completely understood, that it is worth making predictions about them. This is not true of human populations; we know all too little about the forces governing their growth and decline. Projections, on the other hand, assert nothing; they merely show what has to happen *if* certain assumptions hold good over a specified period.

Obviously, there is tremendous scope for error in projecting world population—the longer the projection period, the greater the scope. A small error in the presumed rate of annual increase can throw the projection off by many millions of people. Nevertheless, projections will continue to be made because they are all we have to go on in estimating the number of people for whom space must be available in the future. Table 2.5 is a 1958 summary and projection of populations and rates of increase. These average annual rates seem to be holding up fairly well, though there are some surprises. The 1963–69 average rates recorded by the United Nations were: world 1.9, Africa 2.5, North America 1.2, Latin America 2.9, Asia 2.1, Europe .8, U.S.S.R. 1.1, and Oceania 2.

Figure 2.4 shows a projection of 1970 population growth trends to the year 2000. The result is a doubling of world population, for a total of between 6 and 7 billion people. If the same rates were to continue for six hundred years, each person would have one square yard of the earth to stand on. People will not survive to reach any such concentration as that, of course. But the implication is plain: if human society does not act to control its own numbers, nature will see to it. Short of this point, perhaps man will learn to overcome some of the problems caused by crowding (essay 2.1, p. 34).

POPULATION AND WORLD RESOURCES

The first scientific publication on demography, *Natural and Political Observations Made Upon the Bills of Mortality,* was published in 1662. Its author was John Graunt (1620–74), an English businessman. Others before Graunt had attempted to compile accurate population figures, but he was the first to use such figures for the calculation of survivorship rates —the technique upon which the modern life insurance

TABLE 2.5. Population and population increase, by continent, 1900–2000 (estimates as of 1958)

Area	Population (Millions)					Ave. Annual Increase (%)*			
	1900	1925	1950	1975	2000	1900–1925	1925–1950	1950–1975	1975–2000
World	1,550	1,907	2,497	3,828	6,267	0.9	1.2	2.1	2.6
Africa	120	147	199	303	517	0.9	1.4	2.1	2.8
Northern America	81	126	168	240	312	2.2	1.3	1.7	1.2
Latin America	63	99	163	303	592	2.3	2.6	3.4	3.8
Asia	857	1,020	1,380	2,210	3,870	0.8	1.4	2.4	3.0
Europe (incl. U.S.S.R.)	423	505	574	751	947	0.8	0.6	1.2	1.0
Oceania	6	10	13	21	29	2.3	1.4	2.4	1.6

Source: United Nations, *The Future Growth of World Population* (New York: United Nations, 1958).
*Arithmetic mean of percentage of increase for 25-year periods.

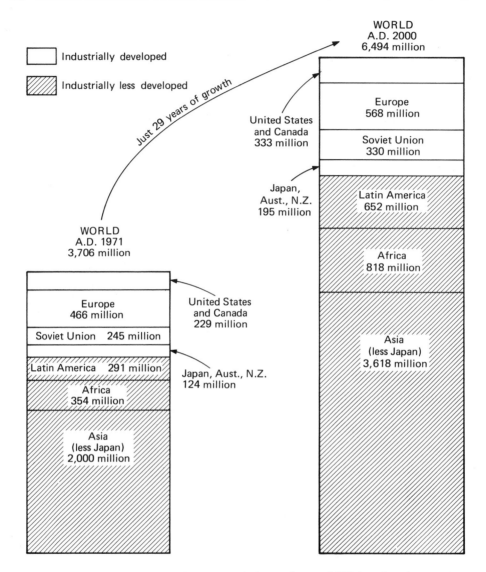

FIGURE 2.4.   Projected growth of world population to the year 2000, based on the "medium" estimate of the United Nations as of 1970. In twenty-nine years the population of the industrially less developed nations alone will be 1.4 billion more than the total world population in 1971. (data from United Nations and Population Reference Bureau)

business is founded. During the following century, population theory engaged some of the best minds. We have already given a brief outline of Thomas Malthus' famous thesis. Here, a few more details of it are worth considering. It is sometimes forgotten that Malthus expounded his views in two distinct works, sometimes called the First and

Second Essays, and that the latter went through numerous editions (our quotation on p. 17 is from one of them). The First Essay is the better known, possibly because it caused greater public controversy on its first appearance. In this work, as Warren S. Thompson and David T. Lewis have pointed out, Malthus laid greater stress than in the later work on the "arithmetical" rate of increase in food supply and general living standards compared with the "geometrical" rate of population growth. Malthus' critics have therefore made much of the fact that although a population, in the absence of limiting factors, undoubtedly grows at what we would nowadays call compound interest rates, there is no reason to believe that agricultural production *has* to grow at a rate that conforms to the arithmetical progression 1: 2: 3: 4: . . . etc. We shall have more to say of limiting factors in chapter 3 (Malthus called them "checks," and argued that man was the only species capable of limiting his numbers voluntarily). The main thing to note here is that although Malthus was familiar with contemporary advances in agriculture, and although he knew that much excellent agricultural land was still waiting to be opened up, he realized that sooner or later increased agricultural development would bring in only diminishing returns, while population would retain the same growth capacity for ever.

The best remedy for overpopulation that Malthus could devise was "proper government of the passions," that is, postponement of marriage and, under certain circumstances, total abstinence from sexual intercouse. Curiously, Malthus never mentioned contraceptive practices, although several were widely practiced in his day (if he knew of them, he probably considered them a form of vice). However, Malthus' name has come to be associated with the advocacy of family limitation by whatever means. This viewpoint is generally labeled neo-Malthusianism. It would not have been approved by Malthus himself, who saw moderate population growth as the natural reward of virtue.

The term "birth control" was first used in 1914, by Margaret Sanger (1883–1966), but birth control for the working classes was being advocated as early as the 1820s, notably by Francis Place (1771–1854). In 1839 the vulcanization of rubber was invented and it became possible to manufacture cheap, efficient contraceptive devices for the first time. Many legal obstacles were placed in the way of their sale. Neo-Malthusian groups had been formed from the 1870s onwards, but it was not until half a century later that the right to practice birth control was finally established. The main purpose of these early efforts was to save the poor from having more children than they could afford; of course, the cost of welfare was also a consideration.

In the 1930s Paul Sears heralded a new direction in neo-Malthusianism. The earlier interest in curbing the spread of poverty now shifted to the impact of whole populations on the environment. Since it was becoming obvious that natural resources were limited, the new goal was to manage and conserve them. In this perspective, population control became a fundamental responsibility. Sears himself was moderate in his approach, but authorities such as Marston Bates and Harrison Brown soon began to take a stronger line. This movement has probably culminated in the writings of Paul Ehrlich, a biologist who regards the present rate of population growth as "the most significant terrestrial event of the past million millenia" (*sic*). However, several of his major points were made two decades earlier by Fairfield Osborn:

> *Some people who are wedded to the magical idea of limitless technological development may say, "Give us time. The day may come when even nuclear energy, in some manner, can be employed as an agent to provide for the needs of innumerable people." Even if we care to envision such a fantasy becoming a reality, we still must ask ourselves," Is the purpose of our civilization really to see how much the earth and the human spirit can sustain?" The decision is still ours to make, assuming we recognize that the goal of humanitarianism is not the quantity but the quality of living. If we evade the choice, the inevitable looms ahead of us—even sterner forces will make the decisions for us. We cannot delay or evade. For now, as we look, we can see the limits of the earth. (Osborn 1953, p. 226)*

Essay 2.1   Human Space

In recent years space has come to be considered as much a natural resource as soil or metal. Human beings need space, not only for such obvious reasons as adequate food production, but for complex biological and psychological reasons which are not yet fully understood. Unfortunately researchers are just beginning to explore the implications of such experiments as ethologist John Calhoun began conducting in 1947 with populations of wild Norway rats. His research over more than 14 years provided some of the first consistent and reliable data on the natural balances between land area, population density, and healthy behavioral functioning. It was he who coined the term behavioral sink, *which he used to describe the gross distortions of behavior which occurred when population density reached certain excess limits. Since publication of his data, environmentalists and social scientists of all persuasions have worked at applying his conclusions to the human population —with mixed results. A great many basic questions still remain unanswered. How much space is required by a human being? By a group of ten humans? By a town of 5,000? By a city of 200,000? Are human spatial requirements innately or culturally determined? What are the effects of lack of space on human behavior? How does one define the word "crowding"? Out of the search to answer such questions have come the interesting observations of anthropologist Edward Hall, who explains in his book,* The Hidden Dimension, *that spatial perceptions and needs seem to vary considerably from culture to*

The Marxist view has always been strongly opposed to the Malthusian one. Marxists point with indignation to the passages in Malthus' writings that seem to accuse the poor of causing their own sufferings. It must be admitted that there is considerable logic in this type of objection. Malthus did not advocate changing the structure of society that existed in his day. Accordingly, if population growth had been limited along the lines he suggested, the main beneficiaries would have been those who were already prosperous. Another standard Marxist argument is that the real cause of the population problem is maldistribution of resources, which in turn results from their being controlled by the wrong people, namely, the bourgeoisie. This, of course, is to redefine the problem altogether. Finally, the very same Marxist theories of the relationship between the bourgeoisie and the proletariat are now being applied with increasing frequency to the relationship between the rich and poor countries. The disparities are certainly immense, as figure 2.5 shows. We will return to these issues in chapters 16–18. Meanwhile,

---

culture. As examples: Arabs in Northern European homes feel confined and oppressed by what they consider rooms of inadequate height and space; Japanese find sleeping in close proximity to others more congenial than sleeping alone or with one other person, as is the American custom; and while the French and Mediterranean cultures have evolved a crowded and interactional public cafe life, other cultures are marked by restrained and somewhat private public behavior. Halls studies have led him towards categories of personal space, which he has termed intimate, personal, social and public respectively. Each represents a somewhat specific set of distances (for example, "personal" space varies from about 1½ to 4 feet) and typical actions which are relatively consistent among members of a common ethnic group. He explains the friction and discomfort that sometimes occurs between strangers of different national or social origins as partially a problem of misunderstood attitudes regarding personal "territorial" limits.

Human beings, like all other animals, have certain spatial requirements. But we are not yet sure what these are. Countries with considerably greater population densities than the United States have not yet reached any clearly identifiable "behavioral sink". But where is the critical point? What will happen if present population growth levels are maintained and world population doubles in the next 30–40 years? There is cause for concern. (Developed from ideas in The Hidden Dimension, *by Edward T. Hall, and* Surviving to 3000, *by Roy Prosterman.)*

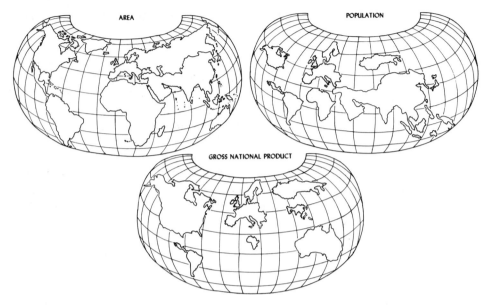

FIGURE 2.5.   The major regions of the world (U.S. and Canada, Latin America, Europe, Africa, Soviet Union, Asia less the Soviet Union, and Australia-New Zealand) are shown according to: land area (top left), population (top right), and per capita gross national product (bottom). It will be noted that the more populous areas are not necessarily the poorer ones, but the poverty of Africa and Asia is readily apparent.

it should be noted that Marxists are far more optimistic than Malthusians about man's ability to provide for himself.

Optimism, however, is no Marxist monopoly. Many people in the capitalist countries believe that technology will provide the key to unlimited economic growth because it is always uncovering new resources. Those who reason in this way do not necessarily advocate reckless squandering of resources. Rather, they tend to feel that hoarding means missing the chance of using a given resource at the opportune time. Thus in an article published in the June, 1952, *Atlantic Monthly,* Eugene Holman put it this way: "I think that under certain circumstances we can forget our fears and entertain the notion of inexhaustible resources." The article was subsequently distributed as a pamphlet by the Standard Oil Company, which is now expressing concern about the so-called energy crisis.

The viewpoint just described has been labeled *technologism.* Its opposite is sometimes called *ultimatism,* because of its preoccupation with the ultimate state of mankind. Ultimatists, or futurologists as they are often known, try to determine the maximum extent of the earth's resources and their capacity to support human life. In order to assess the possibilities of higher food production and greater population density, they borrow technologist theories. This leads them to consider such expedients as human living quarters under the sea or on the polar wastes, so that more of the fertile middle-latitude lands can be freed for food production. But these alternatives are not usually considered in an optimistic spirit. In this the ultimatist resembles the neo-Malthusian: he has a conception of the future, but he does not like it.

The last approach to be considered here is *preservationism.* There is little concern here with demography as such. Critics have said that there is no such thing as a preservation movement, only a collection of special interest groups. It is certainly true that the preservationist, or conservationist, approach tends to be rather piecemeal. Preservationists show up in public to lobby for this or that scenic wonder or endangered species of wildlife, and rarely pause in their agitation to give a systematic account of their philosophy. Their critics, who at one time or another have included most established interests, therefore find it easy enough to point out inconsistencies in their statements and behavior. However, because their objectives are specific and immediate, and because of their perseverance, preservationists have won many small battles. Such groups as the Audubon Society, the National Wildlife Federation, and the Sierra Club work continually to protect what they take to be the public interest. Their ultimate goal is to mobilize public opinion in support of legislation that will preserve environmental quality, and to create the public involvement needed to render such legislation effective.

The precise level at which national governments become involved in environmental protection varies a good deal by country, as does the importance attached by each government to the population problem. Until very recently, as we have seen, almost no countries had national population policies, and these were just as likely to encourage population growth as to discourage it. On the other hand, nearly all countries have policies in favor of increased trade and economic growth. This situation is a legacy from the eighteenth-century doctrine of mercantilism—a doctrine with roots in the great expansion of European trade and commerce that took place in the fifteenth century. The emergence of national population policies is discussed in chapter 16.

CONCLUSION

World population is doubling at shorter and shorter intervals. For some of the less developed countries, rapid population growth has already meant malnutrition or starvation for millions. One reason for this situation is that death rates are far easier to control than birth rates. But the poverty of these countries is due not only to their soaring birth rates, but to their having been exploited for so long by the richer and more technologically advanced countries. The same legacy of exploitation has so far prevented them from reaching the stage in the demographic transition at which they might begin to benefit from such economic growth as their narrow industrial base can provide (figure 2.6).

In sharp contrast, the richer countries have evolved more moderate rates of

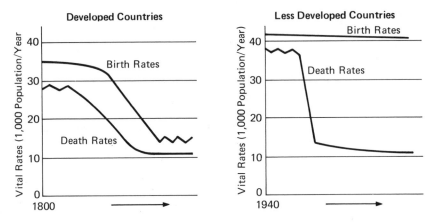

FIGURE 2.6.   The demographic transition: Will the less developed countries follow the developed ones? (adapted from data in congressional hearings on the population crisis, 1966)

increase. Starvation is not an immediate threat to them; it is possible, in fact, that they may be able to postpone it indefinitely by improved technology. What is alarming in these countries is the rate of consumption of resources per person. Since World War I, the United States is estimated to have consumed more mineral resources than the rest of the world in all human history. The United States, as we shall see in chapters 4 and 6, has half the world's industrial capacity and imports more than a third of the basic minerals needed to supply it. Such voracious consumption is a new phenomenon, and its implications are ugly. Resource scarcity (if we exclude scarcity of open space) is not yet a serious threat to the urban-industrial nations, but the by-products of their industrial and agricultural processes are destroying the quality of their environments. Economic growth based on rapid resource utilization means waste, planless development, accumulating scrap and refuse, and increasing **pollution.** The effects of population growth in consumer economies become visible in the scarred and poisoned environment. But even with zero population growth such economies would pollute the environment, since there is no end to what consumers may be persuaded to want.

The inevitable consequences of excessive numbers, or of excessive consumerism, are impairment of renewable resources and exhaustion of nonrenewable ones. The earth is finite, and the number of people it will support is limited. There is no simple formula for man-resource relationships; the concept of optimum population, discussed in chapter 16, is a highly debatable one. Nevertheless, there can be very little meaningful planning until human numbers are stabilized. Malthus was right: technology, however dynamic, cannot possibly keep pace with the inexorable laws of exponential growth. The main question, as Philip Hauser has said, is whether population growth is to be controlled by nature or by man.

REFERENCES

Day, Lincoln H., and Alice Taylor Day, *Too Many Americans* (Boston: Houghton Mifflin, 1964).

Deevey, Edward S., Jr., "The Human Population," in Paul Shepard and Daniel Mckinley (eds.), *The Subversive Science* (Boston: Houghton Mifflin, 1969).

Ehrlich, Paul R., and Anne H. Ehrlich, *Population, Resources, Environment* (San Francisco: Freeman, 1970).

Freedman, Ronald, "Changing Fertility in Taiwan," in Roy O. Greep (ed.), *Human Fertility and Population Problems* (Cambridge, Mass.: Schenkman, 1963).

Harkavy, Oscar, "Impact of Family-Planning Programs on the Birth Rate," paper delivered at the Eighth International Conference of the International Planned Parenthood Federation, Santiago, Chile, April 9–15, 1967. Available as a Ford Foundation Reprint.

Hauser, Philip M., "World Population: Retrospect and Prospect,"in Office of the Foreign Secretary, National Academy of Sciences, *Rapid Population Growth: Consequences and Policy Implications* (Johns Hopkins Press, 1971.).

Malthus, Thomas R., *An Essay on the Principle of Population as It Affects the Future Improvement of Society* (London: Johnson, 1798).

Osborn, Fairfield, *Limits of the Earth* (Boston: Little, Brown, 1953).

Sills, David L., personal communication, June 29,1972.

Thompson, Warren S., and David T. Lewis, *Population Problems,* fifth edition, (New York: McGraw-Hill, 1965).

United Nations, Department of Economic and Social Affairs, *Methods of Appraisal of Quality of Basic Data for Population Estimates,* Population Studies, no. 23 (New York, United Nations, 1955).

3 THE ECOLOGICAL BASIS

We have seen that although the human habitat, depending as it does upon the supply of agricultural land, is a very limited one, the human species continues to grow at an unprecedented rate. Why is this not true of any other species?

This question lies within the realm of **ecology,** the science that deals, in the words of Pierre Dansereau, with "the reaction of plants and animals to their immediate environment." Unfortunately, the word "ecology" has come to be associated, in recent years, with any and every kind of damage inflicted by human beings upon the natural environment. As a result, the scientific content of ecology proper has been neglected (often by those who would gain most support for their cause by studying it), while the impression has been fostered that a great deal more is known about human ecology than is actually the case. Most ecologists would probably agree that there is as yet no truly scientific human ecology, although there is plenty of unrelated information about the human impact upon natural systems. If such a judgment appears to set man up against the rest of nature, then it is very much in the ecological tradition to do so. According to the classic ecological viewpoint, man is always the intruder.

There are excellent scientific grounds for this viewpoint. In ecology the unit of study is the **ecosystem,** or community of organisms considered in relationship not only with each other but with their inorganic environment. An ecosystem can be as small as a tidal pool or as large as a desert; it all depends on the researcher's purpose, and on how complex a set of relationships he is equipped to study. Even in a drop of water relations between organisms can be very complex indeed. The same drop of water, however, does not remain a habitat for very long except under laboratory condi-

3. The Ecological Basis 41

tions. Although much ecological research is now done in laboratories, ecologists are still primarily concerned with what happens to organisms in their natural state. Accordingly, they prefer to study ecosystems that are relatively self-sustaining and in which the **abiotic,** or nonliving, elements _and their effects_ are relatively constant. Almost by definition, these are ecosystems that exclude man. Of course, there are still peoples, such as the Bushmen of the Kalahari Desert, who have adapted themselves so perfectly to local conditions that they are as much part of the ecosystem as the native plants and animals. However, man's adaptability is so great that he soon learns to modify and exploit the environment for his own benefit. Man the hunter is still a part of nature. But as soon as he turns to agriculture his entire way of life becomes ecologically disruptive.

THE ECOLOGY OF LIVING SYSTEMS

All life, as Stanley Cain has said, is associated with environment. Life, however, is more varied than climate, if by climate we mean simply an area's range of temperature, precipitation, and wind velocity. This fact makes it scientifically convenient to divide up the globe into major complexes of ecosystems known as _biomes, formations,_ or _biochores._ The primary division, of course, is between terrestrial and aquatic biomes, the latter being subdivided into fresh water and salt water. Since man has begun major disruption of salt-water systems only within the last century or so, we will say little of them here. Among the major terrestrial biomes are the tropical rain forest, the prairie, and the desert. Within such natural areas the ecologist can expect to find certain broad similarities between the organisms he studies, since all will at least have adapted themselves to local climatic conditions.

This type of generalization does not take one very far. A biome is commonly divided for purposes of study into **habitats,** as when a deciduous forest biome is studied for slight local variations in soil type, moisture, topography, and so on, in an effort to understand why the different species of trees and plants follow certain patterns of distribution. A habitat generally includes numerous _biotopes,_ or microhabitats, each with its characteristic distribution of organisms. Thus a rotting tree stump might be seen as a biotope in a habitat consisting of the thicket that surrounds it. But all this would amount to little more than a specalized form of map making unless the ecologist's spatial units (of which there are many more than the ones cited here) corresponded at each level to different forms of _biocoenosis._ This term, like many others in the ecological vocabulary, tends to mystify on first acquaintance because it is coined from the Greek _(bios_ means "life" and _koinosis,,_ as it was originally spelled, means "sharing"). As an equivalent term to biocoenosis ecologists sometimes use _association,_ but this is not nearly as expressive. In either case what they mean is that the different species found in an environment do not just coexist; rather, they interact in various predictable ways so as to form true _biotic communities._

Nineteenth-century sociologists and novelists were fond of drawing on biological works for parallels between human and animal or insect society. The results were nearly always misleading. It is true, as these writers pointed out, that nonhuman societies often have structures every bit as complex as human ones, and that even within the same species there is room for a great variety of roles. But human beings in themselves do not constitute a species indispensable to the survival of life on this planet. Moreover, very few human societies of any complexity are as wholly preoccupied as most nonhuman societies must be with the one overriding goal of all living things: survival. The means of survival is food, and the organisms in an ecosystem—any ecosystem, large or small—can be divided first of all into **autotrophs** ("self-nourishers"), which convert inorganic substances into food for themselves, and **heterotrophs** ("other-nourishers"), which in turn depend in some way upon the food so produced. Terrestrial autotrophs are for the most part plants and trees that convert water and carbon dioxide into sugar by making use of the sun's energy; in the sea, the same function is performed by algae, which are floating plants. This conversion process, **photosynthesis**, is described more fully below; without it life on earth could hardly exist.

The photosynthetic organisms, with certain types of bacteria that play a lesser ecological role, are generally classified as *primary producers,* or simply **producers**. What they produce, of course, is not energy but stored energy in the form of food. The heterotrophic organisms that depend on them are all either **consumers** or **decomposers** (figure 3.1). Man himself is a consumer sharing the same environment as other consumers. Although broad classification can be even more than usually misleading here (many animals, like man, enjoy a mixed diet), it is sometimes useful to distinguish *primary consumers* (herbivores) from *secondary consumers* (carnivores). A special category should also be reserved for the world's "big game," *tertiary consumers* that feed on primary and secondary consumers alike. Many ecologists would also place scavengers and parasites in this category. Finally, the decomposers—the fungi and bacteria that not only make the process of decay possible but in a very real sense *are* that process—break down dead organisms into chemicals that can then be reused by the producers. Thus there is no waste in nature. Paul Valéry (1871–1945), the great French poet, was expressing sober scientific truth when he wrote:

All things go under the earth and reenter the game.

(*Le Cimetière marin*)

Relations between producers and consumers—often called the **trophic structure** of an ecosystem—can be pictured in the form of a **food chain** (figure 3.2). This is a useful enough device provided one remembers that each organism shown in the chain represents a whole species, and that food chains in real life are not often as simple as they look in textbooks (including this one). One thing, however, the food chain concept does suggest very well, and that is the way in which each species occupies its own *ecological niche.* This is the total role played by the species in the ecosystem, not the area in which it can be found. As Eugene P. Odum has wittily said, if the habitat of a

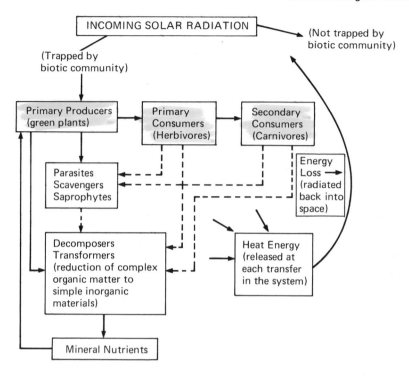

FIGURE 3.1.   The flow of energy in a biotic community. Consumers, parasites, scavengers, and **saprophytes** (plants that grow in decaying matter) are not essential to the system. But the greater the complexity of biological interaction the greater the stability of such a system.

species is its "address," then the **niche** it occupies is its "profession." In older ecological writings the term niche is quite often used as a synonym for biotope. For this reason, some authors prefer to distinguish place niche, or biotope, from functional niche, which refers to the usage just described. In this book, "niche" will be used only in the latter sense.

Niche, of course, is a concept that can also be applied to groups of species; thus all producers, as we have seen, might be said to occupy the same niche. But the level at which the concept becomes a really effective analytic tool is that of the individual species. At this level, the first question it causes us to ask is: How broad is the niche? For it is a major fact of environmental biology that species vary a great deal in their degree of specialization, and so in their adaptability. It is an axiom of experimental ecology that no two species ever have exactly the same niche requirements—that is (to quote Stanley Cain once more), exactly the same way of "making a living." They may have requirements so similar that one species, in the absence of the other, can function as its ecological equivalent. But if such equivalents are placed in the same biotope, sooner or later one will eliminate the other by competing more effectively for the available food supply. One species, one niche—such, it appears, is nature's law. However, the

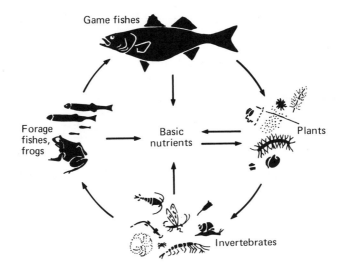

Game fishes

Forage fishes, frogs

Basic nutrients

Plants

Invertebrates

FIGURE 3.2.   Food chain (or web) of a single species of game fish such as the pike, a secondary consumer that cannot exist for long unless there is a plentiful supply of insects, plants, and dissolved nutrients to support the aquatic vertebrates on which it preys. Most game fish have a rather varied diet; salmon, for instance, feed on both crustaceans and small fish. (adapted from "Thermal Pollution and Aquatic Life," by John R. Clark. Copyright © 1969 by *Scientific American, Inc.* All rights reserved)

diversity of species is so great, especially in small organisms, that (if we may permit ourselves for once to use such old-fashioned language) it looks as if nature wants every niche filled. Odum cites the example of oribatid mites, 60 species of which were identified in samples of pine litter (fallen pine needles left to decay under a stand of pine trees) obtained from one part of east Tennessee. The mites all depended in some way on the same pine needles (only two species of pine were involved), but were far from occupying the same niche.

Despite the great diversity of species, only a comparatively small number are ever particularly common. In the mite example, 28 percent of the specimens provided 85 percent of the species, while the dominant species—the one with the most influence on conditions at that level—was represented by over 40 percent. The same effect can be found repeated in almost any habitat, although conditions inimical to life (extreme cold or heat, poor soil, etc.) cut down on the number of species, as does the reduction in the gene pool that results from isolation. It is not always obvious how the dominant species has gained its position, but greater niche specialization often has something to do with it. A moth whose larvae feed only on a particular tree is likely to multiply exceedingly where that tree is abundant. But if the tree succumbs to disease, or (which often comes to the same thing) is singled out by man as particularly useful or valuable, the moth may be unable to change its ways. On the other hand, less specialized species seem to pay for their adaptability by their smaller numbers. Perhaps, since they range more widely, they are exposed to more hazards; perhaps the extra time spent on searching for food tends to lengthen their reproductive cycle or reduce the number of their offspring. In any case, it is lucky for ecologists that dominant species at each **trophic level** are (usually) so easy to identify, since the outline of an entire ecosystem can rapidly be built with them as reference points. But the precise ecological function of the rarer species may well remain obscure even after years of research. In fact, it is not yet known why any taxocene, or array of related species like that of the oribatid mites, tends, in the absence of disturbance from outside the ecosystem or change in its climatic conditions, to remain so stable. This alone is a powerful argument in favor of preserving whole ecosystems, for it is the rarest species that succumb first to disturbance, and we cannot tell what secrets they take with them.

So far we have treated relations between species as if the only form they could take were competition. There are, of course, many other forms, both competitive and cooperative. Competition proper is actually quite hard to observe in a natural ecosystem since even closely related species, as we have seen, tend to adjust to each other's presence by developing more specialized niche requirements. Moreover, what appear at first sight to be the effects of competition can often be traced to slight local variations in terrain or climate. But species with similar requirements undoubtedly do compete for resources such as food and light; the difficulty, in stable ecosystems, is to prove that they have done so, since all that is usually visible is the *result* of competition (a partial exception is the type of ecosystem, such as the seashore, that varies sufficiently in its physical components, even within the same season, to favor now one species and now another). In the laboratory, however, two similar species can be introduced into the same biotope and left to "fight it out." One of them always wins, a fact usually referred to as the *competitive-exclusion principle,* or *Gause's principle,* after the Russian biologist G. F. Gause who verified it by observing two species of paramecium in the same culture. In natural ecosystems a winning species is more likely to be an *invader,* that is, a new species from outside the system. If an invader gains dominance it will of course change the ecosystem completely, giving rise to a form of **ecological succession** (for which see below).

Competition also occurs within species, as when males compete for territory in which to breed. But the competition may be highly functional, for instance by restricting the number of males allowed to breed and so keeping population within food limits. Also highly functional is the interspecific relationship of *predation,* already pictured in our food chain. Under laboratory conditions, as Gause showed, both prey and predator may easily become extinct. In natural ecosystems, however, this is rarely seen; rather, successful predation leads to a smaller population of predators, which then begins to grow again as the stock of prey is renewed. Some types of prey populations would outgrow their food bases if not preyed upon, as in the famous case of the Kaibab Plateau deer herd (p. 328). Others increase when human attempts to control their numbers have the same controlling effect on their predators. Many other factors, such as the relative adaptability of predator and prey, the length of time they have been associated, and the stability of their ecosystem, need to be taken into account. "The long-range trend of such prey-predator interaction," according to Edward J. Kormondy, "would be a system of built-in checks and balances between the two populations as well as between each of them and their myriad other relationships within the ecosystem they occupy."

A relationship not unlike predation is *parasitism,* a term aptly derived from the Greek for a professional diner-out. The parasite, of which the flea is a classic example, actually uses the body of its "host" as a habitat and source of nourishment. Fleas are very accomplished parasites and can often hop from one host species to another without too much difficulty. Other parasites, both plant and animal, are far more restricted in their activities. It is of course not in the interest of parasites to eliminate the host species, but many succeed in doing so because their reproductive rate is so high and they are efficient specialists. Parasites are often virtually impossible to eliminate from an ecosystem unless the host organisms are also eliminated. Nevertheless, they can be of use to man as agents of **biological control.**

It is only a short step from parasitism to *mutualism,* also known as *symbiosis.* This is the kind of intimate mutual relationship that benefits both species. It often pairs animals with plants, especially algae. For example, the zooxanthellae algae that inhabit the tissues of many marine animals both obtain nourishment thereby and have a kind of "supercharge" effect on the metabolism of the host bodies. Lichens are plants that actually consist of algae and fungi in symbiotic combination. Together they are able to survive conditions that would defeat either of them separately. Often distinguished from mutualism is *protocooperation,* a term denoting a relationship that is mutually beneficial but not essential to the survival of the organisms involved. Finally, *commensalism* denotes a relationship from which one species benefits without either benefiting or harming the host species. The term is an expressive one since it suggests people sitting at the same table (Latin *mensa*). This may almost literally occur when a smaller creature, for instance, lives off the unwanted food of a larger one.

Nature, then, is characterized by cooperation as well as competition. Whether one species predominates over the other is probably less important than the question of how natural ecosystems containing many varieties of species can remain stable for so long.

Limiting Factors

The ability of practically any species to reproduce itself without limit is perhaps the most striking of all biological facts. Most organisms seem to act on the assumption that only a minuscule proportion of their offspring will ever reach maturity. On the whole this assumption, if we may call it that, is correct. Without such a profusion of seeds, eggs, or nurslings the species would rapidly become extinct.

Anything that prevents a species from realizing its full reproductive potential is known in ecology as a **limiting factor.** Charles Darwin (1809–82) thought that there were four such factors: food supply, climate, disease, and predation. Contemporary ecologists, despite some differences of terminology, do not reject Darwin's list, but they are inclined to extend it. They have few quarrels, however, with Darwin's general contention that survival is a function of adaptability, and that in this way, as Paul Sears has said, "the pattern of environment is built solidly into that of life." What we have learned since Darwin's time is that the environment, with its inhabitants, is a system.

The study of limiting factors is often distinguished from the so-called ecology of populations, which in recent years has become the largely mathematical study of population growth rates and patterns in nonhuman species. The distinction is an artificial one, the product of historical circumstances. Nineteenth-century ecologists (few of whom would have called themselves that, since the term "ecology" was not in general use until the 1870s) achieved notable successes in relating population growth to such environmental factors as the presence or absence of nutrients in soil. One of these successes is still celebrated in the form of *Liebig's principle* (after Justus, Baron von Liebig, 1803–73), which states that a crop's growth is always limited by the essential nutrient available in least quantity. A resemblance will immediately be noted to the old proverb that a chain is only as strong as its weakest link. Liebig, one of the great pioneers of organic chemistry, helped prepare the way for the modern use of inorganic chemicals in agriculture. It is therefore highly ironic that his principle is now being applied to the study of such limiting factors as chemical pollution. Among the other ecological inputs that can usefully be regarded as limiting factors in this sense are temperature, light intensity, rainfall, salinity and oxygen content (of water), length of day, and fire (not necessarily a negative factor: see p. 127). Of course, whether or not any of these actually becomes a limiting factor will always depend on the ecosystem in question. Rainfall, for instance, is not as likely to become a limiting factor in the ecosystems of northern Oregon, which averages about 37 inches a year, as in those of central Arizona, which averages about 7 inches.

However, there is a large class of limiting factors that entirely escape classification as the weak link in an ecological chain. Rainfall, chemical composition of soil, and so on, are all physical factors that, it appears, a population can do little about. But it is clear from both laboratory and field observation that many populations respond to controls that are, in a sense, of their own making. The general name given to these controls—which, it should be emphasized, we regard as belonging to the general class of limiting factors—is that of *homeostatic mechanisms,* and the process by which they operate is called *homeostasis,* from the Greek for "steady state." The example of homeostasis usually cited in biology textbooks is the human body's remarkable ability to remain at the same temperature. Actually, the body is full of such mechanisms, from the maintenance of blood sugar levels to the workings of the digestive tract. What is more, they are all *feedback systems,* that is, they regulate themselves by "turning off the alarm" once they have adjusted to the new conditions. The obvious mechanical analogy is the thermostat, but the chemical and nervous "switches" of organic systems are far more intricate. It should be emphasized that the condition for which the alarm sounds is one that exists *outside* the system, and that would destroy or at least seriously harm it if ignored. The function of homeostasis is to preserve the system's integrity in the face of all the rival systems that make up its environment.

The remarkable fact about many biological populations is that their growth tends to level off *before* it is stopped by such physical limiting factors, including food supply, as we have just described. This phenomenon has been observed innumerable times (more easily in than outside the laboratory), but is still poorly understood. The key factor appears to be density: growth rates decrease as density increases. In mammals this can often be traced to the reaction of the endocrine system to crowding and greater intraspecific competition. We do not really have a very clear idea of what causes it in organisms of lower orders; all we know is that their numbers grow until, apparently, some sort of equilibrium with the environment is reached, and then (in the absence of disturbances or simplifications of the ecosystem) remain at about the same level. These facts alone suffice to identify the control mechanism, whatever it is, as homeostatic. Not all populations behave in this way, of course; one has only to think of annual plants and other species that have only a seasonal life. Some of these latter seem quite unaffected by density; they just keep right on increasing at a geometric rate until their food supply fails and their numbers plummet. Population ecologists like to identify this type by its J-shaped growth curve, as compared with the S-shaped curve of populations in their early stages of growth toward a plateau. There are also populations (oysters are a good example) that grow fastest at intermediate levels of density—a fact of which conservationists have to take note since it means that the stock may take years to replenish if allowed to fall below a certain level. However, each type of population tends to maintain the same *average* numbers regardless of growth pattern. Those with J-shaped growth curves fluctuate more widely than the others, but the fluctuations are regular ones.

Different species have different ways of regulating their own numbers. V. C. Wynne-Edwards, one of the world's leading experts on animal behavior, has virtually identified such control with the capacity for social organization. He has discovered that many species, particularly those that maintain territorial systems, have adopted one or both of two control methods: limiting the number of adults permitted to breed, and limiting the number of young that each breeding couple can produce. One can easily see how this might arise naturally in, for instance, a population of birds that always breeds on the same cliff, where the number of breeding sites is necessarily limited. Surplus individuals may also be driven away by dominant males and so succumb to predators or starvation. For example, the red grouse of the Scottish moors depend on the supply of heather, which fluctuates from year to year. When heather is scarce, the grouse economize on territory by placing their breeding sites closer together. Even so, there may be too many males of breeding age left over. These are driven away in the manner described. Such practices obviously affect the population's age and sex structures, which represent yet another set of limiting factors. Here, the same kinds of consideration apply as in the study of human populations: indeed, the inexorable mathematics of reproduction know nothing of the human race's supposed uniqueness. In summary, limiting factors are found everywhere in nature, and their operation, while neither uniform nor constant, is as essential to its workings as the fertility they hold in check. The total picture, or what we can see of it, is one of quasi-automatic checks and balances designed to create and preserve homeostasis. Edward J. Kormondy has described the situation well:

At a critical time in the life history of a given population, a physical factor such as light or a nutrient may be significant as a regulatory agent; at another time, parasitism, predation, or competition, or even some other physical factor may become the operative factor. As complex and as variable as the niche of any species is, it is unlikely that this regulation comes about by any single agency. However, there does appear to be considerable and mounting evidence, both empirical and theoretical, to suggest that populations are self-regulating through automatic feedback mechanisms. (Kormondy 1969, pp. 110–111)

What happens when the feedback mechanisms break down? John H. Storer relates one such case. Most pine and spruce forests in the western United States play host to the bark beetle, a **scolytid** that injures and eventually kills trees by feeding on their inner bark. Bark beetles are controlled by two major limiting factors: the sap of younger trees, which repels them, and several species of woodpeckers, which prey on them by drilling through the outer bark. Thus the forest continues to exist as habitat for both woodpecker and beetle. In one Colorado forest this balance was destroyed by a wind that toppled many of the trees but did not quite kill them. The bark beetles, infesting the underside of the fallen trees, were safe from the woodpeckers and undeterred by the sap, the flow of which had weakened. As a result, they multiplied to the point of being able to launch "wave attacks" against the younger, growing trees; the first waves were beaten off, but they damaged the sap flow enough to insure the success of later waves. The woodpeckers were unable to multiply fast enough to control the invaders.

In a few years the entire forest, covering many thousands of acres, was dead or dying. Four thousand million board feet of timber stood rotting where it died, most of it wasted; for in this rough mountain country it was not worth building roads to bring it out. There was no young, productive forest left to justify the cost of these roads.

The entire forest was doomed, and all the great dependent community of living things had lost its food and shelter. This community too must go, simply because one of its smallest members had escaped its natural controls and found too much prosperity. (Storer 1956, p. 66).

Ecological Succession

Pierre Dansereau, drawing on the earlier work of H. C. Cowles, has formulated an ecological "law of succession":

The same site will not be indefinitely held by the same plant community, because the physiographic agents (i.e., such factors as soil composition, contour of slope, etc.) and the plants themselves induce changes in the whole environment, and these allow other plants heretofore unable to

> *invade, but now more efficient, to displace the present occupants.*
> *(Dansereau 1966, p. 459)*

Ecological laws are tricky things to formulate; in the present state of our information they tend to be either too general or too specific. This one, however, could hardly be bettered as a succinct explanation of why ecological succession is such a universal feature of plant life and so also of life at higher levels.

The succession of which we are speaking is not just "one darned thing after another." Rather, it is a process of evolution toward as much ecological complexity as the environment will bear. Succession also means more of everything: as ecologists say, the total *biomass,* or quantity of living organisms in a given area, tends to increase. But let us begin at the beginning. An empty piece of ground (it would have to be *really* empty, like a new island forced up from the ocean floor by volcanic action) becomes a habitat for a few grasses and other plants. Insects fly there to live off the plants; birds, which brought the plant seeds in the first place, soon follow the insects. The resulting ecosystem is an example of *primary succession,* and the stage that it represents in the area's ecological development is called a **sere.** Most primary succession involves autotrophic organisms because it occurs in an environment that is mainly inorganic (*heterotrophic succession* refers to the invasion of organic matter by decomposers and related species). Succession continues from one seral stage to another until the last *successional community* gives way to a **climax community,** capable of reproducing itself and remaining more or less stable in the process. Ecologists also distinguish a type of arrested climax called a *subclimax;* it occurs when an ecological community is prevented from reaching its natural climax because of some recurring factor (often, the activity of man). A somewhat confusing term here is **secondary succession,** which means not everything that happens after primary succession but rather the kind of succession occurring in a habitat that has had its original vegetation removed (as by fire or cultivation) and is then allowed, as the saying is, to revert to its natural state. For instance, when a farm is abandoned (an increasingly frequent occurrence in the contemporary United States), it may become grassland in ten years, chaparral in twenty-five, pine forest within a century, and hardwood forest thereafter. But whether reached by primary or secondary succession, a forest is the climax community for that area.

Nobody knows why an ecological community retains its stability after reaching a climax. Current theory is inclined to credit the increased diversity of species with making this possible: the more complex the ecosystem, so the argument runs, the less likely it is to be thrown off balance by change in any one of its parts. One might add that with the increasing proliferation of niches there is quite literally less room for change, since each species, in order to coexist with all the other species, functions under a more elaborate set of limiting conditions. Of course, the notion of a climax should not be oversimplified. Any *climax area,* or biome consisting of numerous associated climax communities, will contain within its boundaries a substantial minority of communities still undergoing succession. Moreover, some species may actually be less diverse than they were at earlier seral stages; it is the ecosystem as a whole that has gained in complexity. It should also be noted that the increase in complexity does *not* make for corresponding increases in productivity; for instance, the extra leaves in a mature forest do not increase the forest's gross production of photosynthetic energy. Once again, limiting factors are brought into play.

Another important feature of **climax ecology** is the so-called *edge effect,* or ecology characteristic of so-called fringe communities. Such an area is called an *ecotone.* It is not a narrow boundary but rather a place where one community gives way gradually to the other; often, it can be divided into zones. A typical ecotone is a heavily wooded river bank. Elna Bakker has beautifully described a community of this type, set amid the grasslands of California's Central Valley:

> *Many animals use two or all three communities* (i.e., the river, the trees, and the grasslands), *though some confine most of their activities to just one. A kingfisher may choose a limb of a sycamore tree for a pecking site but will restrict the business of food getting to the river. A family of raccoons may hunt for crayfish in a slough, hide in a tree-trunk hole, and raid a farmer's orchard in one twenty-four-hour period. Aquatic insects, on the other hand, tend to remain in water or near it. . . . Tent caterpillars and box alder bugs, which parasitize certain species of riparian trees, pay little or no attention to the river. . . . Attracted by the rich riparian vegetation and its food resources, many other insects are common—butterflies, day-flying moths, wasps, and bees among them. Such a wealth of insect life in turn attracts their feeders. Aquatic insect species are sought by the native and introduced fish of these lowland rivers—carp, squawfish and other local minnows, bass, bullhead, bluegill, and perch. Even though dams prevent their free access to the higher interior streams, salmon, steelhead trout, and lampreys regularly use the Sacramento and San Joaquin riverways for spawning. (Bakker 1971, pp. 130–132)*

LIFE SUPPORT CYCLES

The biological study of ecosystems shows clearly how far more important the system is than the species: the species cannot exist without the system, but what appears to be good for the species may bring the system crashing down in ruins. The other major approach to ecosystems—it is often called *general ecology,* though there is no standard term—shows how they depend on abiotic sources of **energy.**

Virtually all terrestrial energy (about 99.9998 percent of it, according to LaMont C. Cole) comes from the sun. Energy is whatever enables a physical body or group of bodies to do work, that is, to *act upon* another body. There are so many varieties of energy that the full range of its ability to transform itself was not appreciated until the present century. The two with which we are most concerned here are *radiant energy* and *chemical energy.* What makes life on earth possible is the conversion of the sun's radiant energy into glucose and other forms of chemical energy that can be stored by autotrophs and used as "ready-made fuel" by heterotrophs. The distinction between producers and consumers, discussed above (p. 42), is therefore a distinction based on stages in the ecological **energy flow.**

The process that makes this energy flow possible is *photosynthesis,* truly the cornerstone of all ecological structures. The most immediately striking feature of photosynthesis is its productivity : one careful estimate sets the annual sugar production of the world's green plants at about 150 billion tons and their oxygen production (a byproduct of photosynthesis) at 400 billion tons. We say "green" advisedly; chlorophyll, the green pigment found in most plants, gains energy from absorbing light in the red and blue range of the spectrum. As it does so, it not only breaks down water into its compound molecules, thus releasing the oxygen that makes up about 20 percent of the earth's atmosphere, but creates adenosine triphosphate (*ATP*) a co-enzyme that replaces hydrogen with phosphate and simultaneously acts as an energy source. **ATP** enables the hydrogen and carbon dioxide molecules to form **PGA** (phosphoglyceric acid), which then goes on to form the highly stable substance that we know as sugar. Despite the rapidity of this process—experiments by Melvin Calvin at the University of California showed it happening within seconds—the proportion of available energy that it converts is quite small. Plants absorb only about 50 percent of available solar energy and (when allowance is made for the fact that the wavelength used in photosynthesis is shorter than the wavelength of visible light) succeed in capturing only between 2 and 6 percent of this for their own use (the figure is typically somewhere near the lower end of the range). However, the fact that (fortunately for the balance of life on earth) plants are not particularly efficient energy producers on a cosmic scale does not mean that they are unproductive on a terrestrial scale. The *net primary productivity* of most plants— that is, the proportion of what they produce in a given period that is not consumed in the same period for their own respiration and growth—ranges from 60 to 70 percent, though it can be as high as 85 percent in a meadow and as low as 33 percent in a salt marsh. These and other figures are cited by Kormondy, who describes in detail how ecologists study an area's *energy budget.* Another measure used in energy budgets is *gross primary productivity* or total autotrophic biomass including the amount lost in respiration or consumption by heterotrophs. This is usually expressed in terms of kilocalories (**kcal**), because the traditional method of estimating biomass—the so-called harvest method—is to gather, dry, and weigh samples of the vegetation in the area under study, and then convert the weight to approximate caloric content (one kilocalorie is the amount of heat needed to raise the temperature of one kilogram of water from $15°$ to $16°$ centigrade). Of course, allowance has to be made for the biomass lost before harvest. In this way, the gross primary productivity of the world's major biomes can be compared on a territorial basis (table 3.1).

It is important to emphasize at this point that energy cannot be recycled; despite the title of this section, the energy flow is all one-way. Accordingly, energy lost in the transfer from one trophic level to another is energy that is no longer available. We

TABLE 3.1.   Gross primary productivity of major world biomes
(daily kilocalories per square meter)

Biome	kcal/sq. m./day
Deserts	under 2
Deep oceans	under 4
Grasslands, deep lakes, mountain forests, marginal agriculture, continental shelf waters	2–12
Moist forest, secondary ecological communities, shallow lakes, moist grasslands, moist agriculture	12–40
Some estuaries, springs, coral reefs, communities on alluvial plains, intensive year-round agriculture	40–100

Source: Adapted by permission from Edward J. Kormondy, *Concepts of Ecology* (Englewood Cliffs, N.J., 1969), p. 21 (based on E. P. Odum, *Fundamentals of Ecology,* Philadelphia, 1959).

can burn a dead tree, but we cannot burn the energy that it used up while still alive. All this, of course, is in accordance with the Second Law of Thermodynamics (essay 3.1). But we are not concerned here so much with physical laws as with their translation into **biotic** terms. This brings us back to the concept of the food chain (p. 42). With each link in the chain, there is a decrease in *efficiency of energy transfer.* Food chains vary in their overall efficiency according to the number of trophic levels they contain. The same meadow that can support a host of plants and insects provides fodder for, perhaps, only one or two cows, which in turn may support one human baby during a short period of its development or, more likely, supplement the farmer's income through sale of their milk. If the farmer chooses to put the same area into wet-rice cultivation, with a few vegetables on the side, he may just succeed in supporting his family in a good year, though they will be hungry most of the time and become susceptible to diseases associated with protein deficiency.

These topics are discussed more fully below; here, it need be noted only that no food chain can be stretched indefinitely. Various attempts have been made to derive an efficiency-of-transfer formula from the existing studies. One that is often quoted, because it is easy to remember, is that only 10 percent of the net productivity of one trophic level can survive to the next level, or, in more specific terms 1,000 kcal of grass will get you only 100 kcal of beef. This particular formula is based on laboratory studies of ecosystems with algae as the primary producers; other types of ecosystems show both higher and lower orders of efficiency. However, the distribution of stored energy in *any* ecosystem, if diagrammed by trophic level, is shaped like a pyramid (figure 3.3). It is no accident that a diagram showing the number of species at each level will display the same shape. Smaller organisms are more efficient metabolizers than larger ones; that is, they convert more energy for their size. One curious result of this is that the gross weight of a population of producers may sometimes be less than that of the consumer population that has just "worked them over." In the long run, however, the shape of the system *has* to be pyramidal, just as it needs a continuous input of energy to keep it going.

Water

Consideration of the sun's radiant energy has enlarged our viewpoint to include not only terrestrial ecosystems but the entire **ecosphere,** or earth with its **life-support systems.** Water, a simple molecule consisting of two atoms of hydrogen and one of oxygen, has been described by LaMont C. Cole as "the single most important chemical substance in the physiology of the ecosphere." This, if anything, is an understatement. Three-quarters of the earth's surface is water; so is three-quarters of the human brain. Plants and animals alike have a water content that is rarely lower than 60 percent and often exceeds 90 percent. The Greek philosopher Thales (about 640–546 B.C.) is reputed to have said that all things are made of water. He was not far wrong.

Essay 3.1.   Energy and Chaos

Energy, or the ability to do work, is basically of two kinds: potential *and* kinetic. *Potential energy is energy that resides in a situation or condition, like that of a body of water pent up behind a dam. Kinetic energy is potential energy in motion, as when the water is channeled down pipes to turn generators. Thermodynamics was in the first instance the part of mechanics that deals with the conversion of heat into motion, and vice versa. Later, it gave rise to the separate field of chemical thermodynamics. It has been known since the early nineteenth century that heat and motion are only two of the numerous forms that energy can take. Accordingly, there are numerous ways in which it is possible to express the so-called First Law of Thermodynamics. Perhaps the simplest one, for present purposes, is to say that in any isolated or closed system, the sum of potential energy and kinetic energy is always the same. Energy, in other words, is never lost; it only changes from one form to another. Albert Einstein (1879–1955) proposed in 1906 that "every quantity of energy of any form whatever represents a mass which is equal to this energy divided by C^2, where C is the velocity of light." Thus the First Law can be characterized as the law of both conservation of energy and the conservation of matter. But although energy is never lost, it can become unavailable. For instance, the theoretical efficiency of a heat engine was expressed as follows by the French physicist Nicolas L.S. Carnot (1796–1832):*

It was the release of liquid water from the earth's crust by volcanic action that first made the earth habitable. Water vapor in the form of clouds shields the earth from excessive solar radiation (figure 3.4). The earliest forms of life, as far as we can tell, began in the sea.

Water circulates. Through *evaporation* it ascends into the atmosphere, from which it is returned by *precipitation.* Through *interception* (above ground) and *infiltration* (below ground) it is absorbed by plants and becomes part of their metabolism (p. 52). Through *percolation* and *storage* it becomes the *groundwater* that lodges in the **aquifer,** or water-bearing geological stratum. Through **runoff** it makes its way into streams and rivers, if there are any, or becomes a flood that carries all before it until it finds its natural level. Finally, through *transpiration* it is diffused into the atmosphere from the pores of living plants. The entire journey, from the earth to the atmosphere and back again, is known as the **hydrologic cycle** (figure 3.5). Perhaps the most surprising thing about this process—surprising, that is, unless one happens to live in one of the comparatively few places where average annual rainfall is over 80 inches—is how much of it happens every day. Here, too, the sun's role is crucial: most of this water is evapo-

$$\frac{\text{Heat Changed into Work}}{\text{Heat Supplied}} = \frac{(T_1 - T_2)\Delta S}{T_1 \Delta S} = 1 - \frac{T_2}{T_1}$$

Carnot argued that no real heat engine could ever come up to this level of efficiency. His reasoning, which was later seen to be an application of the Second Law of Thermodynamics, was based on the important concept of entropy. Much confusion surrounds this concept because of some of its modern applications. Its original application, however, was simply as a measure of the energy unavailable for work in a thermodynamic system. As the system loses heat, its entropy increases. Heat, as anyone can verify, passes spontaneously from objects to colder ones; if both remain in contact, both eventually reach the same temperature and the energy represented by the heat flow is no longer available. The Second Law is often stated as the tendency of a closed thermodynamic system to maximize its entropy, or (as many chemists prefer to say) reach a state of equilibrium. Entropy can also be interpreted as a measure of a system's randomness, or lack of conformity to any law other than that of chance. From a human point of view, a chance state of affairs would be chaos. Living organisms, no less than inanimate objects, are governed by the laws of thermodynamics; both we and the universe are systems that are continually running down. Kenneth Boulding, a contemporary American economist and philosopher, believes that man's increasing capacity for organization and communication can diminish entropy, and so counteract the universal drift toward chaos. Do you agree with him?

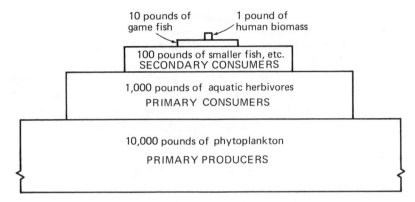

FIGURE 3.3.   Simplified biomass pyramid with man at the top feeding only on second-order carnivores. In this case, the sea must produce 10,000 pounds of organic matter through photosynthesis in order for a man to gain 1 pound in weight. Productivity ratios are (to say the least) schematic, but give some idea of the relative magnitudes involved. If figure were drawn to scale it would run off page.

FIGURE 3.4.   The earth is made habitable by the radiation of solar energy upon vast bodies of water, driving the hydrologic cycle. Water, mostly from the salty seas, is evaporated and purified by solar radiation. The moisture moves through the atmosphere as vapor and clouds, eventually precipitates downward to supply the earth's fresh water resources, and finally returns to the sea. The clouds and waterfall in this photograph of Yosemite Valley in California beautifully illustrate the atmospheric and fresh water phases of the hydrologic cycle. (National Park Service, U.S. Department of the Interior)

rated from the oceans by its action and then returned to them as precipitation. This is called the *short cycle,* in contrast with the *long cycle* by which water is returned to the oceans as drainage from rivers and streams. Some water, of course, evaporates or is transpired directly from the land into the atmosphere. An acre of corn can transpire 3,500 to 4,500 gallons a day, and many lakes lose more water over time from evaporation than they ever get back from runoff, precipitation, or the streams and rivers that feed them. Looking at figure 3.5, we may note another surprising fact: although the world supply of water is vast beyond imagining, the proportion of it that finds its way onto land is quite small—and the proportion of the latter that can be considered easily accessible to man is even smaller. Accordingly, the place of water in ecosystems dominated by man depends on the relationship of *available* water to the demands being made on it. Such demands can be extraordinarily heavy as, for instance, in the manufacture of aluminum, one ton of which requires over 350,000 gallons of water.

The amount of precipitation in a land area, together with its temperature, sets very precise limits on the type of natural ecosystem that can exist there. For instance, according to C.E.P. Brooks a peat bog requires at least 40 inches of rain a year and an average temperature above freezing point. Since air releases its moisture only when cooled, anything that forces air to rise is likely to induce precipitation. It follows that there is really not much we can do about the way in which rainfall is distributed, since it results from the location of hills and mountain chains, on the one hand, and the global circulation of air currents, on the other. An additional point is that what Brooks calls the *biological effectiveness* of precipitation depends on the distribution of

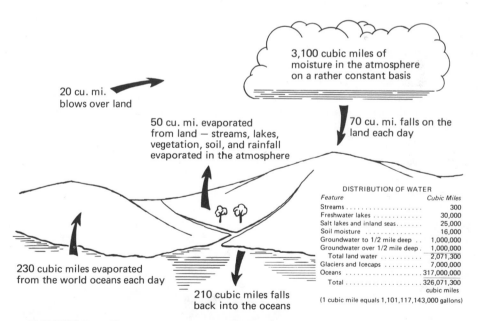

FIGURE 3.5.   The daily quantitative hydrologic cycle of the earth. Note how little of the earth's water supply finds its way onto the land—and how little of that amount is easily available to man.

soil types—some soils absorb more than others—and the presence of vegetation. The latter *is* within man's power to control; when he abdicates that power, as we shall see in later chapters, the consequences can be disastrous.

Chemical Cycles

Before there was life, the earth's atmosphere consisted of free hydrogen (H), water vapor (H_2O), ammonia (NH_3), and methane (CH_4). As can be seen from their chemical symbols, these gaseous substances can all be reduced to four elements: hydrogen, oxygen, nitrogen, and carbon. These, with phosphorus (P) and sulfur (S), are the basic chemical ingredients of life. **Protein,** the name given to a large class of complex molecules that form part of all protoplasm, is essentially an organic product of these six elements. Without the first four, living tissue could not grow or repair itself. Sulfur maintains the structure of the protein molecules, while phosphorus, though not actually part of protein, is the energizer that powers a great many cellular activities, including photosynthesis (ATP, it will be remembered, contains three molecules of phosphoric acid). Protein is made up of the twenty or so *amino acids* synthesized in the first instance by autotrophs, though some of them can be synthesized by heterotrophs as well. Because of their vital functions, the amino acids are often called the "building blocks of life." This is rather misleading: they are only the building blocks of protein! If anything deserves this title it is the purines and pyrimidines, nitrogen-containing bases that, with ribose (a type of **carbohydrate**) and phosphoric acid, make up the *nucleic acids*, so called because they are present in the nuclei of all living cells. Nucleic acids can be classified according to whether they contain two other carbohydrates, ribose or its near relative deoxyribose. In the former case they are known as ribonucleic acid (**RNA**), in the latter as deoxyribonucleic acid (**DNA**). It is the DNA molecule—the famous "double helix" described by James D. Watson and Francis H. C. Crick—that enables life to reproduce itself through the "genetic code" that controls protein synthesis. The main function of RNA appears to be to transmit the code.

Ecologists do not need to become biochemists or geneticists, but they are deeply interested in the ways in which inorganic materials become available to living organisms. Moreover, since the supplies of these materials are finite, they are interested in the ways in which they *remain* available. The outline of this cyclical process has already been given: producers absorb inorganic materials and transfer them in an organic form to consumers, which in turn transfer them to decomposers, which eventually break them down into a form in which they can be recycled. This sounds simple, and the type of diagram all too frequently encountered in textbooks can make it look simple. In fact, it is extraordinarily complicated. Chemical nutrients are not like water; they do not store themselves in convenient reservoirs nor are they recycled as readily.

Many ecologists distinguish two types of **chemical cycle,** according to the habits of the element in question. In *gaseous cycles* the most conspicuous phase of the cycle is when the element is in a gaseous state. Both nitrogen and carbon have gaseous cycles and both are present in the atmosphere, in the former case as N_2 (about 78 percent of pure air), in the latter as CO_2, or carbon dioxide (about .04 of one percent). But their cycles do not correspond in all respects. Atmospheric carbon is directly available to producers by means of photosynthesis and is constantly being returned to the atmosphere by respiration at *all* trophic levels, as well as by nonbiological processes such as combustion. Atmospheric nitrogen, on the other hand, can be biologically fixed only by a rather limited number of bacteria and algae, after which very little of it reenters the atmosphere. The "gaseous cycle" label is misleading in yet another respect: most carbon is stored in the sea, which appears to play a major part in regulating the amount of CO_2 in the atmosphere. The other type of cycle is generally labeled *sedimentary*, since the element in question is stored chiefly in the earth. Both sulfur and phosphorus have sedimentary cycles. Thus hydrogen sulfide (H_2S), released by decomposers from the tissue of dead plants and animals, may become trapped in the sedimentary layer where decomposition took place, or it may be oxidized to sulfate (the more biologically available form) by one of the species of bacteria that flourish under these conditions. Because of the loss from sedimentation, sedimentary cycles are often said to be less perfect (i.e., less efficient at recycling) than gaseous ones. However, a good deal of nitrogen is lost from the soil by *leaching,* or percolation in soluble form. This probably does not have much effect on the world's overall nitrogen budget (there are plenty of nitrogen-fixing algae in the sea) but, as any modern farmer knows, the ecosystem that suffers the loss may not recover for a long time.

Further details of the nitrogen cycle are shown in figure 3.6. The symbiotic nitrogen-fixing bacteria actually take up residence in the roots of certain plants; the nodules so created are depositories of inorganic nitrogen (NO_3). Not all nitrogen-fixing bacteria are symbiotic, but their activity still enriches the soil. Organic nitrogen compounds returned to the cycle as wastes or dead organisms are converted by certain species of bacteria into ammonia (NH_3). Other species convert ammonia into nitrate, a process known as *nitrification.* The same process occurs in aquatic ecosystems, though little is known about the microorganisms responsible. Finally, denitrifying bacteria and fungi convert nitrate into nitrite, ammonia, and even free nitrogen. The entire process is regulated by various feedback mechanisms, many as yet little understood, that adjust the supply of nitrate to the needs of plants at different seasons of the year.

Many other nutrients, from elements as common as magnesium and potassium to ones as rare as molybdenum and vanadium, have been found essential to the maintenance of ecosystems (the common ones are sometimes called *macronutrients* and the rare ones *micronutrients*). Their circulation, like so much in ecology, can be studied by means of **radioactive tracers.** But our general view of their relative importance is unlikely to change; protein, for instance, will remain about 18 percent nitrogen whatever may be discovered about the nutrient functions of tungsten or gallium. For present purposes, it may be of most use to view the major chemical cycles as yet another set of limiting factors. This should cause us to ask certain types of questions. The world may be in no danger of running out of free nitrogen. But what if some widely diffused man-made chemical, such as **DDT,** should wipe out appreciable quantities of nitrifying or nitrogen-fixing bacteria? What if the phosphorus cycle, the least perfect

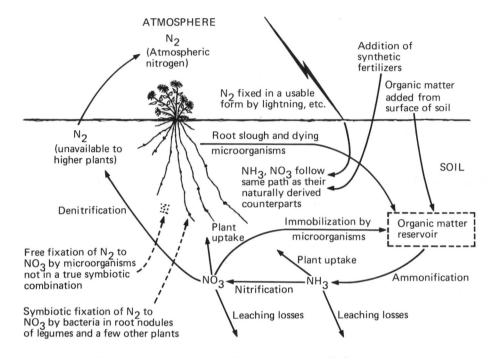

ATMOSPHERE

N$_2$
(Atmospheric
nitrogen)

N$_2$ fixed in a usable
form by lightning, etc.

Addition of
synthetic
fertilizers

Organic matter
added from
surface of soil

N$_2$
(unavailable to
higher plants)

Root slough and dying
microorganisms

NH$_3$, NO$_3$ follow
same path as their
naturally derived
counterparts

SOIL

Denitrification

Plant
uptake

Immobilization by
microorganisms

Organic matter
reservoir

Free fixation of N$_2$ to
NO$_3$ by microorganisms
not in a true symbiotic
combination

Plant uptake

NO$_3$

Nitrification

NH$_3$

Ammonification

Symbiotic fixation of N$_2$ to
NO$_3$ by bacteria in root nodules
of legumes and a few other plants

Leaching losses

Leaching losses

FIGURE 3.6.   The terrestrial nitrogen cycle. Molecular nitrogen (N$_2$) is usable only by a limited number of simple organisms; availability to higher plants is made possible by the intricate activities of *fixing* organisms which change the N$_2$ to NH$_3$ or NO$_3$ or by the *decomposers* which reduce complex organic matter to the same available forms. The whole cycle is regulated by complex but fairly well known feedback mechanisms.

of the major cycles, should break down because the loss of phosphorus, already considerable in natural ecosystems, becomes irreparable through agriculture? According to LaMont C. Cole, 10 percent of the phosphorus is removed from topsoil by a corn crop of 60 bushels an acre. Since the phosphorus cycle has no gaseous phase, it is not easily recovered when leached into the sea. Man puts phosphorus back into the soil as fast as he takes it out, but, as we shall see, world supplies of phosphate rock are already seriously depleted (p. 124). Here, as elsewhere, application of Liebig's principle should give us pause.

The Middle Kingdom

The ancient Chinese called their land the "middle kingdom" because of its ideal situation—midway between heaven and earth. Today, we know that this was a true metaphor of all terrestrial life. The *ecosphere*—the earth with all its support systems—can be said to extend as far as the sun. But the **biosphere,** or realm of life, is

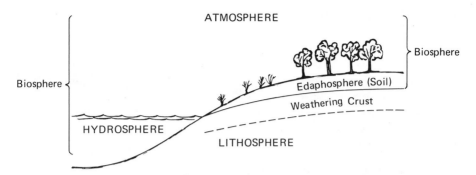

FIGURE 3.7.   The biosphere extends into the soil a few score feet, to the depth of root penetration and microbiological activity, but about 600 feet into the **hydrosphere** (ocean life is found below 6,000 feet, but we are concerned here with the area penetrated by solar energy). The troposphere, which extends about six miles up, is often considered the biosphere's atmospheric limit, but a more realistic one would be the upper flight zone of winged life.

narrower by far; indeed, as Stanley Cain has said, it exists only "at the interface of the lithosphere and the atmosphere" (figure 3.7). Life is a marginal phenomenon even on this greenest and most watery of planets. Meteorological and geological processes take no account of it. For hundreds of millions of years there was no life at all. Perhaps about 2.6 million years ago men appeared. The crocodile and the shrimp have been on earth one hundred times as long. The algae that were the first primary producers date from twice as long ago as that. In the memorable words of René Dubos, the earth became a home for man only after it had become a living organism.

Using the analogy of the biosphere, the paleontologist and geologist Pierre Teilhard de Chardin (1881–1955) has suggested that we also adopt the concept of the *noösphere* (from the Greek *nous*, "mind"), meaning the "sheet of humanized and socialized matter" that man has spread over the face of the earth. By this he meant not just dwellings or artifacts but the entire web of human culture and institutions ("socialized" here is a sociological term meaning "brought under social rules," that is, made part of society). According to Teilhard de Chardin, the most revolutonary change in the earth's makeup since its "greening" through photosynthesis has been the development on it of human consciousness. In particular, man is the first living species capable of planning, and the first to pass on his painfully acquired knowledge by means of education. Partly liberated from instinct and natural heredity, his evolution has been cultural rather than purely biological. Only man has the power of *reflexive consciousness,* that is, the power to become increasingly conscious of his own mental capabilities.

Teilhard de Chardin, a Roman Catholic priest of markedly unorthodox views, was convinced that human evolution is not aimless—that, in his own words, "we are really moving *somewhere* and *forever."* Directly, or indirectly, the rest of this book will be concerned with that "somewhere."

MAN THE INTRUDER

It is no part of this book's purpose to undertake a historical review of agriculture and technology. Suffice it to say with Carl Sauer that "wherever men live, they have operated to alter the aspect of the Earth, be it to their boon or bane." Nor will we attempt an outline of **human ecology**; as we have tried to emphasize, there is as yet no such science.* Three points, however, seem to us of cardinal importance in gaining an ecological perspective on the very diverse types of material we propose to review.

1. *Man is the only worldwide dominant.*   This is not a thought that occurs very often to many of us; man's ecological dominance was won so long ago that he generally takes it for granted. According to Sauer, one of man's greatest advantages is his digestion, which gives him an enormous dietary range—greater, in fact, than that of the proverbial goat. Another advantage (we can be sure it was slowly won) is the reflexive consciousness spoken by Teilhard de Chardin. Kinship may be yet another; the human child is helpless or near-helpless for longer than the young of any other species, a fact that must have served to reinforce the bonds of parenthood. The long immobilization of the mother is thought by many anthropologists to have provided both stimulus and opportunity for invention of the arts on which civilization depends: agriculture, homemaking, the domestication of animals. In these and other cases, man's superior power can be traced to his biology. However, as Paul Sears has eloquently argued, this power has yet to be matched by any corresponding ability to control its consequences. In this connection, it is instructive to read Karel Capek's entertaining ecological fable *War with the Newts* (1935), which pictures man's dominance as being threatened by a highly intelligent aquatic species. We had better believe that something like this might happen!

2. *Man too often disregards the fragility of natural ecosystems.*   We have already commented on how a break in one link of nature's chain may ruin an entire ecosystem. Unfortunately, many of the ecosystems disturbed by man have only low productivity, and therefore take a long time to recover—if they ever do. An example is the arctic tundra (figure 3.8). Often this is due to simple ignorance. Paul Sears has recounted an example: during fieldwork in Montana he and his class noticed that pasture land was being invaded by stands of sage brush that had first taken root in earth turned over by gophers. The gopher explosion, he discovered, was due to the wholesale poisoning of coyotes by ranchers, who wrongly believed that

---

*Sociological studies describing themselves as "human ecology"—notably, the works of Amos H. Hawley and Joseph A. Quinn—actually make little use of the physical and biological sciences, and would be more aptly called "ecological sociology."

FIGURE 3.8.   Erosion across tundra near the Canning River Area of
Alaska's North Slope. The deep scar in this vast plain was made by a
crawler tractor in the process of setting up a seismic exploration for
petroleum. In seismic surveying, small dynamite charges are exploded
from a series of shallow wells so that the reflection of shock waves
passing downward through the various layers of the earth can be picked
up by recording instruments at the surface. Slight environmental disruption usually results from such exploration, but nowhere is the impact
so great as in the fragile ecosystems of the arctic tundra. (Bureau of Land
Management, U.S. Department of the Interior)

the coyote was a menace to their livestock. As a result, the livestock had
less to eat. Ecosystems can also be upset by more indirect means. Thus a
key factor in the invasion of the American West by cheat grass, a weed
unsuitable for fodder in its mature form, was overgrazing. Aldo Leopold's
brief but classic description of this phenomenon is as good an introduction
as any to the science of conservation.

3. *Human ecological succession has entered its climax stage.*   The complexity and diversity of the world's great cities and of the urban civilization for which all mankind seems headed are so great that they constitute
a kind of ecological climax (figure 3.9). Similar climaxes, as we saw in
chapter 1, have been reached in many rural areas. This is not to say that no
increases are possible in the density of human settlement. But what Pierre

FIGURE 3.9.   A man-made ecosystem: midtown Manhattan, with the East River and part of Queens. Such urban agglomeration is certainly an ecological climax, but doubtfully one of equilibrium. (National Ocean Survey NOAA)

Dansereau has called the "scale of human interference" in the landscape has reached such proportions that one cannot imagine it passing on to a *qualitatively* greater stage.

Of course, man exploits natural ecosystems in all successional stages, including the early ones needed for growing crops. But the current rate at which he is withdrawing land from agricultural use proves that he has not yet achieved the mix of stages that would be needed for a stable environment. The task of climax systems, as we have seen, is to reproduce and maintain themselves (p. 50). Nature succeeds in this through homeostasis and the multiplication of niches. Man's homeostatic mechanisms have broken down, as a result of which he is able to maintain himself only by *intensification*. This important concept helps to explain much of what is happening today. In the United States, for instance, virtually all growth and development since 1900, as Frederick J. Smith has pointed out, has been by intensification, that is, by growth within a system that has already reached its territorial limits. The same territory that in 1900 supported 76 million people now supports 205 million. Smith distinguishes two phases of intensification. In the first, which lasted until about 1940, the environment was overexploited and there was a consequent loss of environmental capital through soil erosion and other biological catastrophes. Since 1940, an attempt has been made to use better environmental inputs including artificial fertilizers and erosion control (figure 3.10) as well as alternative sources of materials (usually through

FIGURE 3.10.   Gully erosion was a serious problem in this open-tilled vineyard in Kennewick, Washington until a small increase of complexity was introduced by planting the cover crop of alfalfa in open areas. Agricultural ecosystems often suffer from problems of deterioration similar to those of other man-made systems: soil erosion, like pollution, is the result of simplification. (Soil Conservation Service. U.S. Department of Agriculture)

new industrial technology). But the new inputs, as we shall see, have numerous unintended consequences, and the new technology often results in no more than "running faster to stay in place." More seriously, short-term gains may be long-term losses, as when irrigation of desert areas turns them into smog-ridden suburbs or when plastic substitutes for natural materials consume more energy in manufacture than they will ever save. The truth is that development through intensification is a losing game: in the long run, the quality of life can only deteriorate.

Human Environment and Natural Systems

The relationship of the human environment to natural ecosystems, and vice versa, has become so problematic that some authorities are beginning to talk of sealing them off from each other. Thus Frederick J. Smith, after pointing out that further expansion of the human environment will only bring diminishing per capita returns, argues that agriculture, at least, should be managed as a closed system. Among the possible "advantages" he cites are 100 percent kills of insect pests and avoidance of soil deterioration (a major problem with heavy use of chemical fertilizers) by doing away with soil altogether.

Such arguments only beg the question. Of course any problem can be con-trolled—for a while—in a completely controlled system. But all man-made systems tend to run down; we have not mastered nature's secret of self-renewal, and may never do so. Moreover, it would be folly to pretend that we can predict all the consequences of

FIGURE 3.11.   This Florida cornfield is typical of modern agribusiness. Such extreme mono-culture has a high potential for ecological imbalance, especially in the form of pest problems and attempts at chemical control. (Florida State News Bureau)

interfering with nature to the extent that would be necessary in order to produce an entirely closed agricultural system. To judge from the little we know, such a course would be ecologically unsound because it would cut down on the diversity of species. Diversity, as we have seen, is associated with stability; conversely, extreme mono-culture (figure 3.11) makes for instability. Working with nature is undoubtedly a far more complicated prospect than attempting to cut nature down to human size. But all our experience indicates that it is our only real chance of survival as a species.

On the other side of the equation, operating the human environment as an entirely closed system might well bring psychological costs that we could not bear. Already the mental health problem in our larger cities has far outgrown the society's ability to cope with it. Cities might become self-maintaining in a purely technological sense. But creating citizens to live in them may be beyond our power. Harmonious interpenetration of human environment and natural systems is one of the features by which we recognize a high point in man's cultural history. The following pages will show how far we have strayed from that ideal.

REFERENCES

Bakker, Elna, *An Island Called California: An Ecological Introduction to its Natural Communities* (University of California Press, 1971).

Brooks, C.E.P., *Climate Through the Ages,* second revised edition (New York: Dover, 1970).

Cain, Stanley A., "Biotope and Habitat," in F. Fraser Darling and John P. Milton (eds.), *Future Environments of North America* (Garden City: Natural History Press, 1966).

Cole, LaMont C., "The Ecosphere," *Scientific American,* April 1958.

Dansereau, Pierre, "Ecological Impact and Human Ecology," in F. Fraser Darling and John P. Milton (eds.), *Future Environments of North America* (Garden City: Natural History Press, 1966).

Dubos, René, *A God Within* (New York: Scribners, 1972).

Gause, F. G., *The Struggle for Existence* (Baltimore: Williams and Wilkins, 1934).

Kormondy, Edward J., *Concepts of Ecology* (Englewood Cliffs: Prentice-Hall, 1969).

Leopold, Aldo, "Cheat Takes Over," in *A Sand County Almanac,* enlarged edition (New York: Sierra Club and Ballantine, 1970), pp. 164–168.

Odum, Eugene P., *Ecology* (New York: Holt, 1963).

Sauer, Carl O., "The Agency of Man on the Earth," in William L. Thomas, Jr. (ed.), *Man's Role in Changing the Face of the Earth,* vol. I (University of Chicago Press, 1956).

Sears, Paul B., "The Inexorable Problem of Space," in Paul Shepard and Daniel McKinley (eds.), *The Subversive Science: Essays Toward an Ecology of Man* (Boston: Houghton Mifflin, 1969).

———, "Ecology, the Intricate Web of Life," in *As We Live and Breathe: The Challenge of Our Environment* (Washington, D.C.: National Geographic Society, 1971).

Smith, Frederick J., "Ecological Perspectives," in Ronald G. Ridker (ed.), *Research Reports of the Commission on Population Growth and the American Future: Vol. III, Population, Resources, and the Environment* (Washington, D.C.: U.S. Government Printing Office, 1972).

Storer, John H., *The Web of Life: A First Book of Ecology* (New York: Signet, 1956).

Teilhard de Chardin, Pierre, "The Antiquity and World Expansion of Human Culture," in William L. Thomas, Jr. (ed.), *Man's Role in Changing the Face of the Earth,* vol. I (University of Chicago Press, 1956).

Watson, J.D., and F.H.C. Crick, "Molecular Structure of Nucleic Acids: A Structure for Deoxyribose Nucleic Acid," *Nature,* vol. 171, 1953.

Wynne-Edwards, V. C., "Self-Regulating Systems in Populations of Animals," in Paul Shepard and Daniel McKinley (eds.), *The Subversive Science: Essays Toward an Ecology of Man* (Boston: Houghton Mifflin, 1969).

PART TWO

SUSTAINING THE BASIC PROCESSES

4 ENERGY

The human species survived its earliest days because it consistently succeeded in competition with other organisms for a share of the available energy supply—
food. When men first learned to use fire they achieved modest control of the sun's
energy: they could produce heat and light when they needed it from the storehouse of
plant tissue. In the last few thousand years human society has benefited from continuously increasing stocks of energy and ever more sophisticated knowledge of how to use
them. The industrial technologies based upon fossil fuels began to develop 800 years
ago, and the use of these fuels has increased at an average rate of 4 percent per year
ever since. During the same period human population has increased at an average rate
of 2 percent per year: as the controllable supply of energy was expanded, larger pop-
lations could live on land bases that could not have supported them without it.

The economic well-being of human societies was and is achieved by climbing, rung by rung, the ladder of energy control. On the bottom rung the only energy
supply subject to human control is human energy; on the first rung it is supplemented
by the energy of work animals and fire. Such primitive energy manipulation sustains
only minimal output. Advanced energy technology (figure 4.1)permits lavish production of goods and affluent living standards. The ability of a nation to utilize its energy
resources—and to obtain such resources—determines its economic status in the modern
world.

In developed nations today, the shift from primitive sources of energy to
advanced energy technology is virtually complete. Draft animals are seldom used for
transport, and agriculture relies less and less on either animal or human energy. The

FIGURE 4.1.   The high standard of living that
prevails in industrial societies depends on an advanced
energy technology. As we attempt to forestall the
increasing scarcity of fossil fuels, more and more of
our research and exploration efforts are turned toward
less concentrated sources such as the oil shales. This
experimental oil shale refinery located in western
Colorado could well be the symbol of a coming era of
petroleum extraction that will rival the strip mining of
coal as a destroyer of biological communities and
natural landscapes. (Bureau of Mines, U.S. Department
of the Interior)

same is true of industry; in the United States, for instance, human energy contributes
only a few ten-thousandths of 1 percent of the total industrial work performed.

Energy is extremely versatile. In one or several modes it transforms raw
materials into all kinds of commodities and permits an incredible expansion of human
mobility and communication. Another useful characteristic of energy is its substitut-
ability. This means that in industrial societies increased energy input can be made to
compensate for deficiencies in a wide variety of raw materials. Copper, for example,
can be extracted by intense application of energy from ore containing concentrations
of less than 1 percent. Similarly, energy applied to energy resources acts as a booster,
producing greater quantities or better quality energy supplies. Examples of such fuel
upgrading by energy input are the manufacture of propane from coal and of alcohol
from wood. Cost determines the feasibility of these techniques. Electrically smelted
steel, for example, is superior in quality to steel smelted by coke. But except for such

special products as surgical instruments and razor blades steel will probably be smelted with coke until the cost of electricity declines far below present levels.

Since proficiency in the many uses of energy is the key to abundance, economic progress tends to be cumulative: nations able to afford a high level of energy consumption get richer, while struggling economies with low energy consumption and heavy dependence on primitive sources fall ever farther behind. Because of its size and population, precolonial India must have been among the world's leading energy consumers, yet today it uses fifty-six times *less* energy in a year than the United States. It is no accident that the United States, which has the highest per capita wealth in the world, also has the highest per capita energy consumption.

REQUIREMENTS AND RESOURCES

The minimum human energy requirement is 2,000 kcal per person per day, or about 100 thermal watts. Each person must eat food providing that much energy every day in order to sustain health. At first minimum energy requirement and actual consumption must have been about the same. But when people began cooking food and raising livestock the average daily energy consumption, including fuel and feed, shot up to 10,000 or so kcal. People in modern industrial nations eat foods representing still greater investments of energy. They also consume energy for the construction, heating, lighting, and cooling of buildings, for the manufacture and operation of vehicles, for the manufacture of clothing, and for countless other commodities, conveniences, and services.

In order to maintain its present level of affluence the United States, which represents 6 percent of the human population, consumes over 30 percent of the world's energy output. U.S. consumption of electricity, for example, has grown five times faster than the U.S. population, and is now doubling every six to ten years. The projected rate of increase for the world as a whole is even greater; in fact, there is no foreseeable limit to the demand. Table 4.1 compares past, present, and future energy consumption in the United States and the world. Another set of estimates, developed by the Study of Critical Environmental Problems (SCEP), showed that the United States in 1968 consumed 3.86 trillion **kwh** in solid fuels, 7.10 trillion in liquid fuels, 5.60 trillion in natural gas, .22 trillion in hydroelectric power, and .04 in nuclear power, to make a staggering total of 16.82 trillion kwh. Comparable estimates developed from U.N. figures for 1967 give the United States nearly 35 percent of total world consumption—and the percentages for liquid fuels and gas are even higher (table 4.2). The gap between the "have" and "have not" nations could not be more starkly presented: the "haves" consume nearly 86 percent of the world's energy output (*ibid*).

In 1967 the energy consumed in the United States was divided as follows among the four general sectors of the economy: industry (nonelectric power only), 32 percent; transportation, 24 percent; generation of electricity, 22 percent; and house-

TABLE 4.1. Commercial energy consumption
(in quadrillions of BTUs)

Area	Consumption		Projected Consumption	
	1958	1970	1980	2000
U.S.	41	62	86	170
World	109	189	266	615
	As a percentage of 1958			
U.S.	100%	151%	210%	415%
World	100%	173%	244%	564%

Source: *U.N. Statistical Year Books* and Milton F. Searl, *Fossil Fuels in the Future* (Oak Ridge: U.S. Atomic Energy Commission, 1960).

Note: Projections are based upon an assumed annual rate of increase of 4.2 percent for the world and 3.4 percent for the U.S.

hold and commercial uses, 22 percent. These proportions are shifting, mainly because the use of electricity is growing faster than that of any rival source of energy.

Unlike other resources, energy is theoretically unlimited. Some energy sources are exhaustible, but many others exist in continuous flow. Primitive economies were satisfied to classify energy as either animate or inanimate. But now that advanced technology has introduced the possibility of tapping inexhaustible supplies, a more sophisticated set of categories has evolved. In simplified form it can be presented as follows:

I. *Limited and nonrenewable energy sources*
   A. Fossil fuels
   B. Materials capable of nuclear fission or fusion
II. *Continuous-flow energy sources*
   A. Primary: solar energy by direct receipt
   B. Secondary: solar-energized phenomena
      1. Direct utilization
         a. Downflow of precipitated water
         b. Tidal responses of water
         c. Geothermal pressure
         d. Wind pressure
         e. Animate energy
      2. Indirect utilization through combustion, etc.
         a. Photosynthesized energy (e.g., wood)
         b. Waste products used as fuel

TABLE 4.2. World energy consumption, 1967

Fuel Sector	Solid		Liquid		Gas		Hydroelectric		Nuclear		Total	
Trillions of kwh(t) (kilowatt-hours, thermal)	10^{12} kwh(t)	% (World)	10^{12} kwh(t)	% (World)	10^{12} kwh(t)	% (World)	10^{12} kwh(t)	% (World)	10^{12} kwh(t)	% (World)	10^{12} kwh(t)	% (World)
Developed countries												
United States	3.52	20.2	6.33	35.7	5.58	64.1	0.22	21.8	0.03	25.0	15.68	34.8
Canada	0.18	1.0	0.63	3.6	0.38	4.4	0.13	12.9	–	–	1.32	2.9
Western Europe	3.67	21.1	4.42	24.9	0.33	3.8	0.32	31.7	0.09	75.0	8.83	19.6
Eastern Europe	2.42	13.9	0.37	2.1	0.26	3.0	0.01	1.0	–	–	3.06	6.8
U.S.S.R.	3.47	19.9	2.23	12.6	1.66	19.1	0.09	8.9	n.a.	n.a.	7.45	16.6
Japan	0.61	3.5	1.11	6.3	0.02	0.2	0.07	6.9	–	–	1.81	4.0
Oceania	0.26	1.5	0.24	1.4	–	–	0.02	2.0	–	–	0.52	1.2
Total	14.13	81.1	15.33	86.6	8.23	94.6	0.86	85.2	0.12	100.0	38.67	85.9
Developing countries												
Communist Asia	1.97	11.3	0.13	0.7	–	–	0.04	4.0	–	–	2.14	4.8
Other Asia (exc. Japan)	0.76	4.4	0.85	4.8	0.12	1.4	0.03	3.0	–	–	1.76	3.9
Africa	0.43	2.5	0.29	1.6	0.02	0.2	0.02	2.0	–	–	0.76	1.7
Other America	0.10	0.6	1.14	6.4	0.33	3.8	0.06	5.9	–	–	1.63	3.6
Total	3.26	18.7	2.41	13.5	0.47	5.4	0.15	14.9	–	–	6.29	14.0
World Total	17.39	100.0	17.74	100.0	8.70	100.0	1.01	100.0	0.12	100.0	44.96	100.0

Source: Adapted by permission from study of Critical Environmental Problems (SCEP), *Man's Impact on the Global Environment,* (MIT Press, 1970), p. 294.

Note: Separate data on nuclear energy not available for U.S.S.R.

The Energy Crisis

There are numerous types of continuous-flow sources, but their existence does not guarantee that technology will be able to deliver enough energy in conventional form to satisfy all needs. Although all the sources listed above have been tapped at least experimentally, we do not yet have the technology that would permit transfer of the bulk of our energy requirements to the least troublesome potential supplies.

The nonrenewable sources, of course, will eventually be used up, and there are other serious disadvantages to heavy dependence on them. Nevertheless most of the energy used in the United States and the world is now obtained from fossil fuels, and preparations are well under way to transfer dependence to the other nonrenewable source, the nuclear fuels. The distribution of energy consumption by source for U.S. and world industry in 1967 was as follows:

Source	World (%)	U.S. (%)
Fossil fuels		
Coal	28	28
Oil	} 30	} 68
Natural gas		
Other sources		
Nuclear fission		
Water power	} 42	} 4
Wood, charcoal, etc.		

World dependence on fossil fuels, then, is 58 percent, while the corresponding figure for U.S. industry is 96 percent. In this the United States reflects recent trends, albeit in an extreme form. According to Irving S. Bengelsdorf, half of all the coal burned in the past 800 years was burned since 1939, half of all coal burned in the United States was burned since 1932, half of all the petroleum the world has used so far was used since 1958, and half of all U.S. petroleum since 1954.

One way of grasping the full meaning of these figures is to restate them in terms of a uniform energy source. According to an estimate based on United Nations data, world fuel consumption in 1970 was the equivalent of 6 billion metric tons of bituminous coal. This quantity would average 1.7 tons per capita of world population. But the fuel consumed yearly to maintain the standard of living of the average U.S. citizen is equivalent to 9.8 tons—almost 6 times the world mean.

Fossil fuels (unless one includes natural gas in that category) are still abundant, and absolute scarcity is not yet a pressing problem. However, varying degrees of accessibility or ease of extraction are causing regional shortages. From the conservationist point of view, which embraces a longer time scale, the situation is more serious. By 1969 petroleum was providing 67 percent of the industrial energy consumed in the

United States and 60 percent of that consumed in the world. World petroleum resources are thought to have totaled an original 1,350 to 2,100 billion barrels; at least
566 billion have already been used. Petroleum resources of the **contiguous United
States** probably amounted to some 201 billion barrels originally; 90 billion have been
used so far and about 129 billion will have been used by 1980. It has been estimated
that the middle 80 percent (see figure 4.2) of all the crude oil, natural gas liquids, tar-
sand, and shale oil will be gone by the year 2000. Virtually all U.S. oil will be consumed within 60 to 70 years, including the Alaskan reserves.

　　　　Other authorities have produced similar estimates. Eugene Ayres, for instance, calculated in the mid-1950s that if geologists were right in their estimates of
remaining oil deposits, and if the demand for oil continued to rise, the peak of U.S.
petroleum production would be reached about 1965 and the peak of world production
about twenty years later. By the year 2000, he predicted, the age of fossil fuels would
be over, even though coal and oil would continue to be used for chemical purposes. At
present rates of consumption, we shall be lucky if even this is possible. And yet oil,
at least, is more vital to human well-being as petrochemical stock than as fuel. In a rational world our oil stocks would be placed in escrow for medical and other chemical
needs of future generations.

　　　　World coal resources probably amounted to an original 16,830 billion
short tons, of which 127 billion have been used. Coal is therefore more plentiful than
petroleum; indeed, it could last another three or four centuries if supplemented by

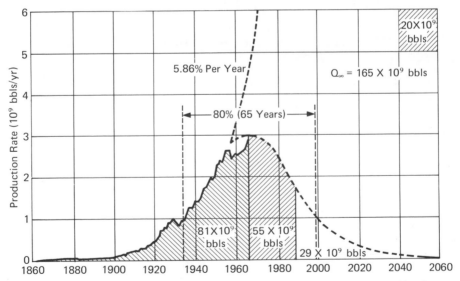

FIGURE 4.2.　　About 80 percent of all U.S. oil reserves will have been consumed by the
year 2000. In this figure, Q_∞ stands for all the oil that will ever be produced in the coter-
minous United States and its continental-shelf areas. (From *Resources and Man: A Study
and Recommendations* by the Committee on Resources and Man, National Academy of
Sciences—National Research Council. W.H. Freeman and Company. Copyright © 1969)

other sources of energy. No such trend, however, appears to be in the making. Thus Hans H. Landsberg and his associates have projected that the annual U.S. demand for coal will increase from 436 million short tons in 1960 to 718 million by the end of the century. The rate of increase is likely to be still greater in countries not as plentifully endowed as the United States with alternative sources of energy.

Altogether, fossil fuels equivalent to 193 billion tons of coal have been burned, half of them in the last twenty-five years. In the next fifty years the world will require more than seven times the energy it has consumed since Christ lived. This acceleration of demand is so rapid that, as we have seen, estimates of remaining use-time require constant downward revision. In any case, it seems that even though more than half the original resources are intact we are well past the halfway point in the era of fossil fuels (figure 4.3).

ENVIRONMENTAL CONSEQUENCES

Depletion of resources is not the greatest danger of fossil fuel use. There are more urgent reasons why it should be phased out as soon as possible.

Atmospheric Pollution

More than 400 billion tons of carbon have been introduced into the atmosphere in the past century. Carbon dioxide is being introduced at the rate of 6 billion tons per year; its tendency to increase heat retention, already evident in large cities, could raise the temperature of the ecosphere to dangerous levels. Airborne particulate

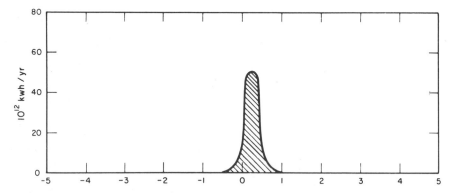

FIGURE 4.3.   The epoch of fossil fuel exploitation. Areas to left and right of shaded portion each represent 5,000 years; height of graph indicates consumption in trillion kwh. (*Energy Resources,* Publication 1000–D, Committee on Natural Resources, National Academy of Sciences—National Research Council, Washington, D.C. 1962)

matter, on the other hand, reflects incoming solar radiation, so that, as Gordon Rattray Taylor has pointed out, the risk of a new ice age seems at least as real as that of "heat death."

Either way, pollution buildup will eventually interfere with incoming solar energy and so with photosynthesis, without which human life could not be sustained at all. The fact is, no one really knows what will be the long-range consequences of disrupting the atmosphere. Meanwhile land and water also suffer pollution from fossil fuel by-products. Such pollution can be *direct*—the effect of the industrial process on the production site—or *indirect,* through fallout of air pollutants. Although the consequences of direct pollution can be spectacular, indirect pollution is the more serious in every way (see chapter 7).

The facts underlying the increased use of fossil fuels should be briefly summarized. Table 4.3 lists the horsepower capacities of the principal animate and inanimate movers in the United States for 1940 and 1965. Total horsepower increased to more than five times the 1940 capacity in this twenty-five-year period. Total nonautomotive horsepower tripled, but automotive horsepower multiplied nearly sixfold. Other sectors with conspicuously rapid increases were mining and farming with respectively five and four times their 1940 horsepower, and electrical generation with six times. The major factor in the increase of mining and farming horsepower was the general trend to large-scale, intensified operations using machinery in place of human and animal energy. By 1965, 95 percent of all horsepower capability in the United States was automotive. Fortunately, the use of automotive vehicles is intermittent; it averages only 10 percent of possible operating time. But automotive vehicles

TABLE 4.3. Total horsepower of all prime movers, United States (in thousands), 1940 and 1965

	1940	1965
TOTAL HORSE POWER	2,773,316	15,096,332
Work animals	12,510	2,000
Inanimate Movers	2,760,806	15,094,332
Automotive	2,511,312	14,306,300
Nonautomotive	249,494	788,032
Factories	21,768	48,400
Mines	7,332	40,300
Railroads	92,361	43,838
Merchant ships	9,408	24,015
Sailing vessels	26	2
Farms	57,472	269,822
Windmills	130	30
Electric central stations	53,542	307,025
Aircraft	7,455	54,600

Source: *Statistical Abstracts of the United States*

Note: Electrical motors that are secondary movers not counted twice. Farm work animals included in the first category.

rely entirely on fossil fuels, and energy conversion in the internal combustion engine is notoriously inefficient.

Electrical generation plants are another main source of indirect pollution caused by fossil fuel combustion. They produce 50 percent of U.S. sulfur oxide emissions, 25 percent of particulate pollutants, and 25 percent of nitrogen oxides. The demand for electricity is so great that the nation's utilities will have to increase their generation capacity from 300 million kilowatts in 1969 to more than a billion by 1979. This means some 250 large new power plants will have to be built. Because the coal and oil burning power plants necessary to keep up with demand represent a huge investment they are certain to be used long after they might have been replaced by plants with nuclear fuel. Sulfur dioxide pollution from power plants alone could amount to 75 million tons annually by the year 2000.

A foretaste of things to come is provided by Four Corners power plant at Fruitland, New Mexico. This plant, the first one built by an association of twenty-three electrical utilities formed to meet the growing demand for power in the urban Southwest, is one of the largest in the world, with a capacity of over 2 million kilowatts. It is also quite possibly the world's single largest source of air pollution. With a daily consumption of 25,000 tons of coal, supplied locally by strip mining on land owned by the Navaho, in 1971 it was emitting about 400 tons of ash particles every day (the corresponding figure for the entire New York metropolitan region in 1966 was 633 tons). According to Roy Craig, who deduced these figures from knowledge of how the plant operates, it also was emitting about 300 tons of sulfur dioxide a day. This was taking place despite company efforts to conform with state air pollution standards and despite use of coal with a low sulfur content. Under certain weather conditions the Four Corners plant has been known to emit a plume of smoke 230 miles long. But Four Corners is small potatoes compared to the Kaiparowits plant, to be built near Lake Powell by the same utilities association. This plant, which will not be in full operation until 1989, will have a capacity of 6 million kilowatts and consume 45,000 tons of coal daily. With plants like these all over the southwestern desert, there will be a very real prospect of smog in the Grand Canyon.

Long-term Consequences

Because the consequences of pollution may be very slow to develop, it is often hard to awaken public concern. Moreover, the slower the rate of pollution, the harder it is to produce the kind of scientific data that will convince legislators and government officials of the need for regulation. Sulfur dioxide, for instance, is invisible; its effects show up in the form of lung and upper respiratory diseases. However, it is not as obvious a fact of life as airborne particles, and little is being done about it. The same can be said about thermal pollution. In 1970 the Committee for Environmental Information produced a report that dealt with these and other long-term dangers posed by the growth in U.S. production of electric power. One of their calculations was that by the year 2000 the amount of excess (i.e., waste) heat emanating from all U.S. power plants, regardless of type, would be enough to raise the temperature of the country's entire annual runoff by 20°F. This figure assumes little improvement in the efficiency with which power plants use heat, but the committee considered this a reasonable assumption. Worldwide, the prospects are still more alarming. If world population by the year 2000 is 6.75 billion, and the entire world somehow reaches the U.S. level of power consumption (7,950 kilowatt hours per capita in 1970), then the waste heat so generated will be enough to increase the total water vapor in the atmosphere by 1 percent. Continued indefinitely, this process would change the earth's climate.

Another long-term effect of reliance on fossil fuels is degradation of the natural environment in the course of extraction. In the case of strip mining, it seems, much can be done to reclaim the landscape so destroyed (see chapter 12). But when the landscape has unique and irreplaceable features, the issue of conservation is presented in its starkest form. Many conservationists believe that the proposed trans-Alaska pipeline is such an issue. In 1968 oil reserves of possibly 9.6 billion gallons were discovered on Alaska's North Slope. For reasons of national security, imports of foreign oil are severely limited by a quota system. Whether national security actually requires this has been much debated; the bulk of U.S. oil imports comes from Canada and Venezuela. But it is beyond doubt that the Middle East, where most of the world's known oil supplies are located, has an uncertain political future. Between 75 and 80 percent of current U.S. demand for oil is met by domestic supplies, but the nation is now using all the oil it produces. By 1985, government economists have calculated, domestic oil—not counting the Alaskan reserves—will supply only about 40 percent of demand, which they estimate will have doubled. Such arguments are supposed to justify exploitation of the Alaskan oil, which constitutes one-quarter of known domestic reserves. It is clear, however, that at present rates of consumption this oil will not last long, and that its potential contribution to the national security is both small and temporary. Nevertheless, the Office of Emergency Preparedness has urged that it be extracted as soon as possible. Heat loss from hot oil pipelines could melt the permafrost (permanently frozen soil) along the pipeline route and damage the vegetation. This is regrettable not only from a botanical point of view; it may also cause erosion and mud slides. Earthquakes are likely to break the pipeline and turn the primeval wilderness into a sticky, sterile morass. There is the additional risk of oil spillage from tankers traveling through the Bering Strait or from the ice-free port of Valdez to San Francisco (see figure 4.4).

Using these and similar arguments, various conservationist groups won a temporary injunction against construction of the pipeline. Many of their objections, however, could be met by the construction of a pipeline through Canada along the valley of the Mackenzie River; in fact the official report on the pipeline, released in March, 1972, found the trans-Canada route the best from both an environmental and a national security point of view. In spite of this, it did not appear likely, as this book went to press, that the trans-Canada route would be used. The reason was that a trans-Alaska pipeline could be put into operation three years sooner! Another possible consideration was that the oil companies had promised to contribute $12.2 million—all but $500,000 of the total—to the cost of the government's report if they were allowed to proceed with the trans-Alaska route.

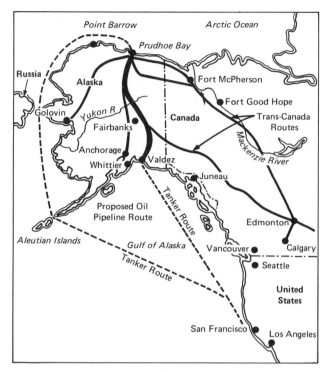

FIGURE 4.4.   Alternative routes for transportation of Alaska
North Slope oil. Trans-Canada route, which would take longer
to construct, is acceptable to most conservationists but is disliked
by the Canadian public. (Reprinted by permission from *The
National Observer,* Copyright Dow Jones & Company, Inc.,
1972)

We linger in the era of fossil fuel use partly because technology has not
opened the door to practical, safe, and economical use of better energy sources. Fossil
fuel reserves may possibly be large enough to supply our gluttonous and shortsighted
appetite for energy until a transition can be made to the less dangerous, apparently unlimited continuous-flow sources. But the environmental risk we are taking in depending so heavily on them is tremendous, and the possible geopolitical consequences are
profoundly frightening.

IMPROVING FUEL USE

Although U.S. energy consumption has increased greatly in the last few
decades, consumption per dollar of gross national product, according to 1964 estimate, has actually declined, from 110,000 **BTU**s in 1940 to 90,000 in 1960. This

decrease only partly reflects technological improvements in the efficiency of consumption; much of it is due to growth in the service sectors of the economy, which use less energy. Accordingly, there is room for much more improvement.

Traditional Fuels

Processes resulting in consumed energy contribute much less pollution than processes that make up for energy lost in conversion and conveyance. Thus consumption of energy for space heating is relatively low and increases slowly. It is relatively efficient because it can be applied directly to the space in question. Most forms of work energy, on the other hand, are relatively inefficient; internal combustion, for example, is disadvantaged by the number of processes it has to go through. As work energy, electricity can be as little as 27 percent efficient by the time it is delivered to the consumer.

In terms of energy, extraction of fossil fuels is an extremely inefficient process, even when cheap transportation is available (figure 4.5). Fully 50 percent of a

FIGURE 4.5.   These Virginia Railroad coal piers in Norfolk, Virginia illustrate the high energy costs required to move fuels from point of extraction to point of utilization. The procedures necessary to prepare the fuel for final use and transport it to the place of consumption often use more energy units than are supplied for final consumption. (photo by Photo Craftsmen, Inc., Norfolk, Virginia, courtesy of Norfolk Port Authority)

coal seam is lost in underground mining operations. Oil recovery is even less efficient: it is calculated that one-half the estimated reserves of crude petroleum in the United States will have been tapped by 1980, with less than one-quarter recovered for use. The most wastefully exploited of all the underground fuels has been natural gas. More of it has been flared off to permit easier access to liquid petroleum than has been harvested for consumption. Now the Federal Power Commission is permitting higher gas prices on the grounds that the gas companies need this extra motivation to look for new supplies.

Improved fuel technology can do little in the face of wasteful practices and attitudes. Whatever savings in energy the American automobile industry may have achieved through more efficient combustion it has dissipated by persuading consumers that they need ever faster and more powerful cars. Consumers, in turn, have done their part by driving without regard to fuel economy. Gasoline is burned most efficiently at moderate speeds of 50 miles per hour or less. Gas mileage for all vehicles averaged 12.4 in 1940 and exactly the same in 1967; for passenger cars alone the figures were 15.3 in 1940 and 14.1 in 1967. According to Barry Commoner, who quotes *Fortune,* American manufacturers are not interested in truly economical, low-powered cars because they would be so much less profitable per unit sold than the present high-powered cars. Whenever sales of economy imports begin to fall off, Detroit begins to soft-pedal the economy features of its own "compacts." One is reminded of the remark attributed to Henry Ford: "They can have any color car they want as long as it's black." In other words, if the only really profitable kind of car is a high-powered one, that is what Americans have to be taught to want. A wholesale change in public attitudes toward automobiles is therefore a major prerequisite for more efficient fuel use.

Further aspects of the automobile pollution crisis are dealt with in chapters 7 and 11. Here it need be noted only that if the desired change in attitudes does not come, technology need not lag behind. Basic research on combustion is investigating ways to reduce the by-products of fire. This may be possible by means of controlled electrical fields acting on ionized particles in the flame. Experiments with this technique have succeeded in reducing the loss of carbon in the burning process by as much as 96 percent. This line of research is not expected to eliminate air pollution by itself, but it may contribute to that end. With cleaner burning, new problems crop up; for instance, there is a slight increase in the quantities of nitrogen oxide and carbon dioxide emitted. Because the source of the nitrogen atoms that form nitrogen oxides during combustion is the air, attempts have been made to cut out the oxides by supplying the oxygen in liquid form. A process based on this approach is already being used in the manufacture of steel; the benefits are said to outweigh the extra expense. Power plants using liquid oxygen would be more efficient and therefore smaller; moreover, they would generate almost no carbon monoxide and almost no nitrogen oxide emissions.

New Nonrenewable Energy Sources

None of the theoretical possibilities uncovered in experiments with energy conversion is more intriguing than the *fuel cell.* It uses the interaction of gases to generate electricity directly by chemical oxidation. This process is two or three times more efficient than the series of thermodynamic and mechanical steps involved in conventional power generation. The cost of hydrogen, one of the gases usually involved, is high. But if fuel cells can be developed for commercial use they will conserve non-renewable resources and reduce by-product emissions. Chemical oxidation in fuel cells is essentially clean; the carbon dioxide end product is the only negative factor, and there is no heat buildup. If coal, oil, or natural gas should turn out to be susceptible to fuel cell conversion the result would be thriftier use of these resources. If unconventional materials prove capable of supplying gases for such chemical conversion, the conservation of fossil fuels would be even greater.

Fuel cells produce direct current, and their efficiency falls as work loads increase. This limits their range of application; large industrial and primary electric plants could not use fuel cells to advantage. They are suitable, however, for small prime mover engines with adjustable work loads.

The ability to tap and use *nuclear energy* seems to promise an inexhaustible power supply. A single gram of uranium-235 yields one thermal megawatt—heat equal to that produced by 13.7 barrels of crude oil. However, U-235 is expensive to produce and the supplies of uranium available to the United States are strictly limited. Hence the importance of **breeder reactors,** development of which has expanded the power potential of this small supply to unknown limits. The breeder reactor burns a core of U-235 which can be surrounded by a blanket of U-238, a more abundant but nonfissionable variety of uranium. The U-235 generates energy while converting the U-238 to fissionable plutonium—about 20 percent more of it than the original quantity of U-235. In this way, the breeder reactor produces more nuclear fuel than it consumes. However, plutonium is extremely poisonous, and the problem of constructing a completely safe breeder reactor has not yet been solved.

Nuclear power stations do not pollute the atmosphere with oxides, but they also have serious disadvantages. Heat buildup is a problem; it affects the air surrounding the power plant, and liquid coolants must be used during operation. Nuclear plants are located on rivers or lakes or beside the ocean in order to have access to the water needed for cooling, but they return the water at temperatures high enough to damage aquatic plant and animal life and upset ecological balance. The long-term effects of this need not be dangerous if proper precautions are taken, but it is not at all certain that they will be (see chapter 8).

More serious, perhaps, is the volume of radioactive waste resulting from nuclear power generation. No method is known of counteracting the biological harmfulness of radioactive substances. They are dangerous to all living creatures for a minimum period of 20 half-lives, which means at least 600 years for such substances as strontium-90 and cesium-137. An advisory committee of the Atomic Energy Commission has set up the following guidelines for the disposal of radioactive wastes:

1. Isolate from the biological environment.
2. Disposal practices must be safe at whatever magnitude of waste production should develop.
3. No compromise of safety in the interest of economy.

Most present operations, however, violate one or all of these measures; for instance, the A.E.C. permits a nuclear plant to release "small" amounts of radioactive waste daily. But the amount released daily by several plants is not small. According to Barry Commoner, the A.E.C. has always done its best to ignore or pooh-pooh reports such as those of John W. Gofman and Arthur R. Tamplin, who have long argued in favor of drastic reduction in the officially permissible levels of human exposure to radioactivity. Even when the A.E.C. does make concessions to its critics it continues to avoid public review. Part of this is due to the way in which the A.E.C. was set up by the original Atomic Energy Act of 1946, when its main job was to manufacture atomic bombs. But, as Richard Curtis and Elizabeth Hogan have pointed out, the A.E.C. may well be trying to conceal the fact that nuclear technology is not yet sufficiently advanced for the nation to embark with safety on a program of widespread nuclear power. The record of other nations is not particularly reassuring. In Great Britain, for instance, the same nuclear power station—Windscale—had major accidents in 1957 and 1970. The one in 1957 resulted in nuclear fallout over an area of 400 square miles.

Public concern in some states has impelled state legislatures to institute stricter standards. Thus in 1970 the state of Minnesota set a limit on radioactive wastes that was one-fiftieth of the amount allowed by the A.E.C. This legislation held up operation of a nuclear plant in construction on the Mississippi River, whereupon the company sued the state (*Northern States Power Company* v. *Minnesota*). Although the courts upheld the A.E.C. standards, the A.E.C.'s authority in this field is now being vigorously challenged by the Scientists' Institute for Public Information, which is invoking the 1969 Environmental Policy Act. The A.E.C.'s reaction was to mobilize its congressional constituency to sponsor legislation that, if passed, would exempt it from the relevant provisions of the act.

The number of complaints and protests by local groups who object to radiation danger, thermal water pollution, or despoilment of scenery has discouraged some power companies from risking investment in nuclear power plants. The construction of new fossil fuel power plants, on the other hand, is often met with equally strong objections. Yet the Federal Power Commission estimates that by 2000 the United States will demand eight times as much power as it uses now. By 1975, there will probably be eighty-four nuclear power plants operating in the United States—over five times the present number. By 1980, such plants may supply 37 percent of the nation's electric power.

Another possibility on the horizon is that domestic energy may be supplied by *nuclear fusion* (essay 4.1). This would generate the same kind of energy as the sun and other stars; its potential is fantastic. The source material is the hydrogen isotope deuterium. One cubic meter of fresh or sea water yields 34.4 grams of it, with the power potential of 269 metric tons of coal. But deuterium must be heated to 180 million °F. for fusion to occur. Fusion energy can be used destructively as in the hydrogen bomb, but the great obstacle to using it constructively is the lack of a container for heat so great that it melts any known substance. A solution may eventually be developed in the form of an invisible but indestructible magnetic "cocoon." Energy from nuclear fusion may some day power virtually pollution-free industrial activity all over the world. Unfortunately, the A.E.C. is not giving research in this area a high priority.

Essay 4.1.   Nuclear Fusion: Energy for the Future

Of all man's present attempts to solve energy shortage problems, the development of nuclear fusion reactors may be the most challenging and the most promising. Fusion reactors use the same energy-producing process as the sun and the stars to generate power for electricity. This process involves compressing a thin, ionized gas composed of hydrogen-heavy atoms and heating it to a temperature higher than the interior of the sun, until the atoms collide with such impact that they fuse and release nuclear energy. To date, scientists in many countries have set up about 200 controlled fusion experiments in an attempt to secure an energy resource that may be available in the next century.

One of the most impressive experiments being conducted in the United States is called Scyllac, at the Los Alamos Scientific Laboratory in New Mexico. The nuclear reaction is produced in a circular aluminum and quartz tube filled with deuterium gas, a heavy form of hydrogen. Since deuterium is obtained from the ocean, the supply of nuclear fuel will be almost inexhaustible. The tube containing the gas is nearly hidden by a seventy-mile network of cables attached to a three-story high bank of capacitors that are charged to 60,000 volts of electricity. When the enormous electrical charge is released into large magnets surrounding the tube, it creates a magnetic field tens of thousands times greater than that of the earth's, compressing the deuterium atoms and heating them to the tremendous temperature required for fusion. Energy released by nuclear fusion in the form of heat is absorbed by a core of liquid lithium that surrounds the tube and is then transferred to a steam generator. The challenge to scientists consists in raising the heat to 180 million degrees F., holding the atoms long enough (two-hundredths of a second) for fusion to take place, and controlling the vast released energies. Scyllac currently reaches a cool 18 million degrees F. and contains the compressed gas a mere five-millionths of a second.

Fusion experiments still consume more energy than they produce, but scientists are optimistic that the reactors can be made to work efficiently. When their goal is achieved, a virtually pollution-free energy supply will be assured for future electric power generation. (Based on "The Search for Tomorrow's Power," an article by Kenneth F. Weaver and Emory Kristof in National Geographic, *vol. 142, no. 5, November 1972.)*

Continuous-Flow Energy Sources

The sun is the *primary* source of continuous-flow energy, but it sustains several processes on earth that can be made to yield this energy flow at second or third hand. One, as we have seen, is photosynthesis, which continually produces plant tissue usable as fuel. If we relied entirely on wood for our energy supply, however, it would soon be depleted; its rate of production is slower than our present rate of energy consumption.

Wood is an *indirect* source because it must be burned in order to release its potential energy. A source of *direct* continuous-flow energy is wind. It will perform local and limited kinds of work, but its energy is too diffused and intermittent to be harnessed for industrial use. Human and animal energy is also directly available for work. Strictly speaking, it is solar energy at third or fourth hand, acquired from the sun via photosynthesized nourishment. Most continuous-flow energy sources have been tapped with some success but can supply only a small part of the total energy demand. All such sources now in use in the United States provide less than one-seventh of the national requirement.

The sun's evaporative function produces the *water cycle,* which can be tapped for direct energy by blocking precipitated water on its way to the ocean. Dams are built on rivers in order to harvest the energy of the impounded water. If the total conventional water power potential of the world were fully developed it would have a 2,857,000 megawatt capacity, a magnitude equal to twice the present world rate of energy consumption. In many countries, however, water power resources have already been developed about as far as is feasible or desirable. Using the rivers of the world to generate electricity has two major disadvantages. One is the inundation of valleys when dams are built. This obliterates millions of acres of fertile and lovely land. The other is economic rather than aesthetic: dams and power facilities are extremely costly to build, and soon after they are completed the artificial reservoirs containing the energy resource begin to fill with sediment. No practical solution has been found for this problem.

The massive and regular ebb and flow of countless billions of gallons of water in response to the gravitational pull of the sun and moon has long attracted interest as a source of energy. Harnessing *tidal energy* does not necessarily destroy scenic value or ecological function. Silting-in is not a problem and few or no noxious wastes are produced. The world's first tidal power dam was finished in 1966 on the Rance River, in France; it harvests the energy of the tides in the English Channel. A U.S. tidal energy project on the Passamaquoddy between Maine and Canada has had a long and troubled construction history. When complete, however, it is expected to attain a peak daily output of 500,000 kilowatts. The estimated potential of the world's tidal energy is small, however, in terms of harvestable power. Economically feasible tapping of tidal energy is possible only at sites with special combinations of geographic and other advantages. Nevertheless, where these advantages do exist tidal power will probably provide economical, convenient and relatively nuisance-free energy for local use.

Steam issuing from the earth can be used as a direct energy source known as *geothermal power.* Surface water that has seeped down to hot regions within the earth's crust expands and is forced upward under pressure. The energy potential of a local steam spout near Lardello in Tuscany was recognized as early as 1904. Specially drilled wells released steam at about 350°F.; later, the steam jets were directed to drive turbine generators that now produce 2 billion kilowatt hours of power per year.

Geothermal power is used to heat 45,000 homes in Iceland and to generate electricity in New Zealand and California. Installation costs are high but subsequent fuel savings make electrical production cheaper than by conventional methods. Of course, steam gushers occur only here and there over the earth. However, according to David Fenner and Joseph Klarmann, if some way could be found to artificially stimulate regions that are already naturally hot, they could be made to supply geothermal power on a hitherto unprecedented scale. Current world output is small, but at least twenty-four countries are said by experts to have unused geothermal potential. Even in the United States, which now produces only 82 megawatts of geothermal power at the Geysers, in northern California, estimates of potential output range as high as 100,000 megawatts, and this is in the West alone. Geothermal power is no panacea—for instance, it may cause harmful chemicals to accumulate—but it could clearly make a substantial contribution if properly used.

From a technical point of view, *refuse* and other kinds of waste must be considered a continuous-flow resource because they are always being produced. Like wood, however, their rate of production is relatively slow, and they have to be burned or processed in some other way in order for energy to be released. The problems of fossil fuel use are grave enough to suggest the substitution of almost any other energy source when possible. On the other hand, refuse disposal has become a serious problem in the United States (see chapter 9). These two environmental problems may have mutual solutions. Not only refuse but garbage, manure, and sewage are potential sources of energy. Peasants of many countries burn dried cow dung in their hearths, and the plainsmen of our own land once relied on buffalo chips for their camp fires. Yet manure piles up unused on dairy farms and feedlots; in fact seven times more solid wastes are produced by animals in the United States than by cities. Both garbage and sewage are now being investigated for energy potential.

Victor Papanek and George Seegers have designed a one-transistor radio that is made from a juice can and operated on paraffin wax, wood, paper, or even dried cow dung. It cannot be tuned, but this does not matter in an underdeveloped country where the government radio station beams only a single broadcast at rural areas. Another approach is the conversion of organic wastes to methane, or natural gas. According to Hinrich L. Bohn, the technology to do this is already available; the main drawback, under existing conditions, is cost. A British farmer, Harold Bates, is already running his car on methane from chicken and pig manure. Urban consumers would doubtless wish to have the odor removed, but this is already being done in the case of fossil natural gas—indeed, the gas companies have to put some odor back in, for safety reasons.

Several long-term economic advantages would result if refuse instead of fossil fuels provided part of our energy supply. Although fuel costs would not be reduced immediately, less uncombusted fuel would be lost to the atmosphere, and refuse disposal expense would be cut. Benefits in terms of conservation would include slower depletion of fossil fuel resources, partial relief from refuse disposal headaches, less pollution of land by dumping of wastes, and reduction of the sulfur oxides and other malignant pollutants near industrial centers.

Partly as a result of the space program, a good deal of publicity has already been given to the idea of solar energy. It is true that two days of sunlight on the United States represent energy equal to that of our total reserves of fossil fuel. If means could be found of making direct use of this primary continuous-flow energy we would at last have a nondepletable and nuisance-free supply abundant enough for all needs. The great difficulty of using solar energy for power is in gathering and concentrating a resource so widely diffused. It is easily used for heat: fish and fruits have been dried for storage by the sun's rays for centuries. Greenhouses and some homes are constructed to take maximum advantage of radiant energy; food can be broiled or fried in solar cookers. The simplest and cheapest use of solar energy is for heat, and the earliest large-scale application of it will probably be for residential space and water heating.

Solar energy now supplies power successfully on a small scale. The most convenient utilization in terms of size and versatility is made by solar batteries, which work well in space satellites and have been adapted for use in radios, fans, and other domestic appliances. But major industrial use of solar power is not a prospect for the immediate future. As Peter van Dresser has pointed out, solar energy devices are the complete opposite of the power generators favored by our current technology, since they are slow to repay capital investment and are in addition nondestructive and non-exploitive. This is probably an area in which we can expect leadership from the developing countries, particularly those poor in fossil fuels. Ultimately, technology may find ways to use solar energy with a degree of versatility equal to our utilization of fossil fuel energy (figure 4.6).

When the production of electricity from solar radiation becomes possible in commercial volume, the ultimate transition to primary, continuous-flow, direct energy will have been made. Energy by direct receipt is the only kind of supply that is free of concomitant pollution buildup, and solar radiation is the only source likely to meet projected long-range demands. It is even possible that once we have stopped polluting the atmosphere some means can be found to use the substitution capabilities of energy to maintain a proper balance of gases in the atmosphere while we attempt to remove or reduce the pollutants we have put there.

ENERGY FOR WHAT?

The absolute supply of energy in the world is great enough to accommodate the most extravagant human usage conceivable. It is likely that technological progress will make one or more of the less limited and less dangerous energy supplies available for widespread use, perhaps within a decade or two. If solar radiation were the source, humanity could enjoy the advantages of high rates of energy conversion without harm to the environment. In the next decade or so, however, we must also solve the problem of sustaining increasing energy demands without damaging the ecosphere beyond repair. We will have to depend as little as possible on fossil fuels, and insist on

FIGURE 4.6.   Prototype desalination
plant for coastal desert zones. Such plants,
now run largely on fossil fuels, would be
ideal candidates for conversion to solar
energy. (Rockefeller Foundation)

the greatest possible efficiency when we must use them. Secondary, continuous-flow
sources such as tidal and geothermal energy should substitute for fossil fuels wherever
conditions permit. The use of energy from refuse should be explored by every possible
means. Fuel cell conversion can fill certain energy needs and newer conversion concepts can be developed to fill others. Many of the sources and techniques of the immediate future will be only temporarily useful. But if they offer improvement over conventional conversion they may provide just the margin of safety we need to tide us
over the interim.

One of the most persuasive programs for conserving energy during the coming decades was proposed in 1972 by Admiral Hyman G. Rickover, in the course of
hearings on the national energy crisis sponsored by the House Interior and Insular
Affairs Committee. The Rickover program consists of the following eight points: (1)
energy resources, particularly enriched isotopes of uranium, should no longer be exported; (2) larger families should be taxed more heavily, as an inducement to have fewer
children; (3) energy of all kinds should be made more expensive, to cut down on use;
(4) current supplies of energy should be used more efficiently (electricity, for instance,
is not an efficient source of room heat); (5) more should be done to save waste heat,
especially from power stations; (6) automobiles should be taxed by size and power, in
order to encourage the use of smaller ones; (7) electrical and other power companies
should *not* be encouraged to expand, since they would only continue to sell the public

on ever more consumption of power per capita; (8) luxury items that consume large quantities of power, such as boats and air conditioners, should be more heavily taxed. Whatever the fate of individual points, some program of this general type will have to be adopted unless the Congress wants to find itself holding exactly the same kind of hearings in about fifteen years' time.

There are many obstacles to putting sensible energy resource management into practice. One is the exclusive concern of vested interests with economic profit. Another is the acquisitive orientation they have encouraged in many industrial societies, especially the United States. Large, powerful corporations making splendid profits from fossil fuels are not likely to accept the substitution of other energy sources without a fight. Nor are the established consumption patterns of whole populations easy to change. Every person, whether he sees himself as producer or consumer (and most of us are both), should be made fully aware that his behavior represents a conscious choice between two values: temporary economic advantage and ultimate ecological sanity.

REFERENCES

Ayres, Eugene, "The Age of Fossil Fuels," in William L. Thomas, Jr. (ed.), *Man's Role in Changing the Face of the Earth,* vol. I (University of Chicago Press, 1956).

Bengelsdorf, Irving S., speech on February 25, 1970.

Bohn, Hinrich L., "A Clean New Gas," *Environment,* December 1971, pp. 4–9.

Cloud, Preston, *Resources and Man* (San Francisco: Freeman, 1969).

Committee for Environmental Information, "The Space Available," in Sheldon Novick and Dorothy Cottrell (eds.), *Our World in Peril: An Environment Review* (New York: Fawcett, 1971).

Commoner, Barry, *The Closing Circle: Nature, Man, and Technology* (New York: Knopf, 1971).

Craig, Roy, "Cloud on the Desert," *Environment,* July–August 1971, pp. 21–24, 29–35.

Curtis, Richard, and Elizabeth Hogan, "The Myth of the Peaceful Atom," in Alfred Meyer (ed.), *Encountering the Environment* (New York: Van Nostrand, 1971).

Darmstadter, Joel, et al., *Energy in the World Economy: A Statistical Review of Trends in Output, Trade, and Consumption Since 1925* (Johns Hopkins Press, 1971).

Fenner, David, and Joseph Klarmann,"Power from the Earth," *Environment,* December 1971, pp. 19–26, 31–34.

Gofman, John W., and Arthur R. Tamplin, "Radiation: The Invisible Casualties," in Sheldon Novick and Dorothy Cottrell (eds.), *Our World in Peril: An Environment Review* (New York: Fawcett, 1971).

Landsberg, Hans H., et al., *Resources in America's Future* (Johns Hopkins Press, 1963).

Man's Impact on the Global Environment: Report of the Study of Critical Environmental Problems (MIT Press, 1970).

Papanek, Victor, *Design for the Real World: Human Ecology and Social Change* (New York: Pantheon, 1971).

Putnam, P. C., *Energy in the Future* (New York: Van Nostrand, 1953).

Scientsts' Institute for Public Information, "Another SST?," *Environment,* July–August 1971, pp. 18–19.

Taylor, Gordon Rattray, *The Doomsday Book* (New York: World, 1970).

U.S. Energy Study Group, *Energy Research and Development and National Progress* (Washington, D.C., 1964).

Van Dresser, Peter, "The Coming Solar Age," in Paul Shepard and Daniel McKinley (eds.), *The Subversive Science: Essays Toward an Ecology of Man* (Boston: Houghton Mifflin, 1969).

5 FOOD

From one-third to one-half the human race is starving to death. It is impossible to give the proportion exactly because the indirect effects of malnutrition are not usually recorded as such. A slow death from anemia or tuberculosis may really be due to malnutrition. If both its direct and its indirect effects are considered, malnutrition is the world's number one public health problem.

Gross world production of food in 1970 was at least 5 billion **metric tons**, up from about 3.5 million tons in 1965. During the same period, world population increased from about 3.3 billion to about 3.6 billion. At first sight, it might appear as if food production were catching up with population growth. Indeed, 5 billion metric tons—5 trillion kilograms—sounds like quite enough even for 3.6 billion people. Any such impression would of course be grossly misleading. The amount of food actually consumed in one year is far smaller than the amount produced. During the mid-1960s consumption was about 1.8 million tons, or about 51 percent of production. Part of this difference can be accounted for by unavoidable shrinkage in processing, storage, and preparation. But a very great deal of unnecessary waste occurs at various points between production and consumption. Problems of transport, finance, and communication also interfere with the transfer of food, making world distribution extremely inequitable. In most industrial nations, food supplies throughout the 1960s were more than enough to provide each member of the population with a rich and varied diet. Elsewhere, however, despite increasing supplies, per capita production has remained at about the same low level (figure 5.1).

We are faced, then, with yet another aspect of what it means to be a poor

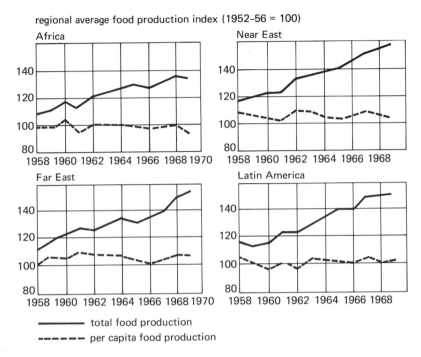

regional average food production index (1952–56 = 100)

FIGURE 5.1.   Food production per capita in the poorer countries has remained
at about the same level despite rising total production. (reproduced by permission
from Donella H. Meadows et al., *The Limits to Growth,* New York, Universe Books,
1972)

nation. The nonindustrial nations of the world are not simply nations that lack industrial equipment; they are also nations that cannot afford to produce or import enough
food to raise the living standards of their rapidly growing populations. Part of the picture is given in table 5.1, which compares the percentage of world population in an
area with the percentage of world food supplies that it produces. It will be seen that
even so heavily industrialized an area as Europe has a much higher agricultural productivity per capita than the largely agricultural nations of Asia, Africa, and Latin
America.

WASTE

The poorer countries also suffer more from all the conditions that cause
food to be wasted. Unfortunately, even reasonably accurate estimates of such waste
are rarely available, though the U.N. Food and Agriculture Organization (F.A.O.) has

TABLE 5.1.   Regional distribution of population and food production (percentage of world total)

Region	Population	Food Production
Asia (Far East)	52.9%	27.8%
Europe	14.3%	22.7%
Africa and Near East	11.5%	8.5%
U.S.S.R.	7.3%	11.5%
Latin America	6.9%	6.4%
Anglo-America	6.6%	21.8%
Oceania	.5%	1.3%

Source: Hugh More Fund.

been doing its best to provide them. But when certain levels of waste routinely occur even in the United States, with its highly scientific and mechanized agriculture, it is reasonable to assume that waste from the same or similar causes is at a much higher level in countries that lack these advantages.

At least 50 percent of the poorer countries' annual harvest is destroyed by pests. On the world scale, according to the president's Science Advisory Committee, a 50 percent reduction in grain losses alone would add 55 million tons to the available supply—enough to fill the basic caloric needs of 500 million people. The **F.A.O.** has estimated (somewhat conservatively) that preharvest losses to insects and weeds cost the world 23 percent of its entire annual crop production. Even in the United States, losses to pests of all kinds run to more than 30 percent (table 5.2). Diseases can be equally destructive: in 1953 and 1954, for instance, wheat rust ruined 60 to 70 percent of the U.S. wheat crop. A good index of the potential seriousness of preharvest loss, at least in developed countries, is the level of expenditure for control. Thus in the United States more than $920 million is spent per year fighting insects, plant diseases, and nematodes, and the annual bill for weed control is $2.5 billion. These are substantial amounts even for a country in which the total expenses for agricultural production are now about $40 billion a year. In tropical or subtropical countries the losses to

TABLE 5.2.   Estimated pest losses in the United States, 1951–60 (percentage of expected harvest)

	Insect	Diseases	Weeds	Combined Loss
Maize	12%	12%	10%	34%
Wheat	6%	14%	12%	32%
Rice	4%	7%	17%	28%
Grain sorghum	9%	9%	13%	31%
Soybean	8%	14%	17%	39%
Potato	14%	19%	3%	36%

Source: Adapted from *The World Food Problem* (note 4), vol. 2, p. 205.

weed growth are still greater; Mexico, for instance, is thought to harvest only half the grain her croplands would otherwise yield. In tropical grazing lands the efficiency of meat production can be reduced as much as 30 percent by invasions of pests and plants.

Diseases and external parasites take a heavy toll of livestock. The U.S. Department of Agriculture has estimated that without modern methods of disease prevention the nation's livestock production would drop by 25 percent. Gordon Wrigley has pointed out that about two-thirds of East Africa, more than one-half of West Africa, and one-quarter of Central Africa are infested by the tsetse fly, which infects cattle with trypanosomiasis ("sleeping sickness"). Once freed from the tsetse fly, large areas of fertile land could be opened up to mixed farming. But progress in this direction has been almost nil, largely because the tsetse fly cannot be eliminated by spraying unless the wildlife and natural vegetation are also eliminated.

Another kind of loss occurs through inefficient harvesting or processing of crops. Mechanical threshing of rice, which is too expensive for most of the world's rice farmers, can produce as much as 10 percent more grain than threshing by hand. The fruit of the West African oil palm yields only about 50 percent of its oil when trodden under foot (the traditional method) but 85 percent when pressed in a factory—and the oil is of better quality. These examples, given by Wrigley, are among thousands that could be cited.

Even more serious, perhaps, is waste that occurs during storage. As much as 35 percent of all harvested grain is spoiled by insects, according to one U.N. estimate. In addition, a great deal of stored grain is eaten or contaminated by rats and other rodents. Georg Borgstrom has reported that rodents annually destroy grain and tubers equal to the average consumption of 200 million people. Such figures refer mainly to bulk storage. But losses in the market and home are also considerable. As much as one-half the world's population cannot afford to can, bottle, or freeze perishable foods for home consumption or display in the market. Understanding of modern methods of food preservation is increasing in these countries, but ability to afford them is not.

In short, the magnitude of the total food waste in the less developed countries indicates that their food stocks could be increased by 25 to 50 percent through more effective pest control and food preservation. This would be expensive, but less expensive than the production of additional food in comparable quantity from the land (according to a 1970 report of the F.A.O., development of new arable land has simply become too expensive to undertake on a large scale). The 1968 grain consumption of the less developed countries was estimated to be 520 million metric tons. Efficient storage and preservation could have added another 100 million tons, thus supplying to the populations of these countries not only the minimum requisite **calories** but a small surplus for investment in the production of animal protein.

Finally, an aspect of food loss that is generally overlooked in world calculations is the waste during processing, preparation, and consumption that is customary in prosperous countries. There was a time when such waste was fed to hogs or chickens. Today, however, it is applied to no productive use whatsoever.

IS WORLD FAMINE INEVITABLE?

Until a few years ago, predictions of world famine were heard so frequently that many people ceased to question them. The appalling Indian famine of 1965–66, which was accompanied by food riots, seemed to bear the predictions out. Immediate and drastic reductions in population growth were urged on the less developed countries. Typical of American policy during this period was the statement of General William Draper, chairman of the Population Crisis Committee, that the peoples of Asia, Africa, and Latin America, were "on a collision course with their food supply." According to the general, the food supply of these countries was increasing by 1 percent a year while their population was increasing by 2 percent. In 1967 the President's Science Advisory Committee concluded that it would be twenty years before programs of family planning could be expected to bring about any long-term improvement. Meanwhile the F.A.O. was warning that world food production would have to increase to 4 percent a year—that is, by 60 percent—for 20 years to supply even minimum critical standards of nutrition for everyone. The race between food and people seemed to be over almost before anyone knew it was going on.

Then, as the sixties drew to a close, the tone of official predictions suddenly changed. In 1967 world per capita agricultural production increased by 3 percent over the year before. It was discovered that Taiwan, a supposedly underdeveloped country to which American aid had ended as recently as 1965, now had exports worth $500 million a year. In 1968 the government of India announced that it expected to become self-sufficient in agriculture by 1971.

What had happened? The answer is generally summed up in three words: the Green Revolution (essay 5.1). These words conjure up a sudden and drastic alteration in the course of events. In reality, however, the Green Revolution itself is nothing new. Rapidly increasing yields of wheat and other cereals, mainly through development of hybrid strains and greater use of fertilizers, have been a conspicuous feature of U.S. agriculture since the mid-1930s. What *is* new is that these same techniques are now being transferred to the less developed countries, often with spectacular success. When one considers that U.S. and Canadian cereal output per acre, once lower than that of either Asia or Latin America, is now by far the highest in the world (table 5.3), then the long-term agricultural prospects for the less developed countries begin to look more hopeful. In addition, the statistics from the F.A.O. and other international agencies showed clearly that, for the less developed countries in general, population is not "on a collision course" with food supply. On the contrary, the decade beginning 1957 showed an overall gain of 4 percent in *per capita* food production for these countries. Although progress was very slow for a while, there was only one year—1966— in which per capita production fell below the average for 1957–59, and by 1967 the trend seemed to be upwards (table 5.4).

Can it be, then, that the world need no longer fear the specter of mass starvation? As of now, very few experts are prepared to give a clear-cut answer to that question. The more optimistic ones temper their long-range optimism with a great deal

Essay 5.1. IR-8 and the Green Revolution

Rice is the staple food in many tropical countries, and yet tropical rice culture always produced much lower yields than that of temperate zones until the International Rice Research Institute in the Philippines set out to develop a rice variety suited to tropical conditions. The first step was to analyze the shortcomings of existing tropical varieties. It was discovered that they grew very quickly at first, easily outstripping the weeds, but that as a result they became too leafy for vigorous growth during the period when the grain was being formed. The tall stems often collapsed before harvest, and the ears of grain tended to shatter. In general, these varieties produced a lot of straw for comparatively little grain. Nitrogen fertilizers only reinforced these characteristics; indeed, when the quantity of fertilizer was progressively increased, there came a point for every variety tested when the yield per acre began to drop. Moreover, the tropical varieties tended to be photoperiod sensitive, that is, they were sensitive to length of day and strength of light during the day. In the monsoon season, the light is not at its strongest and the days are getting shorter. Needed, then, was a variety that was not photoperiod sensitive, so that it could yield both early and late crops. Among the other characteristics sought were shortness and broadness of leaves, strength of stem, good response to nitrogen fertilizers, resistance to shattering and to the commoner diseases, good milling and cooking quality, and tolerance of insect damage. The variety known to I.R.R.I. researchers as IR-8-288-3—IR-8 for short—combines all these characteristics and more; its only major drawbacks are its unappetizing texture when eaten cold and its susceptibility to a number of diseases. How much difference IR-8 could make was seen in 1968, when world rice production showed an 11 percent increase over the 1963–65 average. However, exceptionally favorable weather conditions also played their part, as did massive applications of fertilizers and pesticides that are certain to bring in diminishing returns (they are also very expensive). Increased yield capacity does not exempt the so-called miracle grains from the ecological effects of extreme monoculture (pp. 65–67). Perhaps the best verdict has been delivered by Norman E. Borlaug, in his Nobel Peace Prize acceptance speech of December, 1971: "The Green Revolution has won a temporary success in man's war against hunger and deprivation; it has given man a breathing space . . . But the frightening power of human reproduction must also be curbed; otherwise, the success of the Green Revolution will be ephemeral only."

(Material on IR-8 adapted from Gordon Wrigley, Tropical Agriculture: The Development of Production, *London, Faber and Faber, 1971, pp. 196–199.*

TABLE 5.3.   Trends in grain yield per acre by geographic and economic regions, 1934–38 to 1960

	Grain Output per Harvested Acre (Kilograms)		Percentage of Increase	Percentage of Annual Compound Rate of Increase
	1934–38	1960	1934–38 to 1960	1934–38 to 1960
Geographic regions				
North America	443	927	109	3.1
Latin America	461	498	8	.3
Western Europe	638	876	37	1.3
Eastern Europe and U.S.S.R.	429	514	20	.8
Africa	265	318	20	.8
Asia	508	542	7	.3
Oceania	331	535	62	2.1
Economic regions				
Developed regions	462	699	51	1.7
Less developed regions[a]	468	506	8	.3

Source: Lester R. Brown, *Increasing World Food Output,* Foreign Agricultural Economic Report no. 25, Economic Research Service, U.S. Department of Agriculture, Washington, D.C., April 1965 (reproduced by permission from Clifford M. Hardin (ed.), *Overcoming World Hunger,* Englewood Cliffs, N.J., Prentice-Hall, 1969, p. 64).
[a]Less developed regions are Asia, Africa, and Latin America; the remaining four regions are classified as developed.

of pessimism about the immediate future. The pessimistic ones, who include some of the world's most distinguished scientists, seem reluctant to exclude all grounds for optimism, possibly because they still hope their warnings will have some effect. Unfortunately, the pros and cons cannot be argued here in any detail. But we can give some of the reasons why a so-called green revolution, even when accompanied by slowly but steadily rising per capita food production for the world as a whole, does not necessarily mean the end of the world's food problems.

First, as we have already seen, food production, because of waste, is always much higher than actual food supply. Georg Borgstrom has complained that the official approach takes account of only two dimensions: food and people. Among the other dimensions that should be given equal recognition are food spoilage and utilization, nutritional needs, and disease patterns. Second, the present situation is *already* a disaster. If, as Norman E. Borlaug has said, 50 percent of the world's population is undernourished and 65 percent malnourished, then more of the same is a continuing disaster. Per capita gains of 1 or 2 percent mean very little; indeed, as is evident from figure 5.1, they can be wiped out overnight by bad weather, crop disease, or floods. At the present rate of world population growth, which is about 2 percent per year, there will be about twice as many people in the year 2000 as there are now. These people will need twice as much food as is now produced in order to be fed at the same in-

TABLE 5.4.   World agricultural production, total and per capita, 1960–67 (1957–59 = 100)

Area	1960	1961	1962	1963	1964	1965	1966	1967[a]
					Total			
World (excluding Communist Asia)	106	108	111	114	117	118	122	127
Developed countries[b]	106	107	111	112	116	117	123	126
Less developed countries[c]	107	111	112	117	119	121	120	130
India	110	115	110	117	120	109	107	128
Other less developed countries	106	109	113	117	119	126	125	130
					Per capita			
World (excluding Communist Asia)	102	102	103	103	104	103	104	107
Developed countries[b]	103	103	106	105	108	107	112	113
Less developed countries[c]	102	103	102	103	103	102	98	104
India	105	108	101	104	105	93	89	104
Other less developed countries	101	101	102	103	102	105	102	103

Source: Lester R. Brown, *Increasing World Food Output,* Foreign Agricultural Economic Report no. 25, Economic Research Service, U.S. Department of Agriculture, Washington, D.C., April 1965 (reproduced by permission from Clifford M. Hardin (ed.), *Overcoming World Hunger,* Englewood Cliffs, N.J., Prentice-Hall, 1969, p. 51).
[a]Preliminary.
[b]North America, Europe, U.S.S.R., Japan, Republic of South Africa, Australia, and New Zealand.
[c]Latin America, Asia (except Japan and Communist Asia), and Africa (except Republic of South Africa).

adequate level. Few experts are willing to give any of the less developed countries much hope of improved diets or agricultural self-sufficiency by the year 2000 unless their grain production starts increasing at the rate of at least 4 percent a year by about 1975. This is faster than the rate at which North American grain production has increased since the 1930s (see table 5.3). Amazingly, twelve of the less developed countries have already achieved such rates.* But these represent only about 300 million people, or less than half the combined populations of India and Indonesia.

It is true that the so-called miracle grains produce twice, three times, or even four times as heavily as standard varieties. But they also require tremendous in-

*Brazil, Costa Rica, Israel, Mexico, Philippines, Sudan, Taiwan, Tanzania, Thailand, Turkey, Venezuela, and Yugoslavia. In five of these countries per capita income is over $400, which makes them far from poor by world standards.

puts of chemical fertilizer, which has to be applied in the right way. In fact, such grains are bred for good response to nitrogen, a characteristic that tropical varieties have generally lacked. Trained agricultural technicians, of which there are not nearly enough to go round, are required to introduce the new varieties. Of course, there also has to be sufficient water to sustain this rapid growth (a short growing cycle is another feature of the miracle grains, since it permits double cropping). In short, the investment required is considerable; it is not just a matter of giving the farmer a bag of seed and telling him to get on with it. An invention of which only the more prosperous farmers or countries can take advantage is more likely to cause a red revolution than a green one.

If the poorer nations cannot be expected to feed themselves as long as their populations grow at present rates, can the richer nations do the job for them? Once again we have to remind ourselves that being poor means, among other things, having less money, and that food costs money. In 1967 Thorkil Kristensen, secretary-general of the Organization for Economic Cooperation and Development (O.E.C.D.), calculated that, for the non-Communist world, food supply would continue to balance population growth *provided that the less developed countries were able to import 20 percent of their food.* There is very little hope that they could afford to do so. As time went on, this 20 percent would become an amount so astronomical that the present grain-exporting countries could not possibly supply it—or not without entirely altering the structure of their economies and bankrupting themselves in the process. Writing in the early 1960s, Lester R. Brown projected the need of less developed countries for grain in the year 2000 as two-and-one-half times 1960 levels. The developed countries are not expected to have more than about 8 percent of this amount available for export.

To sum up: worldwide famine is a reality that seems likely to continue. The Green Revolution is also a reality, but in the hungriest nations, such as India, its benefits will be no more than temporary unless population growth is brought under control. In the words of Don Paarlberg, on whose 1969 essay much of this section is based: "Unless the present rate of population growth is checked, there is no solution to the world food problem." To this we would add the present rates of food waste through spoilage and of food loss through crop and livestock disease.

THE ARITHMETIC OF HUNGER

So far we have taken a mainly quantitative approach to world food problems. Since our emphasis has been mainly on the future, we have tended to treat current per capita food production and consumption as if they were satisfactory. But dividing so many people into so many pounds of food is not a very good way of grasping the problem as it actually exists. Moreover, not all food is equally nourishing. Nearly all the people now alive are receiving some food every day. Determining the amount in each case will not tell us how hungry a person is, and still less how long he is likely to live. For this we need to know the nature of his diet.

The F.A.O. has established what it calls the Standard Nutritional Unit (SNU), which consists of 2,350 calories per person per day or 857,750 calories per year. The SNU is based on average caloric need, but it can also be used to imply a particular balance of nutritional elements. Below this average level work capacity falls rapidly. At 1,600 or 1,700 calories per day the body generally reaches the level of basal metabolism, that is, it is barely capable of maintaining the respiratory, digestive, and other basic systems in working order. Most prisoners assigned to hard labor in the Auschwitz concentration camp received between 1,000 and 1,300 calories a day; those who were unable to obtain special privileges died in about three months.

Individual nutritional needs vary with age, sex, body build, activity, and climate. A manual worker in a cold climate may require as many as 5,000 calories. Other things being equal, higher average caloric intake is required in temperate and cold countries than in tropical countries, though the same is not necessarily true of protein requirements. It may seem as if Europeans and those of European origin need more calories, but this is only because a high-protein diet has enabled them to develop to full body size. The F.A.O. now assumes that if this were true of all the world's peoples, nutritional requirements would be about the same everywhere. Figure 5.2 shows average daily caloric intake for the years 1966–68. The areas that fall below the level of the SNU are the larger of the more heavily populated Asian nations, the drier regions of Africa and the Middle East, and much of Central and South America, particularly the Andean nations.

The disparity in quantity is shocking but the difference in nutritional quality is even greater. Some 40 percent of the average daily intake in the United States is in the form of animal protein as compared to only 5 percent in India. Two-thirds of the human population, in fact, averages only one-fifth as much animal protein as the more fortunate one-third consumes daily. A country that needs all the grain it can get is not likely to feed much of it to livestock. Other differences reflect the relative expense of cultivating land for different purposes. Thus about 5 percent of the average U.S. intake consists of fresh fruits and green and yellow vegetables. Land requirements for producing fruits and vegetables are high, and they are expensive to grow and harvest successfully. A far greater quantity of food per acre is yielded by cereals and tubers. The result is chronic malnutrition, which can be defined as the lack of specific nutrients essential to normal growth and functioning. In every region where the average food intake is 70 percent or more from carbohydrates such as grains and starchy tubers, the effects of malnutrition can be seen in the population. Representative food balance sheets for two rich countries and three poor ones are shown in table 5.5.

Most victims of malnutrition are children. This is true not only of those who die before reaching maturity; those who survive despite severe malnutrition are almost always permanently damaged, physically or mentally. Some 350 million children now living have suffered this fate; they represent 70 percent of the world's children 6 years old and under. In India alone an estimated 50 million children will die of malnutrition during the 1970s. For the children of poor nations, the world is a concentration camp.

The damage done by malnutrition is not only physical but mental. Physiologists have established that almost 80 percent of brain growth occurs before the age

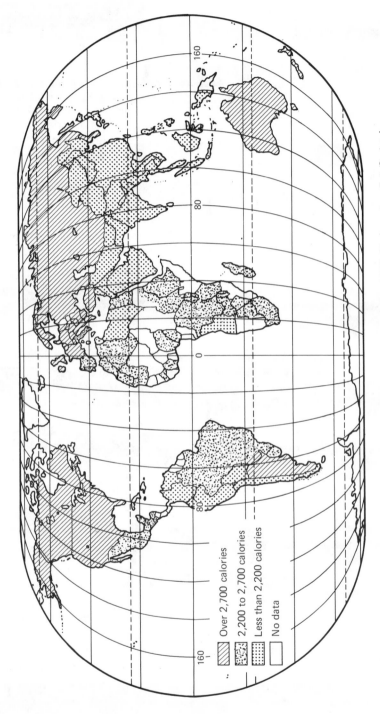

FIGURE 5.2.   Average daily caloric consumption per capita, 1966–68. (based on F.A.O. data)

TABLE 5.5. Per capita net food supplies for human consumption (grams/day)

	Cereals	Potatoes, Tubers	Sugar	Pulses, Oilseeds	Meat	Milk	Fats	Calories, % animal origin	Protein, grams
Afghanistan (1966)	441	1	21	1	31	88	8	1980 (8%)	56
U.A.R. (1965–66)	551	38	49	35	36	122	19	2810 (7%)	81
U.S. (1967)	177	133	133	23	294	665	61	3200 (40%)	96
Denmark (1967)	193	260	130	6	169	700	76	3150 (41%)	89
India (1966)	346	39	50	41	—	113	9	1810 (5%)	45

Source: Food balance sheets prepared by each country in cooperation with the U.N. Food and Agriculture Organization (*United Nations Statistical Yearbook*, 1969, pp. 478–482).

of three. Up to the age of four, children need 50 percent more protein per unit of body weight than adults. As we have seen, in poorer countries the food intake is almost entirely in the form of carbohydrates from grain or tubers, and adult males traditionally eat before women and children thus getting first chance at any high-protein food that may be present. This custom affects both young and unborn children, since protein deficiency in pregnant women impairs the quality of their offspring. Babies born in reasonable health may develop normally until they are weaned, after which loss of the mother's milk deprives them of their only source of protein. That is why the consequences of protein deficiency are commonly known in West Africa as **kwashiorkor,** "the disease the old baby gets when the new baby comes" (figure 5.3).

Lack of essential nutrients is also the chief cause of many chronic diseases in both young people and adults—pellagra, beriberi, scurvy, and others. Moreover, it increases susceptibility to pathogenic diseases, especially malaria, and to parasitic infections. Average expectation of life at birth in more than half of all Asian countries varies between 40 and 55; in Africa the corresponding figures are 30 and 45. The ability to reproduce is little affected by chronic malnutrition: African birth rates, for instance, are regularly two to three times American ones. Of course, this is partly a function of age structure. But the age structure of the poorer countries—a high propor-

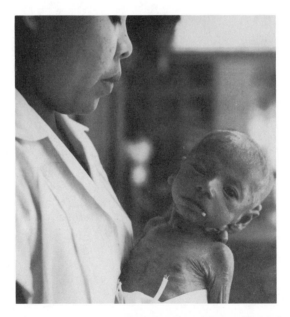

FIGURE 5.3.   This one-year-old Indonesian child is suffering from kwashiorkor, a protein-deficiency disease that often results from a diet of stachy foods such as cassava. The longterm remedy is to make protein-rich foods available to even the poorest families. For this child, however, it may already be too late. (U.N. Food and Agriculture Organization)

tion of dependent preadults coupled with a high proportion of women of child-bearing age— seems to be self-perpetuating.

How useful is the SNU concept for evaluating the world's capacity to produce food? Assessment in purely quantitative terms is simplest: the greatest bulk of food per acre can be harvested in the form of carbohydrates—grains and starchy tubers. One acre of land, producing 44 bushels of wheat per year with energy value of 89,800 calories per bushel, will more than satisfy the caloric needs of four people. Ireland averages 25 metric tons of potatoes per hectare which is equivalent to 7 SNUs per acre. Millet yields as high as 1,069 pounds of grain per acre have been reported in Tanzania when precautions were taken to prevent severe leaching of soil nutrients and chemical fertilizers by heavy precipitation. But it is hard to give any but tentative answers when so many variables are involved. One thing, however, is certain: balanced nutrition draws from a wide range of foods. These include milk, meats, and a variety of fresh fruits and vegetables, all of which have high land requirements. Even under the most favorable cropping, a little more than an acre is needed to produce 1 SNU in milk. Meat is still more expensive in terms of land use: a pound of meat requires about 10 pounds of grain, so that even at the high rate of 44 bushels per acre the meat produced by this technique yields only .4 SNU per acre. Fruits and vegetables vary widely in land requirements, but the high-quality crops typically average 1 SNU per acre.

Thus even under optimum conditions it takes from 1 to 3 acres to produce 1 SNU, if the calories are supplied by foods of quality and variety adequate for normal health. The 3.5 billion acres of arable land now under crop cultivation are not enough to provide the world population of 3.6 billion with adequate nutrition. There are also 10 billion acres of meadow and pasture land capable of meat production. But food gains from this land are offset by the fact that a surprisingly large proportion of meat, milk, eggs, and other animal products are converted from cereals, oil seeds, and other edible foods harvested from the premium cropland.

EXPANDING WORLD FOOD PRODUCTION

Agricultural technology has reached an extremely high level of development in some nations. In spite of this, very little is known about the capacity of the earth as a whole to produce food. There are three general approaches to increasing this capacity: new lands can be cultivated; agriculture on lands already under cultivation can be intensified by conventional means; and new sources and techniques of food production can be developed.

Cultivating New Lands

As we saw in chapter 1, the extent of arable land on the earth's surface is probably about 6 billion acres. This includes the 3.5 billion acres already cropped and the 2.5 billion acres now largely used as pasture. The latter are of borderline quality; the economic value of the energy, equipment, and materials required to make them productive would often exceed that of the expected crops. In addition, the use of marginal land involves problems of ecological balance and threatens soil stability.

Another serious objection to cultivating marginal land relates to the choice between quantity and quality. The 2.5 billion acres in question now yield high-quality protein from the livestock they support. But very large amounts of plant calories and proteins are consumed for a small return in meat. The same land could produce roughly ten times more food in plant form. If the primary goal is quantitative increase, the use of this acreage for pasture is very wasteful. On the other hand, the human species evolved as predators accustomed to a diet that included animal protein. To trade this kind of protein for more carbohydrates or for inferior plant proteins would be a doubtful bargain. At the least, an adequate supply of quality protein would have to be generated from some other source.

On a world scale, however, it seems unlikely that livestock farming of the present type can ever become the chief source of protein. It is simply too expensive. Only 23 percent of the plant protein consumed by a cow is returned to man as milk, and the production of beef is even more wasteful. An acre that yields 800,000 plant calories can provide at best only 200,000 calories in the form of meat. Thus at least 600,000 calories are lost for each acre feeding livestock instead of producing crops for direct human consumption. In many cases the available land might be better used for cultivating fresh fruits and vegetables, for which there is also a pressing need. But it is hard to generalize. Much land on which cattle could be successfully raised is not at all suitable for crops, and cheap protein equivalents, such as urea, can be used to improve low-quality pasture. Moreover, if a society has a tradition of raising livestock, however inefficiently, it is often better to teach them how to improve their existing practices rather than confront them with entirely new ones. This is particularly the case in Africa, where cattle have long been regarded as a sign of wealth. Improved varieties of tropical cattle are now being developed (figure 5.4) and their productivity is being increased through disease control, better feed, and so on. By raising stock *and* cultivating crops—so-called mixed farming—the farmer can hope to get the best of both worlds, since he can use his cattle as draft animals and their dung as fertilizer. If he is able to sell stock and animal products such as milk he may find that keeping one animal is worth more to him than cultivating one acre of land. The problem then, is not only to improve animal husbandry but to develop regional markets. The tropical countries certainly have a long way to go before their cattle become very profitable: according to the F.A.O., a cow in Europe or the U.S.S.R. produces over ten times as much milk in a year as one in Latin America, Africa, or Asia.

Intensifying Conventional Agriculture

Production of any crop requires an investment of energy. Increasing the crop output therefore depends on increasing the energy input. Large-scale agriculture

FIGURE 5.4.   South American cattle crossbred with African zebu for better adaptation to tropical conditions. Productivity of tropical cattle is low, generally because of disease. (Rockefeller Foundation)

in the United States is already intensive and highly specialized; increasingly, manpower is being displaced by mechanical energy. It took 135 man-hours to produce 100 bushels of corn in 1913; today it takes only 15. However, this is not absolute saving, since the input of mechanical energy has increased enormously. Harrison Brown has estimated that U.S. agriculture produces 400 food calories for every calorie of human energy invested and 29 food calories for every carlorie input of other kinds, mostly mechanical. Comparable ratios can be calculated for northwest Europe, Japan, and other highly developed areas. But the ratios for less developed countries are rarely higher than 20 to 1 for mechanical energy and 10 to 1 for human labor. Thus the countries most capable of benefiting from intensification are the ones least able to undertake it. They cannot afford the heavy capital investment in machinery and chemicals, and they lack skilled personnel to introduce and supervise programs involving unfamiliar techniques. These handicaps leave them little choice but to concentrate on the traditional crops—cereals and tubers, which yield the greatest caloric return for the energy invested . Producing food in sufficient quantity to stave off hunger leaves most of them no time or energy for trying to increase production of proteins and other high-quality foods with smaller caloric yields.

The highly productive agriculture of the United States is also the result of enormous capital investment. The investment for each farm worker is over $20,000, compared to $15,000 for each industrial worker. Moreover, the United States has the advantage of having far more land available for agricultural use than most countries. The nation produces its surplus of food and fiber on land farmed at the rate of about

5 acres for each member of the population—2.1 acres in crops and 2.9 in high-quality pasture. By contrast India has .8 of an acre cultivated per capita, and if all of her remaining land area were devoted to pasture there would be less than 1 acre of it per person. Under such conditions, intensification of the American type is out of the question, though certain elements of the American experience, such as highly selective plant and livestock breeding, may be transferable (figure 5.5).

From one point of view, the Green Revolution was an exercise in intensification of a very specialized sort. The increases it achieved were in the yield of cereal grains and, to a lesser extent, tubers. Meat production, however, expanded from 71 million metric tons in 1965 to 76 million in 1968, an increase that barely matched population growth. Production of oil seeds, an important source of vegetable protein, increased only 2 percent in the same three years, while production of pulses, another major source of vegetable protein, declined 3 percent.

This qualified success was further shadowed by negative consequences such as soil deterioration from double cropping and chemical contamination from pestici-

FIGURE 5.5.   An African scientist making a varietal cross by hand pollination of wheat. Research of this kind offers more hope in the long run than simple intensification through use of artificial fertilizers. (Rockefeller Foundation)

des and herbicides. Nevertheless, intensification is commonly accepted as the best, if not the only way to increase short-range food production.

DEVELOPING NEW METHODS OF FOOD PRODUCTION

There is no clear-cut distinction between improvements in conventional agriculture and the development of new forms of agriculture. A new plant breed such as IR-8 rice may or may not be considered exotic, depending on one's point of view. Hydroponics, the growing of plants without soil on nutrients dissolved in water, is clearly exotic, but artificial irrigation of cropland is accepted as conventional. The final criterion is extent of use; the most exotic methods are those that are not in use at all, but exist only in theory. For this reason, and because people are slow to change their dietary habits, we should not expect much immediate help from exotic methods in improving the nutrition of the world as a whole. Local improvements, however, are possible now, and it would be grossly irresponsible to let the wellsprings of research become poisoned by despair.

By far the most visionary of the exotic methods is that of direct synthesis of solar radiation: carbon dioxide, water, and traces of nutrient elements would be used to create starches and fats, bypassing photosynthesis. It sounds very plausible, but there are many drawbacks not the least of which are the economic costs and the absence of adequate technology. Moreover, as Georg Borgstrom has pointed out, to produce enough food just to satisfy the annual net increase in world population would require facilities greatly exceeding the total synthetic-organic industry of the United States. Direct synthesis may come some day, but long before we depend on it there will be extensive use of other exotic methods such as algae culture.

Since exotic methods are slow and expensive, they should be used to improve quality rather than quantity. The crucial qualitative deficiency is that of protein, especially animal protein. Proteins supply the amino acids that are the building blocks of the body. There are twenty-two known amino acids, fourteen of which can be made by the body itself. The remaining eight—sometimes called "essential" although this is true of all fourteen—have to be supplied by diet. A "complete" protein is one that supplies all the essential amino acids in abundance.

The best known complete proteins are all animal products—milk, egg yolk, glandular meats such as liver and kidneys. Roasts and other muscle meats are not far behind, nor are fish and cheese. Less well known, however, is the fact that certain vegetable products, such as soybeans, cottonseed, and wheat germ, are also complete. So is brewer's yeast. Moreover, most beans contain at least some of the essential amino acids. The protein content by weight of vegetables and cereals can be increased by hybridization. Cereal flours, which are not complete proteins, can be enriched with flours made from soybeans, peanuts, and other high-protein legumes. The Institute of

Nutrition, a cooperative research institute in Central America, has developed a complete protein consisting of 55 percent grain, 38 percent oil meal, 3 percent torula yeast, 3 percent leaf, and 1 percent calcium carbonate; the formula does not include animal protein, which is particularly expensive in that part of the world. Swedish nutritionists working in Ethiopia have developed an inexpensive food called *fafa* made of chick peas, dehydrated skim milks, and a local cereal called *teff.* Fafa is subsidized so that it can be marketed cheaply by European standards: a five-day supply for one child costs the equivalent of 10 cents. Programs of this type are under way in other countries; they are important chiefly for the hope they offer children and women of childbearing age. There are also nutritional rehabilitation centers that deal with severe cases of malnutrition and undertake dietary information programs (figure 5.6).

One way to obtain more animal protein is to make use of a greater variety of land animals for food. These could include such familiar creatures as dogs and cats and such unfamiliar ones as hippopotami. They might even include the capybara, or water hog, a web-footed rodent over four feet long that is hunted for food in South America, its natural habitat. Like most rodents it produces meat much more efficiently than any of the traditional meat animals. A further advantage is its preference for marshes and riverbanks—extremely fertile features of the environment that are little used for food production at present. The main problem in such cases is likely to be convinc-

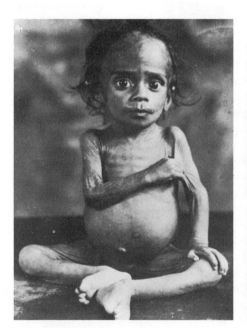 

FIGURES 5.6A AND B.   Malnutrition (marasmus) is curable if caught in time, as can be seen from these photos of the same two-year-old Venezuelan girl. First photo was taken on child's admission to rehabilitation center, second photo ten months later. Rehabilitation included instruction on nutrition given to child's mother. (U.N. Food and Agriculture Organization)

ing people to eat unfamiliar food. Paradoxically, this is often easier in the industrial countries, where people are used to varied diet and are encouraged by advertisers to try new products, than in the nonindustrial ones, where the same limited diet has often been followed for centuries.

The sea is another source of protein from which much has been hoped in recent years. Although only about 10 percent of the world's protein comes from the sea, nations such as Japan have long obtained nearly all their protein from it. But since the early 1960s the world's fishing nations have been engaged in deadly competition to see which one could take most from the major fishing grounds. Huge factory ships and new techniques that have made it possible to extend the season into the winter months have resulted in serious overfishing. In some areas the stocks of fish are almost depleted; in others, the size of fish taken has shrunk drastically. Offshore and freshwater pollution have also taken their toll. In the United States alone, state fisheries reported that fish kills doubled in volume between 1965 and 1970. The U.S. catches of Atlantic cod, flounder, haddock, Pacific halibut, and mackerel have all decreased since 1950, in some cases spectacularly. Countries that have developed major new fisheries—the leading example is Peru—are taking most of their catch in the form of small, bony fish suitable only for industrial purposes. The United States is at last phasing out its whaling industry, at least for the time being. But, as Scott McVay has pointed out, 36,000 of the world's annual whale catch of 42,000 are taken by the Soviet Union and Japan. The International Whaling Commission is fully aware of the fact that the great whales may become virtually extinct. But so far it has made only halfhearted efforts to regulate it members.

Perhaps we are now seeing the last of fresh fish as a regular item of human diet. Only about 60 percent of the world's annual catch now goes to feed people, a decline of some 20 percent over the last ten years. On the other hand, an increasing proportion of it is being used to feed chicken and hogs. This gets round the acceptance problem, since animals will eat fish in forms that people would spurn. But it chiefly benefits the richer countries. A more promising development is the manufacture of a tasteless, odorless fish flour known as fish protein concentrate, or FPC. A teaspoonful of FPC a day will meet an individual's protein requirements and need cost no more than 3 cents. Moreover, FPC can be manufactured out of so-called trash fish, which most people cannot eat. Since the trash fish can be ground up regardless of size, there is no longer any need for selective fishing. According to members of the U.S. Bureau of Commercial Fisheries, a take-all fishing policy is less likely to upset the balance of species. Moreover, catching only big fish is a wasteful habit of the Western nations and is not practiced in the Orient. With Oriental nations exploiting traditionally Western fishing grounds, Western fishermen will have to adopt Oriental methods in order to compete. Finally, even fresh water species can contribute to protein needs. Carp, in their natural habitats, will gain about a pound a year. But with other techniques they may reach 14 pounds in 3 years. They are responding well to breeding techniques aimed at producing natural fillets by increasing the ratio of flesh to bone.

Fish protein, then, is a major element in the world's food supply, and its role seems likely to increase. However, it is unlikely that fish protein by itself will

solve the world protein shortage. As Georg Borgstrom has pointed out, the world's entire catch of fish is only enough to supply the United States with about the same
amount of protein as they now receive from meat.

An as yet little developed source of protein is the culture of microbiological organisms. The general public is familiar with the varieties of yeasts used in baking
and brewing. Health food enthusiasts supplement their diets with yeast products to obtain the high quality protein and generous array of B vitamins they provide. The great
potential of this protein source seems as yet little recognized, however, and its development has barely begun. There are less familiar algae and bacteria that hold equal promise. These micoorganisms may become worldwide staples of the future. Cultivation
of microorganisms involves techniques quite unlike those of traditional agriculture.
One method converts petroleum to protein via yeast: the yeast grows on the waxy paraffin in aerated tanks of crude petroleum. It has been estimated that 2.5 percent of
the world's annual petroleum extraction could produce 22 million tons of protein per
year, an amount equal to the present total production of animal protein.

Bacteria are also extremely efficient producers. The Institute of Gas Technology in Chicago has succeeded in fermenting methane with these single-celled organisms which, when dried, consist of 30 to 40 percent protein. Estimates based on work
by Shell Oil researchers set the quantity of methane needed to produce 1 ton of protein at 200,000 cubic feet. An advantage of gas over petroleum conversion is easier
separation of the protein material from the energy source following the growth process. Another advantage is that methane can be produced from garbage. Protein can
also be produced from hydrogen bacteria fed with carbon dioxide, urea, ammonium
chloride, and potassium nitrate. The first two of these are readily available from
human metabolic wastes.

Fish flour, food from human excrement, huge web-footed rats—none of
these sounds like a very attractive prospect. However, the world food crisis is so grave
that we are forced to consider them. As Americans, consuming an average of 4.5
pounds of food per day with a value of 3,200 calories, we might also ask ourselves how
long we think the rest of the world is going to let us get away with it.

A STATE OF SIEGE

C. P. Snow, leading British author and civil servant, has warned in his address "A State of Siege" that only the richer nations, by learning to cooperate, can
save the world from mass starvation. Another distinguished voice, that of Soviet physicist Andrei D. Sakharov, has been added to this plea. In his essay "Progress, Coexistence and Intellectual Freedom," Sakharov argued that the United States and the
Soviet Union should devote 20 percent of their gross national product (GNP) over at
least a fifteen-year period to a worldwide campaign to control population growth and
accelerate food production. So far nothing of the sort seems likely to materialize. In-

deed, the trend is for foreign aid to stay at about the same level while both **GNP** and defense spending increase (figure 5.7).

There is no doubt that existing forms of agriculture on the present land base could provide enough food for current populations. But they do not; as Georg Borgstrom has said, if all the world's food were evenly distributed, everyone would go hungry. There is likewise no doubt that food production could be increased sufficiently to give everyone in the year 2000 an adequate diet. But it probably will not be. Will mankind break out of the "state of siege" in time? In the view of most experts, the possibility of stabilizing the human population by the year 2000 is extremely remote. But the fault lies in human beings and their institutions, not in technology or natural resources. Perhaps if this truth is repeated often and loudly enough, something may yet be done.

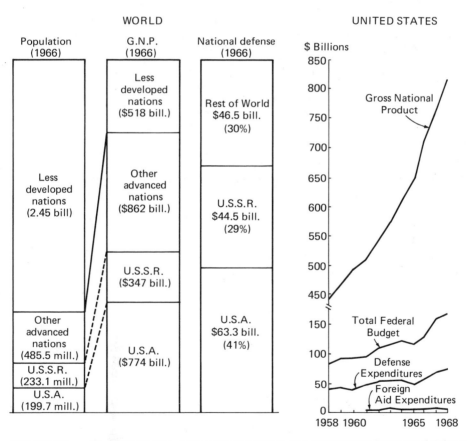

FIGURE 5.7.   World population, gross national product, and expenditures for national defense, compared with the growing gap between U.S. expenditures for national defense and foreign aid. (adapted by permission of the Population Reference Bureau, Inc., Washington, D.C., from "Spaceship Earth in Peril," *Population Bulletin,* March 1969)

REFERENCES

Borgstrom, Georg, *Too Many* (New York: Macmillan, 1969).

——, "The Harvest of the Seas: How Fruitful and for Whom?" in Harold W. Helfrich, Jr. (ed.), *The Environmental Crisis* (Yale University Press, 1970).

Borlaug, Norman E., Nobel Peace Prize acceptance speech, December 10, 1971.

Brown, Lester R., *Man, Land and Food,* (Washington, D.C.: Government Printing Office, 1963).

Cloud, Preston, *Resources and Man* (San Francisco: Freeman, 1969).

Kristensen, Thorkil, paper given at Thirteenth Conference of the International Association of Agricultural Economists, Sydney, Australia, August 23, 1967.

McVay, Scott, "Saving the Whales—Any Hint of Hope?" *Audubon,* November 1971, pp. 46–48.

Meadows, Donella H., et al., *The Limits to Growth* (New York: Universe, 1972).

Paarlberg, Don, "Food for More People and Better Nutrition," in Clifford M. Hardin (ed.), *Overcoming World Hunger* (Englewood Cliffs, N. J.: Prentice-Hall, 1969).

Panel on the World Food Supply, *The World Food Problem: A Report of the President's Science Advisory Committee* (Washington, D.C.: Government Printing Office, 1967).

Population Bulletin, "Spaceship Earth in Peril," March 1969.

Sakharov, Andrei D., *Progress, Coexistence and Intellectual Freedom* (New York: Norton, 1968).

Smith, Nathan J., "Nutrition and Its Effects on Health," in *Man under Stress: Report of the Proceedings of the Second Annual Southwestern Environmental Health Conference,* San Diego, April 15–17, 1970.

Snow, C.P., "A State of Siege," speech at Westminster College, November 12, 1968.

U.N. Food and Agriculture Organization, *Provisional Indicative World Plan for Agricultural Development* (Rome: FAO, 1970),

U.S. Department of Agriculture, *Protecting Our Food, Yearbook of Agriculture, 1966* (Washington, D.C.: Government Printing Office, 1966).

Wrigley, Gordon, *Tropical Agriculture: The Development of Production,* third edition (London: Faber, 1971).

6 MATERIALS

Of all the materials that supply basic human needs, only food and fuel are actually consumed. Shelter, clothing, tools, and weapons—the materials that supply these are fashioned for use rather than consumption. Indeed, their chief merit is that they can stand a good deal of wear. Most of us tend to think of metals in this connection. But stone, wood, and skin were in use long before them. Even fired clay and woven fibers, though of more ancient origin than worked metals, are comparatively recent additions to human technology.

Materials in their natural state are generally described as "raw." The expression is a misleading one because it seems to place them all in the same category as food. It should be clear from the previous chapter that food, with the help of modern agricultural methods, is an almost infinitely renewable resource. The same is true of timber and other organic products, though on a different time scale; given proper management, there is no reason why they should ever run out. But inorganic resources are nonrenewable--or might as well be, considering how slowly they are formed and how fast they are being used up. In chapter 4 we examined the depletion of fossil fuels. Their case should be kept in mind throughout this chapter because at present they are the source of the power needed to extract and process other kinds of mineral resources. Ironically, they also supply the chemical base for many synthetic products widely touted as substitutes for nonrenewable materials.

Besides inventing new materials, modern technology has vastly extended the range of the old ones. Such products as light metals, (figure 6.1), shatter-proof plate glass, laminated woods, wallboard, and paperboard have a versatility that

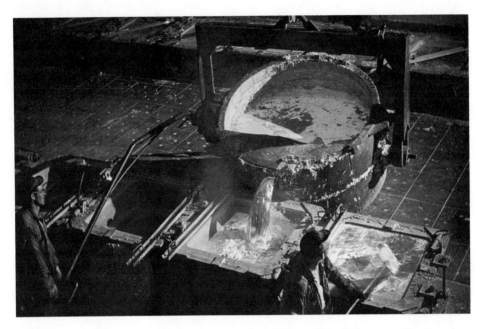

FIGURE 6.1.   Aluminum smelting in progress. Most versatile of the light metals, aluminum is
now used for everything from kitchen foil to airliners. Molten aluminum is produced in electric
furnaces that require a greater energy input than iron or steel furnaces. (Kaiser Aluminum and
Chemical Corporation)

almost obliterates traditional distinctions between classes of materials. Aluminum foil
and cellophane, metal and wood products respectively, are for many purposes inter-
changeable. Such is the complexity of many industrial processes that a new class of
resources has come into being: materials that are hardly ever used in their pure state
but are essential ingredients in some widely used alloy or other compound material.
Modern steelmaking, for instance, depends heavily on the special properties of such
exotic metals as tungsten and vanadium. Here, resources that fulfill this type of function
will be called *auxiliary materials,* in contrast with the *basic materials* of which they
form a part. The distinction is of course a highly relative one: with changing technology,
today's basic material may be tomorrow's auxiliary material and vice versa.

        The supply of any material depends largely on two factors: the level of
demand for it and the rate at which it can be renewed, if at all. Organic materials replenish themselves in a given period of time after harvest if properly managed. But inorganic resources do not, at least on the human time scale. Minerals, especially
metallic ores and fossil fuels, are in greater danger of depletion than any other form of
natural resource. The process of depletion is not visible to the public in the same way
as environmental pollution, but it is just as likely to affect the quality of life.

        Materials become resources when there is a demand for them, and demand
is shaped by technology. The Industrial Revolution was based on a technology that

made heavy demands on mineral resources. The United States attained rapid industrial development after the Civil War by skimming the cream of its own mineral resources, and in so doing developed the technology for economic extraction of less concentrated ores. In time, new power sources—oil, nuclear fission—were also developed. The majority assumption has therefore been that this process can be continued indefinitely—that there will always be, in Eugene Holman's metaphor, a larger room for us to move into as soon as we have learned how to fashion a key that will unlock the door to it. Over the past twenty years, however, evidence has mounted that casts serious doubt on this view. It is true that heavy application of energy and investment in technology permit exploitation of low-grade resources. But natural scarcity of some resources and improvident management of others are pushing the man-resource relationship into precarious balance. Harrison Brown said in 1960 that "if a machine civilization were to stop functioning as the result of some catastrophe, it is difficult to see how man would again be able to start along the path of industralization with the resources that would then be available to him." In other words, you can't skim the same cream twice.

Industrial success has made Americans not only affluent but notably wasteful. In this they are encouraged by their economic system, which woos them relentlessly with an endless variety and volume of goods. If these goods are not intended to be consumed immediately they are either designed to fall apart within a couple of years or are rendered "obsolete" by arbitrary but well-advertised changes in style. No limits are placed on individual consumption.

According to a set of estimates prepared for the 1972 U.N. Conference on the Environment by the National Wildlife Federation, if the whole world were suddenly to begin using metals at the same rate as the United States in 1970, annual world production of iron would have to be increased 75 times, that of copper 100 times, and that of tin 250 times. There is already a serious shortage of copper. Harrison Brown gives 1967 U.S. steel consumption as 634 **kg** per capita. As a measure of comparison, he notes that about one-half the world's population consumes steel at an annual rate of less than 25 kg per capita. Overall, he calculates, some 25 tons of material have to be mined each year in order to support one person at the U.S. standard of living.

Use, with the previously mentioned exceptions of fuel and food, need not equal consumption. Some diminution of any material is inevitable with use. But it can be kept to a minimum, as can the disruption that occurs when it is harvested or extracted. Materials already in use can be better preserved, recovery rates in the extraction of new materials can be improved, substitutes can be found, and the national level of consumption can be reduced.

The greatest losses to materials already in use come from abrasion and chemical alteration or corrosion. Abrasion is caused by the friction of moving parts; a familiar example is tire wear. About 100 million tires are discarded annually in the United States. It is technologically possible to manufacture tires to last 100,000 miles or more, or about the lifetime of the vehicle, but replacement every 15,000 to 20,000 miles is profitable to manufacturers and dealers. The longer-lasting tire would cost more, but not nearly as much as the series of fast-wearing tires the consumer must purchase at present. Losses from corrosion exceed $8 billion per year. Many materials could be kept in service much longer through painting, undercoating, galvanizing, alloying, and other existing techniques. In the United States, however, the cost of labor is so high that it is often cheaper to replace than to maintain or repair. Even when it is not cheaper, replacement is encouraged on other grounds. Buildings that in Europe would be made to last hundreds of years are torn down after fifty. It is far more profitable to construct a new building than to maintain an old one.

Improving the recovery rate of a material may save it from depletion in the short run, but it will also involve greater expenditure of some other nonrenewable resource because of the extra power needed for extraction and processing. It will also involve greater disruption of the environment during extraction and a greater volume of waste materials after. Some wastes cannot be discarded at all without dangerous consequences (see chapter 9).

Many people believe that all shortages of materials can be made up by substitutes. The achievements of industrial chemists lend support to this belief. Many synthetics are derived from nonrenewable materials such as coal and oil, while others present special problems of contamination and disposal. Moreover, they require a very high energy input to produce.

The last resort, then, is also the only certain one: reduce public consumption. This depends, however, on population size and consumption level being brought into balance with the resource and recycling capacities of the environment. Inanimate materials may seem a step removed from direct life-support systems, but they are produced in the biosphere and should be managed as part of it.

NONRENEWABLE RESOURCES: MINERALS AND METALS

Although the smelting of iron probably began around 1400 B.C., heavy use of minerals and metals is a recent practice. For some thirty-two centuries until the beginning of the Industrial Revolution, demand for metals grew very slowly. The turning point, in more ways than one, appears to have been World War II. As calculated by Barry Commoner and his colleagues, per capita production of goods to meet basic needs hardly increased at all between 1946 and 1968—or, to put it another way, increases in these categories kept pace with the overall increase in population, which was 41 percent. Population growth, however, is more an index of real need than of effective demand. This is immediately obvious from some of Commoner's other figures: in the same period, production of air conditioner compressor units increased 2,850 percent; electric housewares, 1,040 percent; consumer electronics, such as television sets, 217 percent; and aluminum, 680 percent.

Here a sceptic might object that since consumption of basic materials such as iron is rising no faster than population, and since population growth is predictable, there will be plenty of time for U.S. society to adjust itself to any shortages that may develop. But, leaving aside the fact that population growth, under present conditions, is *not* predictable, such an objection misinterprets both modern technology and the consumption oriented society that it serves. Thus the ferrous and nonferrous metals are not produced in different economic worlds: because of the complexity of modern products, a shortage of one is bound to affect all the others. Moreover, demand has an alarming discontinuity; it may mushroom almost overnight for any material if there is a quick fortune to be made from some product containing it. Given this condition, adver-tising will create the "need" for the product. An analogous situation exists in the field of national defense. Given the premise that the United States must have the most up-to-date weaponry possible, no limit can be placed on the refinement of military techno-logy. New inventions, unconceivable as yet, may require unprecedented quantities of previously obscure materials. In time, civilian applications may be devised. Already, the technology of weather and communications satellites is affecting home electronics, while campers can use the same protective fabrics as astronauts.

These developments became dramatically evident during World War II and continued to cause serious concern to U.S. authorities throughout the disruptions of the early postwar period. One product of this concern was the 1952 President's Mate-rials Policy Commission, whose report is still the most influential document of its kind. One of the report's projections, as quoted by Samuel H. Ordway, Jr., was that although the demand for iron, copper, lead, and zinc might increase by only as much as 40 to 50 percent over the following 25 years, the demand for bauxite (from which aluminum is extracted) might increase fourfold and the demand for magnesium, an alloy of iron, from eighteen–to twentyfold. Demand for all minerals, including fuel, was expected to double by 1975. This does not seem too serious until placed in historical perspective. Around 1900, the report pointed out, the United States produced about 15 percent more materials than it consumed. By 1950, however, it was consuming some 10 per-cent more materials than it produced (these calculations do not include food, of which the United States has a surplus). "The quantity of most metals and mineral fuels used in the United States since the First World War exceeds the total used throughout the entire world in all of history preceding 1914" (*ibid,* p. 988).

Some of these trends are illustrated in figure 6.2. Clearly visible are the peaks of both production and consumption centering on the two world wars as well as the Korean War, and the trough centering on the Great Depression. Toward the end it will be noted that domestic production (in the case of copper, smelting from domestic ores) falls off quite sharply. From other sources it can be calculated that Americans in 1950 were using three times as much copper as in 1900, three-and-one-half times as much iron, and four times as much zinc. At this point the story is taken up by the import figures. According to Leallyn B. Clapp, it was in 1953 that the United States first began to import iron ore. By 1969, no less than 23 percent of it was being imported, mostly from Venezuela. The principal source of bauxite for aluminum is Jamaica. Other countries supply the United States with much of its copper, zinc, and lead, and with all of its tin. Of the major metals, only magnesium and molybdenum are supplied entirely from U.S. sources. Imports of crude bauxite were valued at $78 mil-lion in 1960; by the second half of the decade, they were regularly over the $140 million mark and increasing. In the same period imports of copper went from $353

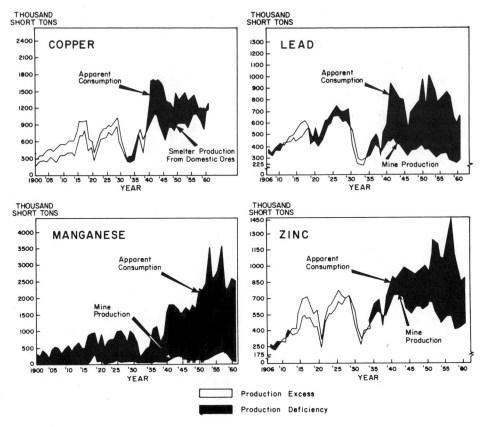

FIGURE 6.2.   Trends in U.S. production and consumption of four important metals. Figures reflect apparent consumption because actual consumption is not known. Note that the consumption peaks reached in World War II have been surpassed in three out of four cases.

million to a level that seemed likely to settle at around $500 million and could go as high as $855 million; imports of nickel climbed from $89 million to over $200 million; and imports of tin more than doubled to reach a level of between $180 and $190 million.

Although a few other countries may eventually reach the U.S. level per capita of metal consumption, it is clear that, for the next few decades at least, the main pressure on world metal resources will continue to come from the United States. And the next few decades will be crucial indeed. According to Preston E. Cloud, Jr., world supplies of at least 8 industrial and precious metals will be exhausted before the middle of the twenty-first century. For the United States, the corresponding figure is 13 (the two exceptions, in a list that includes chromium, nickel, and tungsten, are iron and molybdenum). In several cases, supplies in the capitalist countries are likely to give out first; for instance, the Sino-Soviet bloc has most of the world's tungsten. Cloud's estimates assume that current rates of consumption and ore recovery will continue. Another set of estimates, by Harrison Brown, assume that U.S. demand for metals will increase four-and-one-half times over 1960 levels by the end of the century. These estimates show the United States running out of 11 important metals, including chromium, nickel, tungsten, and zinc, by 1990.

Complete dependence on foreign sources for most strategic metals is not a prospect that pleases the nation's defense planners. We therefore have a so-called national stockpile of these metals. In 1970 this stockpile, with various other emergency stockpiles acquired under federal law, had an estimated market value of $7.1 billion. The total value of U.S. metal production in 1969 was about $3.3 billion, while that of U.S. metal imports (except imports of crude bauxite) was over $4 billion. Simple arithmetic suggests that, given the levels of consumption to be expected in wartime, the protection afforded by the various emergency stockpiles is not very high.

Even if, as Hans H. Landsberg has claimed, technological improvements in ore extraction make it unlikely that the United States will actually run out of metals in the foreseeable future, there is still the problem of rising costs. The price of tin, for instance, increased by nearly 75 percent between 1960 and 1970, and the price of copper by over 80 percent. Indeed, the federal government has been forced more than once to use the threat of releasing metals from the national stockpile as a device for bringing prices down. There could hardly be clearer evidence that the true emergency is not the international situation but the U.S. rate of consumption.

In contrast with metals, sand, gravel, slate, clay, and many other common earth materials are abundant and are used almost as they occur, without processing or refinement except of a simple, mechanical nature. Nevertheless, they can cause environmental problems, especially at the extraction stage. Sand and gravel pits mar hillsides and stream valleys. For convenience and economy, quarry sites are as close as possible to the city, where their ugliness is most conspicuous. Noise and dust are nuisances to nearby residents. As the urban area expands it needs more and more sand, gravel, and cement, yet covers more and more quarry sites with streets and housing. There is very little recovery of used concrete and broken bricks when structures are demolished; the rate of waste is even higher than for the less common mineral commodities. Moreover, the rubble is as bulky as the original quarry material, and is usually dumped on vacant land or tidelands where it remains an eyesore and disrupter of local plant and animal ecology.

Consumption of earth materials has increased greatly since World War II. Harrison Brown has calculated that between 1949 and 1967 U.S. production of stone, sand, and gravel went from 3,300 kg per capita to 8,000 kg per capita. Even greater was the increase in cement production, from 235 kg per capita to 1,000. Substantial increases were also found for clay and lime. Between 1960 and 1969 the amount of sand and gravel sold or used increased by over 30 percent and that of stone by 40 percent. Little attention is paid to the depletion of these particular resources, since they are cheap and plentiful. But the open space that their removal leaves permanently scarred is not at all plentiful. Partial rehabilitation is possible in some cases, but a better remedy would be to design and construct our cities for permanence.

From an ecological viewpoint, depletion of a vital resource over a long period is just as alarming as the short-term depletions that are of immediate economic concern. The U.S. chemical industry, for instance, is consuming phosphate rock, the principal source of calcium phosphate for fertilizers, at a rate that increased from 59 kg per capita in 1949 to 180 kg in 1967. The United States has nearly one-third of the known world reserves of this rock and exports over 10 million short tons of it a year. At the same time domestic producers are mining it at a rate double that of ten years ago. World reserves of potash and phosphate rock are about 50 billion tons: apparent U.S. consumption of both in 1969 was about 34 million short tons. Since both chemicals are essential for soil renewal, the fact that supplies may last to the year 3000 is no cause for self-congratulation. One thousand years is a short period in the life of a non-renewable resource.

An interesting case of an auxiliary material facing depletion is that of mercury. The process of synthesizing organic chemicals, as Barry Commoner has pointed out, requires large amounts of chlorine, the production of which involves mercury. Use of mercury for this purpose has increased nearly 4,000 percent since 1946. Although about 10 percent less mercury was recovered from domestic ores in 1969 than in 1960, its value was over twice as high. The shortage of uranium, in relation to possible future demand, has been mentioned above (p.000). Here, it is sufficient to note that if the United States ever converts entirely to electricity from nuclear fuels, it will have to be by means of the so-called breeder reactor, which converts fissionable uranium into other materials with a higher energy yield. At present, the United States has more uranium than it needs: only $8 million worth of uranium oxide was imported in 1970 as compared with $364 million worth in 1960. But this situation could change very rapidly, especially as other countries develop nuclear power industries.

RENEWABLE RESOURCES: TIMBER

Timber is the most heavily used organic basic material the earth provides. Forests are self-perpetuating resources even under heavy harvest if they are given correct care. But at present, according to Kai Curry-Lindahl, only about 13 percent of the world's 9.8 billion acres of forest are under any sort of management. Forests, as he proceeds to point out, have at least three important functions besides their economic one: they affect the *climate*, by absorbing heat and producing oxygen; they act as *watersheds*; and they conserve regional *ecology*, including habitats for wildlife. Deforestation, on the other hand, destroys ecosystems, erodes soil, and creates serious danger of flooding. In the western United States, some 90 percent of recoverable water supply comes from forest watersheds.

In the last fifty years deforestation has become a problem of world-wide dimensions. Europe has been losing its forests since the Middle Ages, until perhaps one-tenth of them are left. The United States has cut down at least half its forests since the seventeenth century. Now it is the turn of the tropical countries. To cite Curry-Lindahl again: Africa has lost 33 percent of its original rain forests and Brazil 40 percent. In the Philippines, 50 percent of the forests have been cleared in the last fifty years. Much of this damage is due to shifting cultivation, or "slash and burn agriculture," which is practiced throughout Africa and Asia. The method consists in clearing a patch of forest by cutting down and then burning its underbrush. The ashes so formed fertilize a thin layer of topsoil, on which crops are grown. Since nothing further is done to enrich or conserve the soil it is soon depleted. The farmer moves on to another part of the forest, leaving the abandoned patch to be overgrown with weeds and grasses that often prevent reforestation.

Another major threat to the world's last remaining rainforests is U.S. policy in Southeast Asia. In South Vietnam, reports Arthur H. Westing, U.S. bull - dozers had leveled over 750,000 acres by mid-1970. It is not known exactly how much of this was forest of timber quality, but the South Vietnamese forest service calculated its losses at a minimum of 126,000 acres of prime timber land. Altogether, at least 3 million acres of South Vietnam's forest lands have been lost to the war, 1 million of them through the massive U.S. herbicide program. The latter has now been largely abandoned in favor of bulldozing. The purpose, of course, is to deny cover to the National Liberation Front. But the long-term effect will be to destroy watersheds, increase the already considerable danger of flooding, and further weaken the economy of South Vietnam.

The United States has not been notably rational in the management of its own timber resources. In the nineteenth century, the motto was "cut and get out." Unrestrained logging was followed by fires. In 1871, some 1,500 people lost their lives in one such fire, at Peshtigo, Wisconsin. These and other examples of abuse, cited by Michael Frome in his history of the U.S. Forest Service, led to the first efforts at national control of the lumber industry. In 1876 the Department of Agriculture was instructed by Congress to prepare a report on the forest situation. This interest eventually led to the establishment of a Division of Forestry within the department. In 1891 the Forest Reserve Act authorized the creation of national forest reserves on public domain—the beginning of the national forest system. However, nothing very much was done with these reserves until Gifford Pinchot (1865–1946) became chief of the Division of Forestry and obtained the enthusiastic support of President Theodore Roosevelt. This was the beginning of the U.S. Forest Service, which founded its first experimental station in 1907. Thus the agency mainly responsible for the nation's timber resources was called into being by overwhelming evidence of abuse of the public interest by the timber companies, which protested every acre of public land added to the national forest reserves. Pinchot himself finally lost his job because he had openly supported the cause of conservation once too often (the issue was the granting of mining claims in Alaska).

With the New Deal a national timber policy at last began to take shape. The famous Copeland Report, published in 1933, revealed that private forests were eleven times more susceptible to fire than national forests, and that less than 1 percent of the former benefited from selective cutting or systematic replanting. The Civilian Conservation Corps, created the same year, planted an immense number of trees (more than half the number ever planted in the nation, according to Frome) and improved recreational facilities. The logging companies began to learn from government research and example. Nevertheless, in a survey conducted at the end of World War II the Forest Service rated cutting practices in 64 percent of private forests as "poor" or "destructive."

Today, the extension of public ownership envisaged by the Copeland Report and the early conservationists has not yet taken place: only some 187 million acres of forest out of a national total of over 700 million are federally managed—a depressingly small advance over 1940, when the figure was 177 million. Management of most U.S. forests (including some national ones) remains lax; planning often amounts to no more than keeping total cut less than total growth. As of 1963, total U.S. commercial forest lands, including national and state forests, amounted to some 509 million acres covered by 628 billion cubic feet of growing stock. Since 1965, domestic output of industrial timber products from roundwood has averaged about 11 billion cubic feet and consumption of the same about 12 billion cubic feet, the difference being made up by imports. The big increase has been not in the consumption of board lumber, which has remained in the region of 40 billion board feet a year since 1950, but of pulpwood. Measured as consumption of paper and board, this increase was more than 150 percent between 1950 and 1970. In 1970 the United States imported 6.6 million tons of finished newsprint, or twice the amount it produced domestically. This represented an increase of 36 percent over 1950 imports. Meanwhile, the U.S. salvage rate—the proportion of wastepaper being used in the production of new paper and paperboard—declined from 27 percent in 1950 to 18 percent in 1969.

Timber conservation has two main aspects, preservation of wood products and careful management of forests. Where demand for an organic resource is very great, the best form of management may be to convert the natural ecosystem into an artificial one. In agriculture, for example, plant and animal growth and reproduction are almost completely controlled by man. The major European forests are under a system of intensified management that requires high labor input. Under a comparable level of care the annual growth rate of U.S. forests could probably be doubled; certainly, lumber costs would be reduced.

The most important practice in intensified forest management is frequent but highly selective cutting. It stimulates regeneration by encouraging seed stock, provides continuous soil protection and wildlife cover, and generally makes for ecological balance and aesthetic value. All of these benefits are impaired by clear cutting, which is the systematic deforestation of entire areas. Short-run cost accounting favors clear cutting because the initial harvest cost is less. But selective cutting affords timber of more uniform size and quality, and clear-cut areas may be impossible to regenerate. In spite of this, over 60 percent of annual U.S. timber production comes from clear cutting. Another important practice is timber stand improvement, which consists in pruning lower branches and thinning heavy stands and dense underbrush. It accompanies selective cutting and gives the forest an open, park-like character. Water yields are increased and more clear lumber is produced when forests receive this care.

Another important management responsibility, as Smokey the Bear continually reminds us, is fire prevention. What Smokey does not say is that total prevention may not be advisable in all cases. Wildfire is an integral part of the natural ecosystem in many regions, and human success in eliminating it has caused unexpected problems. Undergrowth that is not restrained by periodic burning over (figure 6.3) becomes dense and loses much of its value as watershed. In some cases, absence of burning over sets the stage for fiercer fires that wipe out mature timber capable of surviving less intense ones. Accordingly fire has become a tool of management (essay 6.1). Despite all these precautions, 15 to 20 million acres are swept by fire every year, adding to timber shortages. More selective cutting and timber stand improvement would reduce this hazard.

Fire, however, is not the main cause of timber loss in the United States: insects are estimated to be responsible for twice as much and diseases for four times as much. The danger of both is increased by drought and fire. Present countermeasures are hardly satisfactory. Pest control in forest management is approached with the same broad-spectrum insecticides used in agriculture (see chapter 9). In both cases the result is ecological overkill (see figure 6.4).

A new source of timber damage is photochemical smog. It gradually kills the leaves of a tree, which dies when photosynthetic activity becomes inadequate. Trees of the pine family are most vulnerable. Kai Curry-Lindahl reports that in the San Bernardino National Forest and environs, about 60 miles from Los Angeles, about half the mature ponderosa and Jeffrey pines show some smog damage and 3 percent of them are already dead. Smog is also affecting the Southern California citrus groves. In Beltsville, Maryland, the Plant Industry Station of the Department of Agriculture has observed similar damage on a wide variety of vegetables, flowers, and trees. The

FIGURE 6.3.   Not a pyromaniac but an employee of the U.S. Forest Service engaged in experimental burning under red pine in the Chippewa National Forest, Minnesota. Forest improvement is as important a goal here as fire protection. (U.S. Forest Service)

Essay 6.1.   Fire Ecology and Wood Production

The controlled use of fire to maintain and restore forest resources is known to forestry experts as prescribed burning. *It is not a panacea, but for certain species under certain conditions it can bring numerous benefits. Such is the case with the longleaf and southern yellow pine. Of the four major southern pines, longleaf is the most tolerant of fire as a control factor in its habitat. In earlier times it rivaled the Douglas fir as this country's most valuable timber product. But the virgin supplies were gradually exhausted because hogs ate the seedlings, and because settlers in the southeast coastal plains practiced annual burning, which is too much even for the longleaf. So, too, is total protection from fire. This, however, was the policy later introduced by the U.S. Forest Service. Consequently, the longleaf forests gave way to ecosystems that were no longer "fire climax types," that is, they did not depend on fire for their growth and survival. These "nonfire climax types" were unfortunately not free of fire as a destructive force. Invaded by dense underlying layers of gallberry, wiregrass, and other shrublike species, they were subject to wildfire every six to eight years. Modern forestry research has provided the means to avert this type of climax. The longleaf pine, it seems, is almost unique in its ability to withstand fire after the first year following germination. For the next three to seven years it remains in a grass stage during which it may be starved of sunlight by faster-growing species, especially hardwoods, or attacked by disease. Moreover, when it does begin to grow again it once more becomes vulnerable to fire until it reaches a height of about six feet. For the rest of its life, however, it is practically immune. The burning is usually carried out with a number of goals in mind, but the following procedure is typical. During the summer before the trees are to be cut down, a relatively hot fire is used to clear undergrowth and prepare a seedbed. The actual cutting takes place in the winter, after the seeds have fallen. Three winters later, and approximately every three winters thereafter, the area is subjected to burning in order to suppress vegetation competing with the longleaf seedlings and control the diseases to which they are subject. Douglas fir and even giant sequoia have been shown to benefit from similar treatment; most hardwoods, on the other hand, do not tolerate fire well. Prescribed burning may improve not only the timber quality of softwood forests but also their ecology, aesthetic appearance, and ability to support wildlife. (For more information, consult the proceedings of the* Prescribed Burning Symposium, Charleston, April 14–16, 1971, *published by the U.S. Forest Service.)*

FIGURE 6.4.   Aerial spraying of pesticide for spruce budworm
control, Boise National Forest, Idaho. Problems of scale become
apparent in such measures. It is doubtful that more than 20 to 25
percent of the pesticide settles on the tree cover; the remaining
75 to 80 percent drifts with the air currents, eventually settling on
nontarget soils and water surfaces. The technique is both materially
wasteful and ecologically damaging—essentially biological overkill.
(U.S. Forest Service)

flowering cherry trees of Tokyo have suffered so badly from air pollution that the Japanese government sent to the District of Columbia for new stock. But air pollution in
Washington, as the Nader Study Group has argued, may soon endanger these famous
trees and much else besides.

Wood becomes a useful material only after years of growth and the survival of many hazards. Nevertheless, a great deal of unnecessary waste is allowed to
occur, beginning with the harvest. Quantities of wood suitable for pulp, chip board,
and many chemical uses are lost in the typical logging practice of leaving limbs and
tops behind. This is justified by the logging companies on the grounds of high labor
cost, which are supposed to make removal economically unfeasible. Such an excuse
might do if loss of wood were the only problem; since wood is organic it eventually becomes soil. The accumulated litter, however, increases fire hazard and must be disposed
of in some way. The usual way is to burn it in the winter when snow reduces the danger of fire to the mature timber, but this is to substitute one form of pollution for another. A less risky and more beneficial solution is mechanical mulching and spreading
of the litter after harvest. This, of course, is more expensive, but should probably be

required by law, just as surface mining operators should be required to rehabilitate the land that they disturb (chapter 9). Among the other new techniques that may help to make timber harvesting a less destructive process is logging by balloon, which reduces the need for access roads (figure 6.5).

The greatest loss of wood materials—nearly 50 percent— occurs during processing. About 13 percent of the original timber is generally lost as bark and another 13 percent as sawdust; edgings account for 12 percent and slabs for 6 percent. Finally, 6 percent is lost in seasoning, but this is unavoidable. All the discarded materials are normally burned even though their value is high and increasing. Bark is a source of plywood glues, plastics, insecticides, mulches, fertilizers, and tannin, while sawdust and chunk wood are often suitable for rayon, hardboard, pressed board, roofing felt, and paper. Sweden salvages 25 percent of its pulp from sawmill waste, but most American sawmills do not find it profitable to collect, sort, and transport waste materials to sell for these uses. The so-called timber shortage is in part a result of these wasteful practices. And yet the timber industry never ceases to lobby for more intensive harvesting

FIGURE 6.5.   Blimp logging experiment in the Willamette National Forest, Oregon, July 1966; the airship at right is full of journalists. Despite favorable national attention as a method of reducing the environmental impact of cutting skid trails and logging-access roads through the forest, the technique has remained largely experimental. Apparently blimp logging is not economically competitive under present forest policies. Perhaps if the national forest were to reduce or eliminate road-building credit as part of the payment made by lumber and paper companies for timber resources, the economic feasibility of blimp logging would increase. (photo courtesy of U.S. Forest Service)

of national forest lands. The most serious threat so far from this direction was the proposed National Timber Supply Act of 1969, which would have required an immediate increase in federal logging levels and consecration of more than half of all national forests to logging as the "dominant use." Fortunately, the bill was defeated after Chief Forester Edward P. Cliff and others had testified that the nation's timber supplies could best be increased by improved forestry on presently unproductive private lands.

After timber has been converted to board and sold, its preservation is the responsibility of individual owners or users. Wood is susceptible to weathering and to fire and insect damage. Frequent painting or varnishing will protect it from the weather, but fortification against fire and insects is less simple. The best method is probably chemical impregnation done at the sawmill after kilning, but this is not now widely practiced. The initial cost of treated lumber would be greater, but upkeep costs would be lower in the long run. Another way to save wood is through the use of substitutes such as vinyl, especially in exposed places. Such a development, however, is not likely to be encouraged by the lumber industry. Finally, new varieties of trees have been developed that mature up to twice as fast as unimproved varieties. If enough of the new trees can be planted on private lands, the shortages predicted for the year 2000 may never occur. Short-term shortages, however, seem almost inevitable.

A NATIONAL MATERIALS POLICY?

Although our entire way of life encourages the consumption of materials in increasingly huge quantities, we have nothing that really amounts to a national materials policy. The Bureau of Mines, which oversees our mineral resources, has long been an advocate of the mining industries. The U.S. Forest Service, despite its conservationist heritage, lacks sufficient jurisdiction and is too often forced into the role of having to please everybody. The Environmental Protection Agency (**E.P.A.**) was given broad regulatory authority under the 1969 National Environmental Policy Act (**N.E.P.A.**). But it has to tread warily in fields long occupied by older agencies. The President's **Council on Environmental Quality**, created by N.E.P.A., is simply an advisory body. In general, there is much governmental concern over pollution, but not over preventing the waste that causes the pollution.

A very large part of the problem is the complacency that still prevails even among experts. Thus the Commission on Population Growth and the American Future, in its 1972 report, affirmed its belief that "the United States would have no serious difficulty acquiring the supplies it needs for the next 50 years, even if the population were to grow at the 3-child [per family] rate." This conclusion is all the more incredible because the commission made projections of the demand for 19 important nonfuel minerals, including chromium, nickel, tungsten, and lead, domestic supplies of which are verging on exhaustion. But the shortages, the commission argues, can be taken care of by "tolerable price increases," which will both reduce demand by encouraging recycling, and increase supply by encouraging imports and exploration for new deposits. Finally, we are told that even if world demand rises, the United States will be able to top new supplies by mining lower-grade ores. Although the commission lists several factors that might interfere with this scheme, it clearly believes that the United States can afford to go on using nonfuel minerals at its present rate.

Some of this complacency, it must be admitted, appears to be justified on historical grounds. Around the beginning of the century, conservationists such as Gifford Pinchot were predicting the exhaustion of U.S. timber supplies in a generation and of minerals such as anthracite in fifty years. Neither has come to pass, although domestic anthracite mining is in trouble and domestic timber may well have been saved by Pinchot's own Forest Service. What Pinchot did not foresee then was that technological change would take much of the pressure off both resources. Meanwhile, industry has become far more skilled in resource use. Hans H. Landsberg has listed four areas of which this is true: upgrading old resources; discovering new ones; devising more efficient methods of use; and adjusting to scarcities (e.g., the use of substitute materials). The trouble is that the measures taken in all these areas are partial and sporadic. Neither recycling nor large-scale exploration is undertaken until a material is in really short supply. Thus one-half the nation's copper and two-thirds of its lead, as Richard Saltonstall has pointed out, are already being produced from scrap. But demand for both metals could be as much as 70 times 1960 levels by the end of the century, according to Landsberg. Many people take comfort from the thought that vast new mineral deposits will be found in the ocean bed. Recent geological theory, how- ever, suggests that the larger oceans are much younger than the land—too young, in fact, to contain deposits of the desired size. Mining ores of ever lower quality will only create a new energy crisis on top of the existing one. Contrary to popular belief, nuclear power has not yet been harnessed directly to mining operations, and may never be. It is time for us to stop behaving as if mankind will miraculously come into some rich mineral inheritance on reaching the year 2000. Our only patrimony may well be what we already possess.

What is needed is an entire new philosophy of resource use—a philosophy based on recycling instead of consumption. Only through oxidation or friction can a metal be consumed in the literal sense; all other uses allow it to be reclaimed. Such, however, is the present structure of the U.S. economy that it is generally cheaper to mine fresh ore than to recycle scrap. If mining companies were made to pay the full environmental cost of their operations, they would find recycling more attractive. The alternative is a spectacular increase in commodity prices, all of which will eventually be passed on to the consumer. The wholesale price index for nonferrous metals has almost doubled in the last twenty years—a rate of inflation more than three times that of all commodities. The price of iron and steel has increased almost as fast. The need to recycle organic materials may not seem as urgent, but at least in the case of paper products it could have an immediately beneficial effect on the environment.

Above all, we will have to give up our belief that nature has singled out the United States as the perpetual beneficiary of her abundance. The team that produced *The Limits of Growth* has demonstrated that even if available stocks of natural resources were doubled, continued use of them at present rates would bring about the collapse of the world socioeconomic system through pollution. Decreasing per capita consumption of materials is therefore the goal at which we in the more highly industrialized countries should aim. If we do not plan for scarcity now, waking from the dream of abundance may be unpleasant indeed.

REFERENCES

Brown, Harrison, *The Challenge of Man's Future* (New York: Viking, 1960).
——, "Human Materials Production as a Process in the Biosphere," *Scientific American,* September 1970.
Clapp, Leallyn B., "Can Our Conspicuous Consumption of Natural Resources Be Cyclic?" in Garry D. McKenzie and Russell O. Utgard (eds.), *Man and His Physical Environment* (Minneapolis: Burgess, 1972).
Cloud, Preston E., Jr., "Realities of Mineral Distribution," in Garry D. McKenzie and Russell O. Utgard (eds.) *Man and His Physical Environment* (Minneapolis: Burgess, 1972).
Commission on Population Growth and the American Future, *Population and the American Future* (New York: Signet, 1972).
Commoner, Barry, *The Closing Circle* (New York: Knopf, 1971).
Curry-Lindahl, Kai, *Conservation for Survival* (New York: Morrow, 1972).
Esposito, John, *Vanishing Air: The Ralph Nader Study Group Report on Air Pollution* (New York: Grossman, 1970).
Frome, Michael, *The Forest Service* (New York: Praeger, 1971).
Holman, Eugene, "Our Inexhaustible Resources," in Garry D. McKenzie and Russell O. Utgard (eds.), *Man and His Physical Environment* (Minneapolis: Burgess, 1972).
Landsberg, Hans H., "The U.S. Resource Outlook: Quantity and Quality," in Garry D. McKenzie and Russell O. Utgard (eds.), *Man and His Physical environment* (Minneapolis: Burgess, 1972).
Meadows, Donella H., et al., *The Limits to Growth* (New York: Universe, 1972).
National Wildlife Federation, "World EQ Index," *International Wildlife,* July–August 1972, pp. 21–36.
Ordway, Samuel H., Jr., "Possible limits of Raw-Material Consumption," in William L. Thomas, Jr. (ed.) *Man's Role in Changing the Face of the Earth* (University of Chicago Press, 1956).
Saltonstall, Richard, Jr., *Your Environment and What You Can Do About It* (New York: Ace, 1970).
Westing, Arthur H., "Land War: II. Leveling the Jungle," *Environment,* November 1971, pp. 8–12.

PART THREE

THE PHYSIOLOGICAL IMPACT

7 AIR POLLUTION

Air pollution is the presence in the atmosphere of elements that have adverse effects upon one or more of the following: human health and well-being; property; and nonhuman life forms, both plant and animal. In its broadest sense, then, air pollution includes contamination from volcanic ash and gases, smoke of natural fires, dust, and even pollen. But it is pollution derived from the activities of man that represents the most significant long-term threat to the biosphere.

HOW WE FOUL THE ATMOSPHERE

The earth's atmosphere in an unpolluted state is composed of 78 percent stable nitrogen (N_2), 21 percent oxygen (O_2), less than 1 percent argon and other inert gases, .03 percent or 300 **ppm** carbon dioxide (CO_2), and .01 ppm ozone (O_3). However, naturally occurring O_3 may sometimes be as high as .05 ppm. Water vapor is also present in greatly variable quantities. Carbon dioxide is essential for **photosynthesis,** while oxygen is essential for nearly all forms of life. Ozone helps to protect life by absorbing ultraviolet radiation. In chemical terms, air pollution consists either in an increase in ozone, or in the addition of other active substances, or in both. Each year man puts into the atmosphere some 800 million tons of pollutants. This is *primary pollution,* or pollution before heat, sunlight, and contact of the pollutants with the at-

mosphere and each other have set various chemical processes in motion. Primary pollution in 1970 consisted of 280 million tons of carbon monoxide, 146 million tons of
sulfur oxides, 110 million tons of particulates, 88 million tons of reactive hydrocarbons, and 53 million tons of nitrogen oxides (essay 7.1).

Pollution is generated by three basic processes: *attrition, vaporization,* and
combustion. Attrition refers to foreign matter added to the air through any form of
friction—carbon from automobile tires, for instance, or asbestos from brake linings. Industrial activities such as blasting, grinding, and cutting are also prime contributors.
Vaporization is the process by which liquids become gases and so are diffused in the
atmosphere. Improper storage and handling, together with inefficient energy conversion techniques, cause most pollution from this source. By far the greatest contributor,
however, is combustion, which generates both gaseous and particulate impurities.
Many types of combustion are involved, but in the United States the internal combustion of automobile engines is easily the most serious problem—in fact, it produces
roughly half the contaminants loading our skies.

According to the National Emission Standards Study, the U.S. contribution to worldwide man-made air pollution in 1970 was some 214 million tons of major
pollutants, or about one-third the world total (table 7.1). The derivation of major emissions is shown in figure 7.1. For most regions of the country automobiles and power
plants are the largest and most dangerous contributors, partly because nitrogen dioxide
reacts with the organic hydrocarbons. In some localities reliance upon coal and fuel
oil for space heating adds significant pollution from sulfur oxides. Overall, transportation furnishes approximately 50 percent of U.S. air pollution, industry 16 percent,
electrical power generation 20 percent, refuse disposal 4 percent, and all the rest 10
percent.

There are of course many pollutants beside the ones shown in figure 7.1,
but they would probably add less than 2 percent to the U.S. total given in table 7.1.

TABLE 7.1.   Major air pollutants in the U.S. and world
(million tons)

	U.S. (1966)	U.S. (1970)	World (1970)
Carbon monoxide	94	100	280
Sulphur oxides	31	37	146
Hydrocarbons	29	32	88
Nitrogen oxides	15	21	53
Particulates	22	28	110
Total	191	214	677

Source: *National Emission Standards Study: Report of the Secretary of Health,
Education, and Welfare to the U.S. Congress in Compliance with the Air Quality
Act of 1967,* pp. 80–85; *U.S. News & World Report* Aug. 17, 1970, p. 40; and
Environmental Science and Technology, Vol. 4, February 1970, p. 89.

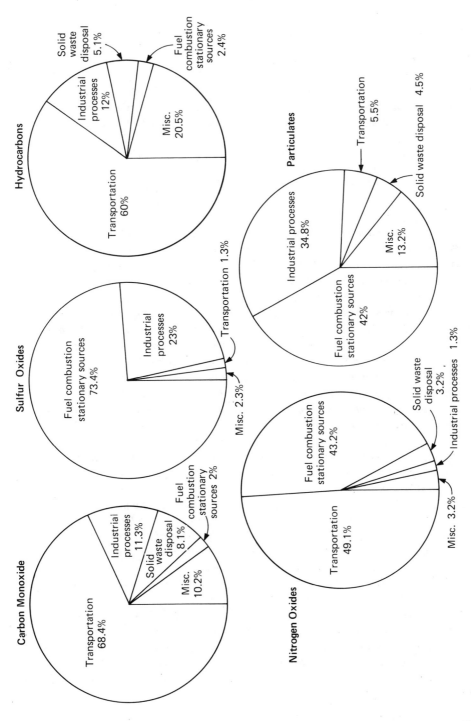

FIGURE 7.1. The major pollutants of air in the United States, and where they come from. (based on same sources as table 7.1)

Essay 7.1   Major Air Pollutants

Carbon monoxide   *In form, carbon monoxide (CO) is a colorless,
odorless, tasteless gas. It results from the incomplete combustion of organic
or fossil materials. Normal background levels of atmospheric CO range from
.025 to 1ppm. However, in a typical American city the range is from 10 to 50
ppm. Some 95 percent of all atmospheric CO is emitted in the northern
hemisphere and at least 65 percent of it is created by gasoline combustion.
Even at low background levels CO affects the blood's oxygen-carrying capacity
by combining with hemoglobin to form carboxy-hemoglobin (COHb). The
normal COHb level for human beings is under 2 percent; death from carbon
monoxide poisoning is likely if the level remains for long near 10 percent.
Such a level may often be reached for short periods in garages, tunnels, and
buildings constructed above highways, in all of which concentrations of CO
may be as great as 100 ppm. Two-hour exposures of 100 ppm. have been
found to increase COHb level to 15 percent. Among the immediate effects
upon humans are dizziness, blurred vision, and distorted perception of time—
certainly hazardous for drivers. Scarcely anything is known so far of the long-
range effects. Worldwide emissions of CO in 1970 were over 280 million tons.*

Sulfur oxides   *The chief pollutant in this group is sulfur dioxide (SO_2),
a colorless gas that can be smelled by human beings when it reaches a concentration of .3 ppm or above. About 5 percent of the sulfur oxides that result
from burning fossil fuels combine with oxygen to form sulfur trioxide (SO_3),
which in turn combines with water vapor to form sulfurous acid (H_2SO_3).
Additional water vapor results in the still more corrosive sulfuric acid
(H_2SO_4). Either acid can do considerable damage to vegetation, fabrics,
metals, paintwork, and even stone; flowers and other delicate vegetation show
damage after exposures of 1 ppm for as little as 1 hour, only .25 ppm above
the threshold for irritation in human beings. It takes about 5 ppm of SO_2 for
1 hour to cause considerable irritation of human throat and lung tissue, with
accompanying bronchial constriction. Concentrations of as few as .08 to .10
ppm for any length of time are considered unhealthy. Worldwide emissions
of all sulfur oxides now total about 146 million tons, of which 93 percent
occur in the northern hemisphere. U.S. emissions were estimated at 37 million
tons for 1970 and projected to go as high as 95 million tons by 1990.*

Particulates   *Unlike the other major pollutants, this is not a class of
chemical compound but merely a generic name for all particles emitted into
the surrounding air through some gaseous or atmospheric medium (smoke,
rain, industrial fumes, etc.). Among the most frequently identified particu-*

lates are fly ash, coal dust, insecticide dust, metallurgical fumes, and oil smoke. These are not to be thought of in the same category as "big, black, floating specks"; many are no larger than one-tenth of a millimeter and most are considerably smaller. General standards do exist for particulate emission. But they are almost impossible to enforce and may in any case be largely meaningless because of the chemical variety of the materials involved. World-wide emissions of particulates as of 1970 amounted to 110 million tons.

Hydrocarbons   As a class of carbon compounds, the hydrocarbons are generally divided into at least six main series: paraffins, olefines, acetylenes, benzenes, naphthenes, and anthracenes. They vary greatly in chemical reactivity, with the paraffins, including methane, as the least reactive. Human activity—notably, the combustion of gasoline and oil—accounts for only about 15 percent of the hydrocarbons in the atmosphere. But this 15 percent includes nearly all the compounds that react with sunlight to cause photochemical pollution. For instance, olefine concentrations of .001 to .5 ppm inflict injury on certain classes of plants. Substances such as formaldehyde (used for pickling biological specimens) and acrolein (used in tear gas) are also produced from hydrocarbons by photochemical reaction. A concentration of .3 ppm of reactive hydrocarbons can result in .1 ppm of photochemical oxidants, a class of pollutants that includes both hydrocarbon and nitrogen derivatives. Worldwide emissions of highly reactive hydrocarbons totaled 88 million tons in 1970.

Nitrogen oxides   Clean air consists of 78 percent nitrogen, 21 percent oxygen, and 1 percent water vapor, carbon dioxide, and other gases. Nitrogen oxides are formed by combustion, the amount formed depending largely on the temperature reached. They are both primary and secondary pollutants. Nitric oxide (NO), the direct product of combustion, may not be a pollutant in itself. But when mixed with air it reacts to become nitrogen dioxide (NO_2), a pollutant that in concentrations as low as .25 ppm for 1 hour can blanket the horizon with a reddish-brownish haze. At 3 ppm for 1 hour it has bronchial effects similar to those of SO_2. Even more important, however, is the ability of NO_2 to combine photochemically with the reactive hydrocarbons to form a wide range of pollutants, including the peroxyacetyl nitrates (PANs), a principal ingredient in smog. Since worldwide natural emissions of nitrogen oxides are 768 million tons compared with man-made emissions of 53 million tons (92 percent of them from the combustion of coal or petroleum products), it is clear that the problem is basically that of how we are using— or misusing—our stocks of fossil fuels.

Unfortunately, many of these so-called minor pollutants are far more poisonous, per unit emitted, than the ones dealt with so far. This is especially true of metals such as lead, cadmium, or nickel, all of which have become quite common atmospheric pollutants in recent years. According to Anthony Tucker, about 1 million tons of lead reach the atmosphere every year from truck and car exhausts—and this is not the only source of man-made lead pollution. In the United States, which has most of the world's automobiles, atmospheric lead levels have been rising in some cities at a rate of 5 percent a year or more. Inhaled lead is absorbed in much larger proportions than lead that is swallowed, and children are more susceptible to lead poisoning than adults. Since many poor families are forced to live near expressways and other main thoroughfares, the rates of lead poisoning among poor children are especially high. Thus in Chicago, as Paul P. Craig and Edward Berlin have pointed out, a testing program in 1967–68 found that nearly 6 percent of the 68,000 children tested had blood lead levels of 50 or more micrograms of lead per 100 milliliters of blood. The California Department of Public Health considers that, for children, 40 micrograms is the highest tolerable level. Introduction of low-lead gasolines and control of related exhaust emissions may eventually solve the problem. But this will not help the children condemned meanwhile to mental retardation and other disabilities because of lead poisoning. The case of lead is fairly well documented. How long will it take U.S. public health authorities to develop figures on cadmium, which causes hypertension and bone porosity, or nickel, which causes lung cancer?

THE CLIMATOLOGY OF AIR POLLUTION

While man generates the major atmospheric pollutants, it is nature that determines how they are spread around. Speed and direction of wind, variation in temperature, the presence of hills, valleys, or large bodies of water—everything, in short that contributes to an area's climate—can influence both the duration and intensity of air pollution. Man, of course, can and does modify the climate. But here we are not concerned so much with this as with the effects of meteorological and topographical factors, regardless of origin, upon the different types of polluting substances.

One such effect is known as *temperature inversion,* or simply **inversion**, because it is the opposite of what normally occurs. In the lower levels of the atmosphere air behaves like a gas, which is to say that, as it rises above the earth's surface and so is subjected to decreasing pressure, it both expands and cools. The rate at which it cools is generally expressed in terms of its *adiabatic lapse rate,* which is a rate calculated under the assumption that no heat is going in or out (according to meteorologists, any large body of air in motion can be regarded for all practical purposes as a closed system). If the air is "unsaturated"—that is, if it does not yet contain all the moisture it can hold at whatever temperature it happens to be at—then its adiabatic lapse rate is about 5.5°F. for every 1,000 feet it ascends. If, on the other hand, the air is saturated, then the rate is about half this. The adiabatic lapse rate is a mathematical constant. This does not mean, of course, that cooling has to take place at a steady and uniform rate. But it does mean that, other things being equal, the average rate of cooling is highly predictable.

Normally, then, at least in the lower levels of the atmosphere, we would expect to find air circulating in such a manner that the warmer air is below and the cooler air above. But sometimes, due to special atmospheric conditions, a layer of warm air fails to cool at the usual rate. Cooler air rising from below cannot penetrate this layer, and so is trapped beneath it and becomes stagnant. This is the phenomenon known as inversion (figure 7.2). Its importance for this chapter is that the trapped layer of air may contain pollutants. Short inversions may cause no more than discomfort, at least in the short run, but long ones can be disastrous. If the lower level of air is prevented from escaping by mountains, or if the region's major air masses for some reason fail to supply the usual cleansing winds, then a whole city or metropolitan region may begin quite literally to choke on its own filth.

One recent inversion episode, the subject of a perceptive article by Donald Jackson, is worth recalling because it shows that air pollution is a very much more serious and widespread public health problem than most people are willing to admit. It happened in Middlesex County, New Jersey, on September 16, 1971. High school athletes in a dozen local schools suddenly began to complain of breathing difficulties as they worked out. Some were in such pain that they had to be hospitalized immediately. In the worst of these outbreaks, the only explanation anyone could think of was that a helicopter spraying the nearby marshes with pesticide might have accidentally contaminated the school athletic field. Public health officials searching for an explanation discovered, almost by accident, that the oxidant levels in northern New Jersey that day had been in the region of .08 to .10 parts per million—certainly unacceptable (see table 7.2, p. 156). But oxidants were not considered a serious problem in the state, despite the heavy motor traffic, and there were only three stations that monitored them. No emergency was declared, although by midafternoon the temperature inversion, aided by a local ridge, had created a low-lying cloud of pollutants some twenty-five miles long and ten miles wide. The high school athletes, of couse, were not the only ones to suffer discomfort. But just because they were exerting themselves they had be-

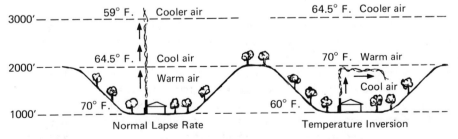

FIGURE 7.2.   Air temperature layers and vertical circulation (diagram assumes that air is unsaturated). Contours are meant to suggest that inversion often occurs where horizontal circulation is inhibited.

come the community's early warning system. However, since this was an area into which people moved in order to avoid big-city air pollution, the warning was not recognized.

Pollution Complexes

It is possible that the world's major pollution complexes share certain broad chemical similarities. But it is the combined effect of weather and terrain on the pollutants that creates the distinctive and persistent local pattern known as a complex. Two great cities, London and Los Angeles, enjoy the dubious honor of having given their names to two different types of pollution complex. The record of London's air pollution goes back to at least the seventeenth century. But it was the smog disaster of December, 1952, that finally showed not only Britain but the world just how dangerous air pollution could be. From December 5 onwards a temperature inversion sealed of off the valley of the Thames, trapping vast quantities of sulfur oxides and particulates over the city. Sulphur dioxide concentrations, typically .1 ppm, rose as high as .7 ppm. The London fog mingling with the smoke of coal fires became a new and deadlier substance: smog. A week later, when the inversion ended and the skies finally cleared, deaths had climbed to 2,482, as compared with an average of 945 for that time of year. Later, authorities calculated that a total of nearly 5,000 people, most of them old, sick, or infirm, had died as a result of the outbreak.

It is doubtful whether London will ever experience another "killer fog." The 1956 Clean Air Act—the first of its kind—gave local authorities the power to set up smoke control zones. According to Ronald C. Denney, by 1978 the entire London area will have been zoned in this way. Smoke emissions have already been reduced by 75 percent and sulfur dioxide emissions by 40 percent. Nevertheless, the London complex can still be regarded as typical of cold season temperature inversion in a valley setting. The high rate of sulfur emission, characteristic of older industrial cities, results from heavy combustion of fossil fuels (in the London case, coal fires in single-family homes, still by far the commonest form of nonindustrial space heating in the British Isles). Examples of the London complex (usually with fuel oil replacing coal for non-industrial use) can be found in such U.S. cities as Nashville, New York, and St. Louis (figure 7.3).

Unfortunately, even in the older cities, the main problem is no longer smoke but automobiles. This is the type of pollution that will always be linked with the name of Los Angeles—perhaps unfairly, because Los Angeles has probably tried harder to regulate its air pollution than any other city on earth. The first indications that Los Angeles had an air pollution problem appeared about 1940, with a significant buildup three years later, but it took over ten years to link it conclusively with motor traffic. The pattern that emerged was an entirely unfamiliar one. Hydrocarbons and nitrogen oxides, trapped from above by temperature inversion and at the sides by the mountains of the Los Angeles basin, were being transformed by photochemical processes into more active substances such as ozone, formaldehyde, and peroxyacetyl

FIGURE 7.3.   Cold season air pollution over St. Louis (photo taken April 1966). The Gateway Arch (in foreground) built to commemorate the city's role in the nation's westward expansion, serves as a backdrop to *London Type* pollution, with its relationship to cold season inversion of atmospheric temperatures and the increase in sulfur dioxide, carbon monoxide, and carbon particulate pollution associated with industrial processes and winter weather space-heating. (St. Louis Post-Dispatch, courtesy of National Air Pollution Control Administration)

nitrate. Heat and sunlight started the reactions so that summer levels were the highest and most prolonged (figure 7.4). This new type of pollution—so-called photochemical smog—was even more frightening than the old-fashioned kind because it involved chemical reactions that no one could control. Moreover, the area's millions of automobiles seemed impossible to regulate.

Even as we have increased our knowledge of London and Los Angeles pollution as two distinct types, most industrial cities of the world have begun to feel the impact of both. Thus winter pollution, fed by space heating and industrial processes, merges almost imperceptibly into summer pollution, as heat and radiation stimulate photochemical pollutants. In such cities, pollution has become part of the climate. The relationship of climatic conditions and chronic pollution is shown for the United States in figure 7.5.

Global Effects

Pollution complexes are by definition exceptional, and as such cause mainly sporadic and local concern. But what if the whole world were to become one

FIGURE 7.4.   Warm season air pollution in Los Angeles—*Los Angeles Type:* three views of City Hall from Arroyo Seco. (Top to bottom) A. Clear day, no atmospheric temperature inversion to trap pollution in basin. B. Dramatic low level inversion layer at about 210 feet above ground. Pollution trapped below this layer is stagnant in the basin. Above 210 feet pollution is dispersed and carried out of the basin by the prevailing westerly winds. C. The more typical inversion at 1,500 feet above ground level over the city is shown here. A ground observer cannot see the top of the pollution layer and stagnant, filth-ridden air permeates the entire basin. (Los Angeles County Air Pollution Control District)

vast pollution complex? The prospect, however distant, cannot be ruled out. There are three main problem areas: the buildup of atmospheric carbon dioxide, the buildup of particulates, and the impairment of the ecosphere's atmospheric recycling capabilities.

Carbon dioxide (CO_2) is not considered a pollutant because it occurs naturally in the atmosphere and plays an important part in many biological processes. However, there is considerable evidence that an increase in the atmosphere's CO_2 level also increases its temperature. In 1967 the President's Science Advisory Council warned that combustion of fossil fuels had increased the world CO_2 level by 14 percent in the last 100 years, and that a continued increase might raise atmospheric temperatures to a level sufficient to melt the polar ice caps, thus raising sea levels by as much as 400 feet. Since CO_2 is a combustion by-product, and since most of the world's fossil fuel stocks have been consumed in the last few decades (see chapter 4), we should not be surprised that scientists have been questioning the atmosphere's ability to keep CO_2 in balance. The surprising fact, really, is that people are not more worried. A 400-foot rise is not very probable, but even one of 20 feet would suffice to drown London and New York. However, the short-range effects of CO_2 buildup may have been counteracted by the accompanying buildup of atmospheric particulates, which reduce the amount of solar radiation entering the atmosphere. As for the long-range effects, it has been pointed out by S. Fred Singer that the oceans contain sixty times as much CO_2 as the atmosphere and seem capable of absorbing even more. Furthermore, increased at-

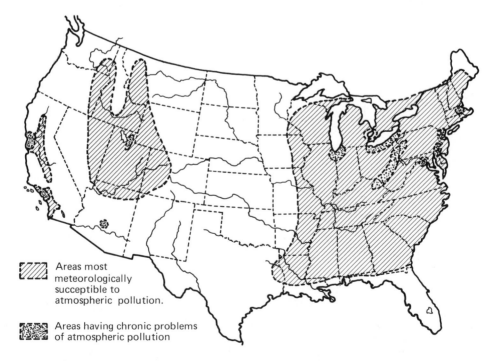

Areas most meteorologically succeptible to atmospheric pollution.

Areas having chronic problems of atmospheric pollution

FIGURE 7.5.   Smog is a chronic problem only in the heavily shaded areas, but could become one in the lightly shaded areas as population density increases.

mospheric CO_2 stimulates the growth of plants. The world's forests, then, can be expected to absorb some of the excess.

Even if the threat of carbon dioxide buildup is more apparent than real (a point by no means settled), there can be little doubt of the threat presented by the buildup in particulates. It has been calculated that until about 1930 the atmospheric dust load was rather constant (figure 7.6). Since that time, however, the amount of dust has gone up—and the temperature has gone down. The U.S. dust bowl of 1933–37 initiated a period of major atmospheric cooling. The dust of agriculture was also increasing elsewhere. In India and China, marginal grasslands were coming under the plow. By the 1960s the Soviets were making notable contributions, comparable to our own dust bowl, as they opened up the "new lands." Agriculture was not the only factor; both industrialization and motor transportation were on the increase. Soviet observations in the Caucasus between 1930 and 1963 found a 19-fold increase in particulates. Similar figures have been reported for other industralizing areas. The contrails left by jet aircraft are another source of worry; according to some meterologists, they have increased cirrus clouds in North America and Europe by from 5 to 10 percent. The net result has been a reduction in the atmosphere's **albedo**, or capacity to reflect solar radiation, and a corresponding reduction of nearly 1 percent in average atmospheric temperatures. This appears to be a reversal of the previous trend. Between 1880 and 1940 average atmospheric temperatures increased by 1°F. But since 1940 there has been a decrease of ½°F., so that 1970 was down to a cold level comparable

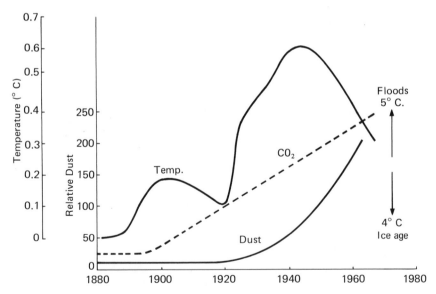

FIGURE 7.6. Effect of dust and CO_2 on atmospheric temperature. An increase of 5°C. in mean temperature could cause worldwide floods, while a decrease of 4°C. would mean the beginning of a new ice age. (adapted by courtesy of Convair Areospace Division, General Dynamics Corporation, from a projection by E.R. Bartle, M. Griggs, and C.B. Ludwig)

to the early 1900s. While a change of 1°F. in sixty years at first seems small, it is estimated that a drop of only 4° to 8°F., requiring 240 years at present rates, would bring
on another ice age. Even at the height of the Pleistocene average temperatures were
probably no more than 5° to 8°F. colder than at present. Some scientists believe the
earth has been cooling steadily since the 1930s.

Another possibility is that we are running out of oxygen. This no longer
seems as urgent a threat as it once did. Biologists used to warn of shortages within
"several" generations as land vegetation was removed and marine phytoplankton poisoned. The marine situation in particular was thought to be extremely critical, since 70
percent of oxygen recycling due to photosynthesis takes place in the oceans. In reality,
however, plant recycling of oxygen amounts to just enough for its own use and for
oxidizing it after death. In other words, animals and bacteria consume oxygen almost
equal to the total product of photosynthesis with very little over for human beings.
This sounds like bad news until one realizes that the reservoirs of oxygen are vast and
well buffered against change for the next thousand years. Nevertheless, according to
Lloyd V. Berkner and Lauriston C. Marshall, if plant activity ceased the atmospheric·
sources of oxygen would be depleted completely within two thousand years. Actually,
for most city dwellers it matters very little how soon oxygen stocks are likely to be depleted, since carbon monoxide will have reached critical levels long before. In any case,
the chief problem is not the availability of this or that gas but the stability of the ecosystems that keep the entire atmosphere in being.

THE COSTS OF AIR POLLUTION

The costs of air pollution are most often stated in terms of the damage actually done. In 1970 the National Air Pollution Control Administration estimated this
figure at $13.5 billion a year. According to the same source it would have cost only
$2.6 billion to prevent this damage. Of couse, both figures are somewhat arbitrary—
damage to human beings cannot be equated with damage to property— but they do indicate how large a gap there is between need and performance. In this section we shall
deal with some aspects of the need, and in the next one with what might be done to
improve the performance.

By 1970, according to N.A.P.C.A., polluted air was costing U.S. agriculture
$500 million annually, of which $132 million was in California. This appears to be a
conservative estimate; other estimates range as high as $240 million for southern
California alone. Most plants are susceptible to a wide range of pollutants. Leafy
vegetables and flowers are most sensitive. But trees suffer too: 1.7 million dead ponderosa pines rim the Los Angeles basin, and citrus yields there have been reduced by 50
percent. Damage to domestic animals appear principally due to secondary pollution
that has settled and accumulated on pasture and forage. For example, fluoride fumes
given off in the production of superphosphate fertilizers and aluminum refining are
protoplasmic poisons with an affinity for calcium. Not only are the bones and teeth of

an animal eating contaminated feed severely damaged but its health, productivity, and lifespan are permanently affected. In dairy stock, milk production and quality decline, while in meat animals the flesh gain may be entirely eliminated (figure 7.7).

Air pollution is generally assumed to have a negative effect on real estate values, but few investigators have succeeded in proving it. One exception, known as the St. Louis–East St. Louis study, succeeded because it isolated the other variables involved. Records of property sales in a heavily polluted area between 1957 and 1964 were compared with those in a control area for the same period. The variables used in the analysis were: (1) air pollution, measured by sulfur diffusion; (2) travel time from central business district; (3) accessibility of highways; (4) accessibility of shopping areas; (5) accessibility of industrial areas; (6) school quality; (7) crime rates; (8) state location (Illinois or Missouri). Variables 4, 5, and 7 were found to exert insignificant influences on property values. But while the average value of properties in the control group was higher at the end of the nine-year period, prices dropped in the polluted area—in individual cases by as much as $1,000. Nationwide estimates have also been attempted; regardless of the actual figures set on the damage, the relationship between soaring pollution and declining property values seems well established (figure 7.8).

A little publicized but economically significant form of loss through air pollution is the combustion of materials in the course of industrial processes. Such materials literally "go up in smoke." Some of them, like manganese, lead, and sulfur, are valuable enough to repay part of the cost of recovery, but most are not and so offer no incentive for restricting emissions. According to E. K. Faltermayer, more than 700,000 tons of manganese—enough for half the nation's needs—are lost to the sky each year. Annual sulfur losses are almost $300 million at the current market value. One encouraging result of this is that some industries are discovering how profitable pollution control can be. Thus the Chemical Division of the Sherwin-Williams Company, according to F. V. Huber, has installed an antipollution system at its Chicago plant that not only cuts out odors but saves $60,000 of chemicals a year.

The role of polluted air in respiratory diseases is obvious from the greater incidence of these diseases in areas of chronic pollution. Figure 7.9 shows the prev-

FIGURE 7.7. This cow has suffered major bone damage due to ingestion of fluorine covered grasses. The gaseous fluorine, a by-product from the manufacture of artificial fertilizers, is adsorbed on the forage and does its damage as a *secondary pollutant*. While small amounts of fluorine may strengthen teeth, high levels can have a harmful effect. Fluorine has a strong affinity for calcium and causes a weakening of the bone and tooth structure to the point that teeth fall out, bones collapse, and animals die. (Photo by Robertson Studios, Bartow, Florida, courtesy of National Air Pollution Control Administration)

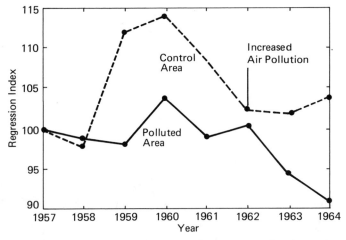

FIGURE 7.8.   Index numbers comparing property values in an area
of heavy air pollution in St. Louis–East St. Louis and a control area
considered normal. Polluted area's values declined sharply after 1962.
(testimony presented by Donald G. Ridker in congressional hearings
for Air Quality Act of 1967)

alence of emphysema in Winnipeg, where air pollution is adequately controlled, as compared with St. Louis, where it is not. For the whole United States, deaths from emphysema in 1969 occurred at a rate of 11.3 per 100,000—an increase of 18 percent since
1965. Death rates from bronchitis show an even greater increase over the same period.
Deaths from bronchitis, emphysema, and asthma for the Pacific States in 1968 were
17.8 per 100,000—an astonishingly high rate considering their mild climate. Rates of
death from lung cancer are clearly related to size of community: other things being equal, inhabitants of cities with populations of 1 million or more are twice as likely to
develop lung cancer as inhabitants of rural areas (figure 7.10).

DEVELOPING QUALITY STANDARDS

Unfortunately for any program of pollution control, pollution and prosperity go together. Since no government, national or regional, wants to kill the goose
that lays the golden eggs, any such program tends to be based on compromise. Regulatory bodies usually attempt to translate all costs into monetary terms, then seek the
point at which the overall costs to the community or region will be lowest. In figure
7.11 pollution losses are depicted as a simple curve. This reflects the assumption that
losses, whether in dollar values or in number and intensity of health problems, will be
greater as pollution increases. The cost curve of "pollution control" assumes that the
closer we approach absolute purity of air, the higher will be the cost of control per

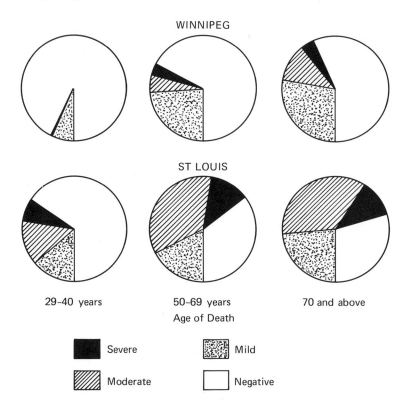

WINNIPEG

ST LOUIS

29–40 years   50–69 years   70 and above

Age of Death

■ Severe   ▨ Mild

▨ Moderate   □ Negative

FIGURE 7.9.   Prevalence of emphysema in two cities with contrasting levels of
air pollution. Data are based on post mortem examination of 300 residents from
each city matched for age at death, sex, occupation, economic status, length of
residence, and smoking habits. (National Tuberculosis and Respiratory Disease
Association)

unit of improvement. The "pollution control" curve can of course move up or down
depending upon technology, economies of scale, and efficiency of application. In any
given situation, the point at which the two curves intersect represents the lowest net
cost to the community by economic standards. Ecologically, however, the only sound
position has to be absolute air purity. In the end, it is a matter of community values.
(essay 7.2). How much does the community really value life, as compared with prosperity and profits? This question, if applied strictly to many American communities,
might produce some uncomfortable answers.

        Pollution control does cost money, however, and it is not at all easy to tell
how much money will be needed to control each type of pollutant. The usual procedure is to determine—or attempt to determine— the *threshold concentration* at which ill
effects begin to be found. This alone involves a major assumption, namely, that a certain amount of pollution will do you no harm. In the case of highly toxic trace metals,
such as beryllium, this may not be true at all. In any case, threshold responses vary

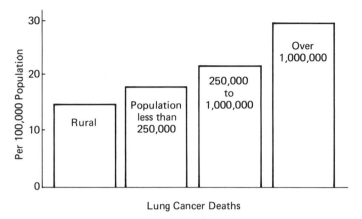

FIGURE 7.10.   Deaths from lung cancer, by city size. (U.S. Department of Health, Education, and Welfare, *Strategy for a Livable Environment,* June 1967)

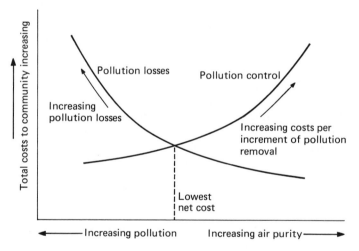

FIGURE 7.11.   Schematic representation of the relationship of
pollution costs to the cost of controlling pollution.

greatly from individual to individual whether the individual is a plant species or man.
This is illustrated in figure 7.12. What proportion of the plant or human population
should constitute a threshold for regulatory action? Should the sufferings of the most
susceptible individuals—shown here by the bottom left-hand portion of each curve—
determine standards for the whole community? Or should these individuals just live
somewhere else? Pollutants seldom occur singly, so that the problem is compounded
again as synergistic effects come into action. For example, it has been found that sulfur

Essay 7.2   Public Concern and Public Control

How much control does the public have over the actions of privately owned companies? In 1970 construction was completed at Four Corners, New Mexico, on the first of a series of enormous coal burning power plants destined to supply electric power to the burgeoning population of the Southwest. Almost immediately the 250 tons of visible pollutants emitted from its huge smokestacks each day and the ravages of local strip mining for fuel (25,000 tons of coal a day) evoked public outcry, first from local Indians, and later from a wide spectrum of conservation groups. A year later, in the summer of 1971, both Indians and conservationists filed a suit against the Departments of the Interior and Health, Education and Welfare for failing to protect the Navajo from air pollution. Another coalition sued the company that furnished coal to Four Corners, charging that the tribal council who gave it mining rights was illegally constituted. To win further public support, these people sponsored a full-page newspaper ad, distributed nationally, expounding their cause. The campaign appeared to work. In response to public pressure, five days of hearings were called by the Senate Committee on Interior and Insular Affairs to discuss the issues. The owners of Four Corners were persuaded to contract nearly 39 million dollars for filters and wet scrubbers capable of reducing particulate emissions to 30 tons a day. Furthermore, the company agreed to pay the Indians 100 million dollars over a period of thirty-five years to reclaim the mesa by filling, grading and seeding. Despite these improvements, it seemed likely in early 1973 that the situation would continue to get worse, though possibly at a slower rate. An Interior Department study released in December, 1972, estimated that energy consumption in the Southwest would nearly double by 1980, and that one quarter of this increase would be supplied by coal-fired power plants in the Colorado River Basin. Even if the visible pollutants are reduced to tolerable levels, there is as yet no indication that the power companies are prepared to invest similar amounts in controlling the invisible pollutants, which include not only sulfur dioxide and nitrogen oxide but toxic metals such as lead, mercury, and cadmium. According to Senator Joseph Montoya (D., New Mexico), when all six plants in the system are finally operating, they will emit 200 tons of particulates, 850 to 1300 tons of nitrogen oxide, and 2000 tons of sulfur dioxide every day, even when the currently proposed anti-pollution equipment is installed. Accordingly, both Senator Montoya and Governor Bruce King of New Mexico have called for a moratorium on the construction of coal-burning power plants in the area. (Based in part on Anthony Wolff, "Showdown at Four Corners," Saturday Review, *June 3, 1972.)*

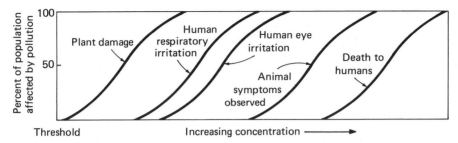

FIGURE 7.12.   Major thresholds in the effects of exposure to sulfur dioxide in increasing order of severity. (adapted from California Department of Public Health, *California Standards for Ambient Air Quality and Motor Vehicle Exhaust*)

dioxide, if absorbed on carbon particulates, is carried further into the lungs. Discoveries like this make quality standards even more difficult to establish.

Air quality standards in the United States were pioneered by the state of California, which in 1959 passed legislation governing both air quality and motor vehicle emissions. These standards were revised in 1965 and upgraded in 1970. Meanwhile, beginning in February, 1969, federal standards were issued by the National Air Pollution Control Administration (now the Air Pollution Control Office of the Environmental Protection Agency). Table 7.2 gives a few examples of the types of standard developed. It will be seen that most standards are set for individual pollutants. The exception is the oxidant, which is any substance that makes oxygen available for further chemical activities— in this case, photochemical changes such as those typical of Los Angeles type pollution. Since the secondary compounds produced by oxidants are much more active than the primary pollutants, their threshold concentrations are much lower (for the sake of clarity it should be noted that the nitrogen oxides are often tabulated under the general head of "oxidants"). For oxidants the threshold criteria have been eye irritation, plant damage, and reduced visibility. For sulfur dioxide the main criterion has been plant damage, with respiratory and eye irritation developing at somewhat higher levels. Criteria for carbon monoxide are based upon interference with oxygen transport in the blood. Lead pollution is even more complicated because its effects are cumulative; standards almost need to be set for the total life span.

Standards of the sort just discussed are generally known as *ambient air standards* because they apply to the air that surrounds us every day. For most scientific purposes, including that of pollution control, the ambient air is regarded as the air that fills the lower atmosphere, or *troposphere.* Emission standards for automobiles or other specific sources of pollutants are calculated on a different scale from the one used for ambient air standards. For example, motor vehicle emission standards set for California in 1965 were by volume: hydrocarbons 275 ppm, carbon monoxide 1.5 percent, and oxides of nitrogen 350 ppm. Here the figures are an attempt to get at the eventual effect of pollutants on the composition of the ambient air. The entire range of factors to be considered in developing standards is shown in table 7.3.

TABLE 7.2.   Quality standards for ambient air: levels considered adverse for four common contaminants, set at various times by California and the U.S.

	California 1965	California 1970	U.S. 1969–70
Oxidant*	0.15 ppm for 1 hour	0.10 ppm, 1 hour	0.10 ppm, instantaneous 0.03–0.05 ppm, hourly ave.
Sulfur dioxide	1 ppm, 1 hour 0.3 ppm, 8 hours		0.11 ppm, 3–4 days 0.04 ppm, mean annual
Carbon monoxide	No "adverse" level set, "serious" level 120 ppm, 1 hour 30 ppm for 8 hours	40 ppm, 1 hour 10 ppm, 12 hours	12–17 ppm, 8 hours
Nitrogen dioxide	0.25 ppm, 1 hour; "serious" level 3 ppm for 1 hour		15 ppm, 24 hours
Particulate	No standard set, just warning of its danger	Lead particulate set at 1.5 micrograms/ cubic meter over a 30-day period	75 micrograms per cubic meter annual average

Source: *Progress in the Prevention and Control of Air Pollution* (Senate Doc. #91–64 April 27, 1970), *Air Quality Criteria for Carbon Monoxide* (H.E.W. March 1970, p. 10–16), and National Air Conservation Commission, Tuberculosis and Respiratory Disease Association, *Newsletter* January 1971.

*Hydrocarbons are not included in this table because of the strong overlap with oxidant. Nevertheless the U.S. standards for hydrocarbons before photochemical changes and excluding methane, were set separately by N.A.P.C.A. at .2 ppm for a 3-hour period. Nitrogen dioxide, which is also strongly reactive to photosynthetic influences, is shown in the table because it is monitored separately.

Once air quality standards have been established there is the problem of control costs. As we have seen, clean air looks like a bargain on paper. But problems arise when the question of who must bear what costs is considered. Since this is essentially a political rather than a scientific question, we must postpone it to the next section.

FIRST STEPS TOWARD CONTROL

Steps toward air pollution control, both in the United States and around the world, have been few and faltering. London has eliminated smog, but Great Britain as a whole has done virtually nothing about automobile emissions. In New York City

TABLE 7.3.   Factors to be considered in developing air quality criteria

Factor	Components
Properties of pollution	Absorbed gases
	Coexisting pollutants
	Kinetics of formation
	Residence time
Properties of pollutant	Concentration
	Chemistry
	Physical state
Methods of measurement	Chemical analysis
	Colorimetric
	Coulometric
	Spectroscopic
	Gas chromatographic
	Sampling techniques
Exposure parameters	Time
	Temperature
	Pressure
	Humidity
Characteristics of receptor	Physical susceptibility
	State of health
	Rate, site, and agent of transfer to
Responses (effects)	
Health	Type of illness
	Diagnosable
	Latent
	Increase in general susceptibility
	Victim
	Animals
	Man
Human welfare	Economics
	Sociology
	Epidemiology
Vegetation	Crops
	Ornamental plants
Material	Objectionable surface decomposition
	Corrosion
	Deterioration
Atmospheric	Radiation
	Temperature
	Diffusion
	Dispersion

Source: Environmental Protection Agency, Air Pollution Control Office, *Air Quality Criteria for Nitrogen Oxides* (Washington, D.C., Government Printing Office, 1971), pp. 1–2.

open burning of garbage has been prohibited since 1968, but the Consolidated Edison Company still operates power stations in the city, and these still emit large amounts of nitrogen oxides. In Los Angeles County efforts to control fixed sources such as refineries and power stations have cut emissions as much as 90 percent in some cases. But control of automotive sources is vested in the state, not the county, and the smog is nearly as bad as ever. Oxidant levels in Los Angeles were higher than state standards on 218 days in 1971, 241 in 1970, and 246 in 1969—progress, perhaps, but not readily perceived as such by the man in the street. County air control offices, according to Earl C. Gottschalk, Jr., are now claiming that the new federal standards may be impossible to meet. Frank Stead, a spokesman for the Tuberculosis and Respiratory Disease Association, urged before the State Air Resources Board in December, 1971, that the state seriously consider such measures as banning cars from certain cities, introducing a statewide four-day week, and staggering working hours for commuters. Los Angeles, however, does not officially recognize air pollution as a public health problem. Thus although the Los Angeles Air Pollution District has about 300 employees and an annual budget of over $5 million, there is no medical representative on its three-man Air Pollution Control Hearing Board.

It must be admitted, however, that the U.S. Air Quality Act of 1967 provides at least the semblance of a new beginning. Unfortunately, it is based on an approach that seems expressly designed to provide a minimum of effective regulation: the federal government sets the standards, but it is the task of the states to apply them. California, of course, already has stricter standards than the federal government for some types of pollutants. But even the strictest standards conceivable are of no use if they remain just standards. When analyzed by John C. Esposito and the other members of the Ralph Nader Task Force on Air Pollution, the 1967 act was found wanting in the following respects:

> 1. It placed all the responsibility for enforcement on the states, even to the point of downplaying the fact that, under the abatement provisions of the 1963 Clean Air Act, a state governor can ask the federal government to intervene.
> 2. It required N.A.P.C.A. to designate so-called air quality regions, but did not make any provisions for cooperation between the various city and state governments involved (according to the task force, voluntary cooperation was virtually nil).
> 3. The "air quality criteria" issued by N.A.P.C.A. lacked the force of law; if any state rejected the criteria, there was nothing N.A.P.C.A. could do except express disapproval.
> 4. Although the 1967 act required the states to hold public hearings on air quality standards, it made no such provisions when the state got to the stage of deciding how it would enforce those standards.
> 5. The entire procedure by which the federal government required the states to produce air quality control programs was subject to intolerable delays.

6. No federal standards had been set for certain highly toxic or irritating pollutants such as asbestos and cadmium—and it did not look as if any would be set for some years.

Given the experience of the Nader Task Force it would be rash to conclude that either the·federal government or any of the state governments is doing anything effective about air pollution. Nevertheless, the Clean Air Act of 1970 does contain provisions that enable the federal government to shut down polluters when air pollution reaches emergency levels. These provisions were successfully invoked for the first time in November, 1971, when the Environmental Protection Agency (E.P.A.), acting at the request of local health officials, obtained a federal court order to shut down twenty-three companies in or near Birmingham, Alabama. Emergency regulations, however, are by definition not for everyday use.

Another way in which the federal government evades its responsibilities is by concentrating on one aspect of a pollution problem—usually the one that still needs more research before it can be controlled—and ignoring others that could be dealt with by existing means. Thus the Environmental Protection Agency has required the major U.S. automobile manufacturers to come up with a means of reducing both hydro-carbons and carbon monoxide to only 10 percent of 1970 levels—and to do so by 1975. But it would be much simpler to tax out of existence automobiles having, for example, over 30 horsepower and weighing more than 2,000 pounds. It is hard not to suspect that the more complicated course is preferred because it can lead to endless compromise and postponement.

What of the future? In 1968 Henry S. Rowen, then president of the RAND Corporation, predicted that the solution to air pollution was less then a decade away. It is probable that technology will yield some answers in that time, but less likely that our social structure will be capable of applying them. In any case, the **systems analysis** approach favored by RAND offers some realistic hope of success. Traditional organization of information into separate categories often misleads us: reality is not divided up in this way. Where the whole environment is concerned, the specialized approach to problem solving does not work; indeed, the solutions it provides often create new problems in related areas. Systems analysis, on the other hand, approaches problems in the broadest possible context of factors, processes, and relationships. Thus it recognizes the fact that pollution is rooted in our highly industralized economy, in the mobile way of life we are used to, in our drive-through cities, and in our individualistic philosophy of consumption. Pursued far enough, this line of thought embraces the total ecosphere. The vast amounts of information available and required can be dealt with only by computers.

Several cities are already using computers to develop a systems approach to environmental management problems. Chicago has a computer-based total management system, to monitor and advise on matters of atmospheric pollution. New York City's Group on Environmental Control plans to integrate responsibility for such factors as noise, air pollution, and garbage disposal: it already makes highly sophisticated use of monitoring devices. One immediate advantage of computerized management is that it yields predictions. Adverse weather, for example, can be foreseen in time to advise heavy polluters to take emergency precautions, to warn especially sensitive citizens, and to restrict private auto use.

Computer simulation, in the form of so-called diffusion models, can be used as an aid to planning. Telemetered data from monitoring networks are easily stored in and recalled from a computer's memory banks. There is even a computerized game, developed under E.P.A. sponsorship, that reproduces the administrative and political dilemmas of air pollution control. Known as APEX (Air Pollution Exercise), the game is used by universities in the training of air pollution control officers. According to Sally Lindsay, a reporter who took part in APEX as an industrialist, the game impresses seasoned pollution control offices as realistic.

If there appears to be no shortage of computerized managerial schemes, there is a definite shortage of basic research. Air pollution effects within ecological systems even less. It has been calculated that air pollution research should be expanded to ten times its present capacity in order to be adequate to its task. When the U.S. Clean Air Act of 1963 was passed, the annual allocation for air pollution research was $12.5 million. The amount has since been more than doubled, but it is still pitifully small compared with, say, the $5 billion a year spent on space research and facilities throughout the 1960s. For establishing air pollution control authorities, planning commissions, and related facilities Congress appropriated $64.2 million in 1968. And yet the statutory report issued in 1970 as *The Cost of Clean Air* estimated the total cost of air pollution control in 1975 as $8.3 billion—about $2.6 billion in capital investment and the rest in annual maintenance. These figures are for four types of pollutants only: particulates, sulfur oxides, carbon monoxide, and hydrocarbons. Meanwhile, federal expenditures for both research and abatement are projected to rise from $132 million in 1970 to $490.4 million in 1975. Clearly, industry is expected to pay for cleaning its own house. In the words of the report, "the annual cost to control these four pollutants is a very very small percentage of the value of shipments in each of these industries—usually less than 1 percent." However, as the report does *not* point out, it is most unlikely that industry will see things this way.

Indeed, the attitude of the major industrial polluters does not seem likely to change very much. The industrial establishment of the United States has fought with every weapon in its arsenal against any form of regulation of emissions. It has vigorously opposed all legislation intended to strengthen enforcement of controls, and has pooh-poohed the very need for them. "People are hysterical about air pollution. There is no proof that it is injurious to public health," a vice-president of Detroit-Edison Company was quoted as saying in 1967. The leaders of industry too often resemble their counterparts in the APEX game, who continually shout such remarks as "If you force us to spend money on controls, we'll move to another state."

It was hoped that the high standards of emission control required by California would force American automobile manufacturers to invest heavily in pollution research. But they have not accepted this responsibility; indeed, they have responded with counterpropaganda designed to show that emission controls are unnecessary. Thus the federal government is forced to shoulder the research burden, with inadequate funds, while auto manufacturers devote $200 million to advertising and promotion in a single year. Steam-driven and many other experimental pollution-free automobiles, though technically feasible, seem unlikely to become economically feasible; electric automobiles, at present, appear suitable only for short trips at low speeds.

For a long time, the public remained apathetic about polluted air, despite the warnings of scientists and medical authorities. By 1971, however, the public mood had definitely changed. Hundreds of groups, such as the People's Lobby in Southern California, formed almost overnight to protest the problem and to bring pressure for stronger restrictive legislation. If this movement persists and grows, it will be effective. It is certainly the only real hope for clean air.

REFERENCES

Angstrom, A. K. "Atmospheric Turbidity, Global Illuminators and Planetary Albedo of the Earth," *Tellus,* vol. 14, 1962, pp. 435–450.

Berkner, Lloyd V., and Lauriston C. Marshall, "The Role of Oxygen," *Saturday Review,* May 7, 1966.

Broecker, Wallace S., "Man's Oxygen Supply," *Science,* June 1970.

Craig, Paul P., and Edward Berlin, "The Air of Poverty," *Environment,* June 1971, pp. 1–9.

Denney, Ronald C., *This Dirty World* (London: Nelson, 1971).

Department of Health, Education, and Welfare, *The Cost of Clean Air* (Washington, D.C.: Government Printing Office, 1970).

Esposito, John C., et al., *Vanishing Air* (New York: Grossman, 1970).

Faltermayer, E. K., "We Can Afford Clean Air," *Fortune,* November 1965, pp. 159–163.

Gottschalk, Earl C., Jr., "Hazy Outlook—Los Angeles Bid to Curb Pollution Makes Critics Wonder If Any City Can," *Wall Street Journal,* April 11, 1972.

Huber, F. V., paper delivered at pollution control roundtable, Kansas City, May 12, 1972.

Jackson, Donald, "The Cloud Comes to Quibbletown," *Life,* December 10, 1971, pp. 72ff.

Lindsay, Sally, "Apex ," *Saturday Review,* May 13, 1972, pp. 55–57.

Robinson, E., and C. E. Moser, "Global Gaseous Pollutant Emissions and Removal Mechanisms," paper presented at the Second International Clean Air Congress, Washington, D.C., December 9, 1970.

Singer, S. Fred, "Human Energy Production as Process in the Biosphere," *Scientific American,* September 1970, pp. 183–186.

Tucker, Anthony, *The Toxic Metals* (New York: Ballantine, 1972).

World Health Organization, *Air Pollution* (Columbia University Press, 1961).

8 WATER: USE AND ABUSE

Water is the universal solvent. Within an organism it carries nutrients into cellular structures and carries away waste products. It has parallel functions in the larger biological community as well as in human resource systems. Since water is a **flow resource** it is constantly recycled. But it is also consumed in ways that severely reduce its mobility, and it is easily overloaded with waste materials.

WATER AS A NATIONAL RESOURCE

In order to establish a standard for minimum human water need, Athelstan Spilhaus invented a mythical being he called the "naked vegetarian." A naked, unwashed vegetarian, he reckoned, would require 300 gallons of water per day: he would drink two quarts, and would need the rest to produce his daily ration of grains and tubers. Not many of us, however, are naked, unwashed vegetarians. Indeed, our condition as Americans represents an opposite extreme; the quantities of water we require to satisfy our demands are phenomenal. Estimated use from the controlled supply alone is 2,000 gallons per person per day—nearly seven times Spilhaus' basic unit. Such prodigious use is linked to our lavish consumption of meat, milk, and fruit, all of which have high water requirements; to our closetfuls of cotton, wool, silk, and synthetic fiber garments; to our nonstop building boom in private, government, and business structures of wood, steel, and concrete; to our millions of vehicles of glass, steel, and rubber, running on petroleum products; and to the countless other commodities that we have been taught to take for granted. This deluge of material goods, on which the nation's so-called economic health is built, depends directly upon the availability of plenty of high-quality water. "Plenty," at present, is 400 billion gallons per day.

The water referred to here is that supplied through controlled or man-made water systems. Water transported artificially for irrigation would be included in these figures, but not the water incorporated naturally into timber, forage, and nonirrigated crops. If all the water that goes into the complete range of forest and agricultural products used by today's average American were included, the individual daily water requirement would be over 6,000 gallons. Only about 8 percent of controlled water use is directly visible in the form of water for cooking, laundry, bathing, and other general and domestic nonagricultural functions. For the remainder we see only the products derived from its uses: about 40 percent goes into agriculture, and the remaining 52 percent is consumed by industrial and steam-electric utilities. Figures for hydroelectric generation are not included because it is not considered a consumptive use. Only since 1955 has industry rather than agriculture been the heaviest user of water. This is mainly because industry has vastly increased its consumption of electrical energy.

As people and economic activities have continued to concentrate in urban areas, it has become increasingly difficult for these areas to obtain adequate supplies of water. Competition between cities for existing water becomes sharper every day but, partly because of outmoded legal barriers, few solutions are available at the local level. Planners have therefore been forced to look toward ever more distant and expensive sources.

The Supply of Water

The quantity of fresh water continuously available to the United States depends upon an average precipitation of 30 inches per year. But 70 percent of this is evaporated. The result is an annual runoff of 8.6 inches, or 1,250 billion gallons per day. Since only about one-quarter of this amount is currently being used, it might seem adequate for the time being. But *possible* water is not *actual* water. Uneven distribution and poor catchments cause much slippage, while much of what is captured becomes useless through pollution. By the year 2000 effective water supply will not cover the projected daily demand of 900 billion gallons.

Uneven distribution of water over the land surface creates special problems. About 60 percent of the contiguous United States receives only 28 percent of the nation's rainfall, and within this area two-thirds of the moisture that falls is concentrated in the Pacific Northwest. Meanwhile urbanization is increasing faster in the Pacific Southwest than anywhere else in the country. Los Angeles, Phoenix, and many other western cities are facing urgent water problems. Surface water is scarce, underground water is receding as existing supplies are not renewed, and population continues to grow. Even though people are attracted by the dry climate, there is still a demand for greenery.

Water Costs

In theory the cost of water should reflect its availability. In practice, however, there is rarely any logical relationship between the cost of supplying water and the charge to the consumer for performing this particular resource function. Uneven distribution, fluctuations in demand, and the existence of countless local vagaries of management all contribute to inconsistencies in the price structure. An urban resident may pay $150 per **acre foot** for water of approximately the same quality that a desert farmer gets for $2 per acre foot. The true costs of provision are masked by subsidies and multipurpose funding, particularly at the federal level. The federal government now invests more than $10 billion a year in water oriented developments, including sewage systems. Much more is spent by state and local agencies. But most of this outlay is for new plant and other facilities; the increasing problem of pollution will require vast new sums. It has been estimated that between $40 and $70 billion will be needed to restore water quality and control pollution by the year 2000. This estimate is certain to be raised as costs increase, and work on the problem has scarcely begun.

The Waste of Water

An adequate water supply is not just a large enough quantity of water; it must also be water of a certain quality. It follows that there are two principal ways in which water can be wasted: *directly,* when water escapes from the human control system, and *indirectly,* when it becomes unfit for human use. In reality, of course, the distinction between these two types of waste is not always clear-cut.

In its broadest meaning, *direct waste* includes the 92 percent of the water that falls on land but eludes human control. More logically, however, it pertains to the way the remaining 8 percent is used after it enters the streams, lakes, and underground stores. Domestic waste is waste that occurs during household or community use of water, or at some point in the system supplying the users. Primary domestic use—drinking, cooking, and personal hygiene—requires water in small quantity but very high quality. Secondary domestic use accounts for most of the 35.5 billion daily gallons of U.S. domestic water; it includes such functions as dilution of sewage, air conditioning, fire protection, recreation, and upkeep of lawns and parks. While these five major functions rank differently in various regions of the country in terms of how much water they take, sewage dilution leads in all urban areas.

Domestic use takes only a minor share of water compared to industry or irrigation. Yet the average domestic consumption per person per day is more than 160 gallons. This figure appears particularly excessive when we realize that the whole range of domestic uses is supplied with the same high-quality water required for drinking and cooking. Whether water is in short supply or not, we continue to flush five gallons of it down the drain in order to dispose of a cup of urine. Multiplied by several times a day and by 200 million people, this is an enormous waste. Many U.S. cities do not meter domestic water but charge flat fees. New York follows this practice, and loses 30 million gallons per day through leaks. It meets the shortages caused by recurring droughts with such stopgap measures as asking restaurants not to serve glasses of water unless customers demand them. Nearly everywhere, dozens of kinds of waste, from poor metering and leakage to excessive lawn-watering and evaporation from uncovered swimming pools, accompany domestic water use. Modern households are geared to high rates of consumption. It is estimated that a typical American household of four individuals will use at least 180 gallons of water inside the home each day, as follows:

Showers, baths	60	Automatic dishwasher	10
Toilet	75	Garbage disposal	5
Automatic washer	25	Miscellaneous cleaning	5

Agricultural waste of water involves much greater quantities than domestic. This is to be expected, because the volume of water used in agriculture is five times greater. But it also has something to do with the fact that cheaper rates and subsidization weaken economic motivation for efficient use. About 63 percent of all water stored, withdrawn, and applied for irrigation plays no part at all in crop growth (author's estimate). Of the total controlled U.S. water supply, 40 percent goes into agriculture. This fact is not lost on city planners, nor is the fact that agricultural use is only about 37 percent efficient. However, the legal apparatus that preserves so-called water rights makes it unlikely that much agricultural water will be diverted to urban use. On the other hand, it must be admitted that the 12 percent of U.S. cropland that is irrigated produces 31 percent of all crops in terms of value. This is because most of the yield from irrigated land is in high-value specialty items, such as green vegetables and citrus. In most urban-industrial nations agriculture must be subsidized by the state in order to be commercially viable. From this standpoint abolishing irrigation subsidies would make sense only where low-yield crops are grown or where the groundwater is subject to depletion.

Controlling waste and balancing the use of water may depend more on how water systems are organized than on how water is used. At present, both industrial and domestic use are often served by the same system. There seems little reason why agricultural use should be excluded. Another consideration is that water of the same quality need not be delivered for all uses; instead, parallel networks could deliver different grades of water for different purposes. A few pioneers, such as the Coachella Valley County Water District in California, are already working along these lines.

Flooding, like other waste, adds to the cost of water. Flood damage in the United States in 1965 caused 119 deaths and cost an estimated $788 million. This is not a record expense for floods, but it does add to the growing evidence that in spite of more than $4 billion in flood control measures the United States is in greater danger of flood disaster than ever. Raymond F. Dasmann has pointed out that, as a result of uncontrolled and destructive logging of Douglas firs, northwest California was suffering disastrous floods as late as 1964—some ten years after the fir boom had ended. As deforestation proceeds, flood danger increases. In semiarid areas even a relatively small rainfall can have the effect of a flood. The main cause in both cases is lack of vegetation. Improved water resource planning would mean not only better but cheaper flood control. It might also cut down the rate of development in areas where the worst floods are likely to occur, and so save the nation from the repetition of major catastrophes such as the Ohio and Indiana floods of 1913, which took place despite advanced flood control measures, or the 1972 disaster in Laredo, West Virginia, which resulted from poor state regulation of strip mining.

Industrial waste of water is very different from simple loss through inefficient use or control. Industrial uses of water are intensely concentrated, and so give rise to severe problems of reclamation. Most of these problems fall under the head of indirect waste, but there is also some *direct waste* due to extravagant use.

The degree of extravagance practiced by an industry seems to be closely related to the price it pays for water. An example of commendably conservative water use is that of the Kaiser Steel plant at Fontana, California. Scarcity drove the price of water up, and the plant found it economical to use its water over and over, up to 40 times. It therefore requires only 1,600 gallons to produce a ton of steel (the national average is 65,000 gallons). The opposite extreme can be illustrated with an example from the paper industry, which has a comparably high demand for water. MacMillan Blodel Limited is located on the Powell River in British Columbia. Because of the abundance of water at this site, little pressure has been put on the plant to practice conservation. It has another advantage in the nearby Georgia Strait for dumping its wastes. All the same, its use of 2 billion gallons of water per day—more than required by the city of New York—is prodigious. We can only speculate what will happen when population growth and new economic development begin to compete for Powell River water. Will the plant's established rights be proof against newcomers? Will it voluntarily install recycling apparatus to cut back waste?

By far the greatest loss of water occurs through *indirect waste* in the form of pollution. According to the U.S. Department of Health, Education, and Welfare, water pollution falls into eight general categories:

1. Sewage   5. Mineral chemical substances
2. Infectious agents   6. Sediments
3. Plant materials   7. Radioactive materials
4. Organic chemical exotics   8. Heat

Some of these categories, particularly sewage and organic chemical exotics, can be further classified as *conservative* or *nonconservative*. Nonconservative pollutants are easily reduced by bacterial action, while conservative ones are not. Most nonconservative pollutants are organic wastes; paradoxically, they cause more trouble in fresh surface waters than inorganic ones because they reduce oxygen and stimulate infectious agents. Some inorganic pollutants also stimulate algae growth, which reduces oxygen still further. The weight of dissolved oxygen required for the biological breakdown of organic matter in water over a specific period (usually five days) is known as biochemical oxygen demand, or **BOD**. It has been estimated that in certain areas of the San Francisco Bay System over 70 percent of the BOD is contributed by waste discharges from local industry. In one area, an average BOD of 298 **mg/l** was recorded during the canning season (the average throughout the system is usually about 1 mg/l).

Conservative pollution is not **biodegradable**—that is, it is not broken down by bacterial action—so increasing the oxygen level of the water, as is usually done in sewage treatment, does not help. Nature has provided no way to get rid of foaming hard detergents, poisonous heavy metals such as mercury, and persistent pesticides such as DDT; they just show up somewhere else in the ecosystem, very often in our food.

Levels of both conservative and nonconservative pollution reflect the concentrations of industrial activity throughout the United States. Even organic wastes are more often derived from industry than from domestic sources. A single beet processing plant can discharge more organic pollution during its season of operation than a city of 500,000 people does in a year. In 1900 the raw sewage of 24 million people and an amount of industrial organic waste equivalent to the raw sewage of 15 million people was being dumped into American streams each year. By 1970 the raw sewage was that of 85 million people but the industrial organic equivalent that of 210 million people. Today, 52 percent of our controlled water goes into industry; most of it is returned to our lakes and streams much hotter than it came out, contaminated with acids and organic debris, and largely depleted of oxygen. In this condition it is less capable of ridding itself even of nonconservative substances. By 1980, according to a 1966 report of the National Academy of Sciences, the volume of this polluted discharge will be great enough to purge all oxygen from the base flow of our twenty-two major rivers. Already, many of the nation's largest sources of fresh surface water have been rendered useless, if not actually hazardous, by pollution. The mighty Hudson River, which has an average daily flow of 11 billion gallons, receives an estimated 400 million gallons of raw sewage each day, of which Manhattan alone contributes 50 million gallons. According to Robert H. Boyle, if New York City had been built 50 miles further upstream, the Hudson would be a dead river by now. As it is, the beautiful upper reaches of the Hudson are now in danger of being converted into yet another reservoir to provide New York City with more water to waste.

The incomparable water system of the Great Lakes, which hold 20 percent of the world's fresh water, has been almost destroyed. Detroit alone dumps 20 million pounds of contaminated material into Lake Erie every day; two-thirds of it is industrial pollution, and the rest is municipal waste. In 1972, with Lake Erie all but dead (but not beyond hope), the United States and Canada finally announced a joint agreement to clean up the Great Lakes. Since U.S.-Canadian relations are now directly involved, perhaps something will be done.

Oil dumping is among the ugliest and most vicious forms of water pollution because it is both deliberate and avoidable. Sensational accidents like the rupture of an oil well in the Santa Barbara Channel in 1969 (the result of a rash decision by the

U.S. Department of the Interior) and the San Francisco Bay Spill of 1971 (the result of careless navigation) have brought to public notice the exceptional ability of oil to foul the marine environment. But oil dumping goes on all the time. Every time a tanker prepares to reload it has to flush out the residue of the previous load in the form of water ballast. Oil slush discharged in this way can amount to as much as 1 percent of total capacity. There are over 3,500 tankers of 1,000 tons or more in operation; according to the 1970 Study of Critical Environmental Problems (SCEP), they are responsible for the *routine* discharge of about 530,000 metric tons of oil into the sea annually. What is still more shocking is that only 20 percent of the tankers discharge over 90 percent of this oil; the other 80 percent take precautionary measures that guarantee a much cleaner discharge. Efforts by international maritime organizations to secure voluntary compliance with majority standards have so far failed to enlist the co-operation of such major polluters as Japan and Liberia. Theoretically, international sanctions could be imposed on the polluters by vote of the U.N. General Assembly. But in practice this would be asking the international oil industry to penalize itself, which is not likely to happen. The problem may eventually be solved by building a new generation of tankers with separate tanks for ballast water. Meanwhile, mankind will have to wait for the old tankers to wear out.

Offshore oil spills, on the other hand, can probably be cut to a minimum by improved coastal navigation systems and stricter regulation of marine traffic. A model system of this kind is now being prepared for the Canso Strait, in Nova Scotia;

FIGURE 8.1.   Oil spillage into a marine environment. The oil on the water to the right, below the drilling platform, is an example of ocean pollution. Although the contamination of marine water, while apparent in food chains, may never significantly alter fresh water supplies, its control remains closely aligned with general abatement techniques and is thus included with the overall water resource problem. (Bureau of Land Management, U.S. Department of the Interior)

in addition to providing one of the world's most advanced radar systems, it will require all foreign vessels entering or leaving the strait to take on pilots. The system is expensive, but it is costing Canadian taxpayers only half as much as cleaning up the one million gallons of oil spilled into the Canso Strait by a Liberian tanker in 1970.

Thermal or heat pollution is probably the most insidious of all, since it can build up for some time without attracting concern, and has mainly long-term effects. It reduces the oxygen supply in bodies of water and so upsets their ecological balance. Many species of fish are spawned in bays and estuaries. Unfortunately, these are also favorite sites for power stations, because of their continual need for water. Discharges of water as hot as $80°$ F. have been registered at stations along the California coast. Water temperatures below $55°$ are considered ideal for spawning most of the fish we eat; many of them, such as trout, cannot live in waters much above $45°$. Power stations in Great Britain are more closely regulated than those in the United States, and are normally equipped with cooling towers that return water to the sea at $60°$ or lower. But even this is barely adequate to safeguard marine life, especially in hot weather. Nuclear power stations, which typically operate at about $4,000°$ F., produce far more waste heat than coal fired stations. So far, however, U.S. electrical utilities show little willingness to conduct environmental studies or even to budget for adequate cooling systems before setting up nuclear plants.

Because the cooling effect of the oceans is so important a feature of the earth's biosphere, the specter has been raised of worldwide thermal pollution. According to the SCEP estimates, global thermal power output in the year 2000 may be as much as six times the present level. Since heat is a form of energy, once it has been produced there is nowhere for it to go except somewhere else on the earth's surface or into space. Building on this principle, some scientists have calculated that it will not be long before not only the sea but the entire globe becomes too hot to support living creatures of any kind—the so-called heat death, when everything will be at the same temperature. This may be too alarmist. It is true that, as pointed out in chapter 3, it would take only a small change in the earth's average reflectivity, or **albedo,** to produce a complete change in its climate. But the albedo of the oceans is very low indeed compared with that of the land; indeed, if it were not for the capacity of the oceans to absorb the sun's heat, the earth would never have become habitable. If the sun cannot cause thermal pollution of the oceans, it is doubtful that human technology will be able to do so in the foreseeable future. In particular bays and inlets, however, thermal pollution promises to become a serious problem quite soon, as indeed it already is in many American lakes and rivers (figure 8.2).

About three-quarters of our planet is sea. It is therefore hard to believe that the main threat to the marine environment at the present time is from pollution by industrial and military wastes. Such, however, is the case. International attention was drawn to this problem in 1970 when Thor Heyerdahl, after a slow crossing of the Atlantic on the papyrus ship *Ra II*, reported that the water was so infested by filth of every description that he and his crew were reluctant to brush their teeth in it. The commonest form of debris was lumps of solidified oil, but there were also empty bottles, tin cans, and even toilet paper. Later chemical analysis of some oil lumps showed

FIGURE 8.2.   Hot outfalls from steel plants polluting the Calumet River, Chicago. Clouds of steam rising from river indicate thermal pollution in its most obvious form. Photo was taken in 1966. (Federal Water Quality Administration, U.S. Department of the Interior)

that they had come from every part of the globe. What, asked Heyerdahl, of the pollution that was *not* visible to the naked eye?

This wretched situation, a product of what Nicholas D. Hetzer has called the "dump and see" mentality, is in the end a matter for international action. But it is hard to be optimistic when the country's principal polluter is the Department of Defense, followed by numerous other government agencies. What if pollution of the oceans is tacitly considered to be in the national interest? The U.N. General Assembly has declared the ocean floor to be the common heritage of mankind. But such declarations carry little weight when set against national sovereignty or military security. Perhaps when the Mediterranean becomes as dead as the Baltic—as it will, if present trends continue—the industrial nations will finally begin to pay more than lip service to the idea of seas and oceans as a common resource. But by then it may be too late.

WATER MANAGEMENT

Discovering fresh sources of water is a very different matter from improving efficiency in the use of existing supplies. Both, however, are important to good water management.

Developing Exotic Water

Finding new supplies has come to mean almost exclusively, in the language of water experts, developing *exotic* water, that is, tapping the hydrologic cycle at some point other than the stores of fresh water on land. Usually, the only points considered are the *saline* and *atmospheric* phases.

The project of desalting ocean or other brackish water has been around for a long time, and is not usually thought of in these terms. However, the desalting technique really amounts to an interruption of the hydrologic cycle for simplified acquisition of water. In the normal process ocean water is distilled when it evaporates to become atmospheric moisture. Eventually it is precipitated, and we collect, store, and reconvey as much of it as we can. In theory, if we could tap this long process at an earlier phase we could obtain very much more water. Unfortunately, the technical and economic breakthroughs that would make this shortcut practical has not yet appeared. For a long time, the cost of desalting has stayed at about a dollar per thousand gallons, or $326 per acre foot. The best rate in practical use so far is 85 cents per thousand gallons, charged for the water supplied by the Westinghouse plant at Key West. In a few instances rates like these are competitive, but in general water from traditional sources is much cheaper. A second major problem is the accumulation of salt as a by-product. A quart of sea water holds an average of one-and-a-half ounces of salt, and an acre foot of such water 50 tons. A plant designed to serve a population of 600,000 would extract some 23,000 tons of salt per day, and a year's continuous production would pile up 8.4 million tons. The United States only uses 31 million tons of salt in a year. The disposal problem would therefore be an extra expense.

Desalting can be no more than a supplement to traditional systems in the foreseeable future. The U.S. Department of the Interior believes that desalting or conversion will supply only 7 percent of the water used in the U.S. by the year 2000. Reseach, both public and private, will continue, but it may be that the most useful result will be to find means of increasing the recycling potential of small water systems in reclaiming sewage and other waste water.

Tapping the atmospheric phase amounts, in all essentials, to rainmaking—an ancient art with dubious scientific credentials. However federal funds have been allocated to research it, beginning with $3.75 million in 1967. Fifty experimental projects are already proposed, and the annual research budget could rise as high as $100 million by 1975. This expense is most questionable. Weather modification, should it ever be successful on a large scale, would cause not only ecological imbalances but the most appalling legal problems. There are better uses for the taxpayer's money.

Improving Traditional Technologies

The tapping, storing, and conveying of fresh water can all be improved without risk or unreasonable expense. Tapping is any method by which runoff or subsurface flow is directed into man-made control structures. Storage and conveyance refer to management of water once it has entered the controlled facilities.

When an area is stripped of vegetation, it provides a much higher initial runoff. However, the flow of water is likely to fall off rapidly unless there is both plant cover and accumulated organic matter in the soil. On the other hand, too much undergrowth will reduce a watershed's contribution to surface flow and groundwater supply. Fortunately, the same management practices that aid timber growth in most forest areas also encourage moderately high water yields. All kinds of suggestions have been made for increasing moisture catchment. For instance, the water take in arid places could be much greater if sandy surfaces were coated with black asphalt, since runoff from the impervious coating would be fast and total.

Underground waters are fed largely from the watershed areas. During precipitation, soil moisture builds up and water flows into underground storage pockets. The **groundwater table** and the **charge** of the underground aquifers depend on the flow from the watersheds. Maintenance of this underground supply is an important part of watershed management. There are areas in which the fresh water supply is threatened because the groundwater is subject to salt water incursion. In some cases salt water has been barred successfully by **recharging** which involves artificially replenishing the fresh underground water. This is done by pumping fresh water directly into wells, and also by letting it seep gradually into the ground. The best known recharging activity in the United States is probably that conducted by the Metropolitan Water District of Southern California. Most of the water for this district is imported from the Colorado River, 300 miles away. To provide a reserve supply and to maintain its natural underground storage facilities this water district uses seasonal surpluses for recharging. The water can then be retrieved from the ground when the demand is at its peak.

Storage and conveyance play a part in all the controlled water we use; their efficiency largely determines how much of it we get. They are affected by natural problems, such as evaporation and seepage, and also by problems of technique and engineering, especially in the design of control facilities.

Surface evaporation is the most obvious natural problem; it causes serious losses in both humid and arid climates. It is worst in dry, hot states like Nevada: Lake Mead, for example, loses the equivalent of an 84-inch layer of water from its vast surface each year. Such losses are hard to control. Evaporation-retarding chemicals can be applied over the water surface; their single molecular layer lets oxygen pass so that aquatic life is not endangered. Most commonly used is some variety of heavy alcohol such as hexadecanol. The alcohols eventually evaporate .

At first U.S. efforts to disseminate retardants were not very successful; there were problems with wind and with the dispensing unit. Recent progress has been more encouraging. For instance, enough water has been saved by evaporation-retardants on Lake Hefner, which is part of Oklahoma City's water supply, to pay the cost of the experiment. A dry powder is now being used that can be mixed with water: 8 ounces of the powder will cover an acre of surface, and evaporation is cut down 50 percent on a calm day. Wind still causes problems, as does recreational activity on lakes where it is permitted.

Losses through seepage vary according to the kind of material a storage or conveyance system is built on. As one would expect, losses are greater through porous substances than through fine or dense ones but they are not always easy to predict. Before Glen Canyon Dam was built, bank seepage from Lake Powell was projected at about 15 percent per year. But when it was finished and filled, losses ran closer to 25 percent—a quarter of the water stored. Not a great deal has been done to check losses of this kind; various linings and sealants all have their advocates, but nobody knows if large-scale use of them would be economically feasible even if the technological problems can be solved.

The Development Trap

Partly because of the difficulties of tapping exotic supplies and partly because earlier large-scale developments have not been wholly successful, state and federal agencies in recent years have tended to plan for ever more grandiose catchment, conveyance, and storage systems (figure 8.3).

In no other area of resource development has man attempted to reorganize nature on such vast scale—and in no other way has the fabric of different habitats been exposed to so much strain. Most of the environmental deterioration of Southern California's coastal plain was made possible by the importation of large amounts of water. Water brought into this semiarid land seemed at first to fulfill the biblical prophecy that the desert would "blossom as the rose." But agriculture gave way to urbanization, and urbanization brought chronic air pollution. The meteorological conditions that gave mild weather the year round were prone to deterioration for this very reason. The movement of water to people rather than people to water has been an ecological disaster. Yet the California Water Plan could provide for twice as many people as now inhabit the coastal plain.

If this unhappy story has a moral it is that the typical American approach to resource planning is to "build it bigger and better"—to tap the distant, costly, and abundant sources just because they will require huge investments of capital and technology. The same capital and technology are then called upon to repair the environmental damage that results.

Planning for Integrated Development

How do we go about planning for more and better water? Building on the principles of watershed management, we can see that the best planning is not the sort that covers a continent with a single massive network to contain every drop that falls. On the contrary, comprehensive planning can best be applied to small units with distinctive problems and logical boundaries. This does not preclude cooperation at numerous levels, but it does bring the planning authority down to the level where the greatest economies of water use can be accomplished.

At the national level, instead of planning and building N.A.W.A.P.A. the same amount of energy should be directed toward coordinating research, disseminating

FIGURE 8.3.   A small section (several hundred square miles) of the Rocky Mountain Trench, which would be flooded if the N.A.W.A.P.A. scheme becomes a reality (essay 8.1). In addition to widespread aesthetic loss, the ecological side effects are incalculable. (Department of Lands and Forests, British Columbia)

technological information, and legislating the control of pollution. Planning for integrated development begins when the resources of the national government are in a position to give the most help possible to the implementing unit, not to be the implementing unit.

A good example of the kind of action needed can be found in the regulation of oil pollution. Even without such spectacular spills as the San Francisco Bay collision of January, 1971, there are 1 million tons of oil spilled on the open seas and 10 million tons dumped and spilled in bays and estuaries each year. Public damage by oil has largely been ignored; in cases where private property has been damaged it has been necessary to invoke laws dating back to 1924 or earlier. Present legislation was pioneered by the 1965 Water Quality Act, while the Clean Water Restoration Act of 1966 strengthened earlier pieces of legislation such as the 1924 Oil Pollution Act. In one fed-

eral case *(California* v. *S.S. Bournamouth,* 1970) discharged oil into navigable waters
was prosecuted as a new maritime tort under the Federal Maritime Act. Nevertheless,
the "navigable waterways" section of the 1972 House Water Pollution Control Bill
(H.R. 11896) has been greatly weakened by amendments, and the bill's definition of
pollution specifically exempts the oil industry (for instance, pollution of groundwater
in the course of oil or gas production is not considered pollution at all). The legislative
situation is further complicated by the fact that, as a result of the present oil import
quota program, the federal government is heavily committed to encouraging the exploration of U.S. offshore oil reserves (see chapter 4).

In the area of flood control, the Department of Agriculture estimates that,
of the 125 million acres of floodplains in the United States, 86 million need some degree of protection. The $4 billion already spent has provided effective control for 27
percent of the tributary areas, 40 percent of the downstream lands, and 31 percent of
the floodplains. This may or may not prove a significant margin of safety. In many
hilly areas, damage to residential property from flooding, landslides, and related dis-
placements is increasing. This reflects poor zoning and insufficient knowledge of soil
and topography. It also reflects the fact that the American home construction industry
will do anything it is allowed to get away with. For many sites, use of steel framing
should be required. The Federal Housing Authority and the Veteran's Administration
have been shortsighted in failing to insist on or even accept these and other safety
measures.

Like many of our resource policies, our flood control measures have
proven penny wise and pound foolish. Channel "improvement" and levee construction
have not paid off. One-third of upstream and two-thirds of downstream flood damage
affect nonagricultural developments—which are much more expensive to repair than
agricultural losses. The disproportionate share of damage to nonagricultural facilities
on the floodplains exposes our bad judgment in planning land use. The logical utilization for most floodplains is agricultural. The great floods that occur statistically once
in a hundred years need cost us only one year's crops instead of wiping out urban-
industrial construction of far greater value. It would be not only cheaper but more
humane to provide crop insurance to agricultural users than to rely solely on emergency
aid to urban flood disaster areas.

Total Development and Total Use

The concept of *total use* of water implies that water is used for various
purposes based upon its quality. When quality becomes too low, provisions can be
made for reclaiming and recycling. Total use involves the integration of the technologies of water supply and liquid sewage disposal.

At the household level implementation of total use may take many forms,
most of which cannot exist unless the consumer is already motivated to save water.
The chief form is recycling. Shower and rinse water from automatic washers can be separated from other discharge and then recirculated to flush toilets, which do not require

Essay 8.1.   The North American Water and Power Alliance

One salient fact about the geography of North America is that the northern portions of it have a great deal of water and the southern ones very little. Much of the fresh water supply flows unused into the Pacific and Arctic oceans, while the need for water in parts of North America is expected to exceed the supply by the end of the century. This has inspired a Los Angeles-based engineering firm, the Ralph M. Parsons Company, to draw up a grandiose plan for channeling surplus water from Alaskan and northwest Canadian rivers into the American West, northern Mexico, and the Great Lakes. High dams would be constructed at the headwaters of rivers to capture their flow. One dam proposed for Alaska's Copper River would reach a colossal 1700 feet—450 feet taller than the Empire State Building. The water would be stored in enormous reservoirs, fifteen of them larger than Lake Mead, North America's largest man-made lake. Among these would reign the Rocky Mountain Trench with a capacity for 518,200,000 acre feet of water or sixteen times as much as Lake Mead. To operate the distribution of water, a computer center would be required with a network of microwave systems, land lines, and relay stations enmeshing a vast region—two-thirds of North America.

Known as the North American Water and Power Alliance (N.A.W.A.P.A.), the plan would use the abundant water from the northern Rocky Mountains to supply irrigation and hydroelectric power for western Canada, create waterways between two Prairie Provinces and the Great Lakes, stabilize the Great Lakes' water levels, increase power production at Niagara Falls, irrigate up to 56 million acres in the United States and Mexico, and provide water to support the growth of cities in the Southwest (see map below). In this form it is backed by at least one influential U.S. Senator, and has been ballyhooed by lobbyists and state legislators. Cost estimates range from $100 billion on up, and construction time might be from twenty to thirty years—perhaps longer if a serious effort were not made at the outset to resolve conflicting international, federal-state, and interstate differences. The Parsons Company claims that the system would pay for itself in fifty years through the sale of water and electric power, but other people have serious doubts about the economic and technological feasibility of the plan, and are wary about the attendant political and environmental problems.

The creation of reservoirs and canals has potentially destructive side effects. At least a thousand miles of valleys, including some of the world's most beautiful, would be permanently flooded (figure 8.3). Several existing communities would be submerged, potential farmland and valuable mineral deposits sacrificed, and physical geology affected by the massive load stress of the reservoirs. Evaporation from the newly formed bodies of water may

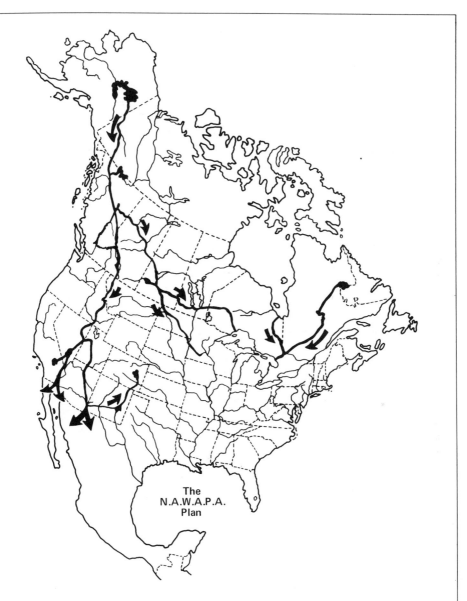

The
N.A.W.A.P.A.
Plan

gradually alter the climate, and changes in the flow of rivers may result in
biological transformations.

Another reason for pause is that the acute water shortage predicted by
the year 2000 may not in fact occur. Is it economically rational to invest
$100 billion in the long-distance transfer of water when there is no guarantee
of actual need and when other methods might well be employed if shortage

does happen? For instance, water could be recycled; water management could be improved to reduce significant wastage; and the price of water could be raised commensurate with the cost of supplying it, thereby encouraging more efficient use and lower requirements.

Although proponents of N.A.W.A.P.A. may envision a technological paradise where reservoirs subdue the wilderness and canals bear the source of life and economic productivity to thirsty regions, is the scheme really practicable, or even necessary? Many questions remain unanswered, and many

water of drinking quality. If we accept the estimates of household use for flushing toilets at 50 gallons per day and of shower and bath use at 60 gallons, it should be a simple matter to save nearly one-third of daily use in this manner. Further savings could be made by simple plumbing changes that take the effluent containing human waste through a simple reclamation process (see figure 8.4). If more water is saved than is needed for household reuse then it will be a simple matter to discharge this cleaner water into separate community lines for uses requiring lesser quality or for recycling to first-quality water. Another technique, developed in Sweden, is based on a vacuum unit for a home toilet; it reduces the water used in a single flushing from 5 gallons to one quart.

At the community or regional level provision can be made for constant reuse through **tertiary treatment** of sewage and other organic waste. In the widely known but little understood project of Santee, California, tertiary treatment is accomplished by stimulating organic breakdown in oxidation ponds, then filtering it through natural sediments in the valley floor (figure 8.5). The recycled water is used to form recreational lakes and for irrigation. This water is actually purer than it was when first used by the residents, but because of the problem of consumer acceptance the water is not returned to the primary supply. Another problem is that once reclaimed water is returned in a system such as this successive uses create unacceptable salt accumulation. Eventually, therefore, it is planned to put a small desalinization unit at the end of the process to treat the more saline waters. Then the only water that will ever leave the system will be that which evaporates or accidentally percolates beyond the recovery boundaries.

Because most areas lack Santee's natural filtration beds the federal government has sponsored research at the site to duplicate the process in a contained system. This prototype has been successful. Thus the problem is no longer one of technology but of convincing communities that the cheapest water is truly in their own backyards. The idea is spreading. Plans have been developed by the Cincinnati Water Research Laboratory for a plant that can convert 20 million gallons of used water to fresh water per day, at a cost of only 10 cents per 1,000 gallons. This is $32.59 per acre foot compared to an estimated cost of water from the California Aqueduct of over $70 per acre foot. The city of San Jose has a tertiary treatment plant already in operation at the southern end of San Francisco Bay.

consequences unfathomed. Current Canadian opinion seems to be against the plan, but so much U.S. capital is already invested in Canada that this may make little difference in the long run. Should the plan ever be implemented, it might just turn out to be the costliest mistake the United States has ever made. (The September 1967 issue of Bulletin of the Atomic Scientists *provides a thorough discussion of the project in a five-article section entitled "Nawapa: A Continental Water System," from which much of the data in this essay are derived.)*

On the whole, however, technologies of water management are advanced far beyond any present application. Sometimes economic factors are to blame for the lag; but very often the problem is a dearth of local leadership. Impetus is to be expected at local levels because it is there that pollution or shortage problems are felt. A regional watershed can be maintained by federal or state agencies, but its value and the

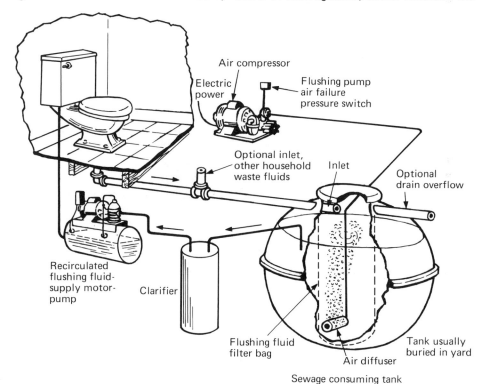

FIGURE 8.4.   Sewerless toilet designed by Carl F. Boester reduces household water consumption by at least 50 percent and requires only as much electricity as a continuously burning 125-watt light bulb. Recirculated flushing fluid is clear and odorless. (redrawn by permission of Sewerless Toilet Company, Lafayette, Indiana)

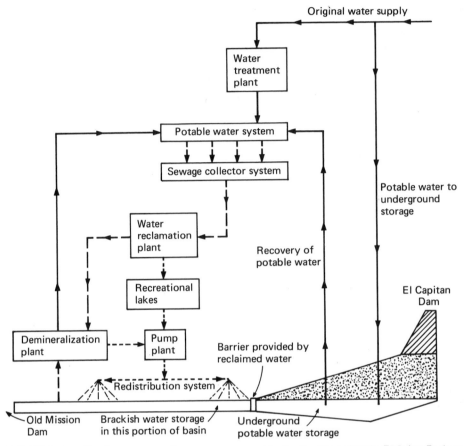

FIGURE 8.5.   Total use system of water management in the Santee–Lakeside–El Cajon Drainage Basin, California. Recycled water is purer than required for domestic purposes but is diverted to nondomestic use because of public acceptance problem. (Santee County Water District)

consequences of its good or bad condition affect the people who live near it. A small stream is of most importance to the nearby community, for which it may be a recreational feature and an aesthetic advantage as well as a water supply. The community that cares enough to foster a recycling or a tertiary sewage treatment system reaps the many benefits itself.

Another factor is that smaller projects are easier for voters to understand. The classic example of a grandiose project that was probably *not* understood by the voters at the time it was put to them is the 1957 California Water Plan. From a strictly engineering point of view, the plan, which is designed to bring water from the Sacramento Basin and northernmost counties to central and southern California, is one of the wonders of the world, involving construction of the highest dam and the largest pumping installation in the United States. The benefits of abundant water are hard for the average citizen to question. And yet, as the plan has taken visible shape, a host of undesirable consequences have begun to appear—the end of wild rivers, irreversible damage to fisheries and wildlife, increased pollution from fertilizers, and, above all, soaring population growth. Moreover, the advantages are temporary; nearly all reservoirs and dams eventually silt up. Even the plan's strongest advocates admit that it will not meet state water needs much beyond 1990.

In the last analysis, the greatest potential for improved water management lies with local planning boards. It is no longer a matter of money; whatever the form in which the 1972 water quality bills eventually become law, they appear certain to provide massive federal aid to local water authorities. The extent to which we can increase our water supplies depends on control of waste, on the one hand, and on our ability to tap the hydrologic cycle, on the other. Less obviously, in a field usually left to experts, it depends on the level of public interest and knowledge. People should know what kind of water system they are voting for, and why. Corporate polluters should clean up—or else. At the international level, experts of all countries must bring pressure on governments to stop using the sea as an open sewer. Despite the possibilities opened up by research, our future will for a long time depend on our ability to use existing supplies of fresh water. Priority should therefore be given to devising methods of extending the fresh water phase of the hydrologic cycle.

REFERENCES

Boyle, Robert H., "The Hudson River Lives," *Audubon*, March 1971, pp. 14–17, 21–24, 41–58.

Carson, Rachel L., *The Sea Around Us* (New York: Mentor, 1954).

Conservation News, "Buffalo Creek Flood Points to Future Strip Mine Disasters," April 1 and 15, 1972.

Dadisman, Quincy, "Not Quite Dead: The Pathology of Lake Erie," *The Nation,* April 17, 1972, pp. 492–496.

Dasmann, Raymond F., *The Destruction of California* (New York: Collier Books, 1966).

Denney, Ronald C., *This Dirty World* (London: Nelson, 1971).

Federal Water Pollution Control Administration, U.S. Department of the Interior, *The Cost of Clean Water,* vol. I, Summary Report (Washington, D.C.: Government Printing Office, 1968).

Gates, David, " Weather Modification in the Service of Mankind: Promise or Peril?" in Harold W. Helfrich, Jr. (ed.) *The Environmental Crisis* (Yale University Press, 1970).

Hawerman, Bertil, "Protecting Areas for Ground Water Sources," in E. Erickson et al. (eds.) *Ground Water Problems* (Proceedings of the International Symposium, Stockholm, October 1966).

Hazleton, Jared E., "Effluents and Affluence," in Marshall I. Goldman (ed.), *Controlling Pollution: The Economics of a Cleaner America* (Englewood Cliffs, N.J.: Prentice-Hall, 1967).

Hetzer, Nicholas D., "Tomorrow's Strategic Sewer: The Ocean," *Ecosphere,* April–May 1971, pp. 3–7, 11–14.

Heyerdahl, Thor, "What We Are Doing to Our Oceans!" *International Wildlife,* May–June 1972, pp. 4–9.

Hill, Gladwin, "The Great and Dirty Lakes," *Saturday Review,* October 23, 1965, pp. 32–34.

Kneese, Allen V., *Water Pollution* (Washington, D.C.: Resources for the Future, Inc., 1962).

Laycock, George, *The Diligent Destroyers* (New York: Ballantine, 1970).

Man's Impact on the Global Environment: Report of the Study of Critical Environmental Problems (MIT Press, 1970).

McCaull, Julian, "The Black Tide," in Sheldon Novick and Dorothy Cottrell (eds.), *Our World in Peril: An Environment Review* (New York: Fawcett, 1971).

National Academy of Sciences, *Report to the Federal Council for Science and Technology,* April 1966.

Novick, Sheldon, "Last Year at Deauville," *Environment,* July–August 1971, pp. 36–37.

Pringle, Laurence, "The Upper Hudson: Whitewater or Washwater?" *Audubon,* March 1971, pp. 88–101.

Reynolds, Malvina, "A Song of San Francisco Bay," in Alfred Meyer (ed.), *Encountering the Environment* (New York: Van Nostrand, 1971), pp. 183–195.

Ross, Charles R., "The Federal Government as an Inadvertent Advocate of Environmental Degradation," in Harold W. Helfrich, Jr. (ed.), *The Environmental Crisis* (Yale University Press, 1970).

San Francisco Bay Conservation and Development Commission, *San Francisco Bay Plan* (vol. 1) and *San Francisco Bay Plan Supplement* (vol. 2), submitted January 6, 1969 (Sacramento: State Department of Documents and Publications).

Squire, James L., "Surface Temperature Gradients Observed in Marine Areas Receiving Warm Water Discharge," Bureau of Sport Fisheries and Wildlife, U.S. Department of the Interior, Technical Paper No. 11 (Washington, D.C.: Government Printing Office, 1967).

Waggoner, Paul E., "Weather Modification and the Living Environment," in F. Fraser Darling and John P. Milton (eds.), *Future Environments of North America: Transformation of a Continent* (Garden City, N.Y.: Natural History Press, 1966), pp. 87–98.

9 LAND WASTES

Garbage, as Kenneth Boulding has said, is the ultimate physical product of economic life. People take resources from the earth, refashion them in various ways for their own use, and then throw away what is left after they have finished with them. Hitherto, new civilizations have sunk their foundations in the garbage heaps of the old. There is reason to believe that this cannot continue.

According to the Council on Environmental Quality, U.S. production of solid wastes in 1969 was over 4.3 billion tons, of which nearly 2.3 billion were from agriculture and about 1.7 billion from mining. Some 250 million tons, of which 60 million went uncollected, were classified as residential, commercial, and institutional wastes, while industrial wastes accounted for the remainder. Altogether the United States is responsible for more than half the world's annual production of solid wastes. Each day's accumulation, *U.S. News and World Report* has estimated, would cover 50 square miles with a 10-foot layer.

The problem of waste goes far beyond the volume of materials needing disposal. Radioactive or highly toxic materials need special treatment even in minute quantities. Others, such as DDT, have peculiar chemical properties that cause them to become involved in various undesirable ways with biotic relationships such as the food chain. In this way they poison not only the earth but the whole biosphere.

All these types of waste are customarily disposed of in the earth. Disposal in the air (through burning) or the sea (through dumping) is also quite common; some of the effects have been dealt with in the previous two chapters. But the commonest method by far is still to rely on the earth's natural recycling capacities. The danger to the earth, as Ronald Denney has pointed out, is threefold: it may be *desecrated* by improper waste disposal; it may be *denuded* by strip mining or other activities that destroy vegetation; and it may be *poisoned* by chemicals or bacteria. Ironically, all these dangers are greater where there is no apparent shortage of land. "Out of sight, out of mind," is the rule with solid waste disposal as with so many other environmental problems (figure 9.1).

Carelessly discarded waste, or *litter,* is a comparatively small proportion of the total. Yet 20 million cubic yards of it were strewn across the nation in 1968—enough to cover a superhighway from New York to San Francisco 1 foot deep. Cleaning up litter is expensive. California alone spends $50 million a year, or $12 per family, tidying its highways and other public places. The expense is borne ultimately by the taxpayers. The same is true of routinely collected solid wastes. The American Public Works Association classifies these wastes into five main categories: *rubbish* (paper, glass, cans, etc.); *garbage* (waste from food preparation); *dead animals; demolition waste* (building materials, including lumber); and *sewage.* Thus the term "refuse" has no precise meaning as far as the association is concerned. Here, it will generally denote a combination of the first four categories, since these are most often disposed of on land. In 1920 municipal refuse from household, commercial, and industrial sources averaged 2.75 pounds per person per day. By 1970 this average had risen to more than 5.3 pounds—a total of 360 million tons per year. These figures will double by 1980 at the present rate of increase. Household refuse alone will exceed 250 million tons by 1980. Refuse production is increasing at the rate of about 4 percent per year—the same rate as the gross national product.

Most of the increase in refuse production consists of *convenience packaging*—throwaway containers of glass, metal, and plastic—and *excess packaging,* designed to bolster the allure of products competing for the consumer's dollar. In 1968, according to a president's Science Advisory Committee report, Americans threw out 50 billion metal cans, 27 billion glass bottles and jars, 67 million plastic and metal caps, and

FIGURE 9.1.   A desert garbage dump.
Open dumps like this one are all too typical of
U.S. dryland waste disposal. (Bureau of Land
Management, U.S. Department of the Interior)

astronomical numbers of paper bags, wrappers, cartons, boxes, and crates. Paper and paper products make up 20 million tons of total municipal refuse—almost 20 percent of the weight but a whopping 45 percent of the volume. Here, too, the consumer pays; 40 percent of the price of a can of beer, for example, is for packaging. An estimated $500 of the average household's annual grocery bill pays for packaging—instant refuse that costs more money to get rid of. By 1969 the nationwide cost of refuse collection and disposal exceeded $4.5 billion, or about one-tenth of all local taxes. This is more than the cost of any other public service except the provision of roads and schools.

METHODS OF WASTE DISPOSAL

In spite of their high cost, most of the current disposal methods are dangerously inadequate. There are from 12,000 to 14,000 land disposal sites in the United States. Some 94 percent of these are *open burning dumps* that pollute the air, contaminate soil and groundwater, create public nuisances in the form of stench and ugliness, and provide breeding places for rodent and insect pests. Dumps of this kind have been declared insanitary by the U.S. Public Health Service, and have been opposed for years by the American Public Works Association. The other 6 percent of land disposal sites qualify as *sanitary landfills.* Here, refuse is deposited in trenches or pits and then compacted with earth-moving equipment and covered at the end of each day with a layer of earth to keep out vermin. Only 25 million tons—one-tenth of the annual total—are disposed of in this way (figure 9.2).

Whatever the exact manner of disposal, 90 percent of all solid refuse is deposited on or under land. Disposal on dry land in open dumps, as described above, has been practiced since at least the age of the Roman Empire. It is an amazing anachronism in twentieth-century urban-industrial society. Dry land disposal at its best involves filling gullies and canyons with refuse that is compacted and then covered with earth to produce usable level land. Most filled sites are aesthetically inferior to naturally contoured areas, and such rapid alteration of natural topography may disrupt surface drainage patterns. More important, although the fill is compacted, buried, and out of sight, its presence as a pocket of potential infection can never be forgotten. Some components of municipal refuse eventually disintegrate and become part of the soil. But others resist chemical decomposition. Glass, aluminum, plastic, and other synthetics are almost unaffected by soil weathering processes. Refuse also includes toxins, hospital wastes, pesticide residues, and innumerable other household and industrial chemicals. Groundwater may be contaminated during heavy rains or flooding, or by ordinary seepage. Dangerous substances can also be exposed by erosion during the continuing natural cycle of denudation and, of course, by future construction on the site. The soil itself may become poisoned (figure 9.3).

The other popular method is *dumping on wetlands.* This has already had serious environmental consequences. Because marshes and tidelands are not valued as

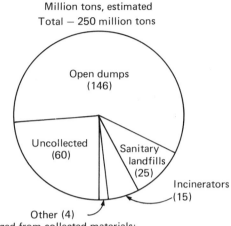

FIGURE 9.2.   Disposal of U.S. residential, commercial, and institutional solid wastes, 1969. The situation is even worse than it seems: not all "sanitary landfills" are truly sanitary. (Bureau of Solid Waste Management, U.S. Department of Health, Education, and Welfare)

FIGURE 9.3   Refuse collected at a sanitary land fill operation. The futility of land fill as a workable disposal method is apparent.(Photo by John Earle)

human habitats they have unfortunately been regarded as good for nothing but refuse dumps. In reality, however, marshes and bay bottoms are potentially the most valuable food-producing areas in the United States, with natural fertility up to six times greater than that of average Kansas wheat land. The estuarine complex that once extended from New England to the Gulf of Mexico was one of the great biological wonders of the world, supporting a phenomenal number and variety of plants and animals. It now affords a good example of an ecological disaster area. According to William A. Niering, only about 60 percent of the original 127 million acres are still left. California and Florida have lost nearly 70 percent of their coastal wetlands to developers, and Connecticut over 50 percent. Chemical plants, petroleum refineries, and pulp mills traditionally locate on estuaries because of their need for water and for access to water transportation. To such industries, the "worthless" marshlands are fair game for pollution. Dredging, filling, and refuse dumping have so altered the tideland ecology that many species have disappeared completely and others are endangered. Waterfowl, fish, crustaceans, and mollusks are all thinning. The total catch of eighteen coastal species of fish, both commerical and sport, dropped from 1.4 billion pounds in 1960 to 700 million in 1965. About 90 percent of this catch depends on the existence of the coastal wetlands. Many species of waterfowl not only breed and feed in the coastal marshes but rest in them during their long migrations. State laws have so far failed to protect the ocean fringes from dumping and other depredations, and federal agencies such as the Bureau of Commercial Fisheries or the Bureau of Sport Fisheries and Wildlife lack jurisdiction over tidal marshes. Meanwhile, cities such as New York continue to fill in their wetlands with solid wastes. Between 1954 and 1959, as Melvin A. Benarde has pointed out, over 13 percent of Long Island's wetlands were used for this purpose; now there is talk of filling in Jamaica Bay.

Other disposal techniques include such familiar practices as incineration. Of some 300 municipal incinerators operating in U.S. cities, at least 70 percent lack adequate emission control equipment or have none at all. They relieve the problem of land pollution only by aggravating that of air pollution. Even after incineration at least 7 percent of the original volume of refuse remains to be disposed of. Some municipalities have been experimenting with techniques designed to make use of waste materials.

Two Florida cities have composting machinery that separates out paper, wood, fabric, and other organic materials and shreds them for mulch. A plant in St. Petersburg converts 100 tons of refuse per day; a Gainesville plant shreds 20 tons per hour and adds digested sewage sludge to produce a cheap, effective organic soil conditioner. However, as Judith G. Meyer has demonstracted, organic compost derived from garbage cannot now compete economically with chemical fertilizers. Both Los Angeles and Houston have tried composting plants, but the Los Angeles plant could not find a market for its product and the Houston plant had to be closed because of odor nuisance. Other cities process refuse with a view to exploiting its structural properties. Minneapolis has a hydraulic press that compacts refuse under 2,800 pounds of pressure per square inch, reducing 5,000 pounds of it to a 4-foot cube; the bales are trucked 17 miles to a landfill site. A giant press in Japan reduces volume by 90 percent; the resulting bales are dipped in concrete, asphalt, or steel sealants and used as road ballast or as foundation blocks in construction. The Aloe Coal Company of Pennsylvania has a $1.1 million contract with the city of Pittsburgh to fill in land disturbed by surface mining with compacted wastes. The process costs the city $6.85 a ton, compared with $25 a ton for incineration, and results in open countryside which is then stocked with game. Precautions are taken against pollution of groundwater. A process called pyrolysis is being tested in San Diego. It decomposes or distills substances in temperatures up to 1,700°F. in sealed, airless ovens. A pyrolysis plant costs about the same as an incinerator, reduces volume by 70 percent, and produces no direct pollution. The solid residue, known as "char," can be used as a cheap and easily transported fuel, while liquid condensed from by-product vapors contains organic compounds that may be salable. A method still in the experimental stage would involve mixing finely ground refuse with water and pumping it to a combination sewage and solid waste treatment plant. The main disadvantage of this method is that it would probably use excessive quantities of water.

Refuse as a Resource

Huge quantities of nonrenewable resources are currently being lost in the flood of waste. As much as $1 billion worth of minerals is thrown away in municipal dumps each year, according to Department of the Interior investigators. Over the same period, refuse burning produces 500,000 pounds of fly ash that contain silver, zinc, copper, lead, tin, and other minerals in economically significant quantities. Over 100 million rubber tires are thown away every year. Experimenters at Texas A. and M. believe that these tires, if reduced to powder, could be used for road building, since rubber makes asphalt more flexible. Independent experiments at the University of Missouri have shown that ground glass granules from discarded bottles can replace the rock aggregates now used in highway construction. A test strip built of "glasphalt" is reported to be very successful.

Refuse can also be used as fuel. Bergen County, New Jersey, operates a swimming pool and a skating rink on power supplied by a trash incinerator with afterburners and pollution control devices. New York City's refuse could, according to one estimate, supply one-quarter of its power needs. One incineration device, called a *continuous refuse gasifier,* can consume up to 200 tons of trash per hour and produce enough heat to operate the largest boilers used in electrical generation. Refuse is cheaper than fossil fuels and its use would conserve the remaining fossil fuel resources. Paper and other combustible trash contains less sulfur than coal or fuel oil, and would cause less air pollution. Moreover, it would be possible to dispose of 93 percent of the refuse in this way. A system now being tested by Combustion Power, Incorporated, in Menlo Park, California, grinds materials that cannot be recycled and then burns them to produce an exhaust that will run turbine generators. The system is being developed under a contract with the Environmental Protection Agency.

The most pressing problem of waste disposal is the environmental one. In the long run, however, there is no solution except to abolish the concept of waste in favor of reuse. A nearly waste-free system could be established if unnecessary packaging and other superfluous materials were eliminated. Goods that could not be conveniently reused would be designed for practical and economical recycling. Even products made of plentiful materials consume energy in manufacture, and all energy generation causes pollution. When refuse is incinerated or shredded, certain components must be sorted out beforehand if they are not to remain as an indestructible residue. So-called disposable glass and aluminum containers are both a nuisance and an expense to get rid of. Plastic film, tubes, bottles and so forth release dangerous polychlorinated biphenyls (**PCBs**) into the environment when incinerated. These materials should not be used at all without a very great deal more thought being devoted to the problem of their disposal. We cannot just take the natural recycling properties of the earth for granted.

It is easy enough to talk of recycling scarce resources, but in truth nothing could be more contrary to our present way of doing things. Meaningless changes of style, deliberately brief product-life, excess packaging, and endless advertising—all these may stimulate buying, but they vastly accelerate the pace at which resources are converted into waste. It will take years to establish a smoothly operating total recycling system, and of course voluntary reform will not come from entrenched economic interests obsessed with their own profits. If reform is to come, pressure must be applied by a concerned public.

SPECIAL DISPOSAL PROBLEMS

Two types of waste, discarded automobiles and spoil banks from strip mining, are so characteristic of our socioeconomic system, and so intractable under that system, that they merit separate treatment.

Discarded Automobiles

In 1969 Americans discarded 7 million cars, some 20 percent of them simply left on the streets or in a field. In New York 54,000 were abandoned on the streets in 1970. The problem is so serious that since 1965 the city has made a policy of towing away unwanted cars free of charge on receipt of a telephone call. Los Angeles, trying to cope with over 33,000 abandoned cars a year, has had to resort to towing them off its freeways after only four hours. Other local authorities are being forced to adopt similar measures, since the value of most old cars to junk dealers is less than the cost of towing and storage. Auto wrecking yards and graveyards are multiplying everywhere; by now they contain over 40 million old cars. Since 1966 many states, in an effort to minimize their ugliness, have required that new wrecking yards be located out of sight of major highways, while existing ones must erect screens or tall fences. Once again, the symptoms are being treated rather than the problem itself.

Recycling of junked auto scrap is inhibited by the cost of collection and storage, the low price it brings, and the steel industry's lack of interest in it. By 1967 only 15 to 26 percent of ferrous scrap used by the industry came from old cars. The alloy content of reclaimed auto metals is high and the big processors' new furnaces are geared for pig iron and pelletized iron ore. The U.S. scrap market, moreover, is depressed. Some attempt has been made to develop foreign markets. Japan, for instance, is buying shredded scrap for its steel mills, and a scrap disposal enterprise in National City, California, hopes to supply the Japanese with 180,000 to 200,000 tons per year. Its main asset is a giant shredder that can chew up a car in 14 seconds and handle 500 cars per day if continuously operated. However, because of high land transportation costs, processing auto scrap for export is economically feasible only for seaport cities.

The present disposal problem exists because the sole concern of automobile manufacturers is profit. Auto scrap is very little used in new car production because pig iron is cheaper for the industry. Consumers pay for this practice through taxes; cities must pay to clear their streets of defunct cars. Getting rid of the millions of cars now rusting in junkyards would mean devising competitive advantages for auto scrap. This would probably depend on direct federal subsidy—another burden for taxpayers. The greatest price, however, will be paid by future generations, whose legacy from the automobile industry and other gross exploiters will be depleted metal and fossil fuel resources.

Surface Mining Wastes

Surface mining (of which strip mining is one form) uncovers the desired minerals by removing the overlying topsoil, rock, and other strata. Enormous quantities of earth are gouged out, inverted, and buried, converting natural terrain into raw , lifeless spoil banks. Between 3.5 and 4 million acres in the United States have been mutilated by all forms of surface mining, and about two-thirds of this acreage has not been reclaimed.

Coal, sand and gravel, stone, gold, clay, phosphate, iron, and copper are taken by surface mining. Strip mining in particular has disrupted more than half the total acreage mined in this way, and two-thirds of all strip mining has been for coal. Before 1920, strip mining was almost completely limited to the taking of iron and confined to the Upper Lake States. Since then, however, it has been increasingly used for coal, and now yields 35 percent of the annual U.S. coal output. The development of giant earth-moving machinery has made strip mining extremely profitable. Its devastating effects on the landscape can now been seen in Ohio, Pennsylvania, Maryland, Virginia, West Virginia, Illinois, Kentucky, and Indiana. The scale of both profit and damage is suggested by the size of the shovel in figure 9.4: the toy-like object beside it

FIGURE 9.4.   A giant shovel engaged in strip mining of coal. The scale of this machine can best be realized by comparing it with the bulldozer on the left side. The bucket of the shovel holds enough overburden to fill two railroad cars and can fill at a height equivalent to a 14 story building and dump on top of a 12 story building a block away. (Marion Power Shovel Company, Marion, Ohio)

is a standard D-8 Caterpillar. Such shovels can scoop up two railroad cars of earth in one pass, or fill at a 14-story height, or dump at a 12-story height from a block away. They easily remove earth and rock 100 feet deep to expose a 3-foot seam of coal.

The giant swathes of scarred land left behind by strip mining operations are ecological ruins. No plant or animal life remains, fertile soils are disrupted and buried, and large areas are isolated by ditches and banks. Watersheds are damaged or destroyed and rapid erosion occurs. Both uncovered strata and piled up materials may shift and flow. Waste banks contain residues of combustible materials that, once exposed to the air, can ignite and burn for weeks, filling the atmosphere with noxious fumes and gases. Erosion results in floods. Where the exposed material consists of high-acid shale and sulfide compounds, rainwater flowing over and through spoil banks becomes highly acid runoff. It pollutes streams and rivers for many miles, killing or diminishing aquatic plant and animal life (figure 9.5).

Strip mined lands *can* be rehabilitated, by grading and reforesting. The cost of reclamation varies from $50 to $2,000 per acre—far less than the company is saving by its use of strip mining rather than underground mining. Federal, industrial, and individual efforts have successfully converted mined out areas to attractive recreational areas, farming and grazing lands, and residential and industrial sites. These are showcase projects, however, and have reclaimed only a fraction of the total damaged acreage. Twenty-eight states now have laws requiring some degree of reclamation by mining com-

FIGURE 9.5.   Mining area in Jefferson National Forest, Virginia, before completion of water-shed restoration project. Most areas eroded as a result of mining are not restored at all. (U.S. Forest Service)

panies of the land they disturb; a permit must be obtained and a bond posted, the amount varying in each state and according to the number of acres to be mined. Failure to rehabilitate to the required extent can mean loss of bond and revocation of or refusal to renew the mining permit. There is no such provision, however, in the Upper Lake States of Minnesota, Wisconsin, and Michigan, or for areas of the other eight states mentioned that were devastated before they passed legislative controls. Even now, the legislation is mostly weak or insufficiently enforced. Moreover, it is aimed primarily at flatland mining areas where reclamation is least costly; repairing mountainous regions is much more expensive and difficult, if it is possible at all. Many companies forfeit bond rather than attempt reclamation, and others, in leveling and recontouring, so compact the material that seedlings will not survive in it.

Six states began reclamation of 45,828 acres in 1967, developing the land for recreational use; meanwhile, according to the Department of the Interior, 45,576 additional acres were being disturbed by mining operations. Of all the land that has suffered in this way, between 2 and 3 million acres remain unreclaimed. The cost of reclamation, estimated at $800 million in 1968, would by now be close to $1 billion. Most mining companies refuse to repair the damage they do, and are lobbying against bills now in Congress authorizing states to develop reclamation standards under Department of Interior approval. The department is prepared to pay some of the cost but wants the mining companies to take the initiative. If they don't, according to Assistant Secretary Cordell Moore, the department will push for much tougher legislation.

That systematic reclamation is compatible with profit has been shown by the example of West Germany, where lignite (brown coal) is mined from the surface by giant wheel excavators. West German law requires the *complete* restoration of land disturbed for this purpose. The program, as described by E. A. Nephew, is so successful that areas have been returned to farming or forestry less than five years after being restored. It is interesting to note that this is a state program, not a federal one, and that its cost, although high, is minimized by superior productivity (about twice American levels) and extensive advance consultation between state and industry officials.

CHEMICAL LAND POLLUTION

Chemical contamination of land is almost invisible compared to the grosser forms of land pollution. But it is far more dangerous to life. Contamination in the United States and worldwide is extensive, and is increasing rapidly from numerous sources. Chemicals often do more harm as secondary pollutants than as primary ones, and can be more dangerous in combination than singly. Natural movement from land to water may have undesirable consequences; phosphate fertilizers, for instance, have caused serious problems in rivers and lakes where they are carried by precipitation run-off. Biocides such as DDT enter the food chain with results that are not fully known even now. The plastics now in use are immune to bacterial action and so cannot be safely or effectively disposed of by the same methods as organic wastes. All of these substances present serious long-term threats to the biosphere.

Air Pollution Fallout

The harm caused by pollutants that settle on land from the air varies in degree according to the nature of the chemical and the place where it happens to fall. Some industrial plants emit quantities of fluorine; there is a high death rate among grazing animals pastured near such plants. Animals that do not die immediately may eventually succumb to starvation as a result of the weakening of their bones and teeth. The effect on humans of ingested fluoride salts is not well known, but they are thought to contribute to bone and joint diseases in later life.

Biocides

The use of insecticides, rodenticides, and herbicides in the United States has increased enormously since mid-century. The national obsession with production, coupled with blind faith in technology and in the chemical industry's promotional claims, erupted in a frenzy of enthusiastic poisoning. In the last decade alone, annual production of synthetic organic pesticides has increased from 294,000 metric tons to over 500,000 (table 9.1). Total production of DDT from 1944 to 1968 was 1.23 million metric tons (table 9.2). These developments were aided and abetted at every stage by the U.S. Department of Agriculture and other federal agencies.

The economic benefits of these new products, which are so lethal that they should be called **biocides**, have been greatly overrated. When originally registered to be marketed, they were not recognized for what they were: a long-range threat to all life. Then, in 1962, Rachel Carson published *Silent Spring.* The book was not only brilliantly written but impeccably documented—and it showed that biocides were defeating the very ends they were supposed to serve. It was an indictment that could not be ignored. The controversy it ignited is still growing (see essay 17.1). Perhaps the most upsetting of Miss Carson's predictions was that mass spraying with insecticides such as DDT would succeed only in creating resistance in the insects themselves—resistance that would take a mere two to six years to develop. In other words, any victories over the insects by chemical means would be of short-term duration. This prediction was dramatically fulfilled in the summer of 1971, when it was officially announced that mosquitoes in fifteen major areas of California had become immune not only to DDT but to every other pesticide on the market.

So many different biocides are now in use or in process of being marketed that simply keeping up with the new ones is a full-time job. Nevertheless, they can readily be sorted into a small number of categories (essay 9.1). Nor are their ecological effects hard to summarize. They are effective pest killers, but being nonselective they also destroy insects that are not pests, including the pests' natural predators. After a period of exposure the pest species often develops a resistant strain, while the predators rarely do. The pest population then multiplies unchecked by either predators or pesticide. In one celebrated case, reported by *Medical World News* in 1965, an epidemic of hemorrhagic fever swept through a small Bolivian town because all the cats, natural predators of the rodents that carried the disease, had been killed off by DDT. The effects of killing off insect populations can be just as drastic. Among the beneficial insects that may disappear are the pollinators. Without pollinating insects there

TABLE 9.1.   U.S. production of synthetic organic pesticides* (thousands of metric tons)

Year	Production
1960	294
1962	332
1964	356
1966	457
1968	545
1969	505

Source: U.S. Tariff Commission and Department of Agriculture data as reproduced in Donella H. Meadows et al., *The Limits to Growth,* New York, Universe Books, 1972 (by permission of the publishers).

TABLE 9.2.   U.S. production and consumption of DDT
(thousands of metric tons)

Year	Production	Consumption
1950	35	26
1952	45	32
1954	44	20
1956	63	30
1958	66	30
1960	75	37
1962	76	30
1964	56	23
1966	64	21
1968	63	15

Source: U.S. Department of Agriculture data as reproduced in Donella H. Meadows et al., *The Limits to Growth,* New York, Universe Books, 1972 (by permission of the publishers).

Note: Total production, 1944–1968 = 1.225 million metric tons.
Ten-year production, 1959–1968 = 676 thousand metric tons.

can be no crops at all except grasses; all other plants depend on them. Frank Graham, Jr., reports that at least 10 percent of the nation's bee colonies were wiped out in 1967; California lost 76,000 and Arizona 70,000. As a result, bees now have to be imported into many agricultural areas. Part of the trouble was that the Department of Agriculture has been promoting the application of certain insecticides to crops in bloom even though the manufacturers' labels clearly stated that danger to bees was likely to result.

The long-term effects are even more sinister. Chlorinated hydrocarbons such as DDT are persistent; they resist disintegration for fifteen to twenty years. Most dissemination is by airplane, and less than half the chemical reaches the target crop. The rest drifts for many miles in air currents and has contaminated the air, water, and land of every part of the world. Derivatives of DDT have been found in all animals on earth that have been examined. The first stage of DDT breakdown is DDE. Unfortunately it is as destructive to organisms as DDT and highly resistant to further biochemical breakdown. Invertebrate organisms ingest chlorinated hydrocarbons from vegetation, soil, and water: the higher up the food chain, the greater the concentration. Charles F. Wurster, the biologist who founded the Environmental Defense Fund, has described how, in research that he conducted with a colleague in 1966, he found that, after sampling for DDT in a Long Island salt marsh and then arranging the sample analyses in order of DDT concentration, he had virtually reconstructed the marsh's food chain. Similar effects have since been uncovered elsewhere. Bottom mud in Lake Michigan, for example, is contaminated by aerial drift and averages .014 ppm of DDE. Shrimp, however, average .44 ppm, chub 4.5 ppm, whitefish 5.6 ppm, and herring gulls 98.8 ppm—7,000 times the concentration in bottom mud. This process is still more insidious

Essay 9.1   Biocides

Biocides may be classified according to their chemical composition, function (e.g., whether they act on the stomach or the nervous system), persistence, toxicity, carcinogenicity (tendency to cause cancer), teratogenicity (tendency to cause birth defects), mobility (tendency to be carried from place to place), selectivity (how many different species they kill), and in many other ways. Since biocides from the same chemical group tend to be similar in other respects, a chemical classification (used here, with one exception) is normally to be preferred. It is also useful from a historical point of view: the synthetic biocides were for the most part developed for agricultural use later than the natural ones.

NATURAL: (1) Plant Products. *Plant extracts have been used for years as nonpersistent, relatively selective biocides of rather varied toxicity. Among the best known are the pyrethrins (from the pyrethrum daisy), rotenone (from plants of the derris group), and nicotine (the only highly toxic member of this class).*   (2) Inorganics. *Among these are such familiar chemicals as arsenic, copper, mercury, and zinc. A compound of lime and copper sulfate known as Bordeaux mixture has long been used as a fungicide.*

SYNTHETIC: (1) Chlorinated hydrocarbons. *The best-known members of this class are DDT, DDE, endrin, aldrin, dieldrin, and the heptachlors, all of which are discussed in the main text. They are highly persistent, mobile, and nonselective.*   (2) Organic phosphates. *The biocides in this class are actually a byproduct of chemical warfare research during World War II. It is not surprising, then, that they are both less persistent and more deadly on contact than chlorinated hydrocarbons. Parathion, which breaks down into the far more toxic paraoxin, has been found responsible for some fatalities and numerous near-fatalities. Organic phosphates sold as garden and yard insecticides include diazinon and malathion; environmentalists are highly suspicious of both.*   (3) Carbamates. *This latest generation of synthetic biocides is less persistent than the previous two and is said to be much safer, although its effect on the nervous system is similar to that of the organic phosphates. The best known carbamate is Sevin (carbaryl), which is teratogenic for some laboratory animals and can be fatal to bees and fish.*   (4) Herbicides. *Increasingly under attack from environmentalists are the herbicides and defoliants, especially 2,4-D and 2,4,5-T, over 100 million pounds of which were sprayed by U.S. planes over 5.5 million acres of Vietnam. Both had long been used in the United States without occasioning any protest since they appeared toxic only to plants. But since they not only upset the hormonal balance of plants but also give them chromosomal defects, H.E.W. has now classified them as carcinogenic and teratogenic. Further informaton on all these classes of pesticides will be found in* Report of the Secretary's Commission on Pesticides and Their Relationship to Environmental Health. *(U.S. Department of Health, Education, and Welfare, Washington, D.C., December 1969.)*

in a marine environment. Thus phytoplankton have .01 ppm of DDE, zooplankton .1 ppm, small fish 1 ppm, large fish 10 ppm, sea birds 10 ppm, pelicans and eagles 50 ppm, and peregrine falcons 100 ppm.

Efforts have been made by the pesticide industry, notably its official spokesman, the National Agricultural Chemicals Association, to dismiss such accumulations as harmless. This they certainly are not. DDT attacks nervous systems—whether they belong to insects, animals, or men. In one carefully controlled experiment, conducted at the Patuxent Wildlife Research Center in Laurel, Maryland, two groups of birds were fed large but sublethal doses of dieldrin and DDT while a similar group received no doses at all. The dosed groups were far less successful at reproducing themselves, and some members died. Symptoms included restlessness in the nest, thinner eggshells, and even a tendency to destroy the eggs by pecking. Similar effects were discovered off the California coast in 1969 by Dr. Robert Risebrough; brown pelicans, in particular, were laying eggs with such thin shells that they almost invariably broke before hatching. Other investigators have since traced abortion in sea lions to the amount of DDT in their blubber—sometimes as much as three-quarters of a pound per animal. Some of this was probably due to the dumping of DDT into municipal sewers by the Montrose Chemical Corporation, which has now desisted from the practice. According to Faith McNulty, it could be thirty years before pollution levels on the California coast begin to decline.

Most meat consumed in the United States is from herbivorous animals, which have lower concentrations of pesticides in their fatty tissue than predators, whether fish, mammals, or birds. Fish can be avoided if necessary, since food is not scarce as it is in so many other lands. However, all U.S. foods are contaminated to some degree. By the early 1960s, average concentrations of DDT in human body fat were found to be over 12 ppm in some areas of the United States (the national average was nearly 8 ppm). Figures from other parts of the world were even higher—19 ppm in Israel and 26 ppm in Delhi, India. Even Alaskan Eskimos, who have practically no use for DDT, averaged 3 ppm.

The official U.S. safety level for DDT in food is 7 ppm. These facts inspired Ronald Denney to remark that Americans had better not take up cannibalism, since they would find most of their compatriots unfit for consumption. At the very least, there is evidence that the proverbial phrases extolling the virtues of mother's milk may be sadly out of date. Levels in human milk range from .15 to .25 ppm; breat-fed infants ingest 4 times the maximum daily intake set by the U.N.— and 10 times the maximum for dieldrin.

Water and air are also contaminated. Clothing, rugs, and furniture are impregnated with chlorinated hydrocarbons from moth proofing and dry-cleaning; theaters and airliners are also regularly sprayed with them. Inhaling these chemicals or absorbing them through skin contact is far more harmful than consuming them in food.

Chlorinated hydrocarbons produce cancer in rats. Human victims of terminal cancer have been found on the average to have far higher pesticide residues in their tissues than persons who die from natural causes. Interviews with relatives of the cancer victims revealed that they were almost invariably heavy pesticide users in home and garden. These chemicals are also believed to cause genetic mutations that could take as long as forty generations to surface. The disquieting fact that 7 percent of all U.S. babies are born with some defect is now under study in relation to chlorinated hydrocarbons and other biocides. Ingestion of a lethal quantity of these chemicals causes death through little understood effects on the nervous system.

The consequences of gradually acquired concentrations can be manifested in a variety of ways. However, the most serious immediate worry is not that great numbers of people will die outright, but that food chains will be impaired. Some scientists fear chlorinated hydrocarbons will cut back the plankton population on which all oceanic animal life ultimately depends for food. In addition, plant plankton recycle 70 percent of the earth's oxygen flow, and recent experiments have confirmed earlier reports that DDT inhibits their capacity for photosynthesis.

England, Sweden, Denmark, and several other nations including Russia have long since banned or drastically limited the use of chlorinated hydrocarbons. In the United States some states have banned the use of DDT in homes or by aerial dissemination, but New York is the only state to have acted vigorously: as of 1971, it has banned the ten most dangerous chemicals and imposed strict controls on sixty others. In 1969, after seven years of controversy, the Department of Health, Education, and Welfare announced cancellation of federal registration of DDT *for certain uses,* amounting to 35 percent of U.S. annual consumption. The balance of use was to be phased out over a 2-year period in order to avoid "excessive economic disruption." The Department of Agriculture sprayed 4.9 million acres with DDT in 1957, 100,000 acres in 1967, and none at all in 1968. But use by all federal agencies accounts for only about 5 percent of annual U.S. pesticide sales. State and local public agencies, private firms, and individuals use only about 20 percent of the 100 to 120 million pounds of DDT produced each year in the United States. The reason is that, although its use *in this country* is now restricted, the Agency for International Development spends $15 million a year on DDT for export to other countries, from which it will be dispersed around the globe by wind and water. Altogether, the people of the United States pay well over $1 billion per year for all pesticides, directly and through taxes. The chemical industry will not willingly relinquish any fraction of this bonanza; it has even challenged H.E.W.'s order to phase out DDT. Cancellation of registration can be legally appealed, and leading manufacturers have initiated appeal. The review process can last for years, during which sales of the cancelled product may continue unless controlled at the state level. Meanwhile, according to the *Wall Street Journal,* chemical companies are turning to "defensive research"— that is, research designed to justify their products.

Although DDT was the first commercially available member of this family of pesticides and is now the most widely researched, it is not the most dangerous. Endrin is from 15 to 300 times more toxic, depending on the organism exposed to it. Although production of DDT is said to be dropping, that of the other chlorinated hydrocarbons is rising and they are being marketed all over the world. Both aldrin and dieldrin were restricted from use on vegetables, grain, and forage crops in 1966 in a sudden reversal of federal assurance that they were "safe"; at the same time, the heptachlors were withdrawn from dairy use. Apart from these tardy and partial measures, the federal government, deeply mired in the conflict of interest between its industrial affiliations and the health of the nation, has made no decisive move to halt or control production or use of the persistent chlorinated hydrocarbon pesticides as a class. As Charles F. Wurster has pointed out, the U.S. Department of Agriculture, which used to administer the federal pesticide registration system until the Environmental Protection Agency took over, never pursued the appeals process to conclusion for any pesticide. And yet aldrin (and dieldrin, to which it is normally converted) has many of the properties of DDT, including persistence. In addition, it is far more soluble in water than DDT, and therefore more likely to be carried through the air. Aldrin and dieldrin have been banned in Sweden. Are Americans somehow less vulnerable than Swedes?

Of course, there are situations in which the use of these chemicals may be less dangerous than the threat at which they are aimed—the control of insect-borne diseases, for example. But there is absolutely no justification for their use in the present quantities. In the decade since Rachel Carson's book was published ample evidence substantiating her warnings has been amassed. Yet pest strips, vaporizers, and bug bombs are still sold in vast quantities for use in homes and restaurants. Stocks of chlorinated hydrocarbon preparations exist in homes everywhere; many people would like to get rid of them but know of no safe way. Jorgen Randers and Dennis L. Meadows have calculated that even if world use of DDT is systematically reduced from 1970 onwards, the level of DDT concentration in fish will not begin to decline until about 1982. It follows from this that levels in animals higher in the food chain will continue to increase for a good deal longer; indeed, we may see no decline from present levels before the end of this century.

Plastics

Even as we begin to comprehend the long-range and ecologically pervasive damage wrought by so-called advanced pesticides, some scientists are already warning us that another family of complex chemicals may be more widespread and just as biologically destructive. The polychlorinated biphenyls are contained in plastics, rubber, paint extenders, and many other common materials of this industrial age. They have been found to cause severe damage to the liver and skin in higher animals. The most serious problem appears to be polyvinyl chloride in the form of plastic packaging. Because of its biological stability it is nearly permanent in the environment, and has become a tremendous waste disposal headache because there is so much of it. The obvious answer would be to burn it, but oxidation releases gaseous poisons that are then carried to all parts of the ecosphere. An even more alarming possibility, as Kevin P. Shea has pointed out, is that phthalate plasticizers, which have been shown to possess both toxic and teratogenic properties, may be absorbed from the plastic bags commonly used in blood transfusions.

Another common plastic, polythene, forms only carbon dioxide and water when burned. However, it shares in common with all plastics the property of being non-biodegradable, that is, unsuitable as food for bacteria. As Barry Commoner has emphasized, it is an unfortunate fact of modern economic life that synthetic materials are valued more highly than natural ones precisely because they are immune to decay. Biodegradable plastics, though theoretically possible, do not even appear to be on the technological horizon. The nearest approach to them are structures that break down after a certain period because they incorporate light-sensitive materials—not very practical for industrial use.

RADIOACTIVE WASTES

Since the early 1950s the Atomic Energy Commission has spurred efforts to get the development of nuclear energy into private hands. By 1970 there were 4,000 U.S. factories, laboratories, and other facilities handling 900 different types of **radioisotopes.** Contaminated wastes from this $2 billion-a-year industry include resins, oils, precipitates, slurries, clothing, rags, glassware, filters, and miscellaneous hardware. Up to 1963 such wastes were disposed of "permanently" by the A.E.C. in underground pits at remote sites, or by ocean dumping in sealed containers.

It is more than a little misleading to speak of permanent disposal for some forms of atomic waste, since they remain radioactive for thousands of years. Other forms are quite harmless after a day or two. Such low-activity wastes are routinely discharged into rivers and oceans. Not all of them are harmless; for instance, they may contain strontium-90, which accumulates in human bones. Many countries use a process called ion exchange to remove strontium-90 and other dangerous radioactive substances from low-activity waste before dumping it. Unfortunately, not all the dangers are known, and even small amounts of radiation turn up greatly magnified at higher levels in the food chain.

In 1963 the first private American firms were licensed to operate nuclear burial dumps. The A.E.C. then refused to accept any more low-activity nuclear waste from commercial firms. Such waste is defined as having no more than 1,000 times the radioactive concentration considered "safe" for direct release to the environment (the A.E.C. sets the safety standards). This action spurred development of a commercial atomic waste disposal industry. In 1970 there were 20 firms that made $1.5 million transporting and disposing of radioactive wastes. The A.E.C. has predicted a $10 million disposal market by 1980 and expressed hope that many states will license commerical burial sites. So far, however, only Washington, Nevada, Illinois, New York, and Kentucky have done so. Meanwhile the A.E.C.'s "permanent" disposal methods are causing alarm. At one of its Washington sites 11 of the 149 nuclear waste tanks have sprung leaks; one of them released 50,000 gallons of radioactive material. A 1966 study by the National Academy of Sciences asserted that the A.E.C.'s four major disposal sites are "in poor geological locations." It added that "current practices of disposing . . . wastes . . . into ground above or in the freshwater zones, although momentarily safe, will lead in the long run to a serious fouling of man's environment."

There have already been a number of disquieting reports of violated regulations and careless practices by some of the commercial firms. They include instances of shipments "lost" or unaccounted for, inadequately fenced waste lagoons from which deer drank radioactive water, and at least one lawsuit by a workman whose handling of a leaky and mislabeled container resulted in loss of an arm through cancer.

The A.E.C.'s latest scheme is to store high-activity wastes in abandoned salt mines. The original idea, as W. C. McClain and R. L. Bradshaw have pointed out, was to exploit salt's geological properties: it is commonly found in large natural deposits far removed from major earthquake zones, and is moreover impermeable and self-sealing. Unfortunately, very little is known about the physical and chemical behavior of salt when exposed to high-level radioactivity over a long period. It is true that salt is a good conductor of heat. But under radiation, according to Edward J. Zeller, it tends to store heat and then release it suddenly. Nevertheless, experiments seem to show that even these variations could be contained if the salt deposits were thick enough and far enough below the level of the ground. The problem has been to relate the experiments, which were necessarily somewhat simplified, to what may happen in reality. The A.E.C. proposes to create a so-called nuclear park (i.e., dump) at Lyons, Kansas, in a salt mine that has been abandoned for some years. If the proposal goes through this mine will become the depository for all the country's atomic refuse from civilian sources. Local engineers and geologists have objected that the A.E.C.'s survey of the mine and its geological setting has not been nearly careful enough. In consequence, reports John Lear, not only the Lyons project but the entire concept of salt mine disposal is now in doubt because of what many consider the A.E.C.'s questionable practices.

Exposure to radioactive materials has such long-term consequences as cancer, reduced fertility, acceleration of the aging process, eye damage, and genetic mutation. It is generally accepted that any amount of radiation, however small, can produce an indeterminate number of undesirable mutations. These are believed to be cumulative.

The history of the fallout controversy, well related by Barry Commoner in *The Closing Circle,* shows that the public safety is not well served by blind trust in such official bodies as the A.E.C. Attempts are being made in the courts by conservationists to have the A.E.C.'s peculiar combination of powers, a product of wartime secrecy, declared unconstitutional. But there is every indication so far that the courts will uphold the A.E.C.'s sole right to set nuclear safety standards. Perhaps the only course left open to us, if the nuclear wastes become unsafe, will be to think of some of the "unthinkable thoughts" proposed by Paul Sarnoff: we can give up nuclear power stations; we can hope there will soon be rain to dilute some of the radioactivity; and we can pray.

THE FUTURE OF LAND WASTES

The future of land wastes disposal will largely determine the future of the land on which we all live. The present picture, though gloomy, is not entirely without hope. Safe and economical refuse disposal *is* possible. Thus the Greater London Council's new incinerator at Edmonton consumes one-eighth of the city's refuse and generates electricity in the process. It conserves water resources by using recycled municipal water and purified sewage effluent, and its smokestacks are fitted with the latest "wet scrubbing" devices to minimize air pollution. Moreover, the plant site is being attractively landscaped. In this country, some hope is offered by the 1965 Solid Waste Disposal Act, which authorizes federal research and a limited amount of federal aid for pilot projects at the local level. The phenomenon of unused federal money is one of the crying municipal scandals of our time, but hopefully citizen pressure can be brought on municipal governments. The only long-term answer to the problem of discarded automobiles appears to be less reliance on the automobile as a means of transportation. Rehabilitation of strip-mined land is within our grasp if only the mining companies are more closely regulated.

Far more serious, alas, are the problems of land pollution from chemical and radioactive materials. In the field of insecticides, some hope is offered by a combination of the highly specific, third-generation insecticides with classic methods of biological control. But pesticide residues will be with us for years to come. Scientists have so far failed to invent a biodegradable plastic, which may in any case be a contradiction in terms. The economics of recycling are as yet poorly understood. The threat presented by radioactive wastes is appalling, no less so because it is mainly in the future. Will a new civilization ever build its foundations on our garbage heaps? It seems unlikely.

REFERENCES

Benarde, Melvin A., *Our Precarious Habitat* (New York: Norton, 1970).

Boulding, Kenneth E., "Fun and Games with the Gross National Product—The Role of Misleading Indicators in Social Policy," in Harold W. Helfrich, Jr. (ed.), *The Environmental Crisis* (Yale University Press, 1970).

Carson, Rachel, *Silent Spring* (Boston: Houghton Mifflin, 1962).

Commoner, Barry, *The Closing Circle* (New York: Knopf, 1971).

Council on Environmental Quality, *Environmental Quality: First Annual Report* (Washington, D.C.: Government Printing Office, 1970).

Denney, Ronald C., *This Dirty World* (London: Nelson, 1971).

Graham, Frank, Jr., *Since Silent Spring* (Boston: Houghton Mifflin, 1970).

Lear, John, "Radioactive Ashes in the Kansas Salt Cellar," *Saturday Review,* February 19, 1972, pp. 39–42.

McClain, W. C., and R. L. Bradshaw, "Radioactive Wastes in Salt Mines," *The Mines Magazine* (Colorado School of Mines), August 1969, pp. 11–14.

McNulty, Faith, "The Silent Shore," *Audubon,* November 1971, pp. 4–11

Meyer, Judith G., "Renewing the Soil," *Environment,* March 1972, pp. 22–24, 29–32.

Nephew, E. A., "Healing Wounds," *Environment,* January–February 1972, pp. 12–21.

Niering, William A., "The Dilemma of the Coastal Wetlands: Conflict of Local, National, and World Priorities," in Harold W. Helfrich, Jr. (ed.), *The Environmental Crisis* (Yale University Press, 1970).

Randers, Jorgen, and Dennis L. Meadows, "System Simulation to Test Environmental Policy I: A Sample Study of DDT Movement in the Environment," as cited in Donella H. Meadows et al., *The Limits to Growth* (New York: Universe, 1972).

Sarnoff, Paul, *New York Times Encyclopedic Dictionary of the Environment,* s.v. "Radioactive Water Pollution," (New York: Quadrangle, 1971).

Shea, Kevin P., "The New-Car Smell," *Environment,* October 1971, pp. 2-9.

U.S. News and World Report, September 8, 1969, pp. 64–66.

Wall Street Journal, "Business Bulletin," April 20, 1972.

Wurster, Charles F., "DDT and the Environment," in Harold W. Helfrich, Jr. (ed.) *Agenda for Survival* (Yale University Press, 1970).

——, "Aldrin and Dieldrin," *Environment,* October 1971, pp. 33–45.

Zeller, Edward J., "Energy Storage in Salt and Its Effect on Waste Disposal Sites," *Abstracts with Programs* (Geological Society of America), vol. 3, no. 3, 1971, pp. 248–249.

PART FOUR

INTENSIFICATION OF FUNCTIONS

10 URBANIZATION

Nearly three-quarters of the U.S. population lives in cities. Only 50 years ago the population was approximately half rural and half urban; today, over 73 percent is urban and is concentrated on a little more than 1 percent of the nation's land surface. Some 53 percent of the population, in fact, lives in 213 cities that together cover only .7 percent of the land. U.S. population per square mile, now about 58, has nearly doubled since 1920.

Urbanization is a worldwide trend. By 1970, some twenty-seven countries had populations classified as over 60 percent urban, as compared with only fourteen countries in the early 1960s. No fewer than fifty countries were reported by the United Nations as having more than 20 percent of their population living in cities of at least 100,000 inhabitants. Some countries have experienced a veritable urbanization explosion. In Ecuador, Columbia, Brazil, and Chile, according to Erich H. Jacoby, net rural-to- urban migration during the period 1950–60 amounted to about 12 percent of the total 1950 population and from 17 to 29 percent of the 1950 rural population. In the less developed regions of the world, according to the authors of *The Limits to Growth,* cities are now doubling their populations in an average of ten years.

The very existence of cities is one sign of man's success in adapting his environment to his own desires. Large numbers of people could not concentrate in any form of urban setting until agriculture was sufficiently advanced to free many of a society's members from the need to work as producers of food. Also vital was the capacity to organize efficient systems of transport, water supply, sewage disposal, fire control, and other municipal services. All these features of urban life were familiar in anti-

FIGURE 10.1.   Urbanscape, U.S.A. About 53 percent of the American people are
crowded onto less than 1 percent of the land space.

quity. Not until the nineteenth century, however, did medical science progress to the
point at which effective public health measures could be taken by city authorities.
Naturally, this reduced urban death rates and attracted people to cities in increasing
numbers. But the main attraction of city life from the earliest times was its variety of
economic opportunities. An industry could become more specialized—and therefore
more profitable—if it was situated next door to another industry capable of providing
the parts or materials that it needed. The presence of wholesale merchants was an
added stimulus, as was that of skilled craftsmen. The growth of cities was also encouraged by what are known as "economies of scale," that is, savings associated with the
size of the production unit and its operations. It was easier to build larger factories in
or near major urban areas because they could act as a base from which to serve many
markets at once. Savings achieved in this way are known as *internal* economies of scale
because they are "internal" to the production units in question. But even more import-

ant, in an urban setting, are the *external* economies to which the internal economies often give rise. Edgar M. Hoover has cited the example of a large commercial testing laboratory. Such a laboratory is profitable only when operating at or near full capacity, and it can do so only when located near industries that will provide it with sufficient work. On the other hand, these industries can have their testing done by the laboratory more cheaply than they could do it themselves. This is an external economy of scale through specialization. External economies of scale are also made possible through the continuing local presence of high demand for some service or product. For instance, an industry that locates in or near an urban area can take advantage of the low transportation costs that exist because there is already a heavy volume of traffic to and from the area. These and other forces acting together produce *agglomeration,* the term economists use for the concentration of economic activities in the same area. With the Industrial Revolution, the advantages of agglomeration were greatly increased, but so also were the external effects of economic activity, many of which represented increased costs to the community even though they were money savers from the business point of view.

America's big cities evolved on sites naturally endowed with great economic potential. Growth was fostered by such resource features as mineral concentrations, fertile soils, and access to transporation. Available labor supply and convenient markets were added advantages. In general, the settlements that prospered were those that occupied key distribution points. Until about the middle of the nineteenth century, the chief method of transportation in the United States was by water. Cities therefore tended to be located near the mouths of navigable rivers. On the Atlantic coast, New York, Philadelphia, and Baltimore became rival ports, displacing the older established port of Boston; on the Gulf of Mexico, New Orleans was without rivals. Trade advanced inland along the country's great rivers—the Hudson, the Ohio, the Mississippi. Since railways tended to follow river valleys, the importance of inland river ports such as St. Louis was enhanced as national rail networks were completed. From St. Louis eastwards, the cities important in the 1850s were, by and large, the cities that are important today. Chicago profited from the agricultural development of the Middle West in the 1880s and 1890s, as did Kansas City; Minneapolis grew on lumber. Between 1870 and 1890, the number of Americans living in cities of 25,000 and over more than doubled. But the most spectacular developments were still to come, as urbanization spread westward. The first transcontinental rail link had been completed in 1869; by 1893 there were three other lines. San Francisco, previously little more than a village, had become a city of over 25,000 during the Gold Rush of 1848; now this initial growth was sustained by the railroads. The Los Angeles oil boom of the 1890s drew many immigrants to southern California, and successive real estate booms, with an expanding agriculture, insured that there would be many more. Today, eight of the twenty largest U.S. cities are west of the Mississippi and three are on the west coast (table 10.1). The westward movement of population has not yet stopped: the "center of population"— that is, the point at which the United States would "balance" if everybody weighed the same—is now rapidly crossing southern Illinois, after being in Indiana from 1890 to 1940. For the decade 1960–70, the West registered a population gain of 24.1 percent,

TABLE 10.1. The westward shift of urban America

Rank				Population			
1970	1960	1940		1970	1960	% Change 1960–1970	1940
1	1	1	New York	7,771,730	7,781,984	-.1	7,450,995
2	2	2	Chicago	3,325,263	3,550,404	-6.3	3,396,808
3	3	5	Los Angeles	2,782,400	2,479,015	12.2	1,504,277
4	4	3	Philadelphia	1,926,529	2,002,512	-3.8	1,931,334
5	5	4	Detroit	1,492,914	1,670,144	-10.6	1,623,452
6	7	21	Houston	1,213,062	938,219	29.3	334,514
7	6	7	Baltimore	895,222	939,024	-4.7	859,100
8	14	31	Dallas	836,121	679,684	23.0	294,723
9	9	11	Washington	764,000	763,956	—	663,091
10	26	20	Indianapolis	744,624	476,258	56.3	386,972
11	8	6	Cleveland	718,956	876,050	-15.6	878,336
12	11	13	Milwaukee	709,537	741,324	-4.3	587,472
13	12	12	San Francisco	704,209	740,316	-4.9	634,536
14	18	41	San Diego	675,788	573,224	17.9	203,341
15	17	36	San Antonio	650,188	587,718	10.6	253,854
16	13	9	Boston	628,215	697,179	-9.9	770,816
17	22	32	Memphis	620,873	497,524	24.8	292,942
18	10	8	St. Louis	607,718	750,026	-19.0	816,048
19	15	15	New Orleans	585,787	627,525	-6.7	494,537
20	29	104	Phoenix	580,275	439,170	32.1	65,414

Source: U.S. Bureau of the Census.

followed by the South with 14.2 percent. The other two regions of the country trailed with gains of less than 10 percent.

A more recent tendency is for the urban population to concentrate along coastlines and around lakes in what is known as the **Mediterranean pattern of settlement**, while the continental interior becomes even more "hollow" in comparison. This trend offers both advantages and disadvantages in terms of land use. If it persists without careful planning it will cover the fertile, low-lying coastal plains—premium food-producing regions—with urban development. Moreover, if coastal cities with doubled and tripled populations continue their present practice of piping sewage into the oceans the continental shelves will be committed to even greater use as cesspools rather than as the producers of high-quality protein that they should be. By 1970, according to William Penn Mott, Jr., Los Angeles was pumping 4.5 billion gallons of sewage a year into the sea and had created a swathe of sterility extending 6 miles downshore from the major outfalls. On the other hand, location near the sea may be an advantage if large-scale desalination of seawater should be needed to overcome shortages of fresh water.

THE SEQUENCE OF CITY GROWTH

Each city has its own unique history and physical features, but there are developmental processes common to all cities as well as structural similarities that arise from these processes. Young communities take their form from the nature of their site, the economic functions they depend on, and the regular activities of the people who live in them. Travel patterns emerge linking residences, sources of livelihood, and community facilities. Well-traveled routes become the thoroughfares along which new public and business structures are built in response to population growth and changing local needs. Residential areas spring up around the business district, which gradually becomes a compact focus of urban functions with little space left for new development. The internal structure of a city is crystallized at this stage of growth. Its core can no longer expand to serve an increasing population; further growth can take place only around the periphery. Whatever their original diversity, cities tend to share a common pattern after this point has been reached.

In the nineteenth century, peripheral urban growth typically occurred in a web-like pattern (figure 10.2). Although the original community became ringed with nodes of new settlement, both old and new development remained focused on the essential services and facilities provided by the core. Radial avenues linking fringe areas with the core became main traffic arteries and eventually secondary urban centers in their own right. Cities of this type, despite their many problems, retained their identity as cohesive communities able to profit from the technology of the period without becoming its victim.

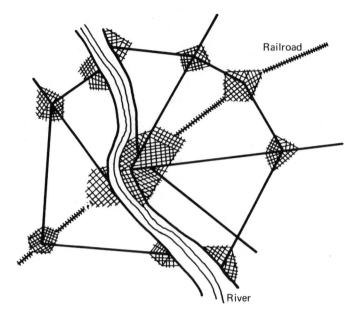

FIGURE 10.2.   A typical gross pattern of the American city before the
dominance of the automobile. Overall size was controlled by the effectiveness of public transportation, especially the railroad; local services were
reached on foot or by streetcar.

Inner-city Decay

For many decades, the population of central cities continued to increase.
Peripheral settlements began to acquire a certain amount of economic independence,
but were still strongly oriented toward the center. Public transport was by rail from
outlying areas and by bus or streetcar in the central business district. Then, around
1920, automobiles began to come into common use, greatly reducing the time consumed in daily travel between the core and the fringe, and providing a far more flexible
link with the central business district than any form of public transportation. Many
urban dwellers saw in the automobile a way to have the best of two worlds: the excite-
ment, variety, and higher income of the city, and the space and quiet of suburban or
rural homes. The practice of commuting began, and ultimately became the dominant
national pattern. Urban growth became a centrifugal process, if it was possible any longer to talk of a center (figure 10.3).

By 1940 a massive mutual escalation of private auto ownership and suburban spread was under way. As more people acquired the flexible and independent mobility that cars provided, distances between residential areas and core facilities increased.
As distances increased more people found it necessary to buy automobiles. Public transit systems could not compete in comfort or practical versatility with cars, and began

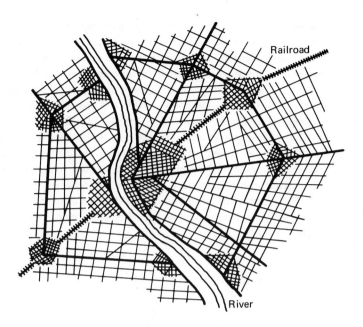

FIGURE 10.3.   The general effect of the automobile upon the
American city has been to expand its limits to the point at which it
becomes wholly amorphous. Open space is filled in, and outlying
nodes become business districts in their own right.

to lose business. The number of cars in cities grew rapidly and soon caused traffic congestion, fumes, and noise, which drove still more people out into the suburbs—and
these people also had to buy cars to commute to the city. And so the process has continued. Suburbanization is still picking up speed and volume, and is by now the prevailing form of urbanization. In 1950 about 25 percent of the total population lived in
suburbs. By 1970 this figure had risen to 35 percent, or about 71 million people, about
59 million of whom lived in the central cities. In terms of land use, suburbanization is
the most wasteful form of urbanization so far. It also contributes to urban problems in
a political sense, because suburbanites continue to benefit from the existence of the
central city without paying their fair share of its upkeep. This problem is discussed
further below (p. 220).

While cities continue to expand outward, their functions change. New patterns of urban interaction develop within the old urban framework, which is unable to
accommodate them. Many of the functions of the city core are transferred to more
accessible locations on the periphery. For these and other reasons, the old core and
much of the inner city is then subjected to decay, as housing abandoned by whites is
occupied by blacks, Mexican-Americans, and other groups who are forced to pay exor-
bitant rents for poorly maintained buildings, and are prevented by racial discrimination from moving elsewhere. In 1950, according to Dick Netzer, about one-quarter of

all inner-city households lived in units classified by the Bureau of the Census as substandard. The term "substandard" is interpreted very strictly by the census enumerators, who classify as "deteriorating" or "dilapidated" many buildings that would look substandard to the average middle-class white. Netzer calculates that if these three categories—"substandard," "deteriorating," and "dilapidated"—are added together and treated as indicative of slum conditions, then in 1960 the proportion of nonwhites living in slums was at least 30 percent in every U.S. city of 500,000 or more except Los Angeles (where the large Mexican-American population is *not* classified as nonwhite) and Washington (which is over 70 percent black anyway). Since then various federal programs have somewhat improved the general picture, at least from a statistical point of view, but as late as 1966 some 16 percent of inner-city nonwhites still lived in substandard housing as compared with only 5 percent of inner-city whites. The dismal history of public housing programs indicates that wholly new approaches will be necessary (see figure 18.3, p. 385).

The Extended City

Urban sprawl is the usual name for the kind of planless urban growth encouraged by the automobile. It was superimposed on most of the older eastern cities as the new growth took suburban form. The old downtown areas, no longer able to accommodate the swelling volume of traffic, tend to be bypassed by new centers, with which they then proceed to compete. The result is much wasteful duplication of functions, as rural areas are carved up into shopping centers and parking lots. Western cities are the greatest offenders in this respect. Los Angeles, with only one-third of New York City's population, covers 44 percent more land. Dallas is even more spread out: its population is one-sixth as great as that of Los Angeles but is scattered over about the same area. But Los Angeles, with its 7,000 miles of streets and freeways, remains the prototype of an automobile city. Some 3 million adults and 4 million automobiles occupy 5,000 square miles of land, and 70 percent of the downtown area is devoted to streets, parking lots, and other automobile facilities. Smog is the most undesirable by-product of such low-density development. According to Frank Tyson, smog will make the Los Angeles area uninhabitable in ten years if present trends continue. But the "spread city" form of development, as it is often called, is wasteful and destructive in many other ways. Reliance on the automobile pushes up transportation costs and results in widespread conversion of farm land into parking lots. Suburban **zoning** laws keep housing costs high, thus preventing the development of socially and racially balanced communities—a legacy for which future generations of Americans will have to pay. Above all, the uncontrolled advance of suburbia makes it impossible to escape the influence of the city, even in the most remote areas. In the words of Christopher Tunnard and Boris Pushkarev, "the entire land area of North America [is] covered by overlapping fields of urban socio-economic influence, emanating from the major centers." There is no longer any such thing as a self-contained settlement.

As adjacent cities grow outwards they eventually merge, so that their boundaries are no longer distinguishable except in a strictly legal sense. Such strip cities appear to be the major form that urbanization is presently assuming. Megalopolis ("Big City") is the name given by Jean Gottmann, a geographer, to the virtual strip city that now extends along the northeastern seaboard from Boston to Washington. Gottman feels that the advantages of such intensive development outweigh the disadvantages. Other qualified authorities disagree. Some urge that the massing of population on such a scale will destroy what little meaning the urban concept has left without putting anything viable in its place. Others have compared the runaway growth of Megalopolis to a cancer. The point at issue is basically how much economic decentralization a heavily urbanized region can take. If present trends continue, the nation's principal metropolitan areas will soon merge into the five strip cities shown in figure 10.4. The U.S. population could top 300 million by the year 2000, when it is anticipated that 58 percent, or 174 million people, will live in these strip cities on 4 percent of the U.S. land surface. Another ten or fifteen smaller strip cities, depending on how the boundaries are interpreted, are now evolving. The fusing of already great urban complexes into giant masses is bound to create serious problems. Already in the mid-1960s the cities of the northeastern seaboard were undergoing critical water shortages. Power supplies were inadequate to meet peak demand for air conditioning—a demand aggravated by air pollution. Social problems were equally threatening. Urban crime seemed altogether out of hand: in 1967, according to Robert Gold, six cities of over 1 million population were responsible for one-third of all violent crime. On the opposite side of the coin,

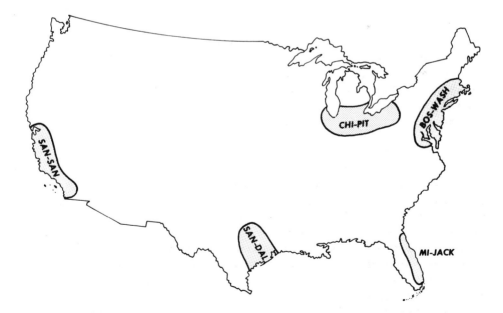

FIGURE 10.4.   The U.S. population is rapidly becoming concentrated into five "strip cities."

police practices were the principal cause of complaint in 14 cities where riots had occurred. From the outside, it looked as if a war was going on. The larger the city, the
more susceptible it seemed to be to every type of disruption.

Finally, it should be pointed out that land lost to urbanization is rarely
regained for other purposes. Since 70 percent of the nation's people occupy only 1 percent of its land, it might seem that plenty of space remains available. But the urban pop-
ulace demands a vast amount of land beyond the city limits to supply it with food, recreation, waste disposal, and so on. Large regions of the nation are poorly suited for
urban use; there is usually a practical reason if settlement is sparse or lacking. Of the
usable rural land, much is already committed to the service of the urban population
and a great deal more will be required as that population grows. There is not a great
amount of suitable nonagricultural land left for urban expansion. According to Robert
E. Dickinson, the cities have been gobbling up agricultural land at the rate of over 1
million acres a year. This cannot be allowed to continue indefinitely. Meanwhile, the
depopulation of rural areas proceeds apace: the National Wildlife Federation reports
that half the nation's counties lost population in the 1960s. We may, as Christopher
Tunnard has remarked, have "plenty of other land to ruin as we choose," but we will
be ruining our way of life in the process. This topic is further discussed in the next two
chapters.

CONTEMPORARY URBAN PROBLEMS

About 150 million Americans are directly affected by the urban environment, with its increasing problems. These problems can be divided into three closely
related categories: operational, sociopolitical, and medical. Most of them receive more
detailed treatment elsewhere in this book, but it may be as well to review them all
briefly under one head.

Breakdown of Operational Functions

The operational functions that have been seriously impaired in many cities
are the provision of sufficient water, the disposal of wastes, and the control of air
pollution. Food and other material commodities are amply provided by the agricultural, manufacturing, and merchandising machinery of the nation. But this machinery
does not of itself provide a livable environment; that function is left to local government or public utilities supposedly regulated by local government. Many cities could
not exist at all if government did not continually insure the means for their survival.

The most serious long-term problem is probably water supply. There is,
of course, nothing novel in this. Southern California, with its combined metropolitan
population of 8 million, has had to import water since 1915, piping it first 160 miles,

then 300, and now 600. Tapping distant sources of water is extremely expensive, and it increasingly involves conflicting claims as cities compete for a share. As local sources become polluted, we can expect more and more cities to compete for ever more distant sources, even in areas with adequate precipitation.

Waste disposal is considered by many experts to be the fastest growing urban problem. Almost every pound of material that enters a city becomes a pound of waste to be disposed of. Each gallon of water entering a kitchen or bathroom leaves as a gallon of sewage. Each ton of newsprint or automobile eventually becomes a ton of trash or junk. Not only population growth but increasing per capita rates of consumption have compounded the problem. Solid waste collections in 1920 averaged 2.75 pounds per person per day; today the average is 5.3, and by 1980 it is expected to be 8 or more. The greatest problem is finding somewhere to put it all. Sewage is piped by most cities into lakes, rivers, and oceans. This practice cannot continue indefinitely without fouling water supplies. Solid waste is hauled to land dumps to be burned and, in a few cases, buried. But, as we saw in the previous chapter, 94 percent of U.S. land disposal operations are no more than open burning grounds. New methods of waste disposal will have to be developed fast in order to avoid a serious public health problem.

The most immediately threatening of all metropolitan problems is air pollution. From 50 to 80 percent of the pollution in the air, depending on the city, is produced by automobiles. Industrial processes and electric power generation are also heavy contributors. The total cost of air pollution per year, including agricultural losses, property damage, and expenses of illnesses, has been set by the federal government at $13 billion, or $65 per person. The possible consequences have already been reviewed in chapter 7; they are serious enough to make many experts call for immediate abolition of the internal combustion engine. This of course raises the question of whether any private means of transportation (except possibly bicycles) should be allowed in cities at all. Certainly, if transportation were regarded as an operational function on the same level as water supply or waste disposal, the way would be open to solving a great many problems (see chapter 11).

Naturally, cities vary in their susceptibility to these and other problems, just as they vary in their occupational and industrial composition. The average proportion of its land devoted by a typical city to major urban uses is displayed in table 10.2. Cities are sometimes classified according to their deviations from this average. Detroit, Chicago and Cincinnati are considered industrial cities because manufacturing occupies more than twice the average proportion of their area. Cities with a very large share of their space in residential use are sometimes called bedroom or dormitory communit-

TABLE 10.2.   Typical distribution of land use within U.S. cities

Residential	45%
Community, Recreation and Open Space	18
Streets and Other Right-of-Way	24
Industry and Railroads	10
Commercial	3

ies; they serve as suburbs to more intensively developed urban centers. Whatever a city's dominant function, its problems are likely to be aggravated with increasing size.

A typical city has between one hundred and two hundred component systems. There are municipal systems for supplying water and removing garbage and sewage, systems for maintaining streets, parks, and public buildings, and systems for social services such as law enforcement, welfare, and education. There are public and private systems of transportation, and systems supplying energy for heat, light, and power to activate machinery. There are numerous systems of communication. Table 10.3 lists the quantities of certain substances typically consumed and eliminated daily in the metabolic functioning of a city of 1 million. The analogy with an organism is obvious.

A single faltering system impairs the functioning of the city as a whole; a breakdown in one system can affect other systems within a short time and cripple the entire structure. Cities that are too large in area and population are most vulnerable to systemic failures because each subsystem is usually overextended, overburdened, and too complex for efficient control.

The Sociopolitical Impasse

Dick Netzer has listed seven major problems of U.S. cities that can be summarized as follows:

1. The central cities contain a growing proportion of poor blacks, Mexican-Americans, and Puerto Ricans.
2. Housing and public facilities in the central cities are decaying from age, and no systematic attempt is being made to renovate them.
3. The entire housing market in the central cities is out of tune with both need and demand.

TABLE 10.3.   Materials consumed and eliminated every day by a hypothetical city of 1 million inhabitants

Daily Intake (tons)		Daily Waste (tons)	
Water	625,000	Sewage	500,000
Food	2,000	Refuse (garbage)	2,000
Coal	3,000	Suspended matter (atmospheric)	150
Oil	2,800	Sulfur dioxide	150
Natural gas	2,700	Nitrous oxides	100
Motor fuel (mostly gasoline)	1,000	Hydrocarbons	100
		Carbon monoxide	450

Source: Data from "The Metabolism of Cities" by Abel Wolman. Copyright © 1965 by Scientific American, Inc. All rights reserved.

4. Jobs have been leaving the central cities for the suburbs.
5. Urban growth has been accompanied by increasing environmental pollution.
6. Urban transportation facilities, both public and private, are totally unsatisfactory.
7. The large cities are on the verge of bankruptcy.

Problems 2 and 5 have been dealt with briefly above, while problem 6 is the subject of the next chapter. No more than a few words can be said about the other problems here. The heaviest migration from the central cities by whites has been in the Northeast and Middle West, which have also seen the heaviest migration to the central cities by southern blacks. Black migration from the South was greatest during World War II, but has continued since then at the rate of 140,000 a year. As of March, 1970, 24.4 percent of blacks in metropolitan areas were living below the federal poverty line; the corresponding figure for whites was 7.3 percent. Urban unemployment rates for nonwhites are regularly at least double those for whites. Nonwhites have much the same housing preferences as whites, and would leave their ghettos for the suburbs if they could. Netzer cites a study from the 1950s that estimated the potential Negro exodus from Chicago as 112,000, if the barriers of segregation were suddenly removed. Victims of poverty and racial discrimination are not the only ones who suffer from the urban housing shortage. Many whites with moderate incomes are trapped in so-called gray areas. These are older urban neighborhoods, originally built to be served by public transport, that are deteriorating because they clearly have no future, but have not yet become slums. Moderate-income families that succeed in moving from such areas to the suburbs are likely to find themselves paying more for housing than they can really afford—just like the central-city poor—and traveling much farther to work than they would prefer. The best most of them can hope for in the suburbs is to become members of the class that has been aptly labeled "the affluent poor."

However, there is one definite advantage in moving to suburbia: better and more plentiful jobs. According to Netzer, while manufacturing employment rose by about 1 million between 1958 and 1963 in all metropolitan areas, it actually declined in the central cities of 17 out of the 25 largest such areas. Similar trends have occurred in the availability of service jobs, as more and more downtown services have been duplicated in suburban shopping centers. All of the above trends acting together have contributed to problem 7, which is basically a matter of the shrinking urban tax base (though the underrepresentation of big cities in state legislatures does not help either). As Netzer says:

> the American system of dividing governmental responsibilities places heavy responsibilities on local governments, including municipal governments— responsibilities for educating children, alleviating poverty, maintaining law and order, and providing basic community facilities like water supply and sewerage. These responsibilities are only partly matched by money- raising powers. (Netzer 1970, p. 23)

Cities still rely mainly on the property tax, a device inherited from a period when the central city included most of an area's taxable activities within its own boundaries. Contrary to popular belief, this falls more heavily on poor people because they pay a larger share of their income for housing. But taxing slum property is not very profitable for the city. The problem is complicated by the fact that, in a large city like New York, many major owners of real estate—religious and charitable institutions, for instance, as well as the independent Port Authority—pay either zero or greatly reduced property taxes. Some cities have experimented with sales taxes and even income taxes. But these, and the higher urban property taxes, only drive more of the well-to-do to the suburbs. Poorer people need more social services, for which the central cities are expected to pay. Federal programs fill the revenue gap to some extent, but the central cities are fighting a losing battle. Things could hardly be otherwise when those who benefit most from city services—the suburban commuters—contribute only a minuscule portion of their cost, and when the city's best potential taxpayers—its high school graduates and college students—are likely to move out as soon as they can.

The Ecology of Poverty

American cities did not begin to be healthy places to live until the 1870s, when most states and cities established health departments and began to concern themselves actively with such things as sewerage and pure water supply. With the development of bacteriology in the 1880s the major urban diseases—typhoid, typhus, and smallpox—were brought under control. Even tuberculosis, the "white plague" that for so long was almost synonymous with poverty, gradually succumbed to public health programs and higher living standards; today, although still a problem, it is no longer among the leading causes of death. But these early gains are now in danger of being cancelled out. We have already seen how urban air pollution increases the risk of major respiratory disease (p. 150). Water pollution from sewage and other wastes is also a hazard; anyone who swallows a mouthful of water from the Hudson River at Manhattan runs the risk of typhoid. In San Francisco and many other cities, ancient sewage systems do double duty as storm drains, with unpleasant consequences in periods of heavy rainfall. But the leading public health problem of American cities is in the ghettos, where standards of medical care are far below those of the general population (essay 10.1).

The central cities also have a growing mental health problem. The Midtown Manhattan Study, undertaken in the early 1960s, found some symptoms of mental disorder in more than half of a large random sample of adult residents; lower socio-economic status was associated with poorer mental health. It has long been known that schizophrenia rates tend to be higher in poorer urban areas. Until quite recently, it was thought that schizophrenics were attracted to such areas; now it appears that the living conditions there may well encourage mental illness of every kind. One index of how desperate the situation may really be is the increased frequency of drug addiction, almost entirely a big-city phenomenon. In 1969 there were about 68,000 known addicts;

Essay 10.1. Black Ecology

Most of the nonurban problems dealt with in this book are not likely to
be among the major concerns of ethnic minorities forced to live in urban
slums and suffer twice or more the general population's risks of unemployment, poverty, and community disorganization. We have already mentioned
that ghetto children are in greater danger than others of lead poisoning from
auto exhausts (p. 142).The bitter irony of this, as Nathan Hare has pointed
out, is that ghetto residents do not own most of the cars responsible for polluting their environment. Other health figures are no less shocking. For
instance, three times as many nonwhite infants as white infants over one
month old die before reaching the age of twelve, and four times as many nonwhite mothers as white ones die in childbirth. It should be noted that
although "nonwhite," in Census Bureau jargon, includes more than a dozen
groups, blacks constitute almost 90 percent of nonwhites. The report of the
National Advisory Commission on Civil Disorders, from which the above mortality statistics are taken, goes on to point out that nonwhites have much
poorer medical services than whites at the same income level. Sanitation services are also inferior in the ghetto. According to a memorandum submitted
to the commission, the reasons were as follows: (1) high population density;
(2) lack of services that should have been provided by landlords; (3) high
turnover among tenants and local businesses; (4) use of streets as recreation
areas (there being little other open space); (5) large numbers of abandoned
cars; (6) infestation by rodents and other pests; (7) interference with garbage
collection by heavy traffic; (8) interference with street cleaning and snow
clearance by parked cars. Such are the ghetto's "environmental problems."
Many black leaders, including Nathan Hare, have dismissed the reformist
intentions of white environmentalists as both inadequate and irrelevent. Inadequate they may be, but their social relevance is continually being demonstrated. For instance, it was discovered in 1970 that DDT and DDE levels are
from two to three times higher in the blood of black than of white children
in Charleston County, South Carolina (Julian E. Keil et al. in Pesticides Monitoring Journal, *June 1972*). Whatever type of solution they propose, it is
time for environmentalists to admit that a system that is not working for
everyone is not working at all. (For more on the black viewpoint see Nathan
Hare, "Black Ecology," The Black Scholar, *April, 1970; and Huey P. Newton,*
To Die for the People, *New York, Random House, 1972.)*

throughout the 1960s, new addicts were being reported at an average rate close to 8,000 a year.

CAUSES AND REMEDIES

Many urban problems developed because the cores of most big cities were shaped at a time when the volume of automobile traffic to come could not have been dreamed of. Nor was it realized that there is a limit to the workable size of a city. Demographers failed to predict both the postwar rise in birthrates and the subsequent flight to the suburbs; indeed, it was widely believed that the end of World War II would be followed by another economic depression. Suburban sprawl was well begun before it was recognized as wasteful and destructive. Meanwhile, both the Great Depression and the war had discouraged urban renovation. By the 1950s most of the larger American cities were in serious trouble, although widespread recognition of this fact did not develop until the 1960s.

The urban crisis was not just the result of temporary circumstances; it stemmed from the basic American conception of a city. In a statement to the press on November 16, 1968, Secretary of the Interior Stewart L. Udall said: "Most of the problems are the result of poor planning, of the old-fashioned industrial approach and indifference to the environment." He was speaking of environmental problems in general, but his remarks applied with particular force to urban ones. Cities, to most Americans, are primarily nodes of intensive economic development in which people exist to serve as producers and consumers. They are not places for people to live in. The most cherished American traditions of community have always centered on the farm or small town, not the city. This remains true despite the American love affair with the automobile. Americans seem to believe that in using the automobile to escape the central city for suburbia, they have somehow escaped the urban environment altogether, instead of creating a new and—some would say—inferior form of it (figure 10.5). As a result, central cities have become ever more ideal environments—for automobiles. We have seen how this process has made the large American cities both unlivable and ungovernable.

Attitudes Toward Land Use

Many environmental problems exist because decisions are made on the basis of traditional values that are no longer appropriate. Thus land in America has always been a commodity to be removed as fast as possible from the public domain and into the hands of private speculators. By the end of the Revolutionary War, as Gustavus Myers has pointed out, although most of the public domain in the North and East had already passed into the hands of a landowning class, large areas of it still existed in the South and Midwest. These tracts were bought up at nominal costs by land

FIGURE 10.5.   Suburban housing in San Mateo, California; foreground shows all that is left of artichoke fields that once covered the whole area. Houses like these inspired Malvina Reynolds to write her famous song, "Little Boxes." (Soil Conservation Service, U.S. Department of Agriculture)

companies, which did not hesitate to bribe the state legislatures, and then resold at an immense profit to settlers. In the nineteenth century, huge tracts of public land were given away to canal and railroad companies by government grant. But the greatest profits were in urban real estate. Thus John Jacob Astor (1763–1848), by far the richest man of his day, profited greatly from the heavy immigration of the 1840s because he had systematically bought up vacant land in and around New York. Cornelius Vanderbilt (1794–1877), who made a fortune out of acquiring railroads and then watering their stock, depended heavily upon blackmail and extortion. Excuses can be made for such "robber barons" on the grounds that they were only the most successful exponents of common practices. But these practices are not needed now, if indeed they ever were.

One out-of-date practice that is clearly no longer in the public interest is speculation in undeveloped urban land. It is profitable to keep such land undeveloped while it appreciates because it is taxed less heavily than developed land. More land remains undeveloped within cities than is generally realized. It has been estimated that enough vacant land exists in the highly urbanized San Francisco Bay area to serve the needs of the state's total population, projected to 1990, if it were used according to a comprehensive plan. The absurdity of taxing unused urban land at a lower rate than used has been demonstrated once and for all by Harry Hyams, a London entrepreneur who made a large profit from empty office buildings. The profits were from selling the stock of his company, which constructed the buildings. There was nothing fraudulent about this. The resale value of the buildings, according to Associated Press reporter

Fred Coleman, increased in eight years to yield a profit over construction costs of 400 percent, and taxes were lower because the buildings were not used.

Another out-of-date practice is boosterism, or proclaiming the advantages of one's own city over its competitors. Today, when many cities suffer from excessive size, boosting is unrealistic and destructive. Yet it persists. Los Angeles, incredibly, still has active boosters who declare it a coastal paradise of unparalleled climate dotted with citrus groves and surrounded by pine-clad mountains. The groves have succumbed to bulldozers and the pines are dying from the smog, but these facts do not deter the boosters. Acquisition of new water supplies has renewed hope of "progress" that may double the present population. Construction continues and land speculation proceeds at the fastest rate in U.S. history—even to the point of developing desert valleys separated from Los Angeles by a range of mountains. One city that renounced boosterism too late is San Jose, which increased its population from 95,000 in 1950 to 446,000 in 1970. The beautiful Santa Clara Valley, once covered with prune orchards, has been subjected to urban development as haphazard as it is ugly. Local planning agencies that might have checked these developments were created only in the late 1960s. The problems that San Jose will face as its overbuilt suburbs degenerate into ranch-style slums could have been avoided if a coherent land use policy had been worked out before the period of growth began.

Other aspects of land use policy are discussed in chapters 17 and 18.

Housing Problems

Housing will be needed for about 100 million more Americans—a 50 percent increase—by the end of this century. Athelstan Spilhaus has calculated that it will have to be built at the rate of one family unit every 27 seconds to keep up with demand. Almost all of it will have to be urban. The federal government is well aware of these facts, and has sponsored various programs to renovate central cities as living areas. The results so far have not been very successful. The 1968 Housing Act, in a move to encourage private home ownership in central cities, empowered the Federal Housing Administration (F.H.A.) to guarantee mortgages in slum areas. Four years later, the Department of Housing and Urban Development (H.U.D.) found itself the owner of some 44,500 substandard houses on which the federally backed mortgages had been foreclosed. The final total, according to reporter Diane K. Shah of the *National Observer,* may be double or triple that amount. The federal housing program, hailed by President Johnson as the most far-sighted in U.S. history, has been exposed as a carnival of crime. The nature of the crime was, roughly speaking, to sell dilapidated houses ("remodeled" for the occasion), at inflated prices, to people who could not afford them. The prices were set by fraudulent or hasty appraisals, backed by inspections that were very often undertaken by the mortgage company seeking F.H.A. insurance. The entire process was helped along by bribery. Among those named in the indictments that followed the scandal were several F.H.A. employees, including one regional bureau chief. Nevertheless, many authorities favor more federal involvement, not less, in order to control the speculators and override local obstacles to development.

Preplanning and the New Town Movement

Rather than repeat old mistakes, it is possible to start again from scratch. New cities can be planned from the outset for a specific population on a predetermined land area, and limited to that size. Planning the ultimate size in advance permits urban land use to bestow its greatest potential benefit: the concentration of people on land in the maximum density consistent with comfortable living. The custom of housing urban families in separate residences spread over many square miles is inconsistent with optimum urban form. A hospitable and satisfying human environment can be created on much less land if better design principles are incorporated.

Innovative architects and urban specialists have designed cities of the future along radically different lines than present cities, some with multilevel facilities using underground and overhead space to extend surface area. Among their innovations are underground factories. Even the more conservative authorities agree that urban structures should use more vertical and less horizontal space. Such extremely thrifty land use may become imperative within the useful lifetimes of structures built in this decade.

Preplanned cities, known in Europe as "new towns," can include generous areas of open space without waste. This is a major consideration. Between 1947 and 1965 suburbia grew at the rate of 1.5 million houses per year. Less than 5 percent of these were designed by architects or functionally planned, according to Wolf von Eckardt. In fact only about 100 people were housed for each 30 acres of land. This population density is too low for efficient provision of municipal services or sensible land use of any sort. Moreover, the results are usually unattractive because construction was planned for maximum profit rather than aesthetic appeal. In contrast, experimental communities such as Reston and Jonathan use open space in a way that is both attractive and efficient.

A city planned in advance can be designed as a whole organism, with essential service systems continually adjusted to fluctuating demand. Among these systems would be a rapid transit network, probably electric. Automobile use within the city would be limited or banned. As a result, much of the space devoted to automobiles in existing cities could be used in other ways. The new city could be prevented from growing beyond its planned capacity by means of the "green belt" device (chapter 13). This would also insulate it from other urban development, preserving its identity. The structure planned for each new city would be influenced by considerations of climate, topography, economic functions, and other local factors. If, for example, atmospheric conditions tended to encourage smog, either the city would be planned for a small population or automobiles would be excluded entirely and no polluting industries permitted.

The main problem in creating new cities has been to avoid making them satellites of existing cities. Preferably, as with the British new towns, the economic base should be built in during planning. Thus the creation of many new cities will necessarily involve economic decentralization. Such a degree of planning at the national level is not easily envisaged in the United States, but it is already a reality at the local level. The most constructive developments in the next decade will probably come from associations of county governments working in cooperation with state and federal agencies.

Cities for People

From a strictly ecological point of view, the modern industrial city is a parasite upon the natural environment, taking resources from it and returning nothing but harmful refuse. In order for any man-made ecosystem to endure it must operate in harmony with the laws of the planet, emulating and fostering natural regenerative processes (figure 10.6). If we want to keep our cities, they will have to change. New cities

FIGURE 10.6.   Fields in Warren County, New Jersey; Delaware River is in middle distance, town of Belvidere at left (photo taken in 1963). A landscape so carefully tended by the hand of man is quite literally a work of art. (Soil Conservation Service, U.S. Department of Agriculture)

cannot achieve immediate equilibrium but they can grant first priority to operational improvements aimed at a better ecological balance. Every city, new or old, should develop the capacity to recycle all of its sewage and other wastes. Metals, paper, glass, cloth, and other materials could be reclaimed for further use; this would both conserve resources and reduce waste disposal problems. Facilities for reconstituting waste could be built in to waste disposal plants, so that very little that is not beneficial would have to be returned to land or water. Such procedures would not only parallel but speed up natural recycling processes. Thus the ecological impact of the city on its surrounding environment could be minimized, while its economic and cultural benefits would be realized to the full.

New cities can and must be planned to eliminate crowding, ugliness, pollution, and other factors that lower the quality of life. Such planning should be more than avoidance of negative influences. Even the most park-like modernistic development will not be a good place to live in unless it inspires its residents with some sort of community feeling. This means that they must be encouraged to get together, not in the impersonal mass settings of stadiums or concert halls, but in their own neighborhoods. The new towns of both Great Britain and Finland include many neighborhood facilities, from playgrounds to clubrooms. Such facilities are often located around "neighborhood squares" that, like the town squares of an earlier period, provide focal points for their communities. The new town of Jonathan, Minnesota, which is less than an hour by car from downtown Minneapolis, is designed to preserve small-town values by having its 50,000 projected inhabitants divided among several "villages" grouped around a single town center (p. 373). Only Village One is in operation so far, but all reports indicate that the structure of the community, which encourages pedestrians and cyclists, is far more relaxed and friendly than that of the average suburb.

The sense of belonging seldom thrives without participation. Residents of new towns sometimes complain that their surroundings are *too* perfect and that they feel superfluous as individuals because there is nothing for them to fix. Perhaps the planning and execution of the finishing touches should be left to the people who intend to live in the city, so that they can feel it really is theirs. Decoration or landscaping of neighborhood streets, parks, and public structures could be undertaken as a community project. Unfinished situations invite creativity and resourcefulness which, once it finds physical expression, attaches the participant to his creation—his neighborhood. Group discussions and group effort hasten the growth of social relationships toward a true community of neighbors.

Another feature of the new urban design is planning for interchangeability of function. One of the factors presently making for decay, both in suburbs and in central cities, is that virtually no allowance is made for the changing age and interests of residents. For instance, retired people need opportunities for leisure activities that will bring them into contact with others of similar age and interests. A man with a full-time job may be quite satisfied with gardening or home repairs as leisure activities. After retirement, however, he is likely to find them poor substitutes for the stimulation provided by his job.

Who Shall Run the Cities?

Even the most creative urban design will be useless unless it is accompanied by equally creative new forms of urban government. It is becoming only too clear that the city governments of the future will have to be closely coordinated at the state and regional level. Only in this way can problems of environmental quality be dealt with in accordance with the guidelines specified in the National Environmental Policy Act of 1969 and the recent federal legislation. According to Robert C. Wood, in 1962 the 212 U.S. "standard metropolitan statistical areas" included more than 18,000 separate local governments. Of the various proposed solutions to this chaos, the most effective seems to be what Wood calls reallocation of functions. Already a number of state governments have passed laws regulating what were previously local functions. In Massachusetts, for instance, local zoning laws have to include adequate provision for low-cost housing. In Vermont, developments over one acre are state regulated. Very large enterprises, such as the new Walt Disney World in Florida, are coming under scrutiny because they affect an area much wider than the one that granted them permission to develop. These and other examples cited by John V. Conti of the *Wall Street Journal* may conceivably be adding up to the much-heralded "quiet revolution in land-use control." Certainly, if no quiet revolution is in the offing, a noisy one is quite conceivable.

REFERENCES

Coleman, Fred, "Londoner Made Millions by Keeping His Office Buildings Empty" (Associated Press dispatch, *Palo Alto Times,* June 28, 1972).

Conti, John V., "A Quiet Revolution: With Little Fanfare States Are Broadening Control Over Land Use," *Wall Street Journal,* June 28, 1972.

Dickinson, Robert E., "The Process of Urbanization," in F. Fraser Darling and John P. Milton (eds.), *Future Environments of North America* (Garden City: Natural History Press, 1966).

Gold, Robert, "Urban Violence and Contemporary Defensive Cities," in Walter McQuade (ed.), *Cities Fit to Live In* (New York: Macmillan, 1971).

Gottman, Jean, *Megalopolis: The Urbanized Northeastern Seaboard of the United States* (M.I.T. Press, 1961).

Hoover, Edgar M., "Spatial Economics: I. The Partial Equilibrium Approach," in *International Encyclopedia of the Social Sciences* (New York: Macmillan and Free Press, 1968).

Jacoby, Erich H., *Man and Land: The Essential Revolution* (New York: Knopf, 1971).

Meadows, Donella H., et al., *The Limits to Growth* (New York: Universe, 1972).

Midtown Manhattan Study, *Mental Health in the Metropolis,* by Leo Srole et al., vol. 1 (New York: McGraw-Hill, 1962).

Mott, William Penn, Jr., remarks in *Man Under Stress: Report of the Proceedings of the Second Annual Southwestern Environmental Health Conference, March 15, 1970* (San Diego: Comprehensive Health Planning Association, 1970).

Myers, Gustavus, *History of The Great American Fortunes* (New York: Modern Library, 1936).

National Wildlife Federation, "1971 EQ Index," *National Wildlife,* October–November 1971, pp. 25–40.

Netzer, Dick, *Economics and Urban Problems: Diagnoses and Prescriptions* (New York: Basic Books, 1970).

Report of the National Advisory Commission on Civil Disorders (the Kerner Commission), with an introduction by Tom Wicker (New York: Bantam, 1968).

Safdie, Moshe, "Can Technology Rescue the Cities?" in Harold W. Helfrich, Jr. (ed.), *Agenda for Survival* (Yale University Press, 1970).

Shah, Diane K., "Housing Mess" *National Observer* (week ending June 24, 1972.

Tunnard, Christopher, remarks in F. Fraser Darling and John P. Milton (eds.), *Future Environments of North America* (Garden City: Natural History Press, 1966), p. 413.

Tunnard, Christopher, and Boris Pushkarev, *Man-Made America: Chaos or Control?* (Yale University Press, 1963).

Tyson, Frank, remarks as chairman, Land Use Committee, California State Environmental Study Council, January 10, 1970.

Wood, Robert C., "City: III. Metropolitan Government," in *International Encyclopedia of the Social Sciences* (New York: Macmillan and Free Press, 1968).

11 TRANSPORTATION

There is one motor vehicle—auto, truck, or bus—for every two people in the United States. California alone has three such vehicles for every five people, plus over a million motorcycles, 1.5 million recreational trailers, and 100,000 dune buggies. Americans, it seems, are always on the move. The U.S. Bureau of the Census has estimated that in any given year at least one-fifth of the population changes residence. Fewer than one-quarter of these do so for purely economic reasons. In the words of Dr. Fred Hacker, a Los Angeles psychiatrist, Americans seem to believe that "going somewhere, going anywhere, is better than just passively enduring." For many, the journey to work resembles mass migration. Already in the mid-1950s, according to Jean Gottmann, rush hour traffic in and out of Manhattan totaled over three million people every weekday.

Private transportation in its present form causes harm in more ways than any other single factor in U.S. society. No part of the nation escapes its destructive power. Depletion of fossil fuels and other raw materials, air pollution, problems of solid waste disposal, damage to national parks, forests, and wildernesses—all can be traced in considerable measure to the private automobile. Use of the automobile has grown much faster than population—twenty times faster, in fact, if rates are calculated from 1915 (figure 11.1). Between 1940 and 1968, the number of passenger car miles traveled per member of the U.S. population increased from about 1,800 a year to about

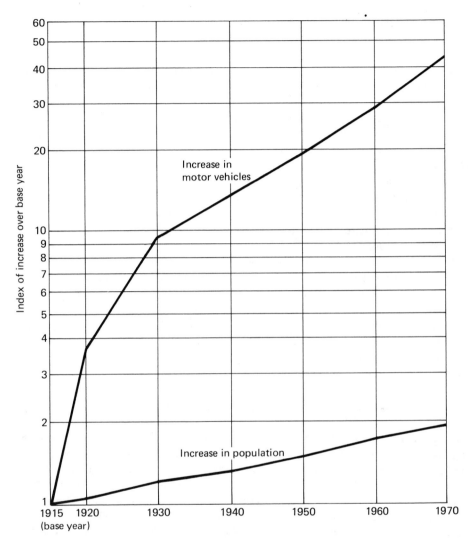

FIGURE 11.1.   Annual increase, 1915–70, for population and motor vehicles in the United States. Note that the vertical scale is logarithmic and so compresses the difference between the two. In 1915 there were nearly 100 million people but only 2.5 million vehicles.

4,000. In 1962, according to Edmund K. Faltermayer, it was proposed at a world urban planning congress that cities with more than 700,000 inhabitants should no longer be built, because their traffic problems would make them unlivable. There is no denying that, in addition to a population explosion and a technology explosion, we are suffering from a mobility explosion.

FROM MOBILITY TO MOTION SICKNESS

Why has the use of private cars for transportation become almost universal in our society? One reason, of course, is that once the automobile became established it helped to create a pattern of settlement that could not exist without it. As a result, people who cannot afford an automobile, or who lack regular access to one, are in a very real sense cut off from full participation in American life. It is also true that, since the U.S. economy now depends upon the automobile, the federal government is an ardent promoter of automobile interests. But none of this would have been possible if the American consumer did not prefer the automobile to any other mode of transportation. The tragedy is that, for all practical purposes, there is at present no choice between the gasoline-powered automobile and the modes that might have replaced it. In order to suggest remedial measures, it is first necessary to understand the stages by which we arrived at this situation.

The idea of a self-propelled vehicle has intrigued mankind's imagination for centuries. The god Hephaestus, in the *Iliad,* is said to have made twenty three-legged tables, with golden wheels, that "of their own accord would go to a meeting of the gods and then run home again—a marvelous sight." In 1769, two years after James Watt patented the steam engine, this vision at last became reality: a Frenchman, Joseph Cugnot (1725–1804) mounted one of the new engines on a tricycle chassis. This vehicle was the original automobile; it could run for 20 minutes up to two-and-one-quarter miles an hour. Nearly a century later another Frenchman, Alphonse Beau de Rochas (1815–93), discovered the 4-stroke principle basic to the internal combustion engine. Thus technology opened the way for a variety of self-propelled vehicles. The world's first auto show was held in 1900, in New York City. At that time it did not seem likely that the noisy, smelly, vibrating internal combustion engine would outlive its steam and electric competitors. Of the 53,000 automobiles in existence by 1903, some 30,000 had been built in France; the United States was only just starting production. In 1912, however, the United States had over a million of them, mostly gasoline powered. By that year, as James J. Flink has pointed out, the automobile had already reached its present form; indeed, the only major technological innovation to be added later was the automatic transmission, developed in the 1920s. Steam-driven automobiles were losing popularity because it took all the skills of a locomotive engineer to drive them. The electrics, although easy to drive, needed frequent recharging and were immobilized while this was being done. They were also comparatively low in horsepower. Gasoline won out because it offered a high ratio of power to fuel volume, plus easy operation and quick refueling.

The popularity of automobiles grew as their dependability increased. Henry Ford's assembly lines turned out cars that were not only cheaper but more dependable; railways and horse-drawn vehicles could no longer compete for local passenger use. The first Model Ts cost $890, but this had dropped to $290 by the time the Model As came out. The mass-produced Model A was the direct ancestor of today's family car. By 1929 automobiles had become a major force in the national economy. There were 25 million of them registered. The automobile industry employed a labor force of 4.7 million, and had become the country's largest single consumer of steel, plate glass, lead, and rubber. Autos were still regarded as luxury items, however, and three years later production was cut by 75 percent with the onset of the Great Depression. By 1940, however, production was up again, and it has expanded ever since. From 27.5 million in 1940, passenger car registration increased to 61.7 million in 1960 and over 89 million in 1970. By the same year there were nearly 109 million cars, trucks, and buses, traveling over a trillion miles a year on nearly 4 million miles of roads and highways occupying 25 million acres of land, burning 90 billion gallons of fuel, and emitting over 140 million tons of atmospheric pollutants each year. Western civilization now depends on the automobile: according to the Organization for Economic Cooperation and Development (O.E.C.D.), four times as many city dwellers go to work by automobile than by all other means combined, while almost all pleasure trips and 85 to 90 percent of total U.S. travel is by automobile.

At first people bought automobiles for their novelty and glamor. But as the general level of prosperity grew, more people became able to afford them. They soon realized that the automobile's greatest charm was its flexibility: the timetables of public transit facilities could be bypassed altogether. For a time automobiles seemed the key to happiness. People wanted the higher pay and other advantages of the city, but as cities grew crowded they also wanted to live on their outskirts. Automobiles brought both within reach, while offering the privacy and prestige so valued by the American middle classes. An uncontrolled suburban expansion began and is still going on; it remains dependent upon automobiles because no system of public transportation could cover such a widely dispersed area without incurring heavy losses. Automobile owners have demanded the streets, parking lots, highways, and freeways necessary to sustain an automotive existence. The impact on the American way of life has been tremendous: complex dimensions of supply and demand have been created and patterns of land use have been dramatically altered. Indeed, it now seems as if we could not get along without it. But it is also clear that we cannot get along with it much longer. The American dream of mobility has become what John Burby has aptly called the Great American Motion Sickness.

AUTOMANIA

The automobile industry's main channel of influence in every state is the highway department. These agencies have become in effect the architects of the nation (figure 11.2). In California the Division of Highways is already the major land use planner; its decisions on highway location, street rerouting, and the building of new interchanges exert more control over the functions alloted to land than any other power in the state. For this reason it has been suggested that the emblem of California should be the clover leaf—in concrete.

FIGURE 11.2.   Freeway under construction in San Diego, California. State highway departments have become the nation's major architects. (Union-Tribune Publishing Company, San Diego)

One very plausible analysis of the "highway bias" has been offered by Dick Netzer. According to Netzer, there are really three separate markets for urban transportation:

1. People who use public transportation for all the trips they take.
2. People traveling to work or to the central business district who have a choice between the automobile and some other mode of transportation.
3. Everyone else, that is, people with a choice of modes who are neither commuting nor traveling to the central business district.

Market 3, since it involves off-peak hours, is dominated overwhelmingly by the automobile. Market 1 contains a relatively small number of people, mostly central-city residents. It is in market 2 that public and private transportation are brought into direct competition (table 11.1). And here the automobile is easily the first choice of most consumers because it is faster, more comfortable, more flexible, and (to all appearances) cheaper. Why should this be so? Highway systems are not cheaper because they are more heavily subsidized. On the contrary, they eventually pay for themselves through taxation of automobile users, while most transit systems are unprofitable. The difference lies in the number of people sharing the cost. Gasoline and vehicle taxes are paid by *all* automobile users, including the substantial number of them in market 3. But for public transportation there is almost no market 3; it runs full during peak hours and nearly empty the rest of the time. Netzer calculates that, in a system that carried 80 percent of its users in peak hours, off-peak users would ride free if peak-hour fares were increased by a mere 25 percent. Motorists, of course, do not pay fares, but taxes constitute a fixed percentage of their operating costs. If the cost of building and operating an urban freeway were to be borne by peak-hour motorists, those taxes would have to be increased more than tenfold. Thus current systems of transportation pricing and financing encourage maximum use of the automobile. Of course, the real cost of running an automobile is very much higher than it appears to most people (essay 11.1).

The existence of the highway bias should not surprise anyone. Popular trends in the United States have steam-roller force. Historically, the trend has been not only toward bigger and more powerful cars but toward fewer passengers per car. In 1940 the number of passengers averaged 3, in 1950 it was down to 2, and in 1960 it was less than 1.5, or about 4 passengers distributed among each 10 cars with drivers. The United States now produces between 8 and 11 million cars, trucks, and buses a year. In 1962, a peak year in which the Federal Interstate System completed 21,051 miles of new roads, some $5 billion were spent on highway construction. Road building at this rate is an alarming consumer of valuable agricultural and residential land, and removes large areas from the tax rolls of local government. Highway departments are naturally concerned with accommodating as many cars as possible as soon as possible, which means building as many freeways as can be funded. But the result is motopia—an environment for cars, not people (figure 11.3).

TABLE 11.1.   Estimated distribution of urban passenger miles, by mode and type of trip[a]: United States, 1965 (percent)

Type of Trip	Mode[b]	
	Bus, Subway, & Suburban Rail	Private Auto
All types	7%	93%
Journey to work	20%	80%
Other types	1%	99%

Source: Adapted by permission from Richard Netzer, *Economics and Urban Problems,* p. 139, © 1970 by Basic Books, Inc., Publishers, New York. (data from Statistical Abstract of the United States).
[a]A "passenger mile" is one passenger traveling one mile, either alone or in a shared vehicle.
[b]Excludes walking, taxi, ferry, and trucks.

Essay 11.1.   The Real Cost of Auto Transportation

According to Henry Ford 2nd, who ought to know, some 20 percent of the country's gross national product is accounted for by transportation—and 80 percent of that amount is spent on motor vehicles. Nevertheless, most Americans remain strangely ignorant of how much their national addiction is costing them. A study conducted in 1972 by the Federal Highway Administration (F.H.A.) presented the following set of estimated costs for a new standard-size automobile kept over a 10-year period:

Gas	$ 2,787
Maintenance and repair	$ 2,147
Insurance	$ 1,350
Garaging, parking, and tolls	$ 1,800
All other (including purchase cost and financing)	$ 5,469
TOTAL	$13,553

On the rather unlikely assumptions that the car is operated only 100,000 miles in ten years, the F.H.A.'s estimated cost per mile is about 13.5 cents. The numerous other assumptions involved are too obvious to need mentioning here (one wonders if the F.H.A.'s statisticians have ever tried maintaining an American car more than five years old). Costs per mile are amazingly similar across the nation: the range, according to the Automobile Legal Association, is from 14.93 cents a mile in Boston to 11.74 cents a mile in Richmond, Vir-

Unfortunately, the automobile is now an economic mainstay. In 1968, total automobile manufacture was valued at $36.1 million, or 4.2 percent of the gross national product. In addition to the manufacturing process, one out of every six businesses owes its existence to the use of private cars for transportation. The advertising business alone makes $500 million a year promoting sales. Since 1968, the total indebtedness on automobiles has ranged from $34.1 to $36.6 *billion* a year. Will this economic dependence make it impossible for us ever to free ourselves from domination by the automobile? The incongruity of this relationship is well expressed by Victor Gruen, who has compared it to

> *a convention of plumbers dictating to architects and the entire construction industry how buildings should be designed, inside and out, in order to (a) increase the employment opportunities in the plumbing fixtures industry, and (b) facilitate their installation. They would dictate that every room in every building must have a bathtub, water closet, and three washstands—otherwise unemployment in the appliance industry might result— and that plumbing pipes of all types must no longer be forced into positions where they are hidden in walls and ceilings. (Gruen 1964, p. 212)*

ginia, and the main variable is insurance. However, the greatest single cost of owning and operating an automobile is depreciation, included in the "all other" section of the table shown above. The F.H.A. estimated that depreciation during the first year of ownership amounted to 16 cents a mile for a standard-size car in suburban use. The University of Michigan Survey Research Center found in 1970 that 20 percent of all American families own two or more automobiles. For these families, then, the costs shown above are at least doubled. In 1969, according to the same source, only 34 percent of new car buyers paid cash, so it is hardly surprising that U.S. automobile loans outstanding in 1970 exceeded $35 billion—a sum six times the gross national product of South Korea. Mabel Newcomer, a consumer adviser in northern California, has reported one estimate of the cost of being a suburban 2-car family on the more realistic basis of seven years' life per car. Her figures are as follows:

Operating costs (including gas, insurance, and repairs)	*$10,290*
Interest on money invested in own garage	*$ 1,099*
Purchase cost (including financing)	*$ 7,272*
TOTAL	*$18,662*

Both cars were cheaper models than the ones in the F.H.A. estimate. Ms. Newcomer suggests that we compare the possible cost of improved public transportation with the $1,333 spent each year for a second car. Even $2 per round trip would only be about $500 a year—a saving of over 60 percent.

It is altogether extraordinary how the automobile has convinced us of its indispensability, when it is unequaled as a consumer of resources, waster of space, polluter of the environment, waster of time—and killer or mangler of human beings. Deaths from auto accidents in 1969 alone exceeded 56,000, while U.S. battle deaths in Vietnam totaled 44,882 from 1961 through 1971. Also in 1969, an additional 4.7 million persons were injured in auto accidents. In 1967, the average family in which there was either death or serious injury from an automobile accident sustained losses of over $10,000. The average loss per death, including loss of future earnings, was almost $90,000.

The loss in natural resources is equally horrendous. Automobile manufacture is the heaviest steel consumer in the nation, using 15 percent of the annual product. Much of this steel is never returned to the active supply pool; at least a million unscrapped cars are abandoned each year. This rush to oblivion is hastened by stylistic change and other forms of built-in obsolescence—in short, by deliberate waste. Only a mammoth corporation could afford the investment that goes into designing and selling annual changes in style. It is hardly surprising, then, that this concept was foisted on the public by General Motors, which then used it to wipe out all effective competition except the Ford Motor Company. Henry Ford's original concept was almost the exact

FIGURE 11.3.   Is this motopia? Los Angeles has been called the "ultimate city"; perhaps it is the ecological climax of Western man. (Newsweek)

opposite: to sell a reliable automobile that would be cheap because it was mass-produced and did not change much. But Ford eventually had to adopt annual restyling out of self-defense. Today, most American cars are marketed in much the same way as women's clothing, except that the clothing is better made. "Planned obsolescence in my opinion is another word for progress," said Jim Roche of General Motors in April, 1970. He omitted to add that in order to sustain this "progress" the United States is using about one-half the world's industrial capacity. Much of this capacity, as we saw in chapter 6, depends on raw materials imported from countries that in time will develop their own industrial programs and so need the materials for themselves. However, this does not deter General Motors and other U.S. auto manufacturers from turning out a product with a median life expectancy of 3 to 5 years. General construction, as the next-to-largest steel consumer, uses only 9 percent of annual output. Moreover, structural steel not only has many times the life span of steel used in cars but is almost 100 percent reclaimable when a structure is demolished. The return of automotive steel for reuse is very low in comparison.

Cars use resources even more extravagantly for their operation and maintenance. Of the 3.3 billion barrels of petroleum refined each year, only 3 percent go into the important petrochemical industry, while 51 percent are used for gasoline and 2 percent for lubricants. We are turning more than one-half of our most valuable chemical base into fuel to be exploded in vehicles that spew most of it over the countryside. Automobiles are also voracious—and unpredictable—consumers of space. Highways already cover 23 million acres of U.S. land; planners insist that much more is needed. The average density of 22 cars per highway mile in 1963 had grown to 26 by 1967. In Great Britain, density even reached 36 per mile by 1960. But then it leveled off as counterpressure developed for agricultural and residential usage. The United States has no such relief in prospect. Appropriation of space by automobiles is most noticeable in U.S. cities, which devote an average of 30 percent of their space to serving cars. Los Angeles, the automobile city par excellence, devotes nearly 70 percent of its downtown area to traffic, servicing, and parking (figure 11.4). It seems that no share of urban resources is too great for the automobile.

Automobiles pollute a broader range of the environment than any other agent. On land this takes two forms: *primary* pollution, as when unscrapped auto bodies litter the landscape; and *secondary* pollution, such as fallout of unoxidized hydrocarbons and tetraethyl lead from the atmosphere. Water also receives secondary pollution, especially near heavily traveled routes. The more serious primary water pollution comes from the industrial processes of auto manufacture and related operations (for pollution of both kinds, see chapters 8 and 9). Air pollution peaks and ebbs in response to levels of traffic activity in our cities. In most cases, the hydrocarbons from internal combustion engines exceed the sulfur oxides typical of industrial pollution. For reasons explained in chapter 7, air pollution from gasoline combustion may well be the greatest long-term threat to life on our planet. The possible effects are so serious that the United States, distracted from action by worry about economic repercussions, resembles a man trying to save his trinkets and currency while his house burns down around him. For purposes of survival, it would be wise to prop, patch, or manipulate our economic structure in any way necessary to wean it from so deadly a mainstay. Internal combustion vehicles in great numbers cause such a variety and degree of damage that they carry the seeds of their own destruction. Either they will be phased out while there is still time, or they will be immobilized along with the society that tolerates them.

Automobiles also waste that most precious of commodities, time. Traffic congestion on city streets is so great that, although the speed potential of automobiles is going up, the speed at which they can travel in cities is going down. In New York City in 1907 the average speed was 11.5 miles per hour, by horse-drawn vehicle. In 1966 the average speed was 8.5 miles per hour—by motor vehicle! Congestion has other consequences: the cost of doing business in Manhattan, according to the former transportation administrator for New York City, Arthur E. Palmer, Jr., has increased as much as 20 percent. During rush hours and on holidays it can take a motorist three hours to drive as little as twenty miles in the Greater Los Angeles area. Inching along in bumper-to-bumper traffic is irritating and dangerous: drivers grow impatient, accidents increase, and cars overheat or run out of gas so that they have to be parked on the shoulder, where they form another lane of motionless traffic. Meanwhile, the air becomes saturated with fumes from the solid mass of idling automobiles. No wonder experts are beginning to speak in terms that suggest the ultimate immobilization of our society. Their prophecies are not groundless: they are based on simple projections of passenger demand, which indicate that travel in California will double in ten years and be five times as great in fifty. Since the ratio of cars to population in other states is now lower than California's, travel demand there will probably increase at a greater rate.

The present situation is not wholly unprecedented, nor are the remedies for which it calls. When the Ohio Valley was opened for settlement, the railroad became the dominant mode of transportation within thirty years of its introduction. Major changes *are* possible. But this time they will have to be the result of deliberation and planning, not a blind response to economic demand.

THE CROWDED AIR

As if our traffic problems on the ground were not enough, we are duplicating them in the air. There is a parallel between acceptance of the automobile for private transportation and acceptance of the airplane as the dominant mode of inter-city travel: both create a dependency that finally leaves the traveler with no practical alternatives. By the late 1960s, according to Edmund K. Faltermayer, there were only one-third as many intercity passenger trains in operation as there had been ten years before. Passenger train service between many major cities less than 300 miles apart was either minimal or had been discontinued: it seemed as if everyone who could afford to was going by air. The resulting air traffic problems were far worse than anyone had foreseen. John Burby reports that 12 airlines were involved in mid-air collisions over airports between 1965 and 1969. Considering that over and near all airports there are about 5,000 near misses a year, the figure for collisions is amazingly low. Many of the accidents and near-accidents are due to private planes operating out of public air terminals, but until 1969 fliers of private planes could fly over the busiest airports without even filing flight plans with the Federal Aviation Agency (F.A.A.). Control facilities have not been modernized to keep pace with the increase in traffic, nor are there enough trained air controllers—as the Professional Air Traffic Controllers' Organization (P.A.T.C.O.) has long complained. Worse still, many smaller airports lack basic safety provisions such as fire-fighting equipment. Airports, it seems, need not meet any federal standards in order to receive interstate flights; half of the airports served by commercial airlines do not even have instrument landing systems. It is a sad but symbolic fact that Transpo 72, the international transportation exhibition presented at Dulles International Airport in 1972, was remarkable mainly for a number of fatal airplane accidents.

Despite the increase in air traffic, travel by air is mainly a privilege of the well-to-do and the wealthy. There are fifty times as many private planes as commercial carriers, and about 30 percent of them are used for business. The total number of private fliers is over 600,000, and they are issued licenses under conditions far less strict than those applied to automobile drivers. They are no longer as heavily subsidized by the U.S. taxpayer as they were before Congress imposed new aviation taxes in 1970. But the pattern of private affluence and public squalor that has established itself on earth seems well on the way to repeating itself in the air. The impression is sometimes given that air travel accounts for most inter-city passengers who use commercial transportation. This is true only in terms of mileage; two-thirds of all passengers still go by bus or train. The dominant mode is actually the private automobile.

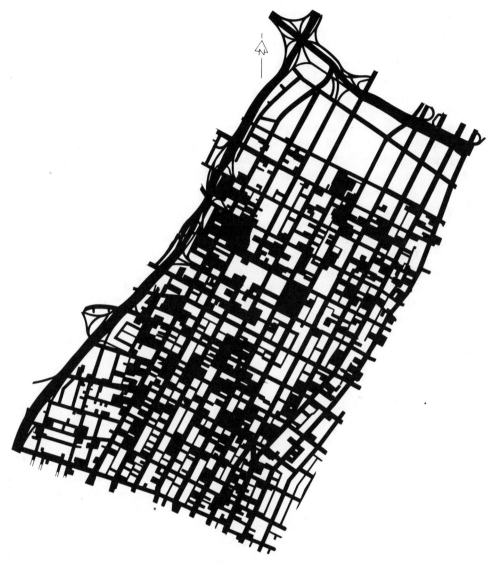

FIGURE 11.4.   Land devoted to automotive uses in downtown
Los Angeles. Seventy percent of this area is used for traffic, servicing,
and parking. (Victor Gruen Foundation for Environmental Planning)

Nevertheless, the existence of airline service is used by railroads as an excuse for phasing out passenger business. Meanwhile, truly rapid and convenient airline passenger service simply does not exist. In many large cities, it takes longer to reach the airport from downtown than it does to fly to the nearest major city. Airports seem likely to consume ever more land while providing increasingly less service. Burby reports that businessmen stalled by traffic jams often run the last mile to Los Angeles International.

If this type of energy were applied to designing transportation systems, many of the problems of urbanization, discussed in the previous chapter, would be well on the way to solution.

Jet aircraft, especially the new supersonic transport (**SST**), are also responsible for new kinds of atmospheric pollution. At 65,000 feet and more, where the SST flies, settling rates are exceedingly slow. Such accumulation of gases and particulate matter at this height could add greatly to the increasing albedo of the earth, perhaps reflecting enough incoming solar radiation to change its heat balance. In late 1970, considerations such as these led the Senate to vote against the proposed SST development program. But the vote was close. Next time, especially if foreign airlines achieve commercial success with *their* SSTs, it could go the other way.

One would have thought that the solutions to the present mess were so obvious that they could have been tried in the first place. Indeed, some of them have been tried: Cleveland, for instance has a rapid-transit connection between its downtown area and its airport. But Cleveland is a solitary exception. It is true that in 1970 the U.S. Department of Transportation, then less than four years old, announced plans to build a 16-mile Tracked Air-Cushion Vehicle (**TACV**) system to serve Los Angeles International Airport. Expensive showpieces, however, will do little to improve the general situation. Meanwhile, according to the department, air freight sent by jet arrives at its final destination no sooner than it used to do when the carrier was a prop-driven aircraft. Not for the first time, technological progress has turned out to be no progress at all.

PLANNING FOR THE FUTURE

John Kenneth Galbraith's characterization of the United States as a land of private affluence and public squalor is nowhere more clearly illustrated than in the field of transportation. It is also clear that millions of cars plus a bare minimum of passenger trains is not a formula for a viable transportation system. In the next twenty years, according to Secretary of Transportation John A., Volpe, the U.S. system will need to double its carrying capacity. Nobody wants a return to private squalor—but we could do with a great deal more public affluence.

Upgrading Public Transportation

Even if we could suddenly buy cars that cost little, used few nonrenewable resources, lasted forever, and were pollution-free, we could not continue to rely so heavily on private transportation. As population and living standards both increased, so also would traffic congestion and pressure on land. At present, as Edmund K. Faltermayer has stressed, most of the country's metropolitan areas completely lack surface transit systems for commuters. Of the few that do exist perhaps the less said the better: the New York rapid transit system, for instance, was accurately described by Mayor John Lindsay as "the most degrading public environment in the world." The sooner we achieve *acceptable* public transportation, the sooner we can expect a decline in the environmental damage caused by cars. The ideal system of public transportation would involve a variety of modes—buses, subway trains, "people movers"—for maximum efficiency and convenience. It would also be sufficiently flexible to vary with the needs of each city. This is obviously a long-range vision. At the other end of the time scale is a change that can be made immediately: reduction of vehicle size and engine horsepower. The old, large buses so familiar to us all could be replaced by smaller ones that run more frequently. This has in fact been tried in several cities including Washington, D.C. Reduced vehicle size has many advantages. Less fuel is used, so less pollution results. In addition, both street and freeway capacity is increased, while bus companies save money on parking and storage space. To be effective, this reduction in size will have to extend to all vehicles, both public and private.

Some of the proposed solutions involve a combination of private vehicles and public control. Public glideways for private cars have been under study for some time. Control of entering autos would be taken over by an electronic system in the road itself; speed and spacing would be determined by computer, and passing and exiting arranged by a signal from the driver (figure 11.5). The object, as described by Melville C. Branch, would be to move traffic at maximum speed by eliminating in-

FIGURE 11.5.   Model of an electronically controlled glideway that includes private cars, commercial trucks, and public transportation. Special feature of model is use of airspace over glideway for residential and recreational purposes. (General Motors Corporation)

dividual idiosyncracies. The whole system would of course be very expensive, and for this reason alone it will be a long time before anything like it is in operation. But if private automobiles continue to be allowed into central cities, the public glideway is probably the only alternative to chaos.

Many aspects of mass transit are being researched by the federal government. In Pittsburgh, a car with dual sets of wheels has been tested. Its operation is as close to automatic as possible, and its main advantage is flexibility. Since it eliminates feeder bus lines and railways, much less reserve equipment for peak loads is needed, as well as less space for storage. The cars pick up passengers along feeder routes and then switch to rails, where they couple onto trains for rapid transfer to urban centers. Some of the cars can switch back to street travel along the way. So far, these versatile vehicles are experimental and are far from completely efficient. Another promising approach is the pneumatic tube train, which combines speed with safety.

The U.S. Department of Transportation has helped to finance two experimental rail vehicles designed for operation on existing railroad systems. The first is the Metroliner, an all-electric two-car train built by a company that had been forced to turn from train to auto parts manufacture for lack of orders. Despite mechanical snags, the Metroliner has increased passenger travel on the 240-mile New York–Washington route, which it can cover in three hours. Another federal grant will soon provide the Long Island Railroad with trains of the same type. The second experiment, not so successful, was with a jet-powered "turbo-train" for the New York–Boston route. Here, the main problem was the track, which allowed the train to run at only half its potential top speed of 170 mph. The department has given so-called seed money to a variety of other rapid transit projects, most of them intended to upgrade rather than replace existing rail facilities. There is even a new government corporation that is supposed to take over "essential" passenger train services that would otherwise be discontinued (its main achievement so far has been to ask for more money). But it will be a long time before there is anything in the United States to match the Japanese Tokaido trains, which cruise at 130 mph on a 340-mile track that they use exclusively. They have been in operation since 1964. Another outstanding transit system is the new Montreal subway, which has elegant, brightly lit stations and rubber-tired trains. Speeds are moderate, but quite sufficient for the 16-mile circuit.

It will be seen from the examples just discussed that the problems of local and intercity travel overlap. In fact, it is hardly possible to distinguish between them any longer in the principal metropolitan areas (figure 11.6). One ambitious project now under construction is the Bay Area Rapid Transit (B.A.R.T.) system based on San Francisco. It will serve Alameda, Contra Costa, and San Francisco Counties with 75 miles of track that follows highway and railroad rights-of-way but is separated from other traffic. It will combine surface, aerial, and subway lines, and include a three-and-one-half-mile tunnel and a slightly longer underwater tube, sunk 70 to 100 feet into alluvial material beneath water up to 130 feet deep—a world record. The entire system from train speeds and spacing to fare collection, will be electronically controlled. B.A.R.T. cars will stop at 37 stations, averaging 2 miles apart, of which 23 will provide free parking for private cars. A B.A.R.T. car will seat 72 passengers in carpeted, air-conditioned comfort, and will average 50 miles an hour. A passenger will be able

FIGURE 11.6.   Local and intercity traffic moving past the Chicago Loop (i.e., old downtown area) on the Dan Ryan Expressway. Note long-distance trucks interspersed with private cars on lane signed for National Interstate Highway 55. (photo by Orlando R. Cabanban, Oak Park, Illinois)

to travel from one B.A.R.T. station to another for about the same money and in about 75 percent of the time that it takes to make the same trip by car (figure 11.7). The automotive cost in this case takes into account only direct expenditures such as gas and oil, not maintenance and ownership. Most of the over $1 billion cost of building B.A.R.T. is being met by a property tax, passed by voters in 1962, that will affect only the three counties it is designed to serve. Other funds are being obtained from tolls paid by users of the San Francisco Bay Bridge, and from various agencies of the federal government, including the Department of Housing and Urban Development and the Department of Transportation. The whole project is the most ambitious attempt so far to supplant the automobile as the mainstay of commuter traffic.

Reducing the Private Sphere

There are both immediate and long-range possibilities for improving private transportation. Most of them are aimed primarily at reducing air pollution, the most serious problem directly related to transportation (see chapter 7). The livability of our cities depends on how soon we replace gas-burning engines entirely. But we

PEAK-HOUR TRAVEL TIMES IN MINUTES

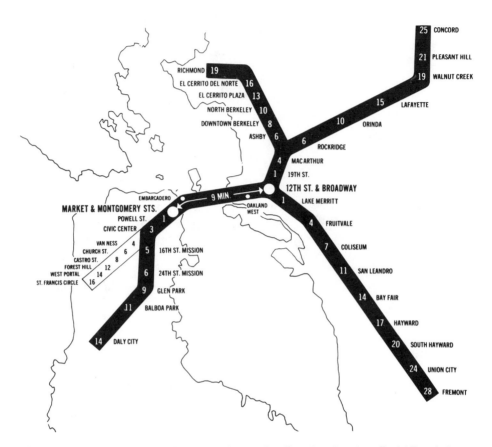

FIGURE 11.7.   Scheduled travel times on the new San Francisco Bay Area Rapid Transit System (B.A.R.T.). Distance from Daly City to Market and Montgomery Streets by expressway is about 8 miles. (B.A.R.T.)

could get some relief from smog at once if we gave up our large cars and drove only smaller models. If automotive power were restricted to 100 horses, pollution from hydrocarbons could be cut by more than half in areas like the Los Angeles basin. This approach to our problems would also ease traffic congestion. Tokyo has already passed legislation limiting vehicle size. But it is not necessary for us to wait for similar legislation—which in any case may never come. Genuinely concerned citizens can turn to small cars on their own initiative. Another action that can be taken by individuals and small groups is the organization of car pools for people who regularly travel the same routes at the same hours. Four people can go to work and back in one car instead of four cars, with a fourth of the resulting pollution. Los Angeles is turning to the computer to organize extensive carpooling. In San Francisco, the Golden Gate Bridge Authority allows car pool users to pass at a nominal toll of $1 a month provided at least three persons are in the car. Authorities in Rome, Italy, have experimented with free rides on buses and streetcars during peak hours (the city-owned transit company was already losing so much money that this seemed a worthwhile method of reducing auto traffic). In Washington, D.C., communal commuting by taxi is a growing trend. Hitch-hiking, though rarely practiced by commuters, is an institution that could be restored to the respectability it enjoyed during World War II. The mess made by gas-burning cars could also be reduced by improving the fuel they burn. According to Edwin E. Nelson, a General Motors research engineer, reduction of the olefinic compounds in gasoline could cut automotive pollution by as much as 56 percent in the cities most affected. Lead, which attacks the nervous and reproductive systems, is added to gas-olines to increase octane ratings. Fortunately for people, it will also gum up catalytic mufflers and for that reason will be completely phased out within a few years.

New fuels offer some hope. Emissions from vehicles burning natural gas or liquid petroleum have been measured with infrared light, and carbon monoxide em-issions were found to average 2 grams per mile as compared to 28 grams from cars burning gasoline. Nitrogen oxides, which are not reduced by smog-control devices on gas-burning cars, amounted to .5 as compared to 4 grams per mile. These tests were carried out by the Pacific Lighting Service Company of Los Angeles, which is convert-ing its 1,100 vehicles to natural gas. In 1969 the federal government began investigat-ing the system for possible use in its own 51,000 trucks and cars, and in 1970 various companies in other California cities were investing in conversion units for their vehicles. Natural gas has other advantages besides reduced emissions: 100 cubic feet of it give 15 percent more mileage than a gallon of gasoline and cost 63 percent less. En-gine oil lasts up to a year because natural gas burns more cleanly; spark plugs fire for 50,000 miles and valve jobs are unnecessary. Present internal combustion engines are retained to burn natural gas, but conversion units must be added. These can be installed with dashboard controls that permit drivers to use natural gas in polluted areas and switch to gasoline on the open road. There are disadvantages, too. Natural gas must be stored in pressure tanks, both in fueling stations and in vehicles. The bulky fuel cylinders fill most of the car's trunk space, and conversion costs about $300. If operating economy attracts more owners of fleets of vehicles, however, mass produc-tion could lower the conversion cost. Natural gas is in short supply, but synthetic equivalents are becoming available. Unfortunately, the only one now being manufac-tured on a large scale is based on naphtha, a petroleum derivative. But, as we saw in chapter 4, methanol from converted organic wastes would be just as effective without depleting irreplaceable fossil fuel resources.

A different kind of proposal would establish central urban car pools that would be individually operated, like U-drive taxis, but publicly or company owned. Theoretically, a commuter could pick up a car near home and drive it to a collection point near his job, where it would be available to the next user instead of being parked all day. The plan would function best if work shifts in large factories were timed to facilitate it. The obvious difficulty would be matching supply and demand closely enough, plus the nuisance of retrieving vehicles from out-of-the-way places. Street vehicles equipped with conversion units for electronically controlled freeway guidance have been briefly mentioned. Not only would congestion be relieved by the greater speed of controlled traffic, but, since the greatest volume of pollution comes from slow-moving vehicles and stop-and-go driving, smog would lessen. And this plan has advantages lacked by others. It might break some of the major political and economic deadlocks in the crisis. Perhaps it would persuade the advocates of open road policies to take a more tolerant view of the wisdom of financing improved transit systems with highway users' tax money. It might also mollify vested interests in the auto industry. It would certainly be less of a shock to the national economy than an abrupt shutdown of gas-burning car manufacture and related enterprises.

If any type of private conveyance is to remain in use, it will have to be built for durability of both design and material. It will also have to be nearly free of pollution. One vehicle that meets nearly all these conditions is the electric car. Even though the generation of electricity still depends mainly on fossil fuels, refueling from some central source of electricity would cause less pollution than the present system. If electric cars can be made economically competitive with gas-powered vehicles, they will free much space for other uses. Solar-powered and air-cushion cars have so far proven too expensive, as well as inadequate in both power output and convenience. Steam-driven cars are perhaps the best potential family transportation. An experimental model now being readied in San Diego will produce about 35 horses, cruising at 45 to 50 miles per hour. It can generate speeds up to 80 miles per hour, but only in short bursts; the steam cannot be condensed fast enough for high speeds to be maintained. Unfortunately, mileage of only 10 miles per gallon of water is expected.

U.S. automobile companies have been hesitant to move strongly into either steam or turbine engines. One large Japanese company, however is planning to mass-produce a steam auto. Hopefully this example will inspire imitation. Steam, electric, and other substitutes for gasoline-fueled cars will probably offer less acceleration and less speed than we are used to. But this is not too great a price to pay for an end to smog and all the problems that it causes.

The most important and difficult thing we are going to have to do about private transportation is to use it less. Technology may give us a kind of vehicle that causes almost no pollution, but it can do little about traffic congestion and space consumption. Public transportation can save us money, but it cannot offer the same kind of convenience and flexibility as the private car, let alone the status differentiation. It follows that our scale of values will have to be changed. This may be difficult. Few people feel enthusiastic about public transport systems today. As a result, our cars have become ends in themselves. Worse, mobility is now valued for its own sake. Our whole society must somehow be brought to see transportation simply as a means to an end. Community welfare must become more important to us than personal indulgence, which means that every adult must be shown the harmful effects of dependence on private cars. Automobile manufacture and the entire complex of related industries, businesses, and services have been basic to the economic growth of this country. But we cannot indefinitely postpone coming to grips with the inherent danger of a national economy that rests in large part on profligate waste, and thrives at the expense of environmental quality and human health.

ALTERNATIVE SYSTEMS

Improvements in transportation, if they are to have any permanent effect, must go far beyond the discovery and testing of new vehicles. Transportation, as Jean Gottman has emphasized, is the basis of urban living; in the urbanized Northeast that he calls Megalopolis, the entire future course of economic and social development will depend on the quality of the transportation services. What is needed, therefore, is transportation planning for development—not an attempt to impose some fixed pattern on an area, but open systems that will lead ultimately to growth instead of strangulation.

Since the needs of each community are different, they must be considered separately. Speed, safety, and convenience should be built into the entire system, as should measures to preserve environmental quality. At the community level, among the determining factors listed by Gottmann are occupational patterns, level of personal income, amount of time and money available for leisure, family structure, distribution of homes and work places, and weather. One would think it obvious enough that a community should both need and be able to afford its new transportation system. Yet this principle has all too frequently been ignored, with disastrous results.

Planning is but half the battle; the other half is putting the plans into effect. This can be done only by regional planning agencies strong enough to cope with conflicting business and political interests, but not so strong that they can afford to alienate local policy makers. Above all, the public must be meaningfully involved. To this end, the planners must be organized and equipped to do a thorough but noncoercive job of public education (see figure 18.5, p. 390). The case of B.A.R.T. shows that voters will recognize their own true interests when these are clearly presented. Perhaps, if the consequences of prolonging future trends are debated often enough, the American public will begin to recover from its motion sickness.

REFERENCES

Branch, Melville C., *Transportation Developments, Cities and Planning* (Chicago: American Society of Planning Officials, 1965).

Burby, John, *The Great American Motion Sickness, or Why You Can't Get There from Here* (Boston: Little, Brown, 1971).

Faltermayer, Edmund K., *Redoing America* (New York: Collier Books, 1968).

Flink, James J., *America Adopts the Automobile, 1895–1910* (MIT Press, 1970).

Galbraith, John Kenneth, *The Affluent Society* (Boston: Houghton Mifflin, 1958).

Gottmann, Jean, *Megalopolis: The Urbanized Northeastern Seaboard of the United States* (MIT Press, 1961).

Gruen, Victor, *Heart of Our Cities* (New York: Simon and Schuster, 1964).

Hacker, Fred, quoted in *Newsweek,* November 30, 1970.

Nelson, Edwin E., testimony before Transportation Committee, California State Assembly, February 18, 1969.

Netzer, Dick, *Economics and Urban Problems* (New York: Basic Books, 1970).

Organization for Economic Cooperation and Development, *Urban Transportation* (London: OECD, 1969).

Volpe, John A., speech on June 19, 1970.

12 ECONOMIC PRESSURES

Material success, both corporate and individual, is a source of great pride in the United States, as is the prosperity of the country at large. The pressure to increase both is unrelenting: every year Americans are expected to produce and consume more. The impact of all this pressure is ultimately borne by the nation's resources and the environmental framework within which they are utilized.

ECONOMIC GROWTH AS NORM: MEANS AND CONSEQUENCES

It was in 1936, while the world was still struggling in the trough of the Great Depression, that John Maynard Keynes published his *General Theory of Employment, Interest and Money.* Ten years later Congress passed the Employment Act, which for the first time established full employment as a national goal. Although Lord Keynes was hardly mentioned in the debate over the act, its passage reflected his influence. Keynesian doctrine advocates manipulation of the economy in order to regulate production and consumption and to minimize the social effects of the business cycle. It does not advocate increased production as an end in itself. However, it was certainly the increased level of production in World War II that lifted the United

States out of the Great Depression. In the postwar atmosphere production seemed the key to everything. With continued population growth, rising consumption standards, and technological advancement, many experts thought that all would be well for evermore. The business community was of course delighted at the prospect of expanding markets, and for this reason was prepared to see the federal government manipulate aggregate demand through such mechanisms as the Federal Reserve Board.

The postwar increase in production has inspired a new economic philosophy to justify it. This philosophy concentrates on certain aspects of production while systematically ignoring others. As John Kenneth Galbraith has pointed out, there are five ways in which production may be increased:

1. Fuller employment of existing resources (i.e., labor and capital).
2. More efficient employment of existing resources, using the technology that already exists.
3. An increase in the supply of labor.
4. An increase in the supply of capital.
5. Improved technology.

It should be noted that under "capital" Galbraith includes both financial capital and available raw materials.

Some interesting consequences can be deduced from this theorem. Galbraith argues that the "conventional wisdom" of economics—that is, the entire complex of currently acceptable economic concepts—emphasizes (5), and (except in time of war) leaves (1) through (4) to take care of themselves. As a result, not only is the chief burden of increasing productivity placed on technology, with a corresponding increase in the consumption of energy and raw materials, but the range of technological innovation is severely restricted, since only a few large industries can afford the necessary research and development. Thus we have galloping productivity increases, at increasing cost to society, in such mammoth industries as automobile manufacturing and petroleum products, but very little improvement in such industries as home construction or passenger transportation, which are dominated by large numbers of small firms. Agriculture, with one of the highest rates of productivity increase, is the exception that proves the rule: the necessary research was performed mainly by the federal and state governments, and by corporations that sell their products to the farmer.

Another curious aspect of the conventional wisdom—curious, until one remembers that governments in the nineteenth century did not have nearly as much power as they do today—is that publicly produced services, such as education, are not thought of as belonging to the same catagory as privately produced services, such as auto insurance. Indeed, the publicly produced services are likely to be denounced as "wasteful" and "inflationary," while the privately produced ones are lauded as the source of the nation's wealth. The fact that insurance companies, for instance, could not operate in the absence of a highly educated labor force is not often made the subject of comment.

It is not surprising, then, that the United States exercises its great capacity for production in a very one-sided way. The "good life" is defined as the consumption of whatever is most profitable to produce. Meanwhile, needs and wants that do not fit into this definition are slighted or ignored. Production, however, is praised to the skies, although no one takes a very close look at what is being produced. In Galbraith's own words:

> *The result has been an elaborate and ingenious defense of the importance of production as such. It is a defense which makes the urgency of production largely independent of the volume of production. In this way economic theory has managed to transfer the sense of urgency in meeting consumer need that once was felt in a world where more production meant more food for the hungry, more clothing for the cold, and more houses for the homeless to a world where increased output satisfies the craving for more elegant automobiles, more exotic food, more erotic clothing, more elaborate entertainment—indeed, for the entire modern range of sensuous, edifying, and lethal desires. (Galbraith 1964, pp. 114–115)*

In short, the basic trouble in the United States is the type of demand regarded as normal. Demand has been built up by persuasive advertising, planned obsolescence, and other devices unknown to classical economics. These practices were not foreseen when the open market concept was originally formulated, nor was the extent to which large corporate producers could stifle effective competition. Nevertheless, the myth that production is controlled by public demand is kept alive by business interests. However, when public demand takes the form of a well-informed, aggressive consumers' movement, business interests do everything they can to combat it. This is not to deny that the United States has achieved remarkable economic success—at a price. The price in question has been the cultivation of economic individualism at the expense of other values. The desirability of sustained economic growth has only recently been questioned; economic depression is generally assumed to be the only alternative. In short, an expanding economy is perceived as equivalent to a healthy society.

At this point many readers may feel like interjecting: Why not? Certainly social equilibrium is affected by economic conditions, and prosperity generally affects it for the good. But the U.S. perspective is skewed to the degree that growth, measured in terms of GNP, has come to seem the ultimate *social* good. This attitude equates prudent resource use with economic stagnation. It appears that American society has adapted to its economic system only to discover that it has placed itself in a position of direct conflict with its own interests in at least two fundamental areas: individual human development and preserving the physical environment.

We are faced, then, with two areas of malfunction in the economic system: the allocation of resources, and the rate at which they are being consumed. Before we can discuss either, it will be necessary to take a closer look at the concept of resources.

THE NATURE OF RESOURCES

To most people, the word "resource" denotes a substance destined for commercial processing. Thus it has distinct economic connotations, acquired gradually through use in economic contexts. The commercial nature of U.S. society encourages the habit of perceiving things in economic terms; disasters, for instance, are always reported as involving so many dollars' worth of damage. This national habit has almost obliterated awareness of the fact that resources have no *inherent* commercial value. Coal and iron, for example, are valued for their *utility,* and only because of this can economic value be ascribed to them. Before the Industrial Revolution, resources were more easily seen in terms of utility. A farmer chopping wood for the winter did not think about its cash value. In fact, he probably thought of it as free, like air or water. He may have valued the time and labor he spent on it, but these were means to an end: warmth. The resource he valued was not the woodpile but its *function.* Functional values were awkward to assess and compare as goods in increasing variety were traded in the developing market economy. The attribution of value accordingly shifted from functions to the physical materials that provided them. Money furnished a convenient common denominator for evaluating diverse commodities.

The perception of resources as substances with price tags was a marketplace expedient. It was not long, however, before the rest of society began to think of them this way. In 1933, when Erich Zimmermann published his view of resources as functions performed by commodities, it was acclaimed as a remarkable clarification of economic thought.

Most resource theorists now agree with Zimmermann's concept. It encompasses functions not derived from commodities: the technology applied to convert "neutral stuff," for example, is as much a resource as the function performed by the converted stuff. Resources of this kind are known as *social* resources, as opposed to natural ones. The social resource system is as open-ended as the society is dynamic. Resources are created and destroyed within cultural frameworks, and both processes are accelerated with increasing industrial prowess and social complexity. The following distinctions, commonly used by economists, need to be discussed before we can deal with the relation between resources and economic ends.

Stock Resources

A **stock resource** is nonrenewable; the supply of it does not increase with time, and once used it is gone forever. A degree of recovery is possible in some cases, as with glass and metal containers, but this is often expensive.

Stock resources can be divided into two groups: those that do not decrease over time unless something happens to them, and those that decrease in any case. Typical of the first group are metal ores and quarry products. The second group includes nuclear fuels, which lose radioactivity slowly but predictably, and petroleum, which is subject to leakage as the volatile components vaporize and the heavy residue forms a tar pit. Also in this category are nonrenewable resources such as national parks. While these do not diminish, there is of course less and less usage of them per individual as population increases.

Flow Resources

The distinguishing characteristic of flow resources is recurrent supply as a result of energy that emanates from outside the ecosphere. The flow itself may be continuous or intermittent and the rate of flow constant or fluctuating. Flow is not to be confused with use: present flow does not diminish future flow. There are two types of **flow resource**. For one, the rate of future flow is not significantly altered by use in a given period. The flow of solar energy, for example, is not affected by human activity, although atmospheric pollution does reduce the amount of it that reaches the earth's surface. For the other, flow may be increased or decreased according to the nature of human or other intervention. Plant and animal tissues such as fiber, meat, silk and wool are of this type.

Some animals may actually become extinct because of their popularity as food. But use of a resource is not necessarily direct; soil formation, for instance, may be impaired by strip mining. Nor is continuous flow a guarantee of plenty. Water is a continuously regenerated flow resource as far as the whole earth is concerned, but local supplies can be exhausted. Groundwater has flow characteristics as long as it is withdrawn at a rate lower than its rate of renewal. A higher withdrawal rate, however, will empty the aquifer, which will then be in danger of collapse or ruin from salt-water intrusion. Such a loss is probably irreversible on the economic time scale.

An important concept often used in connection with flow resources is that of the **critical zone**, or range of rates below which a decrease in flow cannot be reversed with existing technology. Critical zones exist for groundwater, wildlife, plant and animal breeding stock, aesthetic values, and many other flow resources. Even where reversal is technically possible, society may consider the cost in money too high. This is now true, for instance, of certain threatened species of wildlife. Theoretically, there are flow resources in which human action affects future rates of flow but for which there are no critical zones. Cloud seeding, for example, may generate flow that does not affect future flow, although this is not positively established. *Exercise of human ability to manipulate the environment seems to be approaching a level that will leave no flow resources except those vulnerable to interference and subject to critical zones.*

SOCIAL RESOURCES

Such resources as knowledge, intelligence, and physical dexterity are obviously essential to society but do not fit as neatly into either the stock or the flow category as physical resources. Historical or cultural factors may cause them to fluctuate, and they may depreciate very rapidly during periods of social breakdown. Each individual can learn from his mistakes and go on to contribute to the common fund of knowledge. But this fund is not necessarily cumulative since it can be lost by misman- agement. Social resources are also subject to critical zones; they can be so mishandled as to make recovery impossible. Thus most of the books written by the Greeks and Romans have been lost completely, and many of the most important have survived by the merest chance. This was due primarily to social, not physical causes; for instance, there was a long period when hardly anyone in Western Europe could read classical Greek, so naturally copies of Greek manuscripts were rarely made or circulated, and Greek scientific achievements were forgotten.

USING RESOURCES FOR ECONOMIC ENDS

Whether or not the shrinking of our present resource base is a long-term threat to the economy (essay 12.1) knowledge of it has affected economic thought. One response has been an attempt to determine optimum rates of use for resources over given time periods. With the help of such rates it is possible to restrict use of a resource so as to utilize in each period the exact number of units that will provide maximum return without threatening more advantageous returns in later periods. In practice, however, use is generally governed by considerations of short-term economic gain. The following section deals briefly with some methods and concepts that have encouraged this shortsighted view, and suggests a number of changes in perspective.

Resource Discounting

The utilization of privately owned resources is often determined by *discounting,* a method by which future returns are discounted against the going inter- est rate. Use of a resource may be postponed or reduced if future returns appear likely to exceed any of the following: costs of maintenance (including overhead, taxes and insurance); future harvest costs; or the revenue that would be gained in the interval if the asset were sold and the money invested elsewhere. Rapid use yields immediate profit that can provide continuous income if, for example, it is put in the bank. In contrast, resources left on the land are taxed and sometimes require maintenance; they are a continuing cost. Discount theory treats resources in the same way as any capital goods that have value to be depreciated over time. But the discount rate usually favors rapid utilization and discourages conservation.

Discounting has been extended beyond the private sector to become a method for society to determine the allocation of public resources for present and fu- ture use. It involves the dual assumption that each succeeding generation will receive a smaller share of certain kinds of resource, but counts on technology to overcome shortages by substitution. It therefore modifies the Malthusian model of a growing population on a fixed resource base, and assumes a technology capable not only of replacing depleted resources but of maintaining per capita consumption levels. Both capabilities have yet to be demonstrated.

Benefit-Cost Analysis

Benefit-cost analysis has been the major official method of evaluation used in the management of public resources. Before the last quarter of the nineteenth century, management of U.S. public lands was simply a matter of getting them into private hands and onto the rax rolls as rapidly as possible. The first decades after forest and grazing reserves were set aside were spent delineating boundaries and determining control procedures. When population growth began to bring pressure against the reserves in the 1930s and 1940s, Washington officialdom, as Grant McConnell has related, issued a policy centering on the theme of "management for the greatest net public benefit."

Good intentions quickly became mired in the quicksands of bureaucratic fumbling and misplaced faith. The concept of multiple use (p. 285) was favorably received, but efforts to find a workable balance between uses were often disappointing. Terms such as "highest use" and "right-of-way for highest use" sounded good but were hard to interpret. A proposal for a specific highest use often appeared controversial to anyone but the sponsor. Inevitably, given the terms under which federal regulatory agencies had to operate, a bias developed favoring economic benefits to various elements such as towns dependent on logging. With increasing public concern for the management of lands held in trust for the people, the need began to be felt for a systematic, standardized method of determining the greatest benefit of a resource. Benefit-cost analysis gained acceptance near the end of the Great Depression as an aid to government decision making; it seemed to offer greater precision and more comprehensive factor input than had previously been possible. Some of the decisions that had been made earlier, perhaps too hastily or without sufficient information, were regretted, and it was hoped that detailed comparisons of probable returns and losses under alternative uses of a given resource would result in better choices.

Benefit-cost analysis follows a series of steps. First, the legal rights and technical feasibility of a project are determined. Several alternative development possibilities may be investigated, one or more of which will be chosen for detailed economic analysis. Sometimes the information can be summarized in balance sheet form (figure 12.1). Thus a hypothetical project costing a total of $5 million and providing benefits worth $8 million would have a $3 million net benefit and a benefit-cost ratio of 1.6 to 1. If, as is more usually the case, the cost is variable rather than fixed, the ratio is plotted on a curve (figure 12.2). Such analyses are presented at congressional appropriations hearings by resource agencies. If a project is tentatively funded at X (maximum benefit-cost ratio), agency spokesmen will muster convincing arguments for the economic advantages of Y (maximum net benefit). Agencies subject to so-called

Essay 12,1   The Energy Crisis

Historically, America has never had to worry about its energy reserves. Coal, oil, gas, wood, and water have always existed in more than ample quantities, and past warnings that they would one day begin to run short have always seemed implausible. Yet a sad fact of our time is that large scale and growing demands for energy in this century have severely strained our once limitless resource capacity. To believe the energy companies themselves, we are facing a crisis that could significantly affect business, industry, and the quality of domestic life within nine to twelve months. Shortages in fuel oil, gasoline and natural gas such as occurred during the winter of 1972–3 could reach serious and epidemic proportions.

Conservation forces do not disagree with this assessment. Available facts certainly suggest that domestic gas and petroleum reserves will be clearly inadequate by the 1980s (natural gas demand has already begun to exceed supply), that abundant power from nuclear fission will not be available for 10–15 years, and that conversion of raw coal, tar sands, and oil shale into necessary liquids and gas will fail to have any significant impact before 1990.

Where does this leave us?

Commercial interests, extrapolating on our current annual energy demand rate of 4.2% calculate that we will need to double our present level of energy production in 16 years, and so are crying loudly and relentlessly for higher rates and other incentives in order to finance construction of updated and larger processing facilities and promote increased spending in areas of research and exploration. Many conservationists, on the other hand, to not buy this solution. They point out that a massive increase in energy production,

rigid funding levels, which affect benefit-cost ratios, are likely to offer analyses of several alternative developments, counting on approval of the one showing the most impressive maximum net benefit.

Unfortunately for the public interest, benefit-cost analysis favors tangibles over intangibles. The economic values of a proposed dam, for instance, can be described in dollar terms, but not the beauty of the wild river the dam would destroy. Benefit-cost analysis also implies its own definition of the situation—a definition that may be unduly restrictive. The analysis of a prospective dam, for example, may list the recreational values of the future lake but not the recreational or other values of the land to be flooded. Four decades after the introduction of benefit-cost analysis, evidence of its misuse is not hard to uncover. Factual information about the benefits actually realized from completed projects is available for comparison with the original *even if it manages to keep pace with demand, will eventually fall prey to its own excesses. For example, they calculate that if we sustain our current electrical energy growth rate of 7%, we will—by the turn of the century—be discharging heat into the environment at a rate sufficient to raise the temperature of the entire water run-off of the U.S. by 30 degrees, just in cooling power plants. This same growth rate, if continued into the 21st century, would imply releasing energy equivalent to that of another sun over the U.S.*

The problem, argue conservationists, is not one of increased supply and demand, but one of control: national policies which would enable us to eventually stabilize our insatiable power requirements; to develop a broad spectrum of energy source options; to develop energy-efficient lifestyles, and to eventually achieve self-sufficiency in energy resource use.

But such goals raise complicated issues of large-scale impact on contemporary life styles. Will Americans suffer measures such as tax penalties on large families and power consuming appliances and separation from their one or two large and powerful family cars? And will they approve the extensive economic and social planning that will be required to live within the limits of our resources?

Neither businessmen nor conservationists disagree that we must pay some kind of a price in years to come for the security of warm homes, jobs and adequate transportation. But it remains to be decided whether that price will entail simply higher rates and increasingly extensive drilling and mining research plus an enormous expansion of facilities, or whether it will mean a concerted effort to regulate our basic style of life. (Based on "Surviving the Energy Crunch" by Jerome Weingart, Environmental Quality Magazine, *January 1973, p. 29)*

estimated benefits. The greatest discrepancies between estimate and result are to be found in multipurpose water facilities. Hubert Marshall has described how the Missouri Basin Survey Commission investigated a project built by the Army Corps of Engineers on the Missouri River. The original analysis prepared by the corps estimated benefits at $11,795,000 per year and gave the benefit-cost ratio as 1.9 to 1. Actual benefits, according to the commissions's 1953 report, were only $964,000 per year and the ratio therefore a negative one of .8 to 1. Possibly both evaluations were in error, but it does look as if benefit-cost analysis is too elastic to be a reliable measuring device.

Many resource agencies seem convinced that, whatever happens, money must be spent and resources must be developed. This attitude reflects the self-interest of the agency: without the development, employees would be laid off and the agency's power would decline. The undertaking of a benefit-cost analysis is

Benefits		Costs	
Primary or direct benefits	$ _____	Primary or direct costs	$ _____
Secondary or indirect benefits	$ _____	Secondary or indirect costs	$ _____
Total benefits	$ _____	Total costs	$ _____

Benefit-cost ratio $ _____

FIGURE 12.1.   Simplified calculation of benefit-cost ratio when costs are fixed.

generally regarded by the agency as a guarantee that development will occur. As a result, the option of not developing at all—which may be best in terms of conservation—is frequently overlooked, and the agency becomes, in George Laycock's telling phrase, one of the "diligent destroyers."

Investment Theory

What economists call investment theory is an efficient device for increasing profits from privately owned resources; it can generate prosperity for an individual or corporation during a brief period of history. However, this is a dangerously limited rationale for resource use in terms of the whole earth and the future of mankind. The same criticism applies to benefit-cost analysis, which has so often been used to justify agency pork barreling and empire building that it has become discredited. But even if it had been honestly used, with all intangibles excluded from numerical computation, it would have been unsatisfactory. Like investment theory, it is a purely economic yardstick. No mere economic method is capable of assessing the benefits of an ecological steady state or the aesthetic quality of open space. Indeed, economic interests should have only a minor role in determining the use of public resources that feature such values. Both discount theory and benefit-cost analysis are designed for use within the market economy. The most prominent and destructive characteristic they share with it is dedication to productivity and growth as ends in themselves. Economic growth may well be an even greater environmental problem than population growth. Certainly both cannot be sustained for long in a finite world. When shortages are compensated for by increasing energy input (p. 72), then the environmental cost of the goods produced is too high.

Conservation, as Anthony D. Scott has pointed out, is sometimes regarded by economists as a "particular form of investment." But this is very different from the preservation of ecological equilibrium. Conservation does of course include economic considerations. But it extends beyond them into sociology and even philosophy. Moral issues raised by conservationists—present consumption versus conservation for the fu-

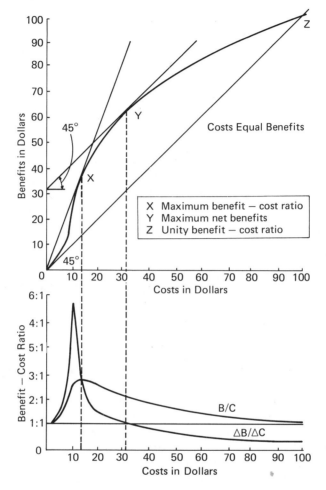

FIGURE 12.2.   Calculation of benefit-cost ratio when costs vary.
Developers rarely pursue a benefit "at all costs"; they are more
likely to ask what they can achieve within certain financial limits.
(reproduced by permission of Information Canada from *Resources
for Tomorrow—a Guide to Benefit-Cost Analysis,* Ottawa, the
Queen's Printer, 1962)

ture—are granted some theoretical validity but disregarded in practice. In effect, the
society's economic institutions behave as if moral considerations did not exist. The
only principles recognized are those of production and consumption—the more of both
the better. In view of this national reverence for economic growth, how could we have
expected our public resources to be anything but plundered? But it is time for us to
come to our senses.

Conservationists are often depicted by business interests as enemies of economic prosperity. But what sort of prosperity is it that allows common property such as water and air to deteriorate and national assets like Lake Erie to be damaged almost beyond reclamation? If these losses are made up and pollution stopped by federal law, it is the taxpayer who will have to foot the bill. Some 46 percent of all federal tax receipts come from individual income taxes; corporations supply only 18 percent, and some very prosperous corporations manage to pay no federal taxes at all. It should be clear that when big corporations talk of prosperity it is their own prosperity, not that of the general public, to which they are referring. The truth is that the profit motive knows nothing of social responsibility. It does not respond to situations or needs unless they promise economic gain. Detroit will not soon develop a nonpolluting vehicle on its own initiative. Oil companies that paid over $1 billion for Alaskan oil leases obviously anticipate continued rapid increase in fossil fuel consumption, and will not passively accept disappointment. It is useless to expect that a society dominated by such interests will ever clean up its environment without undergoing basic reorientation.

PUBLIC PROPERTY: EVERYONE'S AND NO ONE'S

The fate of public property as population has increased was prefigured by the **commons** of colonial times. The commons was the town pasture, owned by no one and used by everyone for grazing the family cow and her calf. A man determined to prosper could graze extra cattle on it; it was free and unrestricted, his books would show a good profit, and the burden of a few more animals on the pasture was negligible—or would have been if everyone had not reasoned the same way. The town population increased slowly but the pasture population grew rapidly. Since no one was responsible for pasture upkeep, the commons was overgrazed, trampled, and finally destroyed. Thus, in the long run, everyone lost.

Among the resources in which the public still retains rights are the ambient air, water, open space, and the seashore. Joseph L. Sax, from whose book this list is taken, points out that although *some* legal protection exists for all of these, legal precedents for protection of the public interest are almost nonexistent. Sax's subject is the United States, but his remarks apply with even more force at the international level. Every nation, as we saw in chapter 4, takes from the sea as much as it is able, and no nation has the authority to administer ocean usage. In the end all will lose.

The concept of public property is workable when population density is low. The earth and all its resources were commons in prehistoric times, but private property gradually extended its sway. Government, so often the servant of private property, added further restrictions. Today, many of these restrictions are accepted as a matter of course. This is not surprising: none of them were imposed any later than the nineteenth century. In order to preserve our remaining public resources new restrictions will have to be adopted fast.

A beginning has been made at the national level with the National Environmental Policy Act of 1969 (actually signed into law on January 1, 1970), which established a three-man Council on Environmental Quality to advise the president. President Nixon subsequently consolidated a number of existing programs, including federal control of water and air pollution, under a newly created Environmental Protection Agency (E.P.A.). Since the job of the council, as Joseph L. Sax has pointed out, is mainly to act as spokesman for the current administration, and since the E.P.A. (as far as one can tell from its record so far) is concerned more with advice than with regulation, it is hard to believe that any fundamentally new principles are being applied. At the international level, the much-heralded U.N. Conference on the Human Environment, held at Stockholm in June, 1972, produced numerous recommendations but hardly any action (the position of the U.S. delegation was notable for its timidity and conservatism).

TOWARD A RATIONAL ECONOMY

The connotations of the words "economy" and "economic," like those of the word "resource," have shifted strangely. Dictionaries list "thrift" and "frugality" as synonymous with economy, and yet in contemporary usage it is associated with a system of deliberate waste. What economics *should* be is the science of allocating resources, from development through distribution and consumption, in order to supply the material needs of a society. It is the responsibility of the economic system to produce and distribute physical goods in quantity and quality adequate for human health and comfort and to do all this with the least possible damage to the environment.

A rational economy, then, would serve social and ecological values rather than manipulating them to further its own growth. Society is more than the economic system, and must make the rules for it. Production and consumption must be recognized for what they are: necessary processes, but not ends in themselves. Conservational, ethical, aesthetic, spiritual, and interpersonal ideals not only afford greater satisfaction but have more survival value. Society is an aggregate of citizens . Since the latter are consumers, and are therefore indispensable to the present economic system, they possess the power to redirect that system by refusing to purchase superfluous or shoddy goods. Offending companies reform their practices with surprising speed if consumers boycott their products. Selective consumption can determine both what and how much shall be produced. It is the responsibility of every citizen to be a selective consumer.

Consumers' movements will achieve no lasting reform unless they are based on solid understanding of how the American economy really works. Ralph Nader has outlined six categories, which he calls "subeconomies," that cover most of the current abuses:

1. *The involuntary subeconomy.*   This is the money that is lost from

short-weighting, deceptive packaging, unnecessary auto repairs, and other common sales practices. According to Senator Philip Hart (D., Michigan) at least $8 billion are wasted annually on auto repairs alone.

2. *The transfer subeconomy.* These are costs passed on by an industry to the consumer, who has no choice but to pay them because he has no alternative source of service. The example given by Nader is pilferage in the freight industry: stoppng it would be more expensive than charging higher rates, which of course result in higher retail prices.

3. *The controlled market subeconomy.* Under this head Nader in- cludes most of the features generally associated with oligopoly, or control of a market by a few firms. Price fixing, resistance to innovation, dilution of quality, artificially created scarcities—these are only a few of the prac- tices by which oligopoly discriminates against the consumer. The fact that such practices are often illegal does not make them any less prevalent. According to Nader, the Federal Trade Commission has estimated that if the oligopolies were broken up, prices within the industries they control would fall by at least 25 percent.

4. *The corporate socialism subeconomy.* This is Nader's ironic name for the way in which corporations, especially large ones, are favored by the U.S. tax structure. For instance, according to Representative Charles A. Vanik (D., Ohio), in 1971 five corporations with profits totaling over $380 million paid no federal corporate income taxes at all. Similar loopholes exist at the local level, especially with regard to property taxes.

5. *The compulsory consumption subeconomy.* Environmental pol- lution—something we did not ask for, but have to suffer—can be regarded as a form of compulsory consumption. As we saw in chapter 7, the annual cost of air pollution has been officially estimated at $13.5 billion. Occupat- ional health hazards fall into the same economic category; thus there are over 80,000 miners presently suffering from black lung disease (the result of inhaling coal dust), and nearly as many widows of miners who have died from it. The question of who is to compensate these victims of ind- ustrial society has not yet been settled.

6. *The expendable subeconomy.* These are the people who, because they are poor, are excluded from the economic mainstream by being de- nied commercial credit, opportunities for investment, access to technical skills, and so on. It should never be forgotten that the poor in the United States represent a minority, although a substantial one. Accordingly, their interests are not adequately represented in the society's major institutions. This is not to say that no one makes money off the poor. On the contrary,

they are often forced to pay higher prices for the bare necessities of life. Some of these problems were touched on in chapter 10. Here, it need only be pointed out that, once again, the economic institutions are working contrary to the best interests of society by helping to perpetuate poverty, and then passing on the bill to the taxpayer in the form of growing welfare rolls.

Nader's criticisms, as he has taken care to point out, are made on behalf of traditional American values—values that are being subverted by the present corporate system. Much of the present situation, of course, is due to the system's failure to cope creatively with social and economic change. Clearly, if the system cannot adjust rapidly enough to changing social and environmental conditions it will have to be modified. Among the questions that should be continually asked of the economy are: Is it achieving a satisfactory relationship with the environment? Is it satisfying the physical needs of all citizens? Is it consistent with the greatest degree of individual liberty possible in a large population? Are there any promising alternatives that are being overlooked? Familiar ways of viewing and doing things, ways that have worked in the past, become ingrained social customs and ideals. The larger and more structured a society is, the more difficult change becomes. The United States will find it very hard to move away from the system to which it has adapted so completely. Indeed, the obstacles to change may appear overwhelming. History supplies many examples of societies that developed highly successful modes of organization but ultimately fell victim to their own rigidity and inertia.

Possibilities for Socioeconomic Change

Warren Johnson has compared the ever-growing economy to a speeding train that must accelerate by 4 percent each year. The increasing speed represents annual expansion. As population and per capita consumption grow, more jobs are created and high employment is maintained. Already, however, the train is going too fast for many would-be passengers—those most in need of jobs—to get aboard, while many riders are not enjoying the frantic trip and would like to slow down or get off. Some are wondering how much faster the train can go, how long it can stay on the track, and where it will find the increasing quantities of energy and materials it must have to keep running. A few are seeking ways to slow or at least stabilize its speed. Alas, it turns out that this formidable train is programmed for acceleration only. It has no built-in mechanism for safe deceleration. Interfering with its operation is an awesome responsibility because of its massive power: a crash would leave most of the nation's millions trapped in the wreckage. Yet it must be slowed.

There have been a few theoretical approaches to achieving a sane rate of economic growth, but no serious administrative attempts. The threat to profits is too great. Yet no problem is more urgent. An annual growth rate of 4 percent means that the United States must double its economic output every nineteen years. Yet it lacks both the technology and the legal machinery to deal with the by-products of such a growth level. Perhaps we need a kind of super Brookings Institution for the environment. But we also need great legislative and educational efforts, and a direct assault on present costing practices.

Easing the Transition

There may be a point beyond which the economy cannot continue to grow without producing all kinds of unintended consequences and side effects. It may even be that this point has already been reached. Many corporations have become too vast and too complex to be controlled by traditional methods; for instance, International Telephone and Telegraph Corporation, the nation's largest communications firm, also owns Levitt and Sons, one of the nation's largest home builders.

Government, like private industry, has a vested interest in economic growth. A change in GNP accounting would help in the transition to a comprehensive costing system. Kenneth Boulding has suggested breaking the GNP into categories distinguishing the portion derived from exhaustible stock resources from that derived from flow resources, and separating constructive from superfluous consumption, or "effluent." This would facilitate a more thorough evaluation of the economy's environmental impact. The extreme difficulty of formulating specific economic policies has much to do with the lack of consensus about social goals. Even terms as familiar as "quality environment" and "social development" are extremely subjective and debatable. Economic goals have at least the advantage of being clearly definable. Given our cultural bias in favor of measurable goals, we will simply have to find ways of quantifying more constructive values.

Ecological-Impact Costing

Formulating a system that accounts for both economic and ecological costs is often referred to as *internalizing the externalities.* The concept is very simple, the accounting highly complex. At present the cost input for prices set by a company on the commodities it sells is based upon the **internal costs** generated in the production and distribution of that commodity. **External costs,** as we saw in chapter 10, have been borne by the larger society. Naturally, such external costs as environmental pollution are not included in the competitive pricing used by the company in marketing its product, so in effect society subsidizes that product by bearing its external costs. In some cases, one type of industry may subsidize another type in the same way. For example, the "free" dumping of wastes from steel mills, paper mills, and chemical industries into Lake Erie has destroyed the product of the fishing industry in that region. Fishing, then, is subsidizing the waste disposal costs of the other concerns. Thus many commodities with high ecological impact are economically competititve only because the heavy external costs of their production are borne by everyone and the profits are retained by a few.

The theory of ecological-impact costing is that the price of the commodity should reflect as completely as possible not only the economic costs but also the ecological ones. Preferably, both sets of costs should be borne by the producer and reflected in his price structure. In some cases the ecological costs may have to be borne by government—that is, by the taxpayer. If the costs are not assigned economically they will be borne by society in some other way, generally in the form of pollution. Realization of this fact is bound to affect consumer behavior. Hopefully, commodities with high ecological impact will become less popular. This should have the initial effect of slowing growth in GNP. But improved technology should continually lower the ecological costs of consumer goods.

There are some signs that the larger corporations are beginning to invest money in antipollution research and other ecological projects. They are doing so, of course, not out of any strong regard for the public interest, but because they think the results will be profitable. For instance, in 1970 the Coca-Cola Company, mindful of the new federal clean-water standards, bought itself a water pollution control company for over $150 million. Often a company required to clean up its own pollution finds that it can save money by starting its own "environmental" division instead of buying pollution control equipment from other companies. One wonders, however, just how far such profit-motivated programs will be able to take us. Companies can be required to clean up their own pollution; they cannot be required to undertake radical technological innovations at the cost of their own financial viability. The only solution available under the present American system would appear to be a greatly increased program of environmental research by the federal government, which already devotes large sums to research in other fields (table 12.1). The example of federal transportation

TABLE 12.1. Federal obligations for research and development, 1960 and 1964–69[a] (millions of dollars)

Research Area	1960	... 1964	1965	1966	1967	1968	1969
Life sciences	511	1,045	1,167	1,301	1,451	1,537	1,501
Psychological sciences	38	95	103	100	108	98	103
Physical sciences	608	1,602	1,705	1,830	1,074	1,131	1,169
Environmental sciences	—[b]	—[b]	—[b]	—[b]	670	663	551
Mathematical sciences	25	93	105	123	130	119	116
Engineering sciences	690	1,450	1,576	1,677	1,555	1,569	1,499
Social sciences	35	102	127	166	189	195	220
Other sciences	33	77	70	74	95	51	80

Source: Adapted from *Statistical Abstract of the United States,* 1971 (92nd edition), table 802, p. 510.

[a]Funds actually spent in a given year may be less than those obligated.

[b]Included in "physical sciences."

research, reviewed in the previous chapter, has not so far been a particularly inspiring one. Far more to the point is the example of the space exploration program, which from 1967 to 1971 cost an average of nearly $4.3 billion per annum. If such a sum were devoted to the environmental sciences, the future might begin to look a little brighter.

REFERENCES

Boulding, Kenneth E., "Fun and Games with the Gross National Product—the Role of Misleading Indicators in Social Policy," in Harold W. Helfrich, Jr. (ed.), *The Environmental Crisis* (Yale University Press, 1970).

Branch, Ben, "The Economics of Reusable Bottles," *Wall Street Journal,* April 20, 1972.

Galbraith, John Kenneth, *The Affluent Society* (New York: Mentor, 1964).

Hannon, Bruce M., "Bottles, Cans, Energy," *Environment,* March, 1972, pp. 11–21.

Johnson, Warren A., "Economic Growth and Environmental Decay," unpublished paper, 1971.

Keynes, John Maynard, *The General Theory of Employment, Interest, and Money* (London: Macmillan, 1936).

Laycock, George, *The Diligent Destroyers* (New York: Ballantine, 1970).

Marshall, Hubert, "Rational Choice in Water Resources Planning," in *Water Resources and Economic Development of the West,* report no. 8, Conference Proceedings of the Western Agricultural Economics Research Council (Berkeley, 1960), pp. 1–18.

McConnell, Grant, "The Conservation Movement—Past and Present," *Western Political Quarterly,* vol. 7, 1954, pp. 463–468.

Nader, Ralph, "A Citizen's Guide to the American Economy," *New York Review of Books,* September 2, 1971, pp. 14–18.

Sax, Joseph L., *Defending the Environment: A Strategy for Citizen Action* (New York: Knopf, 1971).

Scott, Anthony D., *Natural Resources: The Economics of Conservation* (University of Toronto Press, 1955).

U.S. Department of Health, Education, and Welfare, *Toward a Social Report* (Washington, D.C.: U.S. Government Printing Office, 1969).

Zimmermann, Erich W., *World Resources and Industries,* revised edition (New York: Harper, 1951).

PART FIVE

A HUMAN ENVIRONMENT?

13 AESTHETICS AND OPEN SPACE

Economic growth, especially of the Western variety, has generally been accompanied by the concentration of population into cities and industrial areas. The commercial advantages of such concentration are, it seems, great enough to outweigh the often considerable disadvantages. In order to enjoy the supposed benefits of industrialization, people abandon the countryside by the million. They rarely go back, even if the benefits prove illusory.

Major unplanned shifts of population do not encourage consideration of aesthetic values. True, those who succeed in the mad scramble for wealth may appropriate objects of aesthetic evaluation for their own private use. Only later, when society has solidified in a new pattern, do they think of legitimizing their position as the new aristocracy by sharing some of these objects with the public. Meanwhile, a few thoughtful men begin to take the measure of what the public has lost. Cities breed social problems—and cities are crowded, ugly places. Could there be a connection? The issue has rarely been better expressed than in the words chosen by Albert Jay Nock to represent the thoughts of Thomas Jefferson: "Mean and hideous surroundings . . . have a debasing and dehumanizing effect upon the spirit. Cultivation of the instinct of beauty, therefore, is a primary practical concern not only of the moralist but of the statesman. . . . "

Jefferson believed that, just as everyone possessed the same faculty of reason, so everyone possessed some instinct for beauty and an equal capacity to benefit from its influence. Today, we are not so sure what beauty is; tastes differ so much, within as well as between cultures, that it seems impossible to define its nature once and for all. Nevertheless, there are certain very general aesthetic values that are almost universally approved. Thus most people, given the choice, prefer symmetry to asymmetry, regularity to irregularity, and the sense of spaciousness to the sense of being hemmed in. It is difficult to state concisely why streets free from utility poles and cables are more appealing than those so cluttered. When the cables are buried, however, real estate values go up. Much of what people mean when they speak of moving to a "better" neighborhood is that they hope it will *look* better. To them, of course, the preference seems financial rather than aesthetic. But it is a melancholy truth about our society that beauty costs more.

In urban areas, the kind of beauty that contributes most to the quality of everyday life depends on the availability of open space in the city—which is to say, on the world's most costly form of real estate. Yet other civilizations no less mercenary than ours have been able to provide it. Just as the center of every Roman gentleman's house was the open-air courtyard, or *atrium,* so the focal point of every Roman city was the public square. This fortunate heritage was bequeathed to Renaissance Italy. Some of it even found its way to such non-Mediterranean countries as Belgium and England. But despite Jefferson and his admirers, it seems not to have crossed the Atlantic. The nation's capital, one of the few coherently planned American cities, is a partial exception. But it has become two cities, one consisting of parks and the other of slums. Those who could afford it have fled the central cities because they were

FIGURE 13.1.   Cohasset, Massachusetts, settled in 1634, still preserves memories of a way of life centered on church and village green. (photo by John Earle)

starved of the one precious commodity that gives city life dignity and meaning: open space. Only small-town America, or the New England portion of it, recalls a way of life that centered on the church and the adjoining village green (figure 13.1).

DESIGN FOR LIVING

Planners and architects rightly complain that open space is an ambiguous concept. Nevertheless, they tend to agree that in an urban environment it is among the most precious of natural resources, and one that is too often wasted (figure 13.2).

The great name in open space planning is that of Sir Ebenezer Howard (1850–1928), who invented the concept of the garden city, a self-sufficient community of not more than 30,000 surrounded by a "green belt" of open country. Cities like this, Howard argued, would both remove the need for suburban sprawl and, as their name implied, be agreeable places to live in. Although two successful garden cities, Letchworth and Welwyn, were eventually founded in Britain under Howard's auspices, their example has had little influence in Britain or the United States (the so-called new towns movement is really too heterogeneous to be called Howard's brainchild). Most of today's planners have given up dreaming of utopia and are trying instead to make the best of the bad job to be found in existing cities. Thus according to the Housing

FIGURE 13.2. Vacant lot in Cambridge, Massachusetts. (photo by John Earle)

FIGURE 13.3.   Philadelphia: view from the steps of the Museum of Art. The home of American independence has a systematic open space policy. (photo by J.M.B. Edwards)

Act of 1961 open space is "any undeveloped or predominantly undeveloped land in an urban area which has a value as *(A)* park and recreational purpose, *(B)* conservation of land and other natural resources, or *(C)* historic or scenic." Other criteria established for open space typically include absence of man-made structures, the appearance of natural landscape, and relative freedom from vehicular traffic. The main point to note is that urban open space is not simply vacant space; rather, it has a function to perform. The same of course applies to rural open space and even to wilderness. But their functions, although vital, are not as critical in the short run, and do not affect such masses of people. In one of the rare contemporary efforts to construct a theory of open space, Ann Louise Strong has argued that maximization of variety is as ecologically desirable in a man-made as in a natural environment. One of the ways in which variety could be encouraged, she thinks, is by limiting both the size and population density of urban centers. Instead of scattered and haphazard plots of open space, major urban centers would contain systematically planned networks of open space built around the major routes. Some of these ideas have already been put into practice in Philadelphia (figure 13.3).

Psychological needs are rarely mentoned in the fight to preserve open space, yet to city dwellers they may well be the most significant. Three kinds of need are readily discernible: they can be labeled as the needs for *security, identity,* and *stimulation.*

Crowding and Noise Pollution

Higher animals of all types display **territoriality,** or the tendency to define and protect a certain territory as their own. One of the manifestations of this tendency is annoyance at certain levels of proximity. Human beings are conscious not only of the proximity of other humans but also of the closeness of artifacts, particularly structures, that restrict the impression of spaciousness. Other things being equal, a home with a view fetches a better price than a home without one. Yet who knows if the buyer is concerned with the view per se. Perhaps the basic need for man to escape the feeling of being dominated by other men is a more powerful factor. In any case, too much proximity causes stress, as anyone knows who has ever attempted to ride the New York subway during rush hour. Still more alarming than stress is the increased aggressiveness that has been experimentally induced in rats when they are crowded together. Individual behavior degenerates into pansexuality and sadism, while social hierarchies become unstable and territorial taboos are disregarded unless backed by force. The implications for man are only too obvious.

Christopher Alexander has attempted to translate these and other psychological implications into concrete recommendations for city planners. While admitting that his thinking is highly tentative, Alexander takes his stand on some of the most solidly based principles of modern psychology. For instance, since people tend to seek their own kind, a city should have a great variety of people. It has been estab-

FIGURE 13.4.   This lot in New York's Greenwich Village has become a neighborhood bowling alley. Area has low crime rate, thanks in part to high neighborhood solidarity. (photo by J.M.B. Edwards)

lished by experiment that people work better in small, self-regulating groups: the organization of work should therefore be highly decentralized (electronic communication makes this quite feasible). Older people suffer both mentally and physically from isolation—from which it follows that retirement communities should be diffused throughout the community and kept as small as possible. The net result would be a city consisting of numerous "residential islands" linked by freeways. More important than any detail of Alexander's plan is his general concept that cities should make human contact easier, not more difficult, and that each occupational and age group should be made to feel part of the whole by being provided with buildings and open space designed to fit its particular needs. This need not involve vast expense; even a vacant lot can become a valuable neighborhood institution (figure 13.4).

No amount of open space will relieve human tensions if it is polluted by noise. Sound levels in American communities have increased by an estimated decibel per year for the past three decades. A like increase over the next three could prove lethal in some areas. Mice die of external overheating if exposed to 175 decibels for one minute. People who live next to a major airport are being exposed to between 100 and 120 decibels every time a jet takes off (table 13.1). According to William Bronson, claims against industry for hearing loss exceed $2 billion a year.

Noise pollution has three major sources: industry, transportation, and residential activities. Industrial noise abatement can be sought through muffling of direct machine noise, careful placement and orientation of plants, and proper location of loading and offloading activities. Noise from industrial construction is more difficult to control but fortunately does not often last long. Noise from transportation poses quite different problems: for one thing, the source is continually changing position. For highway and air corridors the most effective method of reduction is distance. Design guides for highway noise reduction are available. But, as Louis S. Goodfriend has pointed out, they are often ignored by highway officials, who justify routing highways past schools and through quiet residential neighborhoods as the "price of progress." As for residential noise, before the advent of high fidelity amplifiers and acid rock music it was relatively easy to endure. Apartment dwellers have two courses open to them: either turn up one's own hi-fi, or install a noisy air conditioner. Homeowners may find that simply telling a neighbor to shut up is more effective than calling the police, but neither action is likely to increase neighborhood solidarity.

Fortunately, help is on the way: federal standards of noise emission, though limited in application, are now in force, and a number of states, such as New Jersey, have their own noise abatement programs. More builders are recognizing the need for soundproofing in home design, and more stereo headphones are being purchased. But the overall noise level, particularly from transportation, continues to increase. It is a threat to health and security comparable to any presented by crowding.

The Need for Open Space

The space requirements for security are minimal compared to those for identity and stimulation. Absence of noise and crowding are at best mere negative

TABLE 13.1.   Sound levels and human response

Sound Source	dB (A)*	Response Criteria
	150	
Carrier deck jet operation	140	
		Painfully loud
	130	Limit amplified speech
Jet takeoff (200 feet)	120	
Discotheque		
Auto horn (3 feet)		Maximum vocal effort
Riveting machine	110	
Jet takeoff (2000 feet)		
Shout (0.5 feet)	100	
N.Y. subway station		Very annoying
Heavy truck (50 feet)	90	Hearing damage (8 hours)
Pneumatic drill (50 feet)		
	80	Annoying
Freight train (50 feet)		
Freeway traffic (50 feet)	70	Telephone use difficult
		Intrusive
Air conditioning unit (20 feet)	60	
Light auto traffic (50 feet)		
	50	Quiet
Living room		
Bedroom	40	
Library		
Soft whisper (15 feet)	30	Very quiet
Broadcasting studio	20	
	10	Just audible
	0	Threshold of hearing

Source: U.S. Department of Transportation.

*Typical A—Weighted sound levels taken with a sound-level meter and expressed as decibels on the scale. The "A" scale approximates the frequency response of the human ear.

requirements. To require of urban architecture that it stimulate and provide a sense of identity is to call a civilization into being. A walk in Venice's Piazza San Marco is a civilizing experience; a walk in New York's Times Square is profoundly degrading. Both are the product of urban development, that is, of the conscious use of urban open space for a particular set of functions. Both, in their way, stimulate. But whereas the experience of the Piazza San Marco produces a heightened sense of identity with the community of Venice, the experience of Times Square produces little but self-alienation and disgust. How different the experience of the U.N. Building! Here, fourteen architects from as many nations succeeded in creating a structure that, both inside and out, was designed to provide each individual with an adequate but not overwhelming portion of open space. In both offices and council rooms, the individual was the unit on which all planning was based. One of the fourteen, U.S. architect Wallace K. Harrison, summed up the group's philosophy: "We built one seat at a time."

How does one plan for a civilized, life-enhancing urban environment? Basically, it is a matter of what one wishes to preserve. Almost too late, planners have come to see that open space, since it can rarely be recovered once lost, is the one resource that should shape and guide development. Curiously, New York was once the pioneer in this respect. Thanks to the genius of Frederick Law Olmsted (1822–1903)

FIGURE 13.5.   An agency of the New York Human Resources Administration supplied the portable pool in which these Lower East Side children are escaping the heat wave of July, 1972. Such amenities are lacking most of the year. (New York Times)

and Calvert Vaux (1824–95), Central Park, originally wasteland, became one of the most romantic landscapes ever set down in the center of a city. But there was no systematic effort to follow up this triumph, and New York today is a city where leisure facilities for children have to be provided on an emergency basis by the welfare department (figure 13.5). This tragedy holds yet another lesson for the planner: the only sort of planning that solves more problems than it creates is balanced development for the whole community. Nor is the community always the city: especially in the Northeast, it may be the entire greater metropolitan region. This region, as Jean Gottmann has pointed out, is still mainly farmland or woodland. If this land is properly zoned, for future as well as present use, the northeastern city dweller will be able to enjoy a variety of open space denied to previous generations. The danger is that, amid the conflict of local jurisdictions, the irresponsible private developer will win out.

Accordingly, if the functions of open space are expressed in pragmatic terms they are apt to line up as:

1. Resource protection.
2. Preservation of unique cultural and natural sites.
3. Health and well-being.
4. Public safety.
5. Transportation corridors.
6. Room for urban expansion.

The weight given to each of these functions must vary with each community, according to local needs and resources.

One use for which the available supply of open space is no longer sufficient is the single-family urban or suburban home (essay 13.1). Since the American dream of a house with its separate lot will die hard, builders will be kept busy thinking up plausible substitutes. Some of them are already on the market. All, whatever their attractions, imply greater population density and a less individualistic style of living. The extent to which people accept these new trends is not yet clear. Is it possible that the diseconomics of long-distance commuting will force them into higher density living? One suspects that, Americans being what they are, economics will not have the final say. Community decisions will have to be based upon social and psychic needs to command wide acceptance. In other words, rather than put up with pollution, congestion, and noise, people will move out. The community that does not value open space as one of its most precious resources will soon find that it is no community at all.

ECONOMIC USES OF OPEN SPACE

The rate at which we are losing urban open space in the United States is appalling. California, for instance, is now losing 70 square miles a year of which nearly

Essay 13.1.   Cluster Development: An Idea Whose Time Has Come

The American dream of owning a house on a large property in the sub-urbs is due for revision. The proportion of U.S. population living in urban areas will increase from the present 75 percent to 85 percent by the year 2000. Not only will land near cities become scarce, but its cost will soar beyond the means of the average person. Already developers find their houses are priced out of the market. Still, people want to enjoy the amenities of nature and a home of their own within commuting distance of a city. Is there an accep-table solution to this dilemma? The upcoming generation of homeowners may discover the answer in a new approach toward land use known as clus-ter development.

This approach combines intensive land use with preservation of open space. In a cluster development several houses are built on a relatively small portion of land, and the remaining area is reserved as open space for the use of all the residents. Some of the land can be altered for recreation (swimming pool, tennis courts, playgrounds) and the rest is left in its natural state; main-tenance costs are shared by the homeowners. Houses (or town houses, garden apartments, apartment towers) are built economically because of easier ser-vicing, fewer access roads, and so forth. The layout of the land determines the arrangement of buildings: hills, rock formations, trees, and streams are often featured as the focal point of a community rather than obliterated into lots. Although homes in many cluster developments are set close together, the design creates the feeling of spaciousness.

The idea behind cluster development is not really new—early towns were houses built around a commons. But the practice of sharing land seems to have receded into history around the 1920s when Americans began to dream of leaving the city for the suburbs and a house set as far apart from the neighbors as they could afford. Now heavy demands on the available supply of land call for a revision of values and intelligent planning to preserve the natural landscape and provide homes for people. Clearly cluster development must be an idea whose time has come.

25 are in the San Francisco Bay area. Alfred Heller, president of California Tomorrow, believes the state will need to spend $4 billion by 1984 to stem this tide. He sees this money as being appropriated for some 9.4 million acres of urban and near-urban open lands, all within a 40-mile radius of major urban centers. The California problem is not unique. The pressure on land in the Northeast is so great that rural areas such as back-state New Jersey are hard put to it to supply the recreational needs of the booming urban centers.

Common sense no less than experience suggests that the best way to pre-serve open space is to find an economic use for it. The most obvious of such uses is agriculture. The value of lands near cities combined with a heavy tax load dictates that they be intensively cultivated. Specialty crops, floriculture, and some fruits predominate (dairying, formerly important, has profited from better transportation methods to move farther out). The list of basic economic uses is long: it includes building materials, minerals, forests, watersheds and reservoirs. Recently, in some areas, the need for ground water recharge has been associated with open lands. The now famous Whittier Narrows Recreation Area of Los Angeles provides a valuable open space resource in the spreading grounds used to recharge ground water deposits. By contrast, Nassau County in New York has leased the air rights above one of its recharge areas. The buildings constructed there will have structural supports that elevate them above the basin to insure that recharge can be maintained. Since the money involved is negligible, one wonders what the county thinks it has to gain from this flouting of open space values.

Transportation corridors through open lands pose a special threat. The cost of rights-of-way through developed areas is so great that highway planners choose to build through vacant and open lands wherever possible. Such practices often result not only in loss of tax revenues but in destruction of open space values. Recreational activities, on the other hand, lend themselves admirably to this purpose. Neighborhood parks, scenic corridors, and open canyons usually pay for themselves through the greater tax base of the adjacent lands. Extra revenues can be derived from golf courses, camping, fishing, and boating. In the long run, open space is a good investment.

Preservation and Acquisition

It is always easier to maintain and preserve a resource than to acquire new supplies of it. With open space, however, there has been difficulty in establishing need, so that farsighted planners have been forced to rely on other arguments. Thus the preservation of the best open space has often been accomplished by tying it to other values such as the preservation of historical sites, natural vegetation communities, wildlife refuges, or even geological wonders. It seems unfortunate that planners have had to resort to such devious means, but the nature of a planner's job is such that he has great responsibility but little power. This is especially so in the Midwest, which was settled early and therefore contains few public lands. An interesting case in point occurred in Newark, Ohio, on the scenic Licking River. To the west and southwest of the city lay a group of large Indian mounds that were in need of preservation from real estate developers. Interested groups reasoned that if they could capitalize on the recreation potential of the site there was a chance not only of preserving the mounds but of providing open space as well (figure 13.6). Similarly, it is easier to obtain federal or state funds to hold open lands because they are subject to natural disaster than because they offer a breathtaking view or because the break in development provides a natural division between communities. Frequently, in state legislatures and city councils, the votes for retaining such "hazard lands" are equated with farsightedness, while retention of lands because they are open is often regarded as mismanagement.

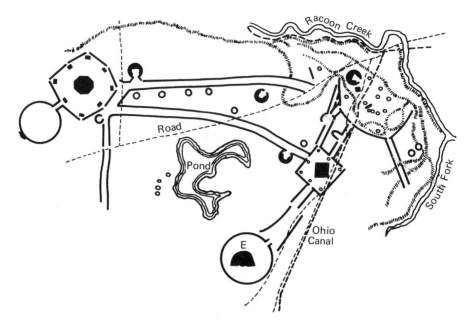

FIGURE 13.6.   Indian mounds in Newark, Ohio. Octagon group at left became site of golf course in 1907, while Great Circle Mound (*E*) was part of county fairgrounds. Such recreational use aided Ohio Historical Society in preserving area from real estate development. (Newark Chamber of Commerce)

Some states already provide tax exemptions for private owners who agree to retain certain classes of land in open condition. Most states provide for acquisition of open lands through purchase, lease, and gift. Still more significant, however, is the pioneer legislation in Pennsylvania according to which open lands can be acquired through **condemnation** backed up by a rotating fund. The condemnation purchase is for fee-simple title. Within two years of acquisition the land must be publicly offered for resale with the purchaser to receive a less-than-fee title guaranteeing open space retention and a lower tax assessment based upon the restriction. Among the obvious advantages of this arrangement is rotation of funds to help purchase other lands.

Tax policies that stimulate open retention are often supplemented by zoning regulations. However, these are easily circumvented by determined land speculators. Often the only alternative has been for the city or state to acquire the land, in which case cost determines how much land can be retained. This is of course an argument in favor of the Pennsylvania plan, since it has been found that less-than-fee ownership is less expensive and just as effective in preserving certain qualities. We are only now coming to realize the potential for resource conservation inherent in various types of landholding. Nor is expense the only problem: priorities are often equally difficult to resolve. How does one balance the need for wildlife lands against the need for flood control corridors? Many would vote unhesitatingly in favor of the latter. But

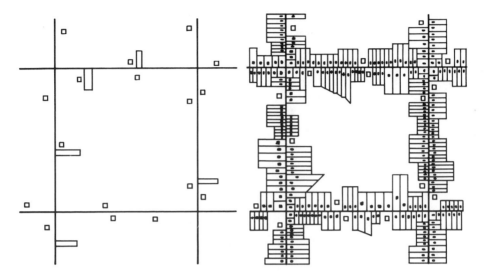

FIGURE 13.7.   A lightly developed rural area (left) may rapidly become an example of poor land use as farmers sell individual homesites along roads (right). Interior of square is of little use at latter stage. (example from the Tri County Regional Planning Commission, reproduced from Christopher Tunnard and Boris Pushkarev, *Man-Made America: Chaos or Control?* Yale, 1963, p. 81)

what if the floods present no danger to human life and occur only in areas with few people but a great many wild animals and birds? All too often the question is settled in favor of the small minority, generally not residents of the area, who stand to profit from additional public works. Unfortunately, wild animals have no vote.

The usual dilemma near large cities is how to control urban sprawl and maintain community identity within the larger metropolitan region without at the same time discouraging the kind of economic change and growth that the city needs. Chauncy Harris has described how urban sprawl can disrupt farming activities without at the same time creating a viable suburban community. This kind of unplanned invasion of the countryside by the city is likely to result in the worst of both worlds (figure 13.7). Legislative devices that give the rural landowner the option of whether or not to develop his land have proved to be costly failures. Far more effective is the concept, pioneered in Britain and Germany, of a "green belt" in which development above a certain density is simply not allowed. The example of Chicago is a heartening one in this respect. Today, Chicago has more natural lands within easy reach of its citizens than any other large city in the United States. This accomplishment required the combined efforts of county and city officials, but the real groundwork was laid over a twenty-year period by a group of public-spirited citizens led by Dwight H. Perkins. This group gained the support of newspapers and discussed the problems with public officials and businessmen. They even conducted guided tours of the proposed open lands in order to demonstrate their potential to Chicago's citizens. After two decades of official roadblocks and numerous difficulties of priorities and funding, the Forest Preserve District of Cook County, Illinois, was firmly established, a lasting monument to the efforts of conservationists. Today the open space values of the district are inestimable. It has helped to limit urban sprawl and make Cook County a far better urban area than it might otherwise have been. Of these efforts Frank Lloyd Wright once said: "No small-hearted city . . . could have established it or made the sacrifices necessary to maintain it."

It also happens very occasionally that affluent families or corporations relinquish valuable open lands to public control. However, the majority of urban open space now held in private hands is in the form of single-family homesites, and there is not much that individual homeowners can accomplish. Indeed, the little conscious thought on the subject that goes on at the individual level is more likely to be directed at blocking off open space in the name of privacy than at enlarging it for the sake of community needs. American building contractors, especially in the West, have recently been experimenting with so-called garden apartments and various condominium arrangements that concentrate housing space and leave the open areas in larger blocks. Some of these designs are attractive and have found acceptance (figure 13.8). But on the whole they are not aimed at households with children, for whom the single-family home remains the cherished ideal. As the price of land, construction materials, and labor goes up, many people who had once looked forward to owning their own home find they cannot afford one. Spurning the more collectivized world of the apartment and condominium, they find refuge in the budget-priced individualism of the trailer park. Serious

FIGURE 13.8.   Victor Gruen's design for the Whitney Estates, shown here, has been widely imitated, especially in the West and Southwest. Few of the imitators, however, can match Gruen's concern with open-space values. (Victor Gruen Foundation for Environmental Planning)

efforts have been made by the manufacturers of so-called mobile homes to upgrade both the quality of their product and the surroundings in which they are placed. But for the majority of mobile home dwellers it is too late. Trapped by the American dream, they have become part of that most American of all open space functions: the parking lot. A far more logical solution, where open space is in short supply, would be the underground home, since it not only preserves space above ground but is cheaper to operate and maintain. But it will be a long time before Americans become accustomed to the idea of living in holes in the ground.

OPEN SPACE MANAGEMENT

Under our present system, open space cannot be managed or even acquired unless there is at least some protection for the interests of three groups: private landholders, the general public, and the government. It is no secret that such protection is not always equally given. Landholders may not receive adequate warning of **eminent domain** proceedings or adequate time to contest the action. Public authorities have been known to abuse their powers of **condemnation**. Legislative hearings are often perfunctory or, which is worse, in secret. The interest that suffers most often is the public's.

Mere retention of open space has proven so difficult that the other aspects of management are often neglected. Once the land is held in public ownership what should be done with it? Is it covered by the city or regional plan? If so, is it being held open for public safety? Will it provide power line corridors or flood channels? Has it any cultural or historical value? Is recreation one of its major functions? The answers to these questions depend on many factors, including location, need, time, and costs. Multiple use is frequently desirable, but if conflicts arise priorities need to be established through the concerted decisions of planners and administrators. The final decision ought to be made by the planners, since theirs is the higher function. But in most American cities the political facts of life are otherwise.

A happy exception is reported by Richard Weinstein. Upon demolition of New York's famous Astor Hotel, the site—in the heart of the Broadway theater district—was expected to be filled by a high-rise office building. The Urban Design Group in the Department of City Planning, of which Weinstein was a member, wanted the new building to include a theater. They were opposed by the developers of the office building and by owners of theatrical real estate who feared new competition. Thanks to the support of Mayor John Lindsay, a theater enthusiast, and various leading producers, actors, and actresses, the New York Board of Estimate approved the change in zoning that made the new theater possible, and the project went through. As so often in American city politics, victory went to the side capable of mobilizing the broadest *inside* basis of support; public involvement was minimal.

Some aspects of open space management extend beyond the lands under

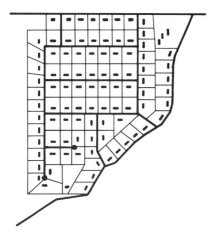

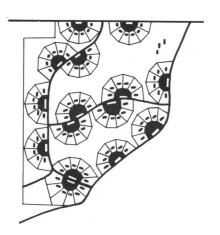

FIGURE 13.9.   Different subdivision
plans preserve different amounts of open
space. Each of these three plans has 94 lots,
but the cluster plan (bottom) uses nearly
half as much space for streets and utilities as
either of the remaining two. (design by
Myron X. Feld, planning engineer, from
the *American City* magazine, copyright
Buttenheim Publishing Corp., 1961)

direct public control. Zoning regulations affect virtually all privately held lands, and
the development of new public and private housing tracts is subject to a wide variety
of additional influences. It is quite possible for a progressive local authority to stimulate building placement in such a way as to retain significant open blocks within
housing areas. There is widespread agreement that the need to improve the spatial
qualities of residential areas is already critical. But pressure on open space is mounting
rapidly as we move from 63.3 million households in 1970 toward an anticipated 84.4
million in 1985. Under such conditions, open space values may simply be jettisoned.

One area in which improvement could be made at little or no extra cost in
design of highway corridors. The same open space, as Christopher Tunnard and Boris
Pushkarev have amply demonstrated, can be divided in many different ways, some of
which will preserve spatial and aesthetic values more than others. This is especially
true of street and subdivision patterns (figure 13.9). If there is extra cost, part of it can

often be paid by recreation. In the desert area of Palm Springs, California, the Coachella County Water Authority has located carefully tended golf courses within the storm channel corridor. This is only one of many multiple-use concepts that have already been successfully tried out. The starting point of all such schemes is the principle that open space is essential to civilized living. If resource conservation is to have any meaning, open space must be preserved even in the city.

REFERENCES

Alexander, Christopher, "Major Changes in Environmental Form Required by Social and Psychological Demands," in Walter McQuade (ed.), *Cities Fit to Live In* (New York: Macmillan, 1971).

Bronson, William, "Ear Pollution," *Cry California,* Fall 1967.

Goodfriend, Louis S., "Community Noise Problems—Origin and Control," in *Proceedings of Rutgers Noise Pollution Conference,* May 22, 1968.

Gottmann, Jean, *Megalopolis: The Urbanized Northeastern Seaboard of the United States* (M.I.T. Press, 1961).

Harris, Chauncy D., "The Pressure of Residential-Industrial Land Use, " in William L. Thomas, Jr. (ed.), *Man's Role in Changing the Face of the Earth,* vol. 2 (University of Chicago Press, 1956).

Harrison, Wallace K., "The United Nations Building in New York," in William A. Coles and Henry Hope Reed, Jr. (eds.). *Architecture in America: A Battle of Styles* (New York: Appleton-Century-Crofts, 1961).

Nock, Albert Jay, *Jefferson* (New York: Harcourt, Brace, 1926).

Strong, Ann Louise, "An Hypothesis for an Adequate Distribution of Open Space," in F. Fraser Darling and John P. Milton (eds.), *Future Environments of North America* (Garden City: Natural History Press, 1966).

Tunnard, Christopher, and Boris Pushkarev, *Man-Made America: Chaos or Control?* (Yale University Press, 1963).

Weinstein, Richard, "How New York's Zoning Was Changed to Induce the Construction of Legitimate Theaters," in Walter McQuade (ed.), *Cities Fit to Live In* (New York: Macmillan, 1971).

14 OUTDOOR RECREATION

Recreation, however defined, is becoming more and more an outdoor affair. Since activities such as hiking, pleasure driving, or sailing require far more space than any indoor form of relaxation or self-improvement, the pressure of population on recreational land has grown correspondingly. Here again the resources available will soon be exhausted by the demands being made on them.

THE DEMAND FOR OUTDOOR RECREATION

The increased demand for outdoor recreation in the United States is not just a result of population growth. Since 1910 the U.S. population has more than doubled, but annual visits to recreation areas, according to Marion Clawson and Jack L. Knetsch, have increased more than five times. Obviously, other factors are at work. Among them are the increasing affluence and leisure of the general population. The steady rise in family income has brought with it distinctive styles of recreation. But increasing affluence would not have had such an effect unless accompanied by upward social mobility. The United States is a highly status conscious society, in its leisure activities as in all else. Parents naturally want to give their children a variety of recreational experiences that they themselves never had. As a form of conspicuous consump-

288

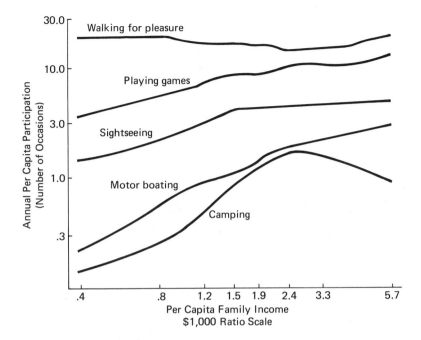

FIGURE 14.1.   Relationship between income level and preference for selected recreational activities; slope of line indicates how closely higher income is correlated with increased participation in an activity. (adapted from Outdoor Recreation Resources Review Commission, Report no. 19, Washington, D.C., O.R.R.R.C., 1962, pp. 67–60)

tion, this is much like higher education. Indeed, a large proportion of higher education, especially at private institutions, consists of acquiring the skills needed for the more exotic and expensive activities. Few upwardly mobile families can transmit such skills to their children; activities that were once traditional seaside or rural pastimes are now taught by professionals, while new types of equipment, such as that of the scuba diver, call new pastimes into being. Since there is money to be made from all this, the techniques of Madison Avenue are applied to selling the equipment and popularizing the activity. The result is an ever-widening circle of enthusiasts with an increasingly sophisticated repertoire of recreational activities and techniques.

Figure 14.1 shows the correlation of various types of leisure activity with family income level per capita. Both sightseeing and boating show a high correlation, as does camping up to a certain point (the very affluent, it seems, do not camp out). Correlations for such expensive activities as sailing and snow skiing, which are not shown here, tend to be much higher, though perhaps not as high as one might expect.

For most Americans, recreation is somewhat more commonplace; mass activities, such as driving or attendance at spectator sports, correspond to the secluded activities of the elite. The leisure time that makes this possible derives from the productivity of the American economic system. There are twenty hours less in the average work week than there were in 1900, plus more annual holidays and longer vacations. The shorter work week alone means over a thousand more hours of leisure a year for each adult in the labor force. There are also 22 million retired people, many of them in good health. A good share of this extra leisure is being spent in outdoor recreation. It is of course no accident that this trend began to accelerate with the introduction of mass-produced automobiles.

Another factor that should be mentioned is the amount of time devoted to "the great outdoors" by the mass media. Enthusiasm for outdoor recreation has been kindled and fanned by television coverage of sports, travel, and scenery. Newspaper and magazine coverage of these topics is also heavy; besides the frequent articles and advertisements in general-interest periodicals there are at least sixteen magazines with circulations over 100,000 that are dedicated to one outdoor recreational interest. Presumably the age structure of the U.S. population has also had some effect. Over 17 percent of all Americans are aged from fifteen to twenty-four. They are eager participants in outdoor activities, and most of them now have access to cars.

A final factor is the effect of urbanization. The more urbanized we become, the more we seem to cherish the thought of open space. Not long ago, however, the opportunity and often the necessity to be in the open was an everyday reality of American life. Access to outdoor recreation was not cherished as it is today, since it was to be had without effort. Indeed, our ancestors would have been amazed at our efforts to achieve it.

RECREATIONAL ACTIVITIES

Three simple activities—driving, walking, and playing outdoor games— dominate American outdoor recreation. The National Recreational Survey shows that nearly 58 percent of such recreation is devoted to these three (figure 14.2). It is significant that these are all simple pleasures, and can be provided quite easily.

Of the recreational activities that do take skill and expense, by far the most popular are water sports, including swimming, water skiing, and the many kinds of boating (table 14.1). Picnicking is also a favorite activity, but the meal itself takes little time; the balance of an outing is spent doing other things. In fact, the list of activities reflects a great deal of overlapping: the camper, for instance, is probably also a hiker and sightseer, and may ride, swim, hunt, and play games. Three broad groups of activities can be distinguished, though a given activity is easily switched from one category to another by special circumstances.

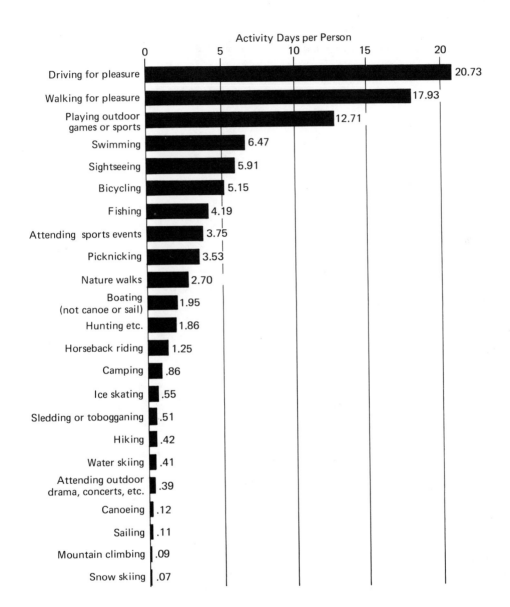

Activity Days per Person

Activity	Days
Driving for pleasure	20.73
Walking for pleasure	17.93
Playing outdoor games or sports	12.71
Swimming	6.47
Sightseeing	5.91
Bicycling	5.15
Fishing	4.19
Attending sports events	3.75
Picknicking	3.53
Nature walks	2.70
Boating (not canoe or sail)	1.95
Hunting etc.	1.86
Horseback riding	1.25
Camping	.86
Ice skating	.55
Sledding or tobogganing	.51
Hiking	.42
Water skiing	.41
Attending outdoor drama, concerts, etc.	.39
Canoeing	.12
Sailing	.11
Mountain climbing	.09
Snow skiing	.07

FIGURE 14.2. America's outdoor recreation habits: number of activity days per person 12 years and over, June 1, 1960–May 30, 1961. A small number of activities account for nearly all the time spent. (adapted from *Outdoor Recreation for America,* Washington, D.C., U.S. Government Printing Office, 1962, p. 34)

TABLE 14.1. U.S. participation in outdoor activities: summer 1965[a]

Activity	Participants (millions)	Avg. Days per Participant	Activity	Participants (millions)	Avg. Days per Participant
Picnicking	80.5	5.6	Attending concerts and plays	15.5	3.0
Driving for pleasure	77.7	12.1	Camping	14.1	6.9
Sightseeing	69.2	6.6	Ice skating	12.7	(NA)
Swimming	67.8	14.3	Horseback riding	11.3	6.8
Walking for pleasure	67.8	15.2	Hiking	9.9	5.1
Playing games and sports	53.7	17.3	Water skiing	8.5	6.6
Fishing	42.4	7.6	Bird watching	7.1	15.9
Attending sports events	42.4	5.8	Snow skiing	5.7	(NA)
Boating[1]	33.9	6.5	Canoeing	4.2	4.5
Bicycling	22.6	20.6	Sailing	4.2	6.2
Nature walks	19.8	5.9	Wildlife and bird photography	2.8	5.9
Sledding	18.4	(NA)	Mountain climbing	1.4	3.1
Hunting	17.0	(NA)			

Source: U.S. Bureau of Outdoor Recreation data, adapted from *Pocket Data Book U.S.A.*, 1969, p. 211.

[a] Except for hunting, sledding, ice skating, and snow skiing, which are for September 1964 through May 1965.

[b] Persons 12 years old and above.

FIGURE 14.3.   Boys playing in swimming hole at Pine Grove Mills, Pennsylvania
(population 950). Such simple country pleasures are fast vanishing from the American
scene. (U.S. Department of Agriculture)

Simple Recreation

The most popular forms of recreation are also the simplest. Varying degrees of skill or training may of course be exhibited. Examples are walking, jogging,
driving, cycling, swimming, tennis, golf, and picnicking. Most of the recreational types
in this group take up relatively little space in proportion to the amount of physical
activity they provide. The old-fashioned swimming hole, once the resort of every
country boy, is the rapidly vanishing prototype of such activities (figure 14.3).

Special-Interest Recreation

Definite skills are necessary for most special-interest activities, and participation in them is often preceded by systematic learning. Bird watching, hunting, fishing, camping, rock collecting, and all kinds of boating are typical special interests. Such
activities consume natural resources at a greater rate than the simpler forms of recreation, and therefore require even larger amounts of space if the resources in question
are not to be depleted. State or federal authorities may have to limit both the number
of recreationists and the amount of the resource consumed by them on each occasion.

FIGURE 14.4.   Climax recreation: river runners taking a break. Unfortunately the residues of civilization now line the banks of our wildest rivers as more people find the time and money for this form of recreation. Because respect for the environment is lacking even by climax recreationists, the Park Service is obliged to run a garbage scow through the Grand Canyon on a regular schedule during periods of heavy use. (photo courtesy of American Rivers Touring Association)

Climax Recreation

Climax forms of recreation are the most specialized of all. There is a difference of degree in the know-how and background required for climax as compared with special-interest activities, and in most instances the degree is great. Considerable danger may be involved, so that skill is as much a prerequisite as physical conditioning. For many people, taking part in a climax recreation is a once-in-a-lifetime experience. Ambitious forms of wilderness exploration such as river running and mountain climbing belong in this category (figure 14.4). Hunting, fishing, and scuba diving also qualify in their more challenging forms—trophy hunting, for example, or highly skilled fly fishing. Climax recreation usually involves longer periods of time and greater expense than other forms, and is even more prodigal of resources than special-interest activities.

Public Resource Management

Since the greatest overall demand of the public is for the simple recreational activities, it might seem at first that the bulk of the resources available should be used in this way. But there are qualifications. Often, part of the volume of simple recreation is incidental to a special-interest or climax activity. Simple recreation not only requires less space but can be accommodated through the widest range of resources. It is possible, and even preferable, that such facilities be placed around urban areas rather than concentrated in one place. But the space requirements for special-interest and climax recreation are greater and more exacting. The resulting problems of public resource management are considerable.

OUTDOOR RECREATION RESOURCES

Resources for recreation total more than 12 percent of all the land in the United States. They include forests, mountains, deserts, rivers, lakes, ocean shores, and city parks. All these resources can be used in various ways, some mutually exclusive and some complementary. The use actually chosen in each case depends on a wide variety of public and private factors.

The National Park System

The National Park Service has a tradition of recreational land use. But this tradition has not always corresponded to public needs. In the original act of 1916 the service was instructed to "conserve the scenery and the natural and historic objects and the wild life therein and to provide for the enjoyment of the same in such manner and by such means as will leave them unimpaired for the enjoyment of future generations." Both conservation *and* public enjoyment—herein lies the core of the dilemma. The national park system occupies only 9 percent of our recreation lands. As of 1971, its 23 categories were dominated by 35 national parks with 14.5 million acres, 85 national monuments with 10.2 million acres, and 13 national recreation areas with 3.8 million acres. A fourth category, national seashores, was represented by a mere 355,000 acres—a national disgrace, considering the extent of the area that needs to be preserved. The pressure upon national seashores such as Point Reyes and Cape Hatteras may soon be commensurate with that found in the Great Smoky Mountains National Park, where more than ten million visitors crowd into 500,000 acres each year. Nowhere in the United States has the cultural heritage of an area been more carefully preserved—and nowhere, as Edward Abbey has pointed out, is it more eagerly trampled underfoot.

The situation in the Smokies is not unique. In 1950 the total park system had only 33 million visits; by 1968 it had 150 million. In 1962 only six parks had annual visits exceeding 1 million. The next year 12 parks had achieved this dubious honor. Air pollution in Yosemite and traffic jams in Yellowstone—such have been the marks of progress. Obviously, the main question about a national park system is whether we can have our cake and eat it too. Park administrations fret over deterioration even as they spend more funds for wider access roads, luxurious campgrounds, and more entertainment. Between 1951 and 1960 nearly $1.2 billion were spent on recreation by the federal government. Some $570 million went to development and construction, but only $60 million for land acquisition. Moreover, funds allocated for acquisition of more seashores and parks go unspent. In 1960, $74 million were expended from the $116 million available to national parks; in 1968 it was $126 out of $183 million. Meanwhile, land prices soar and seashores fall to developers.

Faster roads and more accessible camps to accommodate more people result in a hurried, ever more destructive recreational experience. Perhaps what is needed is a reexamination of basic objectives. The great parks are at the center of the problem. Here, the carnival atmosphere of park camps and activities engender anything but a respect for nature. This is not to argue that all the national parks should be turned into wildernesses. Nor is there necessarily anything wrong with camping in or driving through a park. But there will have to be some form of limitation on these activities if the parks are not to be destroyed by those who come to admire them. There are signs that, in the matter of limitations, some of the park-using public is well ahead of the administrators. A 1968 poll, reported in the Christian Science Monitor, made quite clear that the public wants the national parks preserved even if it involves some personal sacrifice. The public appears ready to give up unlimited access even to the point of drastically limiting the length of park stay and instituting additional fees. Most surprising of all, there was considerable willingness to accept an outright ban on automobiles where necessary and, in cases where autos could be allowed, to keep the existing roads with their speed limit of 35 miles an hour.

Many people feel that, in addition to increased restrictions, there will have to be systematic education for park use. Some users have gone as far as suggesting a required test for campers and backpackers to determine their knowledge of how to use a park without despoiling it. There is also significant opposition to the organized entertainment, ranging from fire falls to rock bands, that some park administrators see fit to provide. It is surely time for the National Park Service to realize that the experience of nature should be enough. Such a course, as Noel D. Eichhorn has argued, would represent not a fundamental change in policy but a reorientation that would preserve the national parks' unique qualities.

Other Federal Recreation Lands

The conversion of large chunks of the once great public domain into federal lands has mainly involved two agencies, the Forest Service and the Bureau of Land Management. Until very recently the Forest Service has been mainly concerned with exploiting timber resources. During the administration of Theodore Roosevelt (1901–09) some effort was made to turn forest rangers into guardians of various resources often only remotely connected with timber. The administrators, however, continued to be largely concerned with the exploitation of timber, and tended to treat recreation as an annoying distraction, forced upon them by interfering amateurs. But continued use of the forests for recreational purposes seems to have wrought a change

FIGURE 14.5. Skiers in Flathead National Forest, Montana; so-called snow ghosts in background are trees covered with snow. Under multiple-use policy more national forests are beginning to provide this type of recreation. (U.S. Department of Agriculture)

in official attitudes. "National Forest, land of many uses," the slogan so proudly displayed in forests today, is a monument to public pressure, not professional concern.

The wonder is that the national forests escaped recreational use for so long. With 226 million acres, eight times the area of the national parks, and with fewer limitations on hunting and vehicular traffic but greater accessibility, they offer scope for recreation lasting anything from a few hours to several weeks (figure 14.5). Visitor days of recreational use increased from 6.9 million in 1930 to 172.6 million in 1970. Bowing to this demand, forest supervisors have hired more recreational advisers, game and fish experts, and even landscape architects. They will be needed. The scenery of a typical forest may be less spectacular than, say that of the Teton Range. But, with the exception of sightseeing, the opportunities for purely outdoor forms of recreation are infinitely greater than on other federal lands.

Of even more recent discovery, as far as the public is concerned, are the lands administered by the Bureau of Land Management. These comprise a catchall category into which were tossed lands too poor to give away. Examples are the basin and desert scrub lands of the West and Southwest. Until about ten years ago, they were thought to be utterly useless: with average annual rainfall ranging from 1 to 15 inches and summer temperatures of 100°F. and above, they were hardly ever visited. It is only the increase of affluence, particularly in the form of trail bikes and four-wheel-drive vehicles, that has brought pressure on these lands (figure 14.6).

Increased access to federal forest and scrub lands has done little if anything to ease the burden upon the national parks. Hopefully, the passage of the 1964 Wilderness Act has initiated a new era in the management of federal lands. But will proper use be made of this opportunity? If present behavior is any criterion, the prospects are not good. Even in primitive and nearly inaccessible areas the American public gobbles down its pleasure as if speed of use were the ultimate value. Education can

FIGURE 14.6.   Motorcycle race on southern California scrub land. Such races often cross miles of open desert and do much harm to wildlife, vegetation, and archeological relics. (U.S. Bureau of Land Management)

achieve something, but it is futile to expect such attitudes to change overnight. Perhaps, as Tibor Scitovsky has claimed, simple enjoyment of life is still not a respectable activity in the United States. The spiritual value of nature contact is unknown to many today (essay 14.1).

State Parks

Many state parks are ideally located for weekend camping and other recreational trips of short duration. Well-developed campgrounds, easy access, and beautiful scenery make many of them as popular as the great national parks, for which they often provide an overflow function. State officials are less than happy over this development, but can do little about it.

One approach that does seem to offer some chance of success is to raise user fees. If fee rates are adjusted to individual parks, with the lowest rates for stays of less than a week and sharp increases thereafter, more people are likely to visit each park in the same period without increasing the strain on its resources. State parks on the whole appear to have more realistic fiscal policies. A comparison with national parks shows the state parks spending more than twice as much and serving nearly three

Essay 14.1   Nature: Resource for Man's Spirit

Desmond Morris, in his book The Human Zoo, *asks us at one point to juxtapose two scenes. The first is 400 square miles of completely virgin land inhabited by all manner of large and small animals. The only people on this land are 60 members of a small tribe. From the top of the tallest point in this geography, you—a member of this tribe—can look out over this enormous stretch of land and know that it belongs exclusively to you and your people. It is your ancestral hunting ground.*

Now, he says, picture that same piece of land, but in a completely civilized and developed state, inhabited by over 6 million human beings and their swarm of houses and machines. From atop the same vantage point as before, the city and its people stretch from horizon to horizon, as far as the eye can see.

Morris' point is that from an evolutionary standpoint, all this has happened in a mere instant of time. Man has evolved spectacularly from one civilization to the other. But at what price; Although man does exhibit many of the abnormalities associated with animals confined in unnatural conditions of captivity, in the main he seems to be able to survive. Remarkably few of our struggling super-tribesmen actually succumb to severe neuroses. In the end, the human species may prove flexible enough to have produced not only the solitary tribesman who lives in intimate contact with all aspects of the natural environment, but also the modern urban dweller who may live in completely artificial surroundings for months and years on end.

Contact with nature has always been credited with a certain therapeutic value, from the time of the ancient Greeks right up through the present day. How necessary is this contact? How practical is it in a society where access to open space must actually be rationed on occasion? How seriously can we ponder the implications of this statement by Henry David Thoreau?

I went to the woods because I wished to live deliberately, to front only the essential facts of life, and see if I could not learn what it has to teach, and now, when I came to die, discover that I had not lived.

times as many people in an area less than one-third as large (table 14.2). Since the national parks are supposed to preserve a national heritage as well as provide recreation, this distribution of use is probably about right. If anything, the state parks should be made even larger, to absorb demand even as the use of national parks is reduced. Unfortunately, state officials will probably not want to spend the money. In that case, the state parks will be overwhelmed and their environmental quality will suffer.

Local Parks

Most parts of the United States lack adequate municipal and county parks. During the early period of economic development industry and transportation got first choice of sites along streams and lakes. Today American cities are faced with a shortage of conveniently situated open land and water frontage, while the cost of obtaining central locations has become almost prohibitive. Nevertheless, new land has been acquired. Between 1950 and 1965 the acreage of municipal and county parks increased from 644,000 to over 1.5 million. But most of this growth was in peripheral areas, away from major cities, and there was actually a decline to 965,000 acres by 1970. Smaller cities thus had the advantage in access to new park lands. Indeed, many of the newer units have been combined municipal-county parks. This is not altogether a bad thing, since units of this kind are more amenable to regional planning. By 1960, some 24,700 of them had been established, involving over a million acres.

Can the municipal-county parks relieve the pressure on the great national parks and even the principal state parks? To some extent they probably can. But they should not be expected to do so. Although the municipal-county parks are presently the bright spot in a gloomy picture, they are no substitute for small, accessible neighborhood parks. And these, unhappily, are in short supply—unhappily, because the neighborhood park should be the foundation of any sane national recreational policy. If outdoor recreational facilities were available to everyone at the neighborhood level, there would be far less abuse of national and state parks. The national park experience should be something rare, even unique. The neighborhood facility, by contrast, should be close enough to be continually inviting. The juxtaposition of plants and man that it provides should develop into a long-term relationship without the frenzy of the annual exodus to large state or national parks in which as much scenery is absorbed in the shortest time possible. A neighborhood park has the potential to become part of an individual's intimate environment. The tragedy is that most Americans now living will never realize this.

Private Recreational Facilities

The link between affluence and recreational demand is nowhere more clearly illustrated than in the development of private recreational facilities. The most expensive outdoor activities are being developed in the private sector. There is a boom in ski resorts, hunting lodges, and fishing camps. Many towns depend on such attractions, and develop them to the full. They are therefore likely to have extremely seasonal incomes. Aspen, Colorado, is typical: oriented to winter sports, all its businesses, including services and professions, fluctuate with the ebb and flow of tourism. In Estes Park, only about a hundred miles away, the season is reversed. With the warm weather, a flood of visitors and summer residents arrive for the season's activities in nearby Rocky Mountain National Park and along the Continental Divide. The winter

TABLE 14.2.   Estimated public expenditures for outdoor
recreation: United States, selected years (millions of dollars)

Year	Federal	State and Local	Total
1951	70	483	553
1960	194	957	1,151
1967	327	1,291	1,618
1971	546	(NA)	(NA)

Source: *Statistical Abstract of the United States, Budget Brief for 1971,* and
Outdoor Recreation Resources Survey.

population of Estes Park is about 3,700 compared with 60,000 in summer. During the peak of the season it is visited by as many as 500,000 tourists a month.

Some lumber companies have opened their private lands to the public. They generally provide minimum facilities, but they do take some of the burden from public recreation lands. Private accommodations to suit every budget generally spring up near state and national parks. Both developments encourage the flow of people to recreation lands. Most destructive of all, however, is the increase in ownership of second homes devoted to recreation. Every year thousands of families move to their summer homes in the mountains, at the beach, or in the woods; a smaller number do the same in winter. Between 1960 and 1970 the number of such vacation homes doubled to reach a total of over 2 million—some 10 percent of the 1970 home market. Partly as a result of aggressive selling by real estate companies, the second home has replaced the luxury automobile as the most prestigious form of conspicuous consumption. In many areas, the result has been disastrous.

ECONOMICS OF RECREATION

Per capita spending for recreation has stayed at about 6 percent of disposable family income since before World War II. In 1950 the total amount was $11 billion, and in 1967 $31 billion. In any given year an estimated one-fifth to one-quarter of total recreation expenditure is devoted to outdoor recreation. This is about 1.4 percent of the national total for personal consumption expenditure. The scale of this consumption can be seen from the fact that in 1969 license fees for hunting and fishing alone exceeded $183 million. In 1965, $721 million were spent for guns and tackle, $655 million for boats and motors, and $257 million for general auxiliary equipment.

The number of participants has also increased rapidly, with corresponding outlays for transportation, lodging facilities, and equipment from yachts to golf balls. The sharpest rises have been in water sports. Although all this still represents only

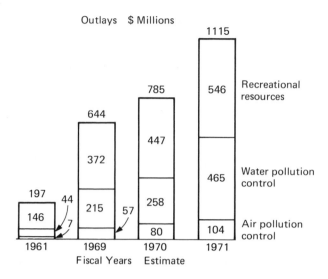

FIGURE 14.7.   Federal outlays on recreation have increased in response to demand, but less than 10 percent of this money goes for land acquisition. (*Budget Brief for 1971,* p. 23)

about 1.4 percent of total personal expenditure, it amounted to between $7 and $8 billion in 1967, as compared with $2.5 billion in 1950. Meanwhile, of course, the natural resources available for recreation have not increased. Since many of these resources are either not renewable or subject to deterioration, the very much greater amount being spent on them should serve as a danger signal.

Public expenditures for outdoor recreation have also increased. Federal, state, and local administrations more than doubled their outlays between 1951 and 1960. Federal expenditures on recreational resources increased more than threefold from 1961 to 1971 (figure 14.7). Part of this rapid growth represents an effort to build up facilities to meet the overwhelming demand. But heavy use has also increased the costs of operation and maintenance. In the rush to satisfy the momentary need, it seems that public planning has done little to provide for the future. Between 1950 and 1970 public expenditures on outdoor recreation were typically allotted as follows: 47 percent for operation and maintenance, 36 percent for development and construction, and only 7 percent for land acquisition.

Attitudes Toward Recreation

Public attitudes toward outdoor recreation are probably more varied than they appear. But the kind of attitude that seems most in evidence is nothing less than a national scandal. For most Americans the word "public" seems to denote "up for grabs." The word "use" does not, for them, imply sharing in common, or enjoying and

FIGURE 14.8.   Vandalism in Saguaro Cactus National Monument: the injuries to these giant cacti are man-made. (National Park Service, U.S. Department of the Interior)

preserving, but rather using up—exploiting and discarding (figure 14.8). In short, the philosophy seems to be that in public parks anyone can do anything, because "after all, I pay taxes." This attitude would not be tolerated on tax-supported highways, or in our neighborhoods. Why should it be acceptable in public recreation facilities? The choice before us is clear: either we impose restrictions on the use of our outdoor resources, or we have complete freedom and no place left outdoors to enjoy it.

Public indifference to the common good is too often reflected in the attitude of local government. Despite the clear need for small urban parks and larger intermediate recreation areas, most local governments are only too happy to let the great parks of the nation carry the recreational burden. This is only part of a general tendency for each level of government to hope that the next higher level will take the initiative—and bear the expense. Many local governments also consider federal and state ownership of recreational lands to be little more than inroads on their own tax bases. Such shortsighted attitudes overlook the capital gain to the community that each tourist represents. In this connection, the chairman of the Oregon Highway Commission has had this to say: "The development of your county's recreation potential is an important link in the total state program, for it is a well-known business fact that adjacent businesses attract customers for each other." He added that if each visitor stayed one extra day, the present Oregon tourist income would increase by $56 million. However, the publication of the National Association of Counties Research Foundation in which this remark occurs is dated 1964. Since then, Oregon authorities have had second thoughts about attracting so many visitors to their state, and have adopted the strictest wilderness regulations in the United States.

Some planners believe that changing tastes in recreation will cause grave problems for conservation planning. But this is doubtful. Given a free choice, people generally favor the simpler recreational activities. This should encourage recreation planners to avoid the trap of overdevelopment. They should also take warning from the example of Oregon that more is not necessarily better.

MANAGEMENT OF RECREATION

Outdoor recreation management, as we have seen, faces a single overriding problem: resources are insufficient to meet demand. It is the ultimate reason for most abuse of such resources by the public. Demand, of course, has been overstimulated without any corresponding increase in user education. But most damage in national parks results from overuse of facilities, and no amount of education can repair it unless the pressure is somehow relieved.

Management in the Big Parks

A typical response to increased demand is to intensify use of already crowded resources and to push for the acquisition of more space. Other things being equal, improved management can compensate for increased usage of a facility. But there is really very little room to maneuver in most cases, and the point is soon reached at which the only hope is to encourage less use. Quotas and reservations have already been instituted in some park systems; no doubt their use will increase. The next major step is bound to be an increase in entrance fees, perhaps differentiated by type and length of use. This would amount to recognition of the principle that the recreational use of state and national parks should by and large be paid for by the users. The primary advantage of this should be a reduction in visitors. But it may also have the secondary advantage of making the visitors more careful with what they pay for. Non-users, on the other hand, will not have to feel that their taxes are being used to finance someone else's activities. The proper application of those taxes is toward acquisition of new park land for generations yet unborn.

In sum, if our great parks are to survive, the National Park Service must seek to discourage simple recreation in favor of special-interest and climax recreation.

Those who argue that this would be an elitist use of public facilities should ask themselves if the national park system is any less valuable than, say, the Capitol or the White House, both of which would certainly be destroyed if visited indiscriminately by all comers. This does not rule out sightseeing or camping, and both can be made available at nominal cost. But even such activities as these should be undertaken in the spirit of one visiting a cathedral, not an amusement park.

Urban and periurban park lands, on the other hand, can be managed in a quite different spirit. For the most part, they were not set up to preserve original environments. Vegetation, landscaping, and facilities can therefore be modified to give maximum flexibility of use. This makes it easier to cushion the impact of use and allows heavier recreational traffic. Most city dwellers cannot usually go far in search of outdoor recreation. Effective park management therefore becomes a matter of providing as much recreation as possible considering the limitations of space and travel time. Such management here is primarily a service to the public, not an attempt to preserve irreplaceable natural resources.

Perhaps the biggest individual problem now facing park management is the shortage of water for recreational purposes. In most areas, crowding of lakes and waterways, especially by vacationers in power boats, has become a serious environmental hazard. Even the most complicated regulations seem to no avail. But when a boat is a symbol of affluence second only to a vacation home, the demand for water is hard to gainsay. Here, too, any substantial improvement will have to be preceded by a change in public attitudes.

In general, it seems that park managers, particularly at the national level, will have to undertake a program of deemphasizing their facilities. The only realistic alternative would be to admit quite frankly that those facilities cannot possibly meet the demands being placed on them. But it is the attitude of the public that is inadequate, not the facilities. Unless that attitude is changed, acquiring new recreation lands will provide at best only temporary relief.

THE FUTURE OF OUTDOOR RECREATION

Increasing pressure on the facilities for outdoor recreation has brought about a devaluation of the experience itself. The pressure comes directly from continued population growth, on the one hand, and increasing affluence and leisure, on the other. These trends will continue. As public facilities become ever more inadequate, those who are affluent enough will buy their own rural sites or join private recreational clubs. This in turn creates still more pressure on public facilities. We seem to be headed for a new form of medievalism: "royal preserves" for the rich, with the "common people" crowded into the least attractive spaces.

Perhaps the vogue for outdoor recreation will decline and people will turn to other forms of leisure. This, at any rate, would be a logical response to the deterio-

FIGURE 14.9.   They tried it—and liked it. Note intrepid look on face of owner of 1923 Chevrolet Truck Camper. Ownership of today's "motor homes" is a more harried affair. (General Motors, Chevrolet Division)

ration of outdoor facilities. There were hints of such a response in 1965 when, after national park attendance had reached a peak in the previous year, there was a decline of over six million visits; indeed, 1964 levels were not reached again until 1968. Vicarious entertainments like television may end up being the only ones our resources can support. Outdoor recreation, after all, still accounts for only a small proportion of the nation's leisure time—perhaps, as Marion Clawson estimated for 1960, as little as 3.5 percent. It is the highly seasonal nature of outdoor recreation away from home that places such a burden on the environment.

The root of the matter here is the interaction of suburbanization with the American life style. By mid-century 25 percent of all Americans lived in suburbia; twenty years later the proportion was already approaching 35 percent. With the great surge of suburban development following World War II it was anticipated that typical family recreation would come to focus on the backyard, each with its bit of open space and perhaps a swimming pool and a few trees and shrubs. As it turned out, the backyard became the focus only for leisure of short duration. Second homes, camping in the great parks, foreign travel—these and other activities away from the family parcel increased with the growth of suburbia. The taste of open space in suburbia seemed only to whet the appetite for ever larger morsels. Thus the American home became a launching platform for the larger world outside. The impact upon recreational resources was beyond anything anticipated (figure 14.9).

The same trend cannot be allowed to continue. We must of course go on acquiring new wildlands, water areas, and parks, while reducing private holdings in

FIGURE 14.10.   "I'm glad we got an early start! Imagine what it's going to be like when school lets out!" (National Newspaper Syndicate, cartoon by John Holm)

the parks we now have. But it is even more important that we seek better guarantees of preservation even if it requires great restriction on the use of existing national parks, national monuments, wilderness areas, and even state parks. There must also be an effort to supply much-needed simple recreation by acquiring some of the less scenic but still usable land near large cities, and by providing more neighborhood parks within walking distance. Limited camping should be available to all within less than an hour's driving time, and as many of the camp grounds as possible should be connected by hiking and bicycle trails.

But perhaps what we need most of all is an "unselling" of outdoor recreation in its present form. Cities and suburbs alike need more open space, and community members should mobilize to see that they get it. If in this way we can divert much of the impact from our great parks there is a good chance that the experience they can offer will not, as now, become progressively cheapened, but will offer the satisfaction of recreation in a completely natural environment. Meanwhile, those who are trying to calculate an optimum population size for the United States will have to take outdoor recreation into account. Long before demand for food-producing lands reaches a critical threshold, our supply of recreation lands will become a measure of our existence.

REFERENCES

Abbey, Edward, *Appalachian Wilderness: The Great Smoky Mountains,* with photographs by
        Eliot Porter (San Francisco: Sierra Club, 1971).

Christian Science Monitor, September 14–16, 1968.

Clawson, Marion, "How much Leisure, Now and in the Future?" in James C, Charlesworth (ed.),
        Leisure in America: Blessing or Curse? (Philadelphia: American Academy of Political
        and Social Science, 1964).

Clawson, Marion, and Jack L. Knetsch, *Economics of Outdoor Recreation* (Johns Hopkins Press,
        for Resources for the Future, 1966).

Eichhorn, Noel D., "The Special Role of National Parks," in F. Fraser Darling and John P. Milton
        (eds.), *Future Environments of North America* (Garden City: Natural History Press,
        1966).

National Association of Counties Research Foundation, *County Parks and Recreation: A Basis for
        Action* (Washington, D.C.: National Recreation Association, 1964).

Scitovsky, Tibor, article published in *Proceedings of American Economic Association* quoted
        in *Palo Alto Times,* June 7, 1972.

15 WILDERNESS AND WILDLIFE

Americans have long both loved and feared the wilderness. But they have not always been willing to grant that wilderness is a resource in its own right. However, just as open space has come to be a valued feature of the urban environment, so has wilderness become the most desirable form of rural openness. Now that man and his economic activities have made such an impress upon the land, there is something inspirational about territories that man has not subdued. From a scientific point of view, the wilderness is also a repository of ecosystems in their natural state.

Just as "wilderness" suggests a place where man rarely goes, so "wildlife" suggests a species from which he is excluded. This is poor biology but good sociology. When people speak of an area's wildlife they generally mean its larger vertebrates, especially the ones hunted for sport, profit, or protection of life and property. Man the hunter is simply another vertebrate predator, even if he does have weapons.

But, unlike the wildlife that he hunts, he is not a prisoner of habitat. Indeed, such is his capacity for social evolution that he can reshape almost any habitat to his own purposes. No longer menaced by wild animals, he is in a position to value them for their own sake. In so doing, he honors his own animal nature and recognizes that, in Aldo Leopold's words, he is only a member of a biotic team. Such an attitude is still far too rare, even among those professionally concerned with wildlife conservation. Here, we can do little more than demonstrate that both wilderness and wildlife are threatened. The extent of this possible loss cannot be shown in scientific terms, but is something for each reader to measure.

THE VALUES OF WILDERNESS

Most preliterate societies appear to have achieved accommodation with wild nature. Indeed, many seem to have meshed readily into the fabric of natural eco-systems, despite or perhaps even because of the difficulty and shortness of their lives. But the advent of agriculture and other civilizing arts brought increased separation from nature. Wilderness became synonymous with barrenness—desolate, hostile, and al-together uninviting.

In North America, members of the native cultures considered themselves part of the cosmic whole. The Zuni and Hopi, for instance, held numerous wild moun-tain peaks and forest springs sacred, and left votive offerings to evoke favor from the deities who they felt sure resided there. European conquest destroyed these beliefs along with so much else. Thus Nathaniel Morton, secretary of Plymouth colony in 1650, described this country as "a hideous and desolate wilderness, full of wilde beasts and wilde men . . . all things stand in appearance with a weather-beaten face, and the whole country, full of woods and thickets, represented a wild and savage hew."By mid-nineteenth century, however, the Romantic Movement in art and literature, with its "back to nature" and "noble savage" emphases, had worked significant change in American attitudes. The educated classes were more disposed toward contact with com-pelling nature. Wilderness for artists like Jasper Francis Cropsey had become incident more than vista, reflecting an acceptance of wild nature's intrinsic values.
But this affected only the educated and urbanized; contemporary American frontiers-men, for instance, still loathed the wilderness for its isolation and indifference to their needs. In 1831 the desire of Alexis de Toqueville to travel for pleasure in the forest wilderness of Michigan was considered absurd by the local settlers. He and his companion invented a tale of interest in land speculation in order to avoid local scorn over their interest in wild nature.

The first American sentiment favoring wilderness for its own sake was born out of mid-nineteenth-century transcendentalism. But this was a small movement, and its views were slow to gain acceptance even among the educated. In any case, there was little in the views of Henry David Thoreau or John Muir to inspire popular acceptance. Far more influential was the national myth of the ever-expanding frontier, with its naive assumption of unlimited resources and its appeal to American individualism and ambition. Only within living memory have attitudes substantially changed. In 1970 the Department of the Interior tabulated over 57 million visits to national parks and re-creation areas—a better than threefold increase in only twenty years. Use of national park facilities is already scheduled to be rationed, though only on a limited and experimental basis. In California, the U.S. Forest Service now requires visitors to its wilderness areas to obtain permits. All these people presumably value wild lands for their own sake. Perhaps they also share a sense that, once lost, the wilderness can never be reclaimed. Man can restore what he has despoiled, but he cannot create wilderness.

Wilderness means many things to many people—sometimes, many things to the same person. To the engineer, its main value may be as primary watershed protection. To the scientist, it is a reference system that cannot be duplicated. Conservationists may see it as the habitat of threatened species, plant or animal. All of these functions can be separated quite sharply from its purely recreational value. At the risk of some oversimplification, we can say that the human use of wilderness must include two aspects: scientific and psychological.

On the scientific side, account must be taken of the wilderness' function as ecological laboratory and genetic bank. Wild areas contain the only control samples that exist for research involving natural climax communities. Perhaps through such studies we can tap the knowledge needed for maintaining man-made climax communities without destroying the environment upon which they depend. Certain complicated interrelationships have already been discovered. For example, use of synthetic nitrogen fertilizers seems to have an enervating effect upon the nitrogen fixing bacteria (for which see chapter 3, p. 59). Such microorganisms seems more than willing to accept the gift of ready-made nitrogen compounds, abandoning their own efforts in the process. As the Green Revolution introduces commercial fertilizers to more and more of the world's crop land, the demand for synthetic nitrates may outrun our capacity to pro-

FIGURE 15.1. "A lovely and terrible wilderness . . . worn until its bones are exposed." Mount Whitney in the John Muir Wilderness, Inyo National Forest, California. This is the highest point (14,495 feet) in the United States that is accessible by trail. (U.S. Forest Service)

duce them. If, at this point, recourse is had to natural methods, it may well be found that the necessary bacteria no longer function properly in the nitrogen cycle. The only alternative might be to search the wilderness for nitrogen fixing bacteria that had not yet lost the use of their natural functions. Even if this particular example is somewhat farfetched, the type of situation that it involves is not. Preserving wilderness ecosystems is essential to our survival.

Recreation is not usually thought of in terms of survival, but the most enduring civilizations and cultures have generally been ones that know how to make good use of their leisure time. The ancient Greeks pursued athletics with religious intensity. Our own outdoor activities take on a new dimension when combined with a wilderness setting. William C. Gibson has gone so far as to call the existence of wilderness a psychiatric necessity. Even if we rarely visit the wilderness, there is a saving grace in just knowing it is there. In the words of Wallace Stegner:

> *It is a lovely and terrible wilderness, such a wilderness as Christ and the prophets went out into; harshly and beautifully colored, broken and worn until its bones are exposed, its great sky without a smudge of taint from technocracy, and in hidden corners and pockets under its cliffs the sudden poetry of springs. Save a piece of country like that intact, and it does not matter in the slightest that only a few people every year will go into it. That is precisely its value . . . they can simply contemplate the idea, take pleasure in the fact that such a timeless and uncontrolled part of earth is still there. . . . We simply need that wild country available to us, even if we never do more than drive to its edge and look in. For it can be a means of reassuring ourselves of our sanity as creatures, a part of the geography of hope.*

THE WILDERNESS SYSTEM

The administrative concept of protected wilderness in the United States was pioneered by men such as Aldo Leopold largely within the framework of the U.S. Forest Service. The first step came in 1924, when the chief of the Forest Service issued an executive order to establish the Gila Wilderness in New Mexico. Subsequent developments were highly sporadic. By the 1950s the Forest Service found itself managing a variety of wild lands under a variety of designations. The result was an uneasy truce between the forces of preservation, spearheaded by the Sierra Club, and the forces of exploitation. Finally, on September 3, 1964, after eight years of legislative hassel, wilderness preservation was established on a more secure foundation by the Wilderness Act. Although the act brought no sudden changes in the extent or administration of wild lands, it provided a framework of congressional assurance.

*For this purpose there is hereby established a National Wilderness
Preservation System to be composed of federally owned areas designated
by Congress as "wilderness" . . . in such a manner as will leave them
unimpared for future use and enjoyment as wilderness, and so as to
provide for the protection of these areas, the preservation of their
wilderness character, and for the gathering and dissemination of information regarding their use and enjoyment as wilderness; and no federal
lands shall be designated as "wilderness areas" except as provided for
in this Act or by a subsequent Act.*

The initial wilderness preservation system included only lands administered
by the U.S. Forest Service: 53 areas covering some 9.1 million acres. But it provided
that additional lands be studied for possible inclusion over a period of 10 years. It
should be noted, however, that the additional million or so acres added between 1964
and 1970 also came mainly from national forest lands. As of October 19, 1972, only
200,495 acres of the nearly 29 million under the National Park System had been
declared wilderness.

From wild lands legislative concern turned to wild waters. The passage in
1968 of the Wild and Scenic Rivers Act is as important a milestone as the Wilderness
Act. Initially, eight of America's remaining natural rivers were protected from dams
and other development. Within ten years, twenty-seven additional streams are to be
considered for possible addition to the system. Again, much of the concern is with the
preservation of natural ecosystems. Despite this legislation, wild rivers continue to be
threatened, especially by the U.S. Army Corps of Engineers and the Bureau of Reclamation. Pork barrel water projects threaten to dam every brook and rill in the nation
(figure 15.2). For the ten years beginning 1957, federal spending for civil projects of
the Army Corps of Engineers went up every year, finally reaching an annual level
more than double the average for the previous ten years. In 1970, the amount spent
by the U.S. government in this way was over $1.2 billion—more than it spent on basic
research in educational institutions. According to George Laycock, the opposition of
Governor Raymond P. Shafer of Pennsylvania to the Ohio canal plan, which would
have linked Lake Erie with the Ohio River, helped to save the U.S. taxpayer over a billion dollars. The plan, typical of many pork barrel projects, almost went through because those responsible for it exaggerated the possible benefits and underrated the
costs.

Until very recently, the arguments of conservationists against such projects were hardly ever taken into account. But the National Environmental Act of
1969 raised protecting—and reclaiming—the environment to the status of a major national goal. Any government agency, unless specifically exempted, is now legally obliged to show how its proposed actions will *not* damage the environment. One result is
that the Army Corps of Engineers is now cooperating with the National Wildlife Federation to work out a flood control plan for the Atchafalaya Basin, in Louisiana, that
will save one of the nation's last wild swamps from drying up. This has raised the
hopes of conservationists because nothing like it was possible before passage of the

FIGURE 15.2. George Fisher's biting cartoon is from 1965; unfortunately, it is not likely to go out of date soon, despite subsequent passage of National Environmental Policy Act. (*The Times,* North Little Rock, Arkansas)

1969 act, and the Atchafalaya had appeared to be doomed. But the corps is only one developer among thousands, and the general prospects for saving the wilderness are nearly as bad as before.

The Fragile Remnant

The total land area of the United States, 2.3 billion acres, was all wild country four centuries ago. Now only 2 percent of this remains in its primitive state. The status of protection for these lands is shown in figure 15.3. According to Stewart Brandburg, less than 20 percent of all publicly owned wilderness lands are now in the wilderness preservation system. Given the present legislative climate, it appears almost certain that we will rapidly and completely lose the more than 24 million acres shown on the left side of figure 15.3. One would have thought it safe to assume that the 10 million acres secured under the Wilderness Act would be relatively safe. Unfortunately, the legal framework for wilderness protection is still incomplete; U.S. mining laws, for instance, apply to all wilderness areas through 1983. The real fight for preservation, however, is now centered on the 14.7 million acres shown in enlargement. These lands were merely earmarked for study and possible inclusion if Congress so desires. The six additions since 1964 represent a somewhat less than encouraging record, since there are 140 units eligible for consideration and the review period is scheduled to end in 1974. As a result, plant and animal climax communities that took millennia to evolve have been and are going to be destroyed. We have nothing better to put in their place

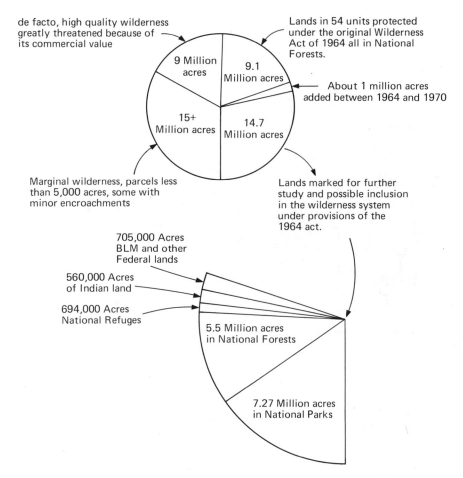

FIGURE 15.3.   Status of U.S. wild lands. Total represents only 2 percent of U.S. land surface. For other legislation affecting the future of these lands, see chapter 17.

than the rural and urban expressions of human technology, or exploited and ruined wastelands, or—at best— anthropogenic climax associations that spring from our pursuit of wealth. Not all anthropogenic climaxes are ugly or bad, but they no longer qualify as natural ecosystems. The tag ends of wilderness contain the only surviving natural climax communities.

Even where there has been no direct cultivation, construction, or other exploitation, signs of human technology are hard to avoid. Bottles and cans are discarded in the back country of the wilderness. Trail bikes and jeep tracks scar the most rugged terrain; fragile meadows show the wear of too many feet; ugly mudflats surround reservoirs built on rivers that should still be wild. The newest form of depredation is caused by sonic booms from jet aircraft, which loosen ancient geological forma-

FIGURE 15.4.   Alpine tundra fringe in Glacier Peak Wilderness, Washington;
Plummer Peak in background. The beauty of tundra, forest, and alpine topography,
in close association and relatively undisturbed in this view, belies the fact that this
area has been prospected for copper. The attendant scars of man's search for mineral
wealth show up in other parts of this wilderness, and like all other "protected" wild
lands it is subject to mineral exploration until 1983. (U.S. Forest Service)

tions. Not long ago in Mesa Verde National Park 66,000 tons of rock were dislodged
in this manner, destroying many prehistoric cliff dwellings in the process. Similar in-
cidents have destroyed delicate geological formations in Bryce Canyon National Park
and in Death Valley National Monument. The wilderness areas that remain unexploited
are mostly regions with topographic or climatic characteristics that originally made
them uninviting or hard to reach. They were considered poor economic investments,
and so have been able to survive as natural climax associations. A few such examples
will be dealt with here.

Alpine Tundra

The delicate vegetation climax of the alpine tundra is well adapted to the
high elevations in which it occurs (figure 15.4). But it cannot survive the mass intrusion of man. Grazing of domestic animals in the high meadows has done some damage,

as has accumulation of skiing litter when the snow melts. But the greatest threat is the sheer volume of summer recreation. The grazing and trampling of pack animals and the impact of extended campsite occupation are changing the balance of the plant communities. Grass cover is showing wear; many flowering species are disappearing, exotic weeds have come in, and the shoddy look of secondary succession (chapter 3, p. 50) is replacing the tundra's original aesthetic appeal. Native animals, particularly the large carnivores and the mountain sheep and goats, are getting scarcer each year. Thus although it is one of the most inaccessible of biotic communities, the remaining alpine tundra is endangered because of its fragility.

Desert

The most diversified plant community in the United States is the complex of desert vegetation, annual grasses, woody perennials, and spiny succulents found in the Southwest. The only climax association with a greater number of species is the tropical rainforest. The closest rival for variety within our borders is the Florida Everglades. Desert plants, no less than those of the alpine tundra, are delicately attuned to their environment, especially its climatic factors. They are therefore highly sensitive to the impact of civilization in the form of grazing and traffic. A desert climax association takes at least 200 years to mature; any serious damage it sustains will remain visible for that long as a scar on the desert floor.

The inhospitable climate of the desert, its lack of water, and its monotonous appearance to the casual observer all discouraged large-scale intrusion in the past. Recently, however, its charms have been "discovered" and popularized by real estate companies. It is also being invaded by swarms of recreation seekers and amateur explorers equipped with four-wheel-drive vehicles or motorcycles. But the responsible authorities have been slow to act. For instance, no part of the Sonoran desert region in Arizona was officially protected as wilderness until a few years ago. There are now two Sonoran preserves, Mazatzal Peak and Superstition Mountains (figure 15.5), but both are small. Representative Sonoran vegetation is constantly being modified by use. No wilderness units yet exist to protect Mojave Desert rock formations, and there are only two such units sheltering Great Basin plant associations—both even smaller than the Sonoran units. Fortunately, other types of preserves exist in both areas. But it seems likely they will only retard the process of destruction, not prevent it.

Tropical Marshlands

More accessible than either alpine tundra or desert are tropical marshlands. In consequence, they have been attacked from all sides with plow, saw, and match. The best remaining example is the Everglades. How long it will remain is anyone's

FIGURE 15.5.   Spring kingdom in Superstition Mountains Wilderness Area, one of two small nature preserves in the Sonoran desert region of Arizona. Plant in foreground is cholla cactus, other cacti are saguaro. (U.S. Forest Service)

guess. Over 40 percent of the Everglades has already been drained for development purposes, while nearly half is under the joint jurisdiction of state flood control authorities and the Army Corps of Engineers. The Everglades National Park occupies a mere 7 percent, and was established only after nineteen years of effort by a handful of dedicated people. Threats to the park in recent years have included drastic reductions in its water supply, in the name of flood control, and a plan to establish an international jet airport on private land just north of it. Both threats receded as a result of public outcry, but they may well recur.

The Big Thicket in Hardin County, Texas has been similarly ravaged. All that remains of this biologically superb formation is owned by five lumber companies; according to Orrin H. Bonney, they are clearing it at the rate of 50 acres a day. In this way it has been reduced to one-tenth of its original 3 million acres. Three bills to set up a Big Thicket National Park are now before Congress. Rep. Bob Eckhardt (D., Texas), sponsor of the most ambitious of the three, is trying to persuade his colleagues that only a single large park of 100,000 acres would save the area's ecology. But the lumber interests favor one of a mere 35,000 acres, broken up into numerous parcels—an ecological disaster.

Both the Everglades and Big Thicket have articulate defenders who may eventually be able to save at least a part of what is threatened. Many examples could be given of areas that are not so fortunate. The reason in every case is some form of commercial exploitation. As Havelock Ellis once remarked, the sun, moon, and stars would have disappeared long ago if they had happened to be within reach of predatory human hands.

PROBLEMS OF MANAGEMENT

Wilderness cannot survive too many visitors and retain its natural character; often it must simply be left alone. Even benevolent human interference in the form of fire protection has its negative aspects. Periodic fires were once part of the normal course of events in all areas. In forests this helped reduce underbrush and litter, while doing little damage to mature trees. The absence of periodic fires creates dense underbrush and natural litter, so that when fires do occur they destroy the mature trees as well.

Administrators are unwilling to leave the wilderness alone; they have to find a use for it. According to James P. Gilligan, from 1930 to the early 1960s the U.S. Forest Service opened one million acres of primitive land *per year* to development. The service now subscribes to a multiple-use policy. This may be suitable for some of the lands it administers, but not for the wilderness areas—indeed, "wilderness" and "use" are contradictory terms. Of the 15 million acres that await consideration for official protection by 1974 under the Wilderness Act, more than one-third are national forest lands. They are highly vulnerable to uses that could cause their ultimate exclusion before that time. Some uses are compatible with preservation: research and educational studies, for instance, make few demands on natural ecosystems. Acting as a watershed is a natural function of wilderness rather than a use. But recreation and commerce are not compatible with preservation. In the case of recreation, the damage done by admitting a certain number of people can be weighed against the recuperative power of natural communities. But commercial exploitation is in theory completely excluded.

Wilderness administrators are therefore in an ambiguous position. The existence of stronger legislation to protect wilderness lands depends largely on greater public awareness—which leads to an increase in the number of people who want to visit wildernesses. The presence of people in significant numbers, *whatever* they are doing, rapidly alters biotic communities, pollutes land and water, and generally modifies the entire primitive environment. Oregon has become the first state to establish really severe anti-pollution regulations for wilderness visitors: they may not make any sound louder than the wind, or be responsible for any visible air pollution or measurable water pollution. It remains to be seen, however, whether these standards can be enforced.

Conflicts frequently develop between preservation and recreational use. For example, developers acting with the concurrence of the Forest Service had for many years pushed to establish facilities in the San Gorgonio Wild Area of the San Bernardino National Forest, near Los Angeles. Fortunately, the combined efforts of the Bear Valley Water District and the National Parks Association enlisted the support of enough people to prevail against such development, at least for the time being. The Forest Service, noting the trend, now feigns neutrality or even support of the wilderness concept. But its record does not inspire confidence.

ZONING TECHNIQUES

Zoning is an obvious and frequently proposed method of deflecting use away from prime wilderness. One of the more elaborate systems has been proposed by Ezra Bowen, who believes that wildernesses should be zoned in concentric rings according to density of use. Thus the innermost ring would be for backpackers on extended trips, the outermost ring for those who needed regular resort facilities, and the middle rings for those able to undergo wilderness conditions, but with limited time to spare. At the very least, such a measure would eliminate the array of lodges, camp grounds, and access roads that crowd to the very edge of most areas presently designated as wilderness.

Could commercial uses be zoned as well? Obviously, extractive measures such as clear-cutting and strip mining would be unacceptable. Probably the only kind of exploitation allowed would be carefully supervised grazing and forestry activities. Such grazing would require that adequate water be available without modification of natural drainage and that ranges could maintain their natural composition. Controlled wood extraction would be more difficult but not impossible; the use of logging blimps and selective cutting could minimize the physical impact. In some cases it might be possible to use temporary access roads that would be blocked and reseeded as soon as the operation was complete. The concept of a buffer zone is relevant here. Access trails to the wilderness can be laid out across the most scenic part of the buffer, thereby retaining a wide unmodified corridor secure against extractive activities. A semi-wilderness buffer not unlike Ezra Bowen's scheme has been in use in Canada to protect the wilderness sections of Algonquin Provincial Park in Ontario. The policy has been to keep commercial recreation facilities on the park fringes and return most of the park to a natural condition. In effect the nature conservance areas are buffered by semiwilderness. The same policy is reflected in the Canadian national parks system, which provides for five zone classifications: primitive, wild river, nature reserves, natural environmental, and a catchall classification entitled heritage and recreation. In the United States, on the other hand, administrative acceptance of the semiwilderness concept has been poor. This is not surprising in view of the policy complications involved. The pressures against any such use by commercial interests, including both the recreation and the extractive industries, are probably too strong for any government agency to withstand without strong legislative support.

Rationing, already in force in California, is the most drastic management technique to be suggested here. It is also probably the best way to preserve primitive nature without completely excluding people. As visits increase, however, it raises complex questions of eligibility. Who may enter, how long may they stay, and how often may they return? There are no easy answers to these questions. Perhaps, as Homer Aschmann has argued, all our efforts to preserve wilderness are futile. But if we give up, we only play into the hands of the exploiters. David Brower, founder of Friends of the Earth, has summed it up: "The wilderness can't be won once and for all; it can only be lost once and for all."

ANIMAL EVOLUTION AND HUMAN DOMINANCE

In nature the evolution of biological communities leads ultimately to dynamic equilibrium: a climax ecosystem in which plants, animals, and the physical environment maintain a balanced relationship. Alteration of any variable changes the equilibrium and sets off a renewed drive toward another climax. In a relatively balanced ecology, evolutionary processes bring about dynamic changes, but over very long periods of time compared to the human lifespan. By contrast, the changes made by human technology are extremely rapid. Among the results of such changes are imbalances in wildlife populations; some species have become extinct, some are declining, and some are increasing.

The disappearance of some species and the appearance of others are natural evolutionary events. The relationship between developing and failing species is part of the slowly shifting ecological balance; vacated niches are filled by new species better equipped for survival. But the rise and spread of the human species has decreased the potential for evolutionary change. As a result of man's intervention, the variety of species is being reduced faster than new forms can evolve (figure 15.6).

Nonspecialized animals have great ability to adapt to change. An example is the opossum, which will eat almost anything. Opossums have survived in essentially their present form for one hundred million years; they were among the earliest mammals to appear, and have accommodated themselves repeatedly to changes of habitat.

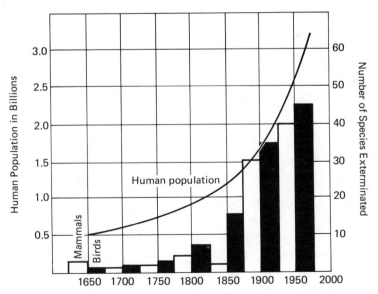

FIGURE 15.6.   As human population increases, so does number of extinct species of mammals (light bars) and birds (dark bars). Each pair of bars represents fifty years of this process. (adapted by permission from Vinzenz Ziswiler, *Extinct and Vanishing Animals,* New York, Springer-Verlag, 1967)

Like cockroaches, they fit easily into a commensal relationship with man, and will probably exist as long as man does not completely destroy the biosphere. Specialized animals, on the other hand, are often highly successful competitors because they have evolved a unique and sophisticated response to their environment. But environments change. When they do, overspecialized species are the first to die out. Saber-toothed tigers were well adapted to prey on large, thick-skinned herbivores such as mastodons. Near the close of the Pleistocene, overhunting by both tigers and men caused the extinction of these big creatures. The saber-toothed tigers vanished along with their prey; they were too specialized to be able to change. Specialized species are usually hardest hit by human encroachment. The outlook for the large predatory animals of the United States is not good; they can only withdraw into the remaining wilderness, and their numbers dwindle as the wilderness shrinks. Waterfowl, as Glen Sherwood has pointed out, are threatened not only by drought and by loss of their natural habitat through drainage, but by the indiscriminate killing that goes on even in the face of state and federal game regulations.

One might argue that, although man has crowded out some wild species, he has also created new ones through domestication. But these are few and highly specialized; dependent on human care, they do not begin to equal in number the natural species that have been lost. In recent decades, the number has been increasing at

FIGURE 15.7.   The wetlands in which these wild geese breed and raise their families are threatened by drainage, dumping, and chemical pollution. (Michigan Department of Natural Resources)

an accelerated pace. Extinct species of the better known mammals and birds alone add up to a depressing list. It must be repeated that human activities are not responsible for all cases of extinction and partial extinction. But they do account for most of the recent ones. All human societies affect wildlife to some degree, and fast-growing industrial societies like ours affect it drastically.

CHANGES IN WILDLIFE POPULATIONS

It is probable that more species have been lost in North America in the last century than in Europe in the last ten centuries. Part of the reason is that Europe was more populous at an earlier date than the United States, so that susceptible wild species were eliminated longer ago. But the rate of U.S. population growth has also been a powerful factor, as has the variety of the American people's activities. Some species have been destroyed by unrestrained hunting, others by pollution of their food supply. But the greatest disaster for animal life has been the steady removal of its habitat. All the buffalo hunters and pigeon fowlers combined have not had one-tenth as much impact on wild populations as this relentless eviction.

Biological Extinction

According to Ralph Shaw, vertebrate animals are now becoming extinct at the rate of one species every nine months, compared to a rate of one per 1,000 years before man came on the scene. Biological extinction has overtaken at least twenty species of large and well-known animals in the United States since 1776. Recent examples include the Arizona wapiti, last sighted in 1906; the Newfoundland wolf, 1910; the passenger pigeon, 1914; and the California grizzly bear, 1922.

Regional Extinction

The disappearance of a species from part of its range may result from human settlement; from environmental changes such as loss of food supply or cover; or from growth in the population of another species. Thus wild turkeys, once plentiful in the forested parts of the United States, have been hunted almost to extinction; the giant sable antelope, finest of all African antelopes, is being forced out of the grasslands on which it depends; and ground-nesting birds are endangered by sharp increases in the population of skunks, with their fondness for eggs. **Regional extinction** is a danger signal that should not be ignored; it is usually the prelude to **ecological extinction.**

Endangered Status and Ecological Extinction

Animals whose populations have decreased greatly or are shrinking very rapidly are said to be endangered. According to Bil Gilbert, eighty species in North America are considered endangered; fourteen of these are mammals, thirty-six are birds, six are reptiles or amphibians, and twenty-two are fish. Many endangered species are already ecologically extinct, which means that there are too few of them left to have a significant impact on the ecology of their habitats.

The American bison or buffalo is a classic example of ecological extinction. The huge herds, estimated at 60 million head, that once roamed the plains were methodically slaughtered by whites in order to deprive the Plains Indians of their livelihood. By the 1870s the few surviving animals were practically museum specimens. But from 969 animals in 1900 they have increased to some 30,000. Protected by law, they no longer face biological extinction, but their broad ranges are gone and they can no longer interact at will with a variety of natural environments. They are as dependent upon man as they would be in a zoo.

The Pacific salmon is not ecologically extinct, but it is perilously close to endangered status. Salmon have a four-year spawning cycle. In 1913, railroad building disrupted that cycle for the first time. The catch immediately began to drop; by 1928 only 90,000 cases of salmon were canned from the Fraser River run, as compared with 2.4 million cases in 1913. Yet it was not until 1937 that the U.S. and Canada signed a fishing treaty protecting salmon in the marine littorals as they returned to spawn—and by that time the damage had been done. It has been the same kind of story for most of the streams in the Northwest. The other giant spawning water, the Columbia River, was at low run in the summer of 1965. Even so, at least 80,000 chinook—the most important and most threatened species of salmon—should have moved up river to spawn in Idaho streams and so maintain the population. But there were only about 12,000. Fishery biologists found that major losses of fish eggs had resulted from erosion, as gravel beds were shifted. Most of the shifting was caused by the moving of logs on the river, yet this practice is not restricted either in British Columbia or in the U.S. Northwest. Investigation has shown that other ways of moving logs would be almost as economical for logging companies, but the inertia of vested interest resists change. Salmon have already been reduced by overfishing. If their spawning territory continues to be disturbed by logging, pollution, increased water temperatures, power dam construction, and other human interference, they will certainly become extinct in an ecological sense, if not in a biological one.

The dismal tale could be continued at length. Poachers have almost eliminated the American alligator for the price of its hide. In 1972 a Georgia grand jury brought a federal indictment against an alligator poacher who was doing a business of over $100,000 a year in alligator skins—nearly two years after killing alligators had become illegal under both state and federal law. Alligator skins, according to George Laycock, are worth $5 or more a foot, and as many as half a million American alligators may have been illegally killed for profit since 1968. Some of the skins have been shipped to Japan in boxes labeled "small scale crocodiles." Meanwhile the whooping

Essay 15.1.   Wildlife Poisoning: Control or Massacre?

"*The Division of Wildlife Services of the Department of the Interior is probably indirectly the greatest killer of certain endangered species which the Department is supposed to be protecting.*" *This surprising charge was made on December 14, 1971, by Senator Birch Bayh (D., Indiana) in testimony before a subcommittee of the Senate Appropriations Committee. In 1963, federal poisoning programs had caused the deaths of 90,000 coyotes, 300 mountain lions, 21,000 lynx and bobcats, and no fewer than 73,000 other animals. In addition to the mountain lions, members of endangered species killed in this way included California condors, Utah prairie dogs, and American bald eagles. During the previous five years, employees of the Division of Wildlife Services (D.W.S.) had baited the nation's public lands with 2.3 million pounds of poisoned meat and a similar amount of poisoned grain. Among the poisons used were Compound 1080 (a rodenticide), strychnine, and thallium sulfate. Quite apart from the fact that bait so widespread often poisoned species for which it was not intended, the majority of the animals for which it was intended were not actually preying on domestic livestock. On the contrary, as we have already seen (p. 62), upsetting natural predator-prey relationships—for instance, by killing the wild rodents fed on by coyotes—was more likely to work out to the livestock's disadvantage. All these facts had long been known to environmentalists; indeed, they were available in the famous 1964 report of the Leopold Committee. But it took another report by another, equally prestigious committee, to evoke government action. In 1971, the Council on Environmental Quality and the Department of the Interior together appointed an Advisory Committee on Predator Control headed by Stanley Cain (pp. 41, 61). The committee's report recommended that all federal poisoning of predators be discontinued immediately and that the poisons in question be banned. These recommendations were carried out in part on February 8, 1972, when President Nixon issued an executive order to discontinue the poisoning of predators on public lands or by federal employees anywhere. A month later, the Environmental Protection Agency either suspended or canceled the registration of several poisons used in predator control. Senator Bayh, however, claimed in August that the President's order contained too many loopholes (for instance, use of Compound 1080 had continued). Other conservationists were wondering if most state legislatures were either able or willing to replace wholesale poisoning with selective trapping. A crucial factor appeared to be whether the D.W.S. could upgrade most of its field agents to the level of wildlife biologists. (For additional information, see Report of the Advisory Committee on Predator Control, Washington, D.C., U.S. Government Printing Office, February, 1972.)*

crane is disappearing because trash dumps are crowding it out of its marshy nesting grounds. Four species of cutthroat trout are dying out from the effects of polluted water. Even the bald eagle, prototype of our national emblem, is endangered. It is failing to reproduce; the shells of its eggs are too soft, apparently the result of its primary diet of fish contaminated by pesticide. The bald eagle is now protected by federal law. But the law still encourages widespread poisoning in the name of so-called pest control (essay 15.1).

Recovering and Thriving Species

While some wild animal populations are declining others are growing. But they are the exceptions. In a few instances the danger has been recognized and the trend to extinction reversed. Thus the pronghorn antelope, which had been reduced to 30,000 head in 1922, was increased by careful management to 378,000 by 1955. They are now second only to deer as a big game species in the United States. Another recovering species is the wood duck. Many endangered species attract little public notice, but the plight of the wood duck, with its beautiful markings, aroused the concern even of people not ordinarily interested in wildlife. Its population is now growing again and, free from the pressure of hunters, it may succeed in adapting to the proximity of civilization. Unfortunately, species really close to oblivion, such as the whooping crane with 43 individuals, the California condor with 51, and the Everglade kite with 22, can seldom be expected to make a significant comeback. Even the little key deer of Florida, whose numbers have climbed from 32 in 1951 to more than 300, is scarcely a recovering species, although there is just a chance that its genetic pool may be diverse enough to permit survival in the wild state.

Opponents of conservation will sometimes argue that there is more wildlife today than ever before. In purely quantitative terms they may be right. But the variety and quality of species has declined. Conditions favor the survival of species that can adapt to what man has made of his environment. The outstanding examples of such species (if we except cockroaches) are rats and mice. Skunks, ground squirrels, raccoons, and oppossums have also done well. These hardy, venturesome, nonspecialized creatures turn human encroachment into an advantage: they multiply and prosper in places from which many of their natural predators must flee or be killed. The white-tailed deer has shown more adaptability than any other large mammal. There are now more than 15 million of the species in the United States, and they have moved into regions where they were unknown a few decades earlier. Thus they are filling ecological niches left open by less fortunate species, niches to which they can adapt more successfully than any other candidates. A larger cousin, the Jackson elk, is also doing well in localities previously occupied by other similar species.

Birds that feed at lower levels of the food chain, accumulating lesser quantities of biocides from their food supply, have been more successful at surviving than many mammals, reptiles, or fish. Ducks, which feed on aquatic plants rather than insects or fish, are also plentiful. So it is that we have 20 million ducks, but no passenger pigeons. White-tailed deer are easy to find, but even a poacher is hard pressed to bag a desert bighorn. Since the diversity of the organisms supported by an environment is one measure of its health, it is about time that we stopped considering ourselves immune to the same ecological laws as the rest of nature.

MAINTAINING HABITATS FOR WILDLIFE

To the competent biological researchers and administrators involved in wildlife protection there are few technical problems that cannot be cared for rather quickly and well. The reasons why one species thrives while another cannot compete are not usually difficult to understand. But corrective measures cost money, whether indirectly in the form of commercial opportunities foregone, or directly in the form of government protection programs. The American philosophy of land use favors intensive development, which is generally hostile to variety and quality of wildlife. Thus the greatest problem is the acquisition and maintenance of adequate wildlife habitats.

The steady loss of good habitat on private and public lands alike remains largely beyond the control of wildlife administrators. Cover removal destroys food sources, shelter, and breeding grounds, forcing wild creatures to withdraw. Many species likewise have been dispossessed by dredging, filling, and refuse dumping in tidelands and other wet habitats. Many areas not otherwise hostile become unacceptable to some species because of rising levels of pesticides and other pollutants. The shrinking of all habitats hits the already endangered animals hardest, especially such large and widely admired predators as the cougar, Mexican grizzly, bald eagle, and American alligator.

Loss of environment is, unfortunately, a problem that we can expect to grow more serious. The increase and spread of the human population and its demand for outdoor recreation means further invasion of areas now sheltering wild creatures. Faced with such pressure it does not seem likely that wildlife management will be able to prevent increasing loss of quality and variety in the future.

The focus of wildlife protection is increasingly on habitat. Traditional state refuges have been largely opened to hunting. Fortunately, the National Wildlife Refuge System has enlarged itself to compensate for part of that loss. The national system has 297 separate units totaling 28.6 million acres. The first refuge, Pelican Island in Florida, was set aside in 1903. It was considered a general purpose refuge, but is primarily a haven for marine birds. From this small beginning, the system grew in diversity and sophistication as well as size. Some much larger units have been added, and these are more meaningful from an ecological point of view. The Arctic National Wildlife Range, for example, covers 89 million acres; it is a magnificent wilderness that protects a wide variety of Alaskan species in their natural associations. In contrast, Cedar Island Refuge in Oregon occupies only a few acres and has a single purpose: it protects a nesting area for blue herons. Small as it is, it is the largest heron nesting site in the Northwest. No one can visit it; boats are not permitted to approach its shores. It is a valuable miniwilderness.

These examples suggest the variety of provisions for wildlife protection under the present system. Ideally, such a system should have been established a hundred years ago, but at that time we were still enthusiastically butchering buffalo. Some of the survivors of that carnage are now sheltered by the refuge system; its very existence, however tardy, shows quite a change of attitude in one century.

The 1.2 percent of U.S. land in national refuges is really only a pittance considering how much wildlife protection is needed on other public and private lands that are not refuges, nor necessarily should be. Encouraging wildlife is not an American pastime; seldom does the U.S. farmer leave a hedgerow or wooded patch. Timber exploitation increasingly takes the form of clear-cutting, which devastates total habitats —cover, food supplies, and water resources, Little wonder that grizzlies give way to coyotes, or that quail and bobcat give way to such lesser commensal animals as skunks and other rodents. This loss of quality is a result of man's thoughtless domination.

The Use of Wildlife

From the point of view of ecological balance it would be ideal if man's numbers and impact were no greater than those of other high-level predators. In such a case wildlife communities could maintain themselves, and all human uses would be consistent with ecological equilibrium. This, alas, is only a dream. Human use of the environment runs counterproductive to the maintenance of wildlife habitats. The level of habitat maintenance and potential use of wildlife are directly dependent upon how much society is willing to pay, and on whether control is to be at the federal or local level. The question of level is usually controversial. Strict preservationists tend to favor federal control, feeling that it is less vulnerable to encroachment. Hunters traditionally favor more local control because it gives them greater access. Ultimately, however, all access is dependent upon maintenance. The most suitable level of control really depends upon the nature of each animal. For this it is necessary to have close cooperation between government at different levels, something that has not been too much in evidence in the past.

Balancing Disrupted Communities

As a simple biological agent man was just another predator. His hunting practices were absorbed by the total system and balance was maintained. But aggregate human intervention is another matter: natural balances are upset and natural predators eliminated. Attempts to maximize the numbers of certain species have often backfired as ranges were overgrazed and animals starved. Cyclic productivity has been impaired so that both animals and plant life have suffered, not to mention the soil.

A famous example is the Kaibab deer range in Arizona. In 1906 the

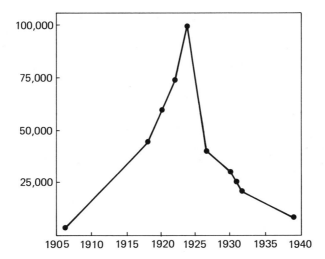

FIGURE 15.8.   Population curve of Kaibab Plateau deer
before and after destruction of predators. Between 1905 and 1915
some 600 cougars were killed; by 1925, all wolves had been ex-
terminated and 3,000 coyotes killed. (adapted by permission from
Vinzenz Ziswiler, *Extinct and Vanishing Animals,* New York,
Springer-Verlag, 1967)

Kaibab portion of the Grand Canyon Forest Reserve became the Grand Canyon National Game Reserve. Predator control programs eliminated the cougars, and the
perfectly balanced ecosystem of some 4,000 deer, which depended on surplus forage
production and was kept in balance by predation, fell apart. Deer increased at the
rate of about 20 percent a year, reaching a peak of 100,000 by 1918. The browse was
severly damaged and soils depleted so that starvation and disease cut the herd to
20,000 by 1930 (figure 15.8).

Today hunters take significant numbers of animals each hunting season,
thus in part crudely replacing the function of the top-level predators. Perhaps the
reintroduction of cougars would also be advisable to give a more finely tuned balance.
But in deference to the traditional fears of stockmen Arizona still maintains a bounty
on cougars. If man is careful there is no reason why finely tuned natural ecosystems
cannot sustain reasonable sport hunting, but he must take into account the other
pressures on a given species or habitat.

The variety, quality, and numbers of individuals in a community of wildlife are directly related to the condition of the habitat. In an unaltered ecosystem the
outside limits of population growth are controlled by the energy available through
photosynthesis, and by shelter and cover, water supply, and climate. Predators,
parasites, disease, and other forms of biological stress normally function as balancing
agents. But as man interacts with and controls wildlife communities he knowingly
or unknowingly alters habitat and stress factors, thereby reducing both the number
of species and the number remaining in each species.

There are various approaches to restoring balance in disrupted wildlife communities. The eventual result, however, tends to be the same: a degree of variety and quality somewhat below the stable optimum of an unaltered community. Man's interference has usually meant a declining growth curve for the large and well-known species. The best that man can achieve in the way of restoration is to control environmental stress at a level at which all species in the habitat can interact in an ecologically significant way—that is, at a level above ecological extinction. As people flock to the wilderness, and as our air and water become increasingly polluted, the prospects for attaining even this modest goal do not seem good. Indeed, it is only too likely that within 25 years 75 to 80 percent of all species of living animals will be extinct.

WHAT PRICE WILDLIFE?

The human species, having assumed stewardship of the earth and all its creatures, has an unconditional obligation to fulfill this responsibility with the greatest possible foresight and wisdom. But preserving wildlife may also be a matter of basic prudence. Wild animals are accurate barometers of any environment's livability. All species are, in the long run, threatened by incautious human manipulation of the earth, and the human species is no exception. Where wildlife survives, the air, water, and land are generally safe for people. Where wild species are thinning, we can often consider ourselves warned.

Some people may consider this an exaggeration. After all, human life is ultimately dependent upon photosynthesizing plants and certain invertebrate organisms such as bacteria. There is no firm evidence that man cannot survive at least without vertebrate wildlife. Simple biological survival, however, is a pitifully inadequate goal. Furthermore, as we have seen, ecological complexity can only increase our chances of survival.

If arguments addressed to the quality of life seem hopelessly idealistic in a profit oriented society, consider the money to be made from a well-managed wildlife system. According to the Bureau of Sport Fisheries and Wildlife, sportsmen spent $4 billion on hunting and fishing in 1965. For comparison, in the same year only $6.6 billion were spent for all the electricity used for household operation throughout the nation. Peter H. Pearse and Gary Bowden report that in 1964 a take of 14,000 animals in the east Kootenay region of British Columbia contributed more than $2 million to the economy, including $145,000 for licenses, $700,000 for transportation and lodging, and $350,000 for food and drink. Thus returns from the provision of habitats for game animals compare favorably with those from such other possible uses as grazing livestock, farming Christmas trees, or even cropping, and the initial investment is much less. Hunting wild animals is certainly preferable to poisoning them. But intelligent management of the nation's wildlife resources will cost money, and the U.S. Bureau of Sport Fisheries and Wildlife lacks funds either to increase or to upgrade its field personnel to the necessary level. State regulations, with very few exceptions, have proved inadequate. Here, then, is another area in which public opinion should be mobilized before it is too late.

REFERENCES

Aschmann, Homer, in *Yearbook of the Association of Pacific Coast Geographers,* Volume 28 (Oregon State University Press, 1966).

Bonney, Orrin H., "Big Thicket," *Sierra Club Bulletin,* May 1968, pp. 8–10.

Bowen, Ezra, interview on radio station KCBS, San Francisco, February 16, 1972.

Brandburg, Stewart, *New Challenges for Wilderness Conservation* (Washington, D.C.: Wilderness Society, 1968).

Frome, Michael, *The Forest Service* (New York: Praeger, 1971).

Gibson, William C., "Wilderness—a Psychiatric Necessity," in *Wilderness in a Changing World: Wilderness Conference Proceedings, 1965* (San Francisco: Sierra Club, 1966).

Gilbert, Bil, "A Look at Wildlife in America," *Saturday Evening Post,* September 9, 1967.

Gilligan, James P., "Our Wilderness Today," in *Tomorrow's Wilderness: Wilderness Conference Proceedings, 1963* (San Francisco: Sierra Clubs, 1963).

Laycock, George, *The Diligent Destroyers* (New York: Ballantine, 1970).

——, "The Gator Killers Never Stopped," *Audubon,* May 1972, pp. 104–106.

Leopold, Aldo, *Sand County Almanac* (New York: Oxford University Press, 1949).

Morton, Nathaniel, *New-England Memorial* (Boston: Boone, 1721).

Pearse, Peter H., and Gary Bowden, *Big Game Hunting in the East Kootenay* (University of British Columbia Press, 1966).

Ripley, S. Dillon in *Outdoor Recreation Action,* April 1970, p. 2.

Shaw, Ralph, personal communication, Kamloops, British Columbia, July 1967.

Sherwood, Glen, "If It's Big and Flies . . . Shoot It!" *Audubon,* November 1971, pp. 72–99.

Stegner, Wallace, quoted in Francois Leydt, *Time and the River Flowing* (San Francisco: Sierra Club 1964).

Tocqueville, Alexis de, *Journey to America,* tr. George Lawrence (Yale University Press, 1959).

PART SIX

ACHIEVING AN OPTIMUM

16 POPULATION LIMITATION

Any systematic program to limit human numbers bases itself on the idea that there is a range beyond which the ratio of population to resources should not be allowed to vary. However, attempts to specify this range have not so far been very successful. Scientists have not even decided whether the optimum population for a modern industrial state is necessarily static or, in other words, whether population growth as such is unacceptable in a finite world. But they do tend to agree that a stabilized population is far easier to plan for than any growing population. On the other hand, many national governments feel that there is strength in numbers, and that population control is not something they need to advocate at the present time. Perhaps the concept of optimum population is too subjective for the scientist to handle with comfort. Nevertheless, as with population projections, science can show that certain consequences follow from certain assumptions.

OPTIMUM POPULATION AND
ZERO POPULATION GROWTH

Demographers and other students of population have long been intrigued with the notion of *optimum population,* or the best population (in composition as well as size) for a given area. However, as Alfred Sauvy has pointed out, the *purpose* of this optimum needs to be specified; it really does not help to define the optimum as the "happy medium" between underpopulation and overpopulation. Moreover, discussions of the optimum tend to become embarassingly utopian. Does a nation want to be a major military power, have a high standard of living, outshine other countries in its cultural activities, and maintain full employment? With the means at its disposal—not to mention the accidents and vicissitudes to which countries, like individuals, are subject—these ends may be simply incompatible. And if, by some devious arithmetic, we arrive at an optimum number that is either greatly above or greatly below the actual one, what are we to do then? Any humane solution (and few governments today will consider any other type) is bound to be years in the future.

It therefore becomes necessary to consider *optimum growth rates.* But in relation to what? This is just the problem: everyone has his own list of desirable ends. We have already made clear the grounds on which we favor zero population growth: the human species has to limit its numbers or the biosphere will cease to support it. However, mere survival is not much of a goal; we must decide *how* we want to survive—or, in other words, what things are truly important to us. Citizens of the United States have more of a choice in this regard than citizens of most other countries. We should listen, then, to the projections of such authorities as J. J. Spengler, who has made a systematic comparison of the foreseeable advantages and disadvantages of zero population growth. Among the advantages are higher investment per capita; a larger working force; more stable patterns of consumer demand; more stable family life; less pollution and lower population density (as well as the chance of more dispersed job opportunities). Among the disadvantages are an older and so presumably more conservative, less dynamic population; less rapid promotion; and more inflation. The lesson is clear: we cannot have everything. As Spengler has written in another paper, quoted with approval by two dissenting members of the Rockefeller Commission:

> Today it is assumed that the economic circle can be squared; for . . . it is supposed that a society may have guaranteed full employment, price-level stability, strong producer pressure groups . . . and freedom from direct economic controls. In reality, of course, it is impossible for these four objectives to be realized simultaneously; only two, possibly three, are compatible. The policies driving the American economy are much more directionless than those which animate the Strassburg goose and the Sumo wrestler to eat continuously, the one to become liver pâté and the other to "belly" one of his kind from the ring; for this economy, with its momentum based upon destruction of a finite earth's depleting resources, neglects the fundamental requirement for survival, namely, conducting its affairs in keeping with an infinite time or planning horizon. (Spengler 1972, p. 274)

MAN, AN ENDANGERED SPECIES

World population, as we have seen, is growing at an average rate of 2 percent per year; in 1972 alone there was a gain of more than 72 million people. At least

70 percent of the children in the world do not receive adequate food or medical care: of the over 8,000 or more of them born each hour, only about 5,700 survive the first year of life.

Changing population distribution is almost as much of a menace as population growth. The next generation will see 4 billion people out of a world population of 7 billion massed in urban nodes each containing more than 100 thousand inhabitants, for many of whom even ordinary sustenance and social stability will be unattainable goals. Present rates of growth also make disease, famine, and war increasingly probable in most parts of the globe.

All these problems are compounded by pollution. The earth can supply the needs and absorb the insults of great numbers of people as long as the natural recycling processes, functioning according to their own timetables, can handle the waste products. When populations "explode," these processes are overloaded and pollution accumulates. Any finite environment in which a population produces wastes faster than the environment can recycle them becomes progressively poisoned. Finally, the population dies. In industrially and technologically advanced countries like the

FIGURE 16.1.   People, people everywhere . . . a typical rush hour scene on John Street, lower Manhattan. (photo by J. Sherrick Soroka, Silverton, Colorado)

United States, the ravages of famine and disease can be held off longer than in less developed countries. But accumulating wastes threaten the quality of life sooner. The dangerous levels of pollution already existing in our nation have been described in previous chapters. They are a function not only of population size but of high consumption standards. In addition, urbanization concentrates both people and pollution. Intelligent and beneficial long-range planning cannot be undertaken if numbers are increasing at exponential rates. Under such conditions as figure 16.1 suggests, it takes a society's best efforts merely to preserve the existing balance between population and resources. The most likely result is the overorganization that leads to what Aldous Huxley called a "new medieval system"—in other words, the end of freedom as we know it.

If population stopped growing now, existing technology and social institutions could alleviate the problems of both food supply and pollution. But to preserve disappearing natural ecosystems and create decent urban environments will require changes in values and perhaps a smaller population than we have now. In any case, as long as we continue to grow, as long as we fail to establish an equilibrium between population and environment, all other conservation measures will be no more than postponements of catastrophe.

The analogy between the present state of the human population and the "swarming state" so often observed in other biological species is one that many scientists find irresistible. The old density regulating mechanisms—famine, disease, war, and natural disasters—are beginning to break down, and nothing so effective has been put in their place. According to L. S. B. Leakey, the celebrated anthropologist, if man does not act immediately and effectively against pollution and overpopulation, he will certainly become extinct, perhaps in 50 years from now. The fact that most human beings refuse to take this possibility seriously is perhaps the most alarming sign that the human species may be doomed.

BIRTH RATE AND BIRTH RIGHT

Nobody wants a return to the bad old days. But if the human race is to avoid a fate similar to that of the Gadarene Swine it will have to order its affairs differently. The first prerequisite is birth control; without it, as U Thant pointed out in 1966, most U.N. programs are condemned to be of a stopgap nature. And yet there is much resistance to birth control, from both institutions and individuals. To the latter, being asked to limit family size often seems an infringement of personal freedom. Population control may be pictured as a move toward totalitarian regimentation. Such indignation is misplaced, for two reasons: first, there is in fact no such thing as free choice, if by this is meant freedom from social pressures; and second, it is population growth that is more likely to bring regimentation, not population control. In order to substantiate these propositions, let us briefly examine some of the influences for and against population growth.

Influences for Growth

The procreative instinct is a biological universal that is generally strongest in the young. How far this instinct is also socially conditioned is still a matter for speculation. But since young adults are more fertile than older ones, it is quite likely that society, by sanctioning the youthful procreative urge, is providing for its own survival. However that may be, young adults in modern industrial society are encouraged to think of reproduction as a personal matter. It was not always so. In the past the economic interests of individuals fostered the belief that children are good investments. For elderly members of tribal societies old-age security still rests on the backs of many sons. In our society, however, children are no longer financial assets to their parents; instead, they fall more in the category of consumer goods. Fathers of large families are more likely to end up poor than prosperous.

Ethnological factors propagate attitudes that population is power, that growth entitles nations to expand their territories, that armies of youth are needed to keep the world safe for democracy or to spread the gospel of Communism, and so on. Within nations, interethnic rivalry is often expressed by a breeding contest. Such attitudes are transmitted through religious, political, and military institutions—and, of course, the family.

Influences Against Growth

The instinct for survival is probably the strongest of all biological instincts. It is all the more tragic, then, now that mankind's survival depends on controlling or even eliminating population growth, that this instinct should continue to be exercised in favor of having children rather than not having them. Unfortunately, it has been proved time and time again that appeals to reason or patriotic duty do no good. Whether the spectacle of a steadily deteriorating environment will motivate people to limit their families is something that has yet to be seen. It is known, however, that human fertility tends to decline in the presence of three social forces: urbanization, industrialization, and economic depression. Although the three are of course related, each has effects distinctive enough to be treated separately. In addition, the effects of education are to a great extent independent both of religion and of ethnic background, at least in the United States. Lower education is reflected in higher fertility rates, presumably because of lesser ability to follow a contraceptive routine. Results are serious, for both society and the individual. According to D. F. Bentley, a Canadian estimate published in 1967 showed that two-thirds of all pregnancies in Canada were unwanted and half the babies born unwelcome. Between one-third and one-half of all babies born in the United States are unwanted, according to similar estimates. The

Canadian study also indicated that unwanted children were the greatest single factor perpetuating poverty in families.

HOW MUCH CONTROL?

Paul Ehrlich, a biologist who has made himself the nation's leading advocate of zero population growth, believes that the ideal population size for the United States is 150 million—60 million less than at present. However, he regards the immediate goal for the United States and the world as reducing birth rates to a level where they just balance death rates. This level would vary not only with actual death rates, but also with life expectancy levels. If such an equilibrium were ever reached, then it would be possible to consider letting birth rates fall below death rates in order to establish a more reasonable population for our ecosphere. In the United States, the zero growth level would be statistically equivalent to 2.2 children per bearing couple (the average exceeds two because some couples have no children). Only with zero population growth, according to Ehrlich, can we hope to deal effectively with such problems as food supply and the environmental impact of technology.

The question of whether Ehrlich and his followers are right is discussed further in chapter 18. In this chapter we shall be concerned mainly with current approaches to population control, and the means by which they are implemented. Demographically speaking, of course, there are only two possible approaches: raising mortality or lowering fertility. Both have been practiced on occasions in human history when demographic control became necessary. The natives of Hawaii, for example, long before the arrival of Europeans in their island, faced the horror of overpopulation. They practiced infanticide as the only way to protect the ecological balance of their society. Only female babies were put to death; the institution of one woman being married to several men evolved in order to accommodate the resulting imbalance of the sexes. Infanticide was also frequently practiced in China, Japan, and ancient Greece. In Japan, where it was called "weeding" *(mabiki),* infanticide helped to maintain the population at about 26 million for over three hundred years. But raising mortality rates is not an acceptable solution for most modern societies. Stability will have to be achieved by reducing birth rates.

Present-day China has been quite successful in discouraging marriage until couples are in their late twenties or early thirties; at the same time, it has instituted compulsory abortion for illegitimate conception. While some will think this is too drastic, not a few population experts feel that measures of this nature are overdue. Our Western traditions make us shrink from compulsion in this sphere. However, as Norman Douglas has sarcastically demonstrated, we impose licenses and other restrictions on all kinds of activities with which no self-respecting Oriental would tolerate interference. If freedom means no more than blind pursuit of private advantage, then it is clearly

FIGURE 16.2.   A well-to-do Indian family (with mother-in-law) against a background of government birth control propaganda. This family may get the message, but most of India's millions have not. (Black Star)

something we can no longer afford. Moreover, we cannot hope to educate the majority of the world's peoples in all the ecological ramifications of birth control. It will be enough if they understand the immediate advantages to themselves of having smaller families. This is in fact the approach taken by many governments, including the government of India (figure 16.2). But motivation is useless without techinque. Here, then, is the truly formidable educational task that governments face. The task is complicated by the variety of techniques available and the varying sociocultural contexts in which they are applied. The techniques are of two kinds, physical and social.

Physical Techniques

Birth rates can be reduced by terminating pregnancies or by preventing them. In the United States there is considerably less objection to prevention. The contraceptive methods available for this purpose are generally classified as either artifical or natural. Of the latter, the most widely advocated (because of its acceptability to the Roman Catholic Church) is the so-called rhythm method, developed in the 1930s. This method, based on the fact that conception is possible during only a few days of the menstrual cycle, is sound enough in theory. However, its effectiveness is accurately reflected by an old joke to the effect that those who practice it are known as "parents." A far more effective natural method, believed to be of great antiquity, is *coitus interruptus,* or male withdrawal prior to ejaculation.

Artificial techniques were known and used in ancient China, India, Persia, and imperial Rome. Post-coital douches, insertion of a sponge in the vagina before intercourse, and innumerable drugs supposed to induce abortion—these and other devices were all used with varying degrees of success. Some of them belonged to folk medicine, while others were upper-class inventions that diffused slowly, if at all, throughout the larger society. Most of the population remained too poorly informed to prevent repeated pregnancies even for urgent health or economic reasons.

Today a much wider variety of artificial techniques are known. The most effective is sterilization by surgery; both men and women can be rendered infertile by surgical operations that do not affect sexual performance or pleasure, and fertility can sometimes be restored through further surgery. Sheaths or condoms for male use are widely available and easily used. The diaphragm, which applies the same principle to female use, requires individual fitting by a trained person and is more expensive. Since the diaphragm is designed for repeated use it is actually much cheaper in the long run than the disposable condom. Reusable condoms, still popular in some countries, are even cheaper but, like diaphragms, they need systematic care, and this reduces their usefulness to poorly educated people.

Chemical contraceptives for female use are manufactured in the form of suppositories, foams, and douches. In rich nations the favorite women's contraceptive in the last decade has been "the pill," a steroid chemical, taken orally, that suppresses ovulation. It is highly effective but has been shown to have undesirable side effects in the form of nausea, bleeding, and even a slightly increased risk of death.

According to the British studies that established the relationship, deaths from pulmonary embolism attributable to the pill number 1.3 per 100,000 users between 20 and 34 years old, and 3.4 per 100,000 aged 35 to 44. Some U.S. studies indicate a similar danger of brain embolism. Deaths from all risks of pregnancy, however, are 22.9 per 100,000 for the first age group and 57.6 for the second. Thus the chances of death from pregnancy complications are seventeen times greater than from use of the pill in both cases.

Intrauterine devices (IUDs) are rings, coils, or loops made of chemically inert material that are inserted in the uterus and that, by some mechanism not yet understood, prevent fertilization of the ovum. The great advantage of the IUD is that once inserted it can be left in place. Widespread tests also seem to have vindicated its effectiveness. However, some women involuntarily expel their IUDs or suffer from irritation of the cervix.

A number of new contraceptive technologies are now in the experimental stage. Some are refinements of old methods, while others are based on principles never before put to this purpose and even on new physiological and chemical discoveries. According to Oscar Harkavy and John Maier, of all the new methods the one on which research has been carried farthest is contraception by means of progestins alone (the oral contraceptives now licensed for use are a mixture of progestins and estrogens). Interest in this method was stimulated by the fact that the major undesirable side effects of oral contraception were due to the estrogens. Low doses of synthetic progestins have been found effective in clinical tests, but the side effects (mainly, irregular bleeding) are still undesirable, and tests on animals have thrown doubt on the long-term safety of this method for human beings. Among the other experimental methods listed by Harkavy and Maier are: male chemosterilants that inhibit sperm production; reversible female sterilization (also by chemical means); reversible male sterilization (by surgical-mechanical means); postcoital estrogens and estrogen inhibitors (the so-called morning-after pill); postcoital antizygotics (these actually destroy the fertilized ovum); **luteolytic** compounds (as their name implies, these dissolve the *corpus luteum,* persistence of which is essential to the growth of the fertilized ovum); prostaglandins (fatty acids that appear to have a luteolytic effect); and releasing-factor inhibitors (a general name for any method that controls the LRF, or luteinizing hormone release factor). All these approaches are years away from fruition, and many of them already seem too dangerous for general use. The anti-LRF approach, however, is considered extremely promising because it would control the entire hormonal chain of events through one link in the chain. Presumably this would minimize the side effects.

Contraceptives vary not only in effectiveness, cost, and the risk they present to health, but also in social acceptability. Condoms and oral contraceptives are popular in urban-industrial societies but have not worked well in underdeveloped countries. Continuing cost is a disadvantage of both, and the pill requires strict adherence to a calculated schedule, an idea so foreign to village folk that they do not credit its importance; the schedule is "loosely" followed and, of course, the pill does not work.

Despite all these drawbacks, it is a scientific fact that we now have the contraceptive technology to make zero population growth physically possible. Making it socially possible is the task of education. Contraception is likely to remain the preferred technique for control because it is more achievable than continence and less repugnant than abortion. While the latter has long been publicly condemned and legally prohibited in many societies, it continues to be practiced secretly in these same societies. Women who can afford premium prices receive competent medical care from professional abortionists; those who cannot—the overwhelming majority—are left to the mercy of quacks or to any self-administered measures their own desperation may suggest. The results are appalling.

To sum up: there is no longer any good reason why a woman should bear a child she does not want. The prospects are not good for the mother, the child, or the population. The fact that so many unwanted children are born even in urban-industrial

---

Essay 16.1. Education for Tomorrow

Ecological concepts have been with us for centuries. Voices from many ages have cried out for responsible environmental thought and action. St. Francis preached equality of all living creatures in the early 13th century, and citizens decried London's smog problem in the 14th. Malthus worried about the population explosion in the 18th century, and the word ecology itself appeared in the 19th. But how many people listened then? And how many listen now? Certainly the popular press is rife with sensational articles and many basic ecological terms have recently slipped into the popular lexicon; but it will require more than a sudden rash of articles or the concern of scattered groups and individuals to ensure that our descendants will manage their environment more intelligently than their forefathers.

Public education and commitment will be a critical factor in the success of current and future campaigns against environmental irresponsibility. Scattered individuals may be able to garner a certain amount of temporary publicity and public attention, but no lasting changes in public policy can be effected without the participation and support of a large and active body of concerned citizens. Unfortunately, a large segment of today's public has been conditioned over many years to accept flagrant abuses of our natural resources, and still confronts the environmentalist's outcry passively and refuses to participate in policy reform. Recognizing this problem, environmentalists have begun to stress the need for youth education, feeling that while the citizens of today may be able to afford apathy, those of tomorrow will not have this luxury. The increasing pressures of organization, industrialization, and increased population will force solutions upon them whether they are prepared or not.

Present environmental youth education programs are few and generally inadequate. Despite the wealth of information published by private and government groups, there remain too few systematic national, state and local

---

societies where contraceptives are easily available shows that an equivalent number of women still lack adequate information about birth control technique or are intimidated by social prejudice. It points again to the urgent need for intensive educational campaigns (essay 16.1).

Social Techniques

Penalties and rewards, like the sticks and carrots that persuade lazy donkeys to move along, can elicit cooperation in birth control programs. Once the major-

programs. In addition, many of our existing programs, both public and private, lack coordination, numbers, and substance. There are insufficient curricula, inadequate standards of instruction, and too few classroom materials for the job. There is too little active cooperation among school administrators, and too little public funding available for concerted programs. Yet meanwhile, the crisis is all around us. We needn't look in most cases further than our own front doors to discover pressing problems of transportation, urbanization, air and water pollution, population growth, and energy supply—to name just a few.

Organizations such as The Conservation Education Association, Inc. have offered plans for state education programs. These include recommendations in areas of curriculum, standards of instruction, materials evaluation, teacher preparation, administration liason, budgeting and resource development. State and local committees have been proposed in various places to coordinate the efforts of teachers and school administrators, women's clubs, youth groups, churches, conservation agencies, community planners, farm organizations, PTAs, and parent groups; but much effective organizing remains to be done. Certain states—Oregon, for example—have developed such outstanding programs as the reforestation program in the Tillamook Burn utilizing the participation of adults and youth of all ages; but in too many locales there are gaps: lack of funds, powerful opposition groups, widespread public apathy, uninformed public leadership and plain lack of experience and training.

Children and young people learn what they live. If the public mind continues to feature the outmoded and disastrous concepts of the past, our future leaders will possess no wisdom and experience upon which to draw when they assume power. We must insist now on educational training to prepare them and their constituents for the complex and difficult job of managing our planet.

ity of a population has been awakened to the dangers of unchecked growth, social disapproval of individuals with large families can act as a deterrent. Provision of free contraceptive, sterilization, and abortion services can act as an incentive to their use. Some countries even award cash payments to men or women who volunteer for sterilization. Rewards and penalties can also be administered through taxation—that is, if a country has an efficient taxation system, which most do not. In the United States, the plans suggested range from allowing the present tax exemption only for the first two children in a family to giving every woman of childbearing age a stipend of, say, $500 for every year she does not have a child. J. William Leasure has computed the amount

TABLE 16.1.   Payments that could be made to women without increased cost to taxpayers, for not having children

Years Following Birth	Value
1	$379
2	313
3	318
4	319
5	325
6	324
7	322
8	319
9	311
10	301
11	271
12	233
13	265
14	163
15	117
16	98
17	62
18	48
19	43

Source: Adapted by permission from J. William Leasure, "Some Economic Benefits of Birth Prevention," *Milbank Memorial Fund Quarterly,* October 1967.

Note: Costs have been discounted at 5 percent and shifted up so that the large payments begin immediately.

that could be paid to each woman for each successive year she avoids having a child. Only women with at least two living children and with a family income under $3,000 per year would be eligible and the scheme would not cost the taxpayer an extra penny. The figures given in table 16.1 are based on North Carolina data; for states like New York or California, where taxes are higher, the savings would be much greater, so that payments could be higher or the surplus funds put to other constructive use.

Of course, once a child is born both it and its mother have certain rights, all of which should be protected far more carefully than they are at present. But this is not the same as a pronatalist policy. The entire complex of issues involved here is weighed rather carefully in the report of the Commission on Population Growth and the American Future, which concludes that it is perfectly equitable to distribute child-rearing costs throughout society because the whole society has an interest in seeing that the next generation is properly raised (pp. 156–161). Discrimination against the children of poorer parents by reducing the public funds available to them is therefore unacceptable. There is also some suspicion that financial incentives for not having children would be equally discriminatory, because they would be most attractive to the poor. The argument that welfare mothers are encouraged to have more children is based on false information. For instance, as the report points out, although welfare payments in New York City went up steadily in the 1959–70 period, "the percentage of welfare mothers bearing children each year dropped from 18.9 percent in 1959, to 11.3 percent in 1970." All the talk of social penalties and deterrents should not be allowed to obscure the positive aspect of a zero growth policy: those who wanted to bring up children would be able to do so under more favorable circumstances than before, since there would be more public funds available for maternal and child welfare.

ORGANIZED OPPOSITION TO POPULATION CONTROL

Individual opposition to population control can generally be excused on grounds of ignorance. By contrast, organized opposition must be considered a socially dangerous anachronism. Here, we shall deal with three varieties of such opposition: religious, ideological, and nationalist.

Religious Opposition

The Roman Catholic Church is the most important religious group opposing artificial methods of contraception. Its importance is due not only to its size—an estimated 580 million members worldwide—but to its influence in areas of high population growth, especially Latin America. Contraception by any method was condemned by a papal encyclical in 1930. This position was only slighly modified in 1951, when use of the rhythm method was deemed acceptable. Nevertheless, a Harris Poll in 1965 revealed that 78 percent of American Catholics believed birth control devices should be available to all who wished to use them. In the atmosphere created by Vatican II (the Second Vatican Council, convened in 1962) many people hoped that the Catholic hierarchy would abandon its rigid position. But all hopes were dashed by Pope Paul VI in his 1968 encyclical, *Humanae Vitae* ("On Human Life"). This document seems to have closed the door on change for the near future, since it reiterated that "every marriage act [*quilibet matrimonii usus*] must remain open to the transmission of life" —a doctrine taken directly from St. Thomas Aquinas (1225–74). Meanwhile many respected Catholic priests and laymen, including doctors, lawyers, and scholars, are using their considerable influence in favor of limiting families. One of them is Dr. John Rock, prominent gynecologist and pioneer in developing oral contraceptives, who

Marxism - agst. birth control

affirms the need to halt population growth. Countless individuals of the Catholic faith are following the lead of such men.

Ideological Opposition

Malthus' dire predictions were rejected by Marx, who laid the blame for poverty on inequitable distribution of goods and mismanagement of the factors of production. As a result, Communist propagandists today are still asserting that all will be well once production is controlled by the working class. But the anti-Malthusian stance of Communism is apparently more important as an ideological weapon than as practical policy. In the U.S.S.R. after the 1917 revolution the sale of contraceptives was authorized and the legal ban on abortions repealed. In the 1930s, however, after the losses of the Civil War, Soviet authorities were faced by a declining labor force at the same time that they were embarking on a period of economic expansion. Accordingly, they devised tax inducements to encourage large families, awarded medals for motherhood, and in general emphasized the relationship of declining fertility to capitalist decadence. After Stalin's death, however, birth control information again became widely obtainable. Throughout these changes in policy the Soviet birth rate has steadily declined, so that today there is little difference between the crude birth rates of the U.S.S.R. and the United States. Economic and social changes, including urbanization, have played a larger part in Soviet demographic trends than Marxist theory. The same is true of other Communist countries.

Nationalist Opposition

Some nations still actively promote population growth, implementing their pronatalist policies with economic benefits to large families. Many of them are nations generally thought of as industrially and culturally modern; their objective is military and political strength through large populations. France, for example, still cherishes her dream of 100 million citizens, an imperialistic relic of past ages, instead of counting herself fortunate that her excellent agricultural resources are more than sufficient for her present population. Countries peopled largely by immigrants also tend to adopt pronatalist policies. Canada, for instance, is still paying a baby bonus of $30 per month for each child.

All these efforts, it seems, are in vain. The population of Canada is increasing at a rate of only 1.7 percent a year, and that of France at a rate of less than 1 percent. Pronatalist measures had very little effect in Nazi Germany and Fascist Italy. On the other hand, when governments have introduced birth control programs the results have often been spectacular, especially when such programs included easy access to abortion. Thus before 1966 a Romanian woman could get an abortion at a cost equivalent to less than $2. The crude birth rate had dropped to a low of 14.3 per 1,000 for 1966. In November of that year abortions were outlawed because of government fears that the low birth rate would decimate the future labor force. The crude birth rate jumped to 27.1 per 1,000 in 1967. In subsequent years it has somewhat declined, as the people of Romania have begun to adjust to the use of contraception. In general, it seems that if people really want to limit their families, there is very little governments can do to stop them. Many population experts find this a hopeful sign.

SOME NATIONAL POLICIES AND PRACTICES

Only a few nations have explicit population policies. More often the position of a given nation with regard to population growth is left implicit in its legislation, its tax structure, its economic system, and its traditions. The fact that a country has a policy does not necessarily indicate that it is coping successfully with its population problems. Among the first countries to take an official stand in favor of limitation were Pakistan, Puerto Rico, and India, all of which are still far short of their goals. On the other hand, such countries as Japan and more recently S. Korea have reduced their birth rates without formulating a national policy for control. The crucial factor, of course, is the existing sociocultural base. Even the most progressive national policies are slow to take effect on peoples still in the grip of religious and social prejudice. In some cases sheer ignorance of reproductive processes is a formidable barrier to progress; a population cannot be charged with lack of motivation when 80 percent of its members do not know that conception is preventable. For example, less than one Turkish woman in ten has any idea on which days of her fertility cycle conception is possible.

Japan, India, and the United States have been chosen here for more detailed discussion because each represents a different degree of success in diagnosing and coping with indigenous population problems. Together they suggest the variety of economic, sociological, political, and other conditions encountered by control programs.

Japan's Success

Japan recently halved its birth rate in less than a generation—the fastest such decline in demographic history. Japanese population troubles were acute after World War II: no fewer than 73 million people were crowded into an area one twenty-fifth the size of the United States. At that time, abortion was illegal and distribution of birth control information prohibited. A postwar marriage boom soon made the birth rate one of the highest in the world and tripled the growth rate. In 1948 the Japanese

Diet, desperate for a solution, took a radical step: it passed an abortion law that could be interpreted liberally. By 1955, eighteen times as many abortions were being performed annually as had been reported in 1948. At the same time birth control information was being disseminated as widely as possible, originally at the instigation of Dr. Yoshio Koya, director of the National Institute of Public Health. Dr. Koya disapproved of repeated abortions because of the possible consequences to health, and his efforts were intended to influence the government in favor of promoting contraception. He was assisted by volunteers associated with the new Family Planning Federation; together they set up a basic program rated by experts in the late 1960s as the world's most sensible. They started with the very poor and found them not indifferent, as they are often assumed to be, but pitifully eager for help. Since Dr. Koya's department was not authorized to push such a program, he at first raised funds himself in order to distribute a variety of contraceptives without charge. Later many large firms volunteered to pay the costs of free birth control services and equipment for their employees.

A government family planning program was established for indigents in 1955. By 1964 the Health and Welfare Ministry had begun training 50,000 midwives and nurses, was providing financial aid to private agencies, and had set up the first of a chain of birth control centers that now number about 900. Japanese information media gave strong support to all these efforts. Finally, the responsibility for control was shifted to cities, towns, and villages, with financial assistance supplied by the government. By 1966 the Japanese crude birth rate was 13.8—less than half what it had been at the height of the postwar baby boom.

The success of the Japanese program was followed by a reaction. Around 1969 Japanese business and industrial interests began to exert pressure in favor of increasing the birth rate. Labor had grown expensive and a population increase, they reasoned, would lower wages. The success of these efforts is not yet known. At first they seem to have been partially realized in an upswing of the crude birth rate, which in 1970 was about 19. But this may have been largely the result of the postwar babies growing up and having babies of their own. In any case, if the Japanese birth control movement is to consolidate its earlier gains it will have to educate the present generation of Japanese women as successfully as it did the previous one. But whatever happens, the Japanese achievement is not likely to be surpassed for some time.

India's Failure

In 1970 India's population reached some 550 million—an increase of more than 14 million over the previous year. India comprises about one forty-fifth of the world's land area and is occupied by nearly one-seventh of the world's population. The Indian growth rate for the period 1963–70 averaged 2.5 percent per annum, as compared with a world growth rate of 2 percent. However, the average annual increase in

Indian food production has been only 2 percent, and is not likely to be much higher in the near future.

Efforts to lower the Indian birth rate began in the early 1950s when the World Health Organization (W.H.O.) introduced the rhythm method to India. Each woman contacted by the W.H.O. workers was given a string of beads to help her keep track of her fertility cycle day by day; the menstrual period was represented by red beads, the "safe" days by green beads, and the days when conception was likely by black beads. The result was a fiasco. Some women assumed that possession of the beads provided automatic protection, others that the cotton thread they were strung on was taboo on certain days or that safety was assured if they flicked to a green bead. Even if the purpose of the beads had been understood the scheme could not have worked: menstrual regularity cannot be maintained on an unbalanced and inadequate diet.

Oral contraceptives were tried next. But the women did not understand the schedule for taking them, or did not realize that adherence to the schedule was vital, or perhaps were not completely committed to avoiding pregnancy. In any case, this method also failed.

During the 1960s intrauterine devices and sterilization were most strongly promoted. Intrauterine devices failed; the number rejected almost equaled the number inserted. The main reason seems to have been that this procedure is rarely effective until a woman has borne children. A second problem resulted as some women removed the device in order to collect again the small payment offered for insertion. The program was reevaluated at the end of the 1960s and the government decided to redirect its energies into the domestic production of condoms.

The Indian government has also conducted a major sterilization program, for both men and women. By 1970 some 8 million sterilizations had been performed, three-quarters of them on men. This is more than have been performed in all other countries combined, yet less than 1 percent of India's population is affected. Even this program has run into logistic problems. First, the transistor radios given as a bonus for having the operation are costly, and the fledgling Indian electronics industry cannot meet the demand. More difficult is the problem of finding enough medical personnel to man a program of the required dimensions. India now has 26,000 family planning centers, 9,000 hospitals, 13,000 doctors, and 120,000 paramedical workers. But the impact of all these on her population growth has been almost nil. The *gross reproduction rate* was 2.7 in 1961; by 1970 it was still about the same. Among the obstacles still to be overcome are the sheer numbers to be persuaded, ignorance of reproductive processes, illiteracy, poor mass communications systems, and pronatalist social and religious traditions, including the view (natural in an agricultural society) that children are economic assets, especially in old age. Another major obstacle is the fact that Indian women traditionally marry soon after puberty. In 1961 some 81 percent of all Indian women in the 15 to 24 age group were married—a very high proportion even by Asian standards. A 1964 survey, based on a sample of 66 towns with a total population of nearly 25 million, showed that about 12 percent of all live births in that year were to teenage mothers. But there are tremendous social pressures against raising the marriage age.

U.N. demographers now project that India's population will be larger than China's by the year 2000. This is in spite of or perhaps because of India being the most "aided" nation on earth. It has received 10 percent of all loans made by the World Bank plus billions of dollars' worth of food and other aid from the United States and elsewhere. And yet, according to one estimate, India now needs an additional 4 million jobs, 2.5 million houses, and 126,000 schools. Clearly, international aid to India cannot continue to be increased to match her population growth. Perhaps massive aid has been a mistake insofar as it has spared the Indian government the harsh decisions that might have curbed population growth and given economic development a chance.

The most optimistic estimate of the population total at which stabilization will be possible is 700 million, to be reached in the late 1980s. But it is more likely that the population will continue to increase well past the billion mark now projected for the year 2000. Over 40 percent of the present population is under 15 years old, and 48 percent of all women are over 15 and under 50. There is no sign of change in the growth rate and at this point there seems to be no humanitarian solution to the problem.

India is one of the first countries to reach a helpless condition of runaway population growth. But other countries with high growth rates, especially in Latin America, will be at the same stage in a decade or a generation.

The United States: Stabilization or Chaos?

The United States has never had an official population policy. Restrictions have been imposed on immigration, but despite the 1972 report of the Commission on Population Growth and the American Future (of which more below) there has so far been no official attempt to stimulate or retard the birth rate. Dissemination of contraceptive information and devices is still subject to various restrictions in more than twenty states, but for moralistic rather than pronatalist reasons. Until recently, the nation's resources seemed abundantly able to support the demands of the growing population, and family size was regarded as an entirely private concern.

Today, it is becoming evident that our resources are not infinite, and that one kind of pressure on them is population growth. At last we are ready to appreciate our family planning pioneer, Margaret Sanger (1883–1966). She was half a century ahead of her countrymen when she opened the nation's first birth control clinic in Brooklyn in 1916. It was received with outrage; Mrs. Sanger was called a "lascivious monster bent on murdering unborn children." The previous year she had served 30 days in jail for sending birth control information through the mails. Times have changed. Today some cities are receiving federal funds in order to operate birth control clinics. In 1966 President Johnson received the Margaret Sanger Award for his "vigorous and farsighted leadership in bringing the U.S. government to enunciate and implement an affirmative, effective population policy at home and abroad."

President Johnson certainly deserved credit for his action, but the policy could hardly be called effective. Many of the reasons for this are historical. For at least two decades after the beginning of Margaret Sanger's crusade opposition to birth control remained strong. Even the medical profession ignored the issue. Dr. Ralph L. Hoffman has recounted how "in medical school at Michigan in 1932, Dr. Norman Miller presented to us behind locked doors the first lecture on contraception given to a medical school class at that institution. The start was slow; it wasn't until 1958 that the ban on contraceptive services in New York City hospitals was removed." Finally, in 1964, the American Medical Association published a statement that read in part: "The medical profession should accept a major responsibility in matters related to human reproduction as they affect the total population and the individual family." It had at last begun to relinquish its neutrality. Politicians and statesmen also sidestepped the issue as long as possible. If pressed for a statement their responses were likely to resemble that of President Eisenhower: "This government will not . . . as long as I am here, have a positive political doctrine in its program that has to do with this problem of birth control. That's not our business."

Ironically, it was our first Roman Catholic president, John F. Kennedy, who in 1963 first took a stand in support of birth control research. In 1961 he had stated that population growth was threatening standards of life throughout the developing world and announced U.S. willingness to support family planning programs in countries receiving U.S. aid. Nevertheless, budgets for such programs under the Agency for International Development remained tiny until 1968. In that year a more reasonable $34.7 million was allotted, and for fiscal 1971 the amount was more than doubled. Meanwhile, there has been some federal support for domestic birth control programs, though it has been increasing at a slower rate. By 1969, the Institute of Child Health and Human Development (Department of Health, Education, and Welfare) was spending nearly $6 million a year for the study of reproduction and the development of effective and acceptable contraceptives. Grants for family planning services received by the Health Services and Mental Health Administration, also under H.E.W., increased from $18.4 million in 1969 to $49.8 million in 1971. These services were offered to low-income families, but were reaching such a small minority of the 5 million eligible women that as late as 1969 the Office of Economic Opportunity still felt it necessary to run a parallel program of its own. Similar services are provided by the Department of Defense for military families and by the Department of the Interior for Indians, Eskimos, and the peoples of the Pacific Trust Territories. The total amount the government spends on all these agencies, however, is minute compared to the billions poured into the space program or military research and development.

Population research has fared a little better with the private foundations. The leader here has been the Ford Foundation, which has granted sums of money that have increased from $2.9 million in 1963 to a total, divided among various organizations, of more than $39 million in 1969. The fact remains, however, that all domestic government programs are still oriented toward family planning—giving parents the information to make their own choice—rather than population control. Naturally, the message of family planning has been directed almost entirely at the poor; neither President Johnson nor President Nixon has suggested that those who want and can afford large families need consider anything beyond their own inclinations.

The Rockefeller Commission

It is sometimes argued that the United States does not have a population problem. Our problem is indeed different from India's or Japan's but unless our growth rate is modified we will see a steady deterioration in our quality of life. There is also our global responsibility to consider. We consume a great deal more than the people of the developing countries; although we have only 6 percent of the world's population we use 50 percent of its nonrenewable resources. One U.S. child will cause *at least* 25 times the stress on his environment that an Indian child will. All our efforts to aid and promote population limitation in developing countries will ring false, and our motives will be suspect, unless we demonstrate willingness and ability to practice what we preach.

It is in this context that we should read the report of the Commission on Population Growth and the American Future, otherwise known as the Rockefeller Commission, after its chairman, John D. Rockefeller 3rd. Among the report's major conclusions and recommendations were the following:

1. Neither the economic health of the country, nor the vitality of its business, nor the welfare of its average citizen, depend on continued population growth.
2. A population in which parents on the average had just enough children to replace themselves (the "two-child projection") could afford much better educational services than a society in which parents produced an average of one extra child (the "three-child projection"). Welfare expenditures, however, would remain about the same under the two-child projection as under the three-child projection unless reforms were undertaken.
3. There would be ample manpower under the two-child projection to insure the nation's military security.
4. Intensive education on the facts of population growth and the means of birth control should be undertaken throughout the population, including the public schools (to this end, the commission actually called for a Population Education Act.)
5. Sex education (as distinct from population education) should be avail-

able to all, especially through the schools, as the best means of discouraging unwanted pregnancies and venereal disease among young persons.

6. Adequate child-care services should be available to all who want them, especially working mothers.

7. Adoption should be encouraged by extra subsidies, removal of legal obstacles, and, above all, information programs stressing its positive aspects.

8. In order to encourage women to take up careers other than childbearing, the Equal Rights Amendment should be approved and government at every level should work to eliminate discrimination against women.

9. All state restrictions on access to contraceptive information and supplies should be abolished, and special programs should be established allowing minors to receive such information and supplies under supervision.

10. Abortion, although not to be considered "a primary means of fertility control," should be made available on request under the same legal conditions as it is now available in New York State, and should be not only supported by federal grants in states that allowed it under such conditions but also included in all comprehensive health insurance programs.

This last recommendation was declared unacceptable by President Nixon, who also made clear his displeasure with the report on other grounds. Several members of the Rockefeller Commission dissented from one or more of its major recommendations, and in general it was received as a highly controversial document. And yet very little was said in the public debate about the facts on which the recommendations were based.

The report also made quite clear that U.S. population problems could not be blamed on the poor. For instance, less than one-third of all children born in the 1960–65 period had poor parents (figure 16.3). Moreover, sample surveys indicate that preventing unwanted births to well-to-do parents would have a far greater impact on the U.S. birth rate than preventing such births to poor parents (figure 16.4). Thus no matter how much birth control propaganda is aimed at the poor it will not change the overall picture. The poor are not in the majority, and neither are their children. If government birth control efforts are not directed at the whole society, then the poor will quite rightly suspect that the society has no use for them. A better recipe for a revolutionary situation could hardly be imagined.

What is needed far more than a Malthusian campaign against the poor is change in the nature of the middle-class family. Companionate marriage, communes, parents without partners, and many other variations on the conventional nuclear family are all compatible with lower birth rates, if not with greater appreciation of children. These are of course suggestions for the future, but the social experiments of the present generation may have pointed the way.

WORLD POPULATION POLICY

Sir Julian Huxley has recounted how, as director general of **U.N.E.S.C.O.** in 1949, he suggested that the subject of population be included in the U.N. Conference on World Resources then about to be held at Lake Success. The reply was that technical, political, and religious difficulties made such a thing impossible. Five years later, a U.N. Conference on World Population, the first of its kind, was held in Rome. During that interval, comments Sir Julian, world population had increased by over 130 million.

The United Nations now has a small budget for action programs in the field of population control, but its main function in this field continues to be one of collecting and analyzing demographic statistics. The Population Branch of the U.N. Bureau of Social Affairs now publishes the *Demographic Yearbook* (since 1948), the *Population Bulletin* (since 1951), and a lengthy series of technical reports under the rubric of *Population Studies*. Largely thanks to the United Nations, the basic demographic facts about the developing countries have now been made available (in many cases, they were compiled by U.N. trained demographers). The demography of these areas was one of the main topics discussed at the Second World Population Conference, held in Belgrade in 1965.

Despite all this activity, the United Nations continues to fall far short of its full potential as an agency for population control. In a report prepared for a presidential committee in 1959, William H. Draper demonstrated that $5 invested in population control was worth $100 in economic aid of other kinds. Now, more than a decade later, world population problems have assumed such proportions that a third zero could reasonably be added to the second of Draper's figures. The principle, however, is still valid, and one logical application of it might be to require "demographic creditworthiness" of nations seeking aid from U.N. funding agencies or from other nations.

Investment in population control will not only reduce the amount of assistance ultimately required by undeveloped countries; it will also result in positive economic benefits to these countries. According to Stephen Enke, cutting a 3 percent gross reproduction rate by half over a 30-year period would result in a 3 percent per

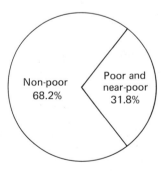

FIGURE 16.3.   Fewer than one-third of all U.S. children born in the 1960–65 period had poor parents. ("Population Challenge of the '70s," *Population Bulletin,* February 1970, by permission of the publisher, Population Reference Bureau, Inc., Washington, D.C.)

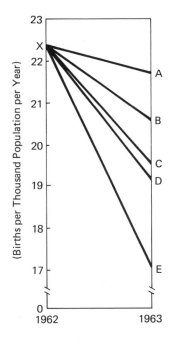

FIGURE 16.4.   "Unwanted" births among the well-to-do in 1963 accounted for a larger share of U.S. births than did "unwanted" births among the poor and near-poor. Here, *A* = actual 1963 birth rate; *B* = theoretical birth rate if poor and near-poor in 1960 had had as few "unwanted" births (proportionately) as non-poor in 1963; *C* = theoretical birth rate if poor and near-poor had had no "unwanted" births in 1963; *D* = theoretical birth rate if non-poor had had no "unwanted" births in 1963; and *E* = theoretical birth rate if entire U.S. population had had no "unwanted" births in 1963. (adapted from "Population Challenge of the '70s," *Population Bulletin,* February 1970, by permission of the publisher, Population Reference Bureau, Inc., Washington, D.C.)

capita increase of income in a typical undeveloped country. Additional benefits would accrue from a 33 percent increase in the productive labor force. Even with the added cost of contraception, a benefit-cost ratio of about 80 to 1 would result. The optimistic possibilities suggested by this and similar studies brighten a dismal picture, but the discouraging fact remains that thousands of millions of human beings are totally unaware of them. Millions still do not know that reproduction can be a matter of choice. Curbing of the human population explosion depends on reaching every one of these millions with a convincing explanation of why and how to avoid pregnancy.

REFERENCES

Bentley, D.F., Canadian press release, datelined University of Alberta, July 26, 1967.
Commission on Population Growth and the American Future (the Rockefeller Commission),
        Population and the American Future (New York: Signet, 1972).
Douglas, Norman, *Good-bye to Western Culture* (New York: Harper, 1930).
Ehrlich, Paul R., and Richard L. Harriman, *How To Be a Survivor* (New York: Signet, 1971).
Enke, Stephen, "Birth Control for Economic Development," *Science,* May 16, 1969.
Harkavy, Oscar, and John Maier, "Research in Reproductive Biology and Contraceptive Technology:
        Present Status and Needs for the Future," *Family Planning Perspectives,* June 1970
        (also available as a Ford Foundation reprint).
Huxley, Aldous, "Over-population Means Over-organization," in Marian Maury (ed.), *Birth Rate and*

Birth Right (New York: Macfadden, 1963). Reprinted from Huxley's *Brave New World Revisited.*

Huxley, Julian, "World Population," *Scientific American,* March 1956.

Leakey, Louis S.B., quoted in *Conservation News,* January 15, 1972.

Leasure, J. William, "Some Economic Benefits of Birth Prevention," *Milbank Memorial Fund Quarterly,* October 1967.

Sauvy, Alfred, "Population: Population Theories," in *International Encyclopedia of the Social Sciences* (New York: Macmillan and Free Press, 1968).

Spengler, J.J., "Economic Growth in a Stationary Population," Population Reference Bureau selection no. 38, July 1971.

——, "Declining Population Growth: Economic Effects," cited in "Separate Statement of Otis Dudley Duncan," concurred in by Paul B. Cornely, M.D., in Commission on Population Growth and the American Future, *Population and the American Future* (New York: Signet, 1972).

17 ENVIRONMENTAL CONTROL

Despite a number of problem areas, such as automobile manufacturing, consumers of durable goods are reasonably well served in the United States. The supply of services is not nearly so varied or reliable, but the middle-class consumer who lives in a major population center can generally find the service he needs at a price he can (just) afford. Social welfare functions are grudgingly and inadequately performed by government at various levels, but the poor are not usually allowed to starve. The public interest, however, is quite systematically neglected. In theory, it is supposed to be preserved through the unfettered operations of enlightened self-interest. It should be quite clear by now that even enlightened self-interest has been less than successful in providing clean air and water, open space, quiet, and a generally livable environment.

Unfortunately, there is no simple or direct alternative to the present system. Violent revolution, even if it were possible, would probably have such a deleterious effect upon the general quality of life that environmental issues would be all but forgotten. Environmental quality, one aspect of the public interest, can only be promoted through step-by-step improvement within the existing framework. No existing political system offers a model of how to deal with the environment.

One thing, at least, is obvious: in order to safeguard the public interest, we need more effective public control. We also need a new definition of prosperity. Individualistic consumption of goods and services must give way to cooperative striving after the common good. Government should function freely in this arena, for it is one in which people acting as individuals can do relatively little for themselves.

GOALS AND OBJECTIVES

The public interest in the environmental field can be summed up in a single word: livability. This has been defined by the U.S. Department of Health, Education, and Welfare as a convenient, healthy, comfortable, and attractive environment for all. Although there is bound to be some disagreement about the precise application of these terms, they clearly imply a need for ecological balance, on the one hand, and improved urban conditions, on the other. In other words, we must improve the man-made environment even as we preserve the natural one.

Toward a More Livable Environment

The process of acquiring a more livable environment necessarily involves reducing pollution of the ecosphere. In practice, however, this has often meant little more than shuffling pollution from one part of the ecosphere to another.

It is tempting, for example, to regard so-called **wet scrubbers** as the final answer to industrial stack emissions, although in effect they merely transfer pollution from air to water. The long-term acceptability of this type of trade-off is questionable.

If the battle for environmental control is ever to be won, it will have to proceed simultaneously on at least eight different fronts, as follows.

1. There will have to be more population research and population control, so that population growth can be reduced and finally eliminated.
2. Man-made air pollution will have to be controlled at a level that allows natural recycling of the atmosphere while maintaining ambient air quality at a level fit for human, animal, and plant life.
3. Water quality will have to be restored and then maintained, probably with the help of novel use patterns and man-made recycling schemes.
4. There will have to be integrated programs for disposing of solid, liquid, gaseous, and nuclear wastes, with massive federal aid to local governments so that they can afford to develop new systems for treating and recycling such wastes.
5. The use of chemical products of all kinds will have to be far more carefully controlled in order to avoid danger to health and damage to the environment. Wherever possible, chemical control of insect population's should be replaced by biological control (essay 17.1).
6. Both the concept and the reality of the American city will have to be thoroughly reexamined with a view to eliminating congestion, excessive noise, and other stress-inducing factors.
7. The large corporations that between them control most of the country's resources will have to be brought to a new sense of social and

Essay 17.1. Biological Control

    In 1970 some 75,000 acres of Texas cotton were spoiled by the tobacco budworm, which had already ruined the entire cotton-growing industry of northeastern Mexico. The budworm was periodically drenched with synthetic biocides, including the latest organic phosphates and carbamates (essay 9.1), but to no avail: it had become immune. Events such as this have rekindled interest in the ancient art of biological control, often defined as control of insects through their natural predators and parasites. Actually, this definition somewhat begs the question, since if the natural predators and parasites were doing their work there would be no problem of control. The classic opportunity for biological control arises when a pest seems to have no natural predators, usually because it has been imported from another area or country. The problem then becomes one of finding a predator or parasite—a search that often leads far from the pest's country of origin. Today, biological control also includes the use of pathogens, or microbial agents that reduce pest populations by disease, as well as the so-called sterile-male technique, which consists in sterilizing large quantities of insects by radiation and then setting them free to mate with nonsterilized insects. Various chemical lures, especially the attractants emitted by the female of the pest species, are also in process of development. The ideal, of course, is a technique that achieves complete control, that is, permanent reduction of the pest population to a level at which it is no longer a pest. One of the most celebrated examples of complete control involves not two insect species but an insect and a plant, the Klamath weed, which formerly infested some two million acres of north California range land. Two species of leaf-eating Chrysolina beetle, originally from France and England, were imported in 1944 from Australia, where Klamath weed was also a problem. By 1954 they had eaten up 99 percent of the Klamath weed—and the situation remains stable to this day. In Australia, however, the same degree of success has not been achieved. Farmers unwilling to wait for perfect control (which may never come) are more likely to opt for integrated control. This has been defined by Francis R. Lawson, retiring director of the U.S.D.A. Biological Control of Insects Research Laboratory in Columbia, Missouri, as "the use of biological and cultural control whenever possible, with insecticides used locally and in small amounts, but only when necessary to prevent economic loss to the farmer." Perhaps the best we can hope for in the immediate future is reduction of pest damage to acceptable levels. (Based on Julian McCaull, "Know Your Enemy," and Kevin P. Shea, "Old Weapons Are Best," both in Environment, *June 1971; for further information see Scientists' Institute for Public Information,* Pesticide Reevaluation Task Force Report, *New York, 1972).*

environmental responsibility, if necessary by the most stringent legal measures.

8. The federal government will have to be far more responsive to state and local needs in the environmental field, and will have to develop programs sufficiently flexible and imaginative to meet those needs without strangling local initiative in red tape.

According to the report of the Commission on Population Growth and the American Future, even if the average number of children per family drops to two, there will still be over 80 million more people living in U.S. metropolitan areas by the year 2000 than there are now. (The reason why an average of two children per family would not immediately result in zero population growth is that the number of women of childbearing age will continue to increase for some time.) If the 3-child family becomes the norm, then the increase will be nearly 130 million. Obviously, it will help a great deal if some of this increase can be channeled to smaller cities and towns. But the commission estimates that these communities would have to grow at a rate of 50 percent per decade in order to carry any substantial burden of growth for the metropolitan areas. Hopefully, there will be a demand for more new communities, especially the planned ones known as "new towns." Surveys cited by the commission show that more than two-thirds of all Americans would prefer to live in a small town or rural area within commuting distance of a major city. If this preference is to be realized, there will have to be far more planning and development of middle-sized communities. So far we have succeeded neither in this nor in lightening the burden of the major metropolitan areas (figure 17.1).

Reducing the Impact of Growth

Significant as the population factor is, it will, as far as the United States is concerned, be almost insignificant over the next three decades compared with economic and technological factors. If we fail to control the unintended consequences of our advanced industrial technology, then we have nothing to look forward to but increasingly rapid environmental deterioration. Since this technology exists in order to serve our insane habits of mass consumption, basic changes in our way of life will have to be instituted—changes that will be fought every inch of the way by powerful vested interests.

Maintaining an Equilibrium

We can never return to an ecological Garden of Eden. But we can make sure that a balance is reached between the natural and man-made environments. Our model, as Ian McHarg has emphasized, should be the landscape gardener. In other words, we must work with natural processes, not against them. This does not mean

FIGURE 17.1.   Manhattan skyline seen from borough of Queens. How long can these single-family homes resist increasing pollution and loss of open space to the automobile? (New York Times)

jettisoning our advanced technology; rather, we must use it more wisely. Technology itself is not the villain, only man's misuse of it. Above all, we must have planning—planning for land use. In the long run, however, our success in maintaining a livable environment will depend on whether or not we can achieve not only zero population growth but zero environmental deterioration as a result of consumption patterns. Hopefully, improved technology will provide us with greater flexibility in this respect. For instance, our high consumption of electrical power would have far less environmental impact if it were derived from nuclear fusion than, as at present, from the combustion of a heavy fossil fuel. The need is both wiser use of what we have and an equilibrium of use with impact. From such a basis we must devise our strategy for insuring the common good.

The principal danger, in a political system so hospitable to private business as ours, is that nothing effective may be done. Government and business alike may pay lip service to "environmental needs," "quality of life," and so forth, while proceeding exactly as before. For instance, in the 1970 Report of the National Goals Research Staff, *Toward Balanced Growth,* all pessimistic views of our long-term environmental outcome are lumped together as the "doomsday" model and dismissed as fallacious. Instead of such "extreme" solutions as lowering the rate of conventional economic growth, the report prefers a "mixed strategy" in which the "market mechanism" (i.e., private enterprise) would, it seems, play as important a role as the government (pp. 66–75). It should be added that one of the market mechanisms favored by the report's authors is making producers pay the costs of pollution; their theory is that higher prices for polluting products would mean fewer consumers of them and so less pollution. But would it really work that way? In a prosperous society that encourages consumers to think in terms of "low, low monthly payments" rather than real costs, can higher prices make enough difference to matter? And what if the environmental crisis *is* a crisis, and not (as the authors of the report suggest more than once) the result of our so-called technological success combined with a change in environmental philosophy? Chapter 11 of this book should alone suffice to dispel the illusion of that success. As for the philosophy, it is being changed because people can see and judge for themselves that the quality of their life is deteriorating. Ecological problems do not (except possibly in New York and Los Angeles) appear as signs in the heavens; instead, they have a way of accumulating slowly—as slowly as any other ecological process. But once part of the environment, they are as hard to remove as cancer.

STRATEGY

From an ecological perspective—the only viable one, as we have demonstrated—the necessary strategy is to attack boldly the problems of the total environment rather than react piecemeal to single problems as they become too bothersome. Unfortunately this ideal is more easily stated than implemented. But we are at last beginning to acquire the technology that will make a global view possible. Indeed, we may have progressed already to a point at which we need new laws more than new machines.

Monitoring

We have already seen how monitoring techniques can help us to understand total ecosystems. Far more common, however, is their use for surveillance, most often as alarm systems for public health authorities but increasingly as mechanical witnesses for agencies charged with enforcing the new environmental laws. In this latter capacity they are often a community's only source of scientific information on levels of air and water pollution. This is unfortunate. What most urban communities need is not just a series of early warning signals that tell them when pollution levels are about to become even worse than usual, but an integrated information system for environmental management. Monitoring in the purely negative sense of detecting hazards or violations will succeed only in telling us how badly off we are. Even the monitoring

FIGURE 17.2.   Marine biologist measures live English sole for ongoing sample survey of fish in San Francisco Bay; record keeper (with clipboard, left) and assistants are all volunteers. When completed, survey will show how anti-pollution measures are affecting bay's ecology. (Marine Ecological Institute, Redwood City, California)

equipment now commonly available is far more versatile than the uses to which it is generally put. A community's monitoring system should feed into an ongoing program of scientific research at both a local and a regional level(figure 17.2). The air pollution episode recounted in chapter 7 (p. 143) vividly illustrates the shortcomings of a local-ized approach employing only a narrow range of monitors. Something like environ-mental systems engineering will be required if our highly complicated urban civilization is to avoid total breakdown in the not-too-distant future. Universities and corporate think tanks are already at work on a variety of regional planning models derived largely from systems concepts. However, there are many cultural obstacles that may prevent these models from becoming reality.

The Tragedy of the Commons

It scarcely has to be emphasized here that the allocation of resources is an area in which private interests often conflict with public needs. All the same, we

should remind ourselves that public needs tend to be described in negative terms—
avoiding pollution, staving off famine, and so forth—and that this can be misleading.
The fact that, as John Kenneth Galbraith has said, the United States is in many
respects a land of private affluence and public squalor may blind us to the possibility
of private *and* public affluence. The very word "republic" comes from the Latin for
"public property." And yet we are brought up to believe that the only kind of property worth having is private.

　　　　Our ancestors' failure to preserve the New England commons was discussed in chapter 12. There are virtually no more commons left in the United States.
Land held by the federal government is just that; the public is admitted only under
conditions set by the federal agency that has jurisdiction over it. In any case, nearly
all the land on which people live and work is under the jurisdiction of state or local
governments, which have powers that our ancestors would have found outrageous.
However, such resources as the atmosphere, the oceans, and even fresh water systems
are still regarded as commons in the sense that nobody can claim exclusive ownership
of them (no doubt they would if they could, but the point is that they cannot). If
individuals, corporations, or governments abuse their access to these larger commons,
the public has few means of redress. In modified capitalist systems such as ours, the
government usually appoints so-called watchdog agencies. The disgraceful record of
these agencies in the United States has made "Who will watch the watchers?" a
perennial question of American politics.

　　　　The question then of how to deal with the commons is an increasingly
agonizing one to which we tend to have no answer but vague plans for "educating
the public" or "getting involved." Such messages may well succeed only in giving the
impression that the individual is a fool to stand aside and let the rest of us exploit the
commons. To Garrett Hardin, who perhaps has written more eloquently than anyone
else on this subject, the preservation and sustaining use of the commons lies in "mutual
coercion, mutually agreed upon." In other words, social arrangements that produce responsible actions are based upon social coercion. The example of the Pueblo Indians
is well known: they used what in essence was a system of social ostracism, through
exclusion from clans and fraternities, in order to enforce tribal custom. Of course, the
system could not survive contact with the white man. Nevertheless, it is to certain
forms of tribal behavior, according to Beryl Crowe, that we may have to return. "As
we stand on the 'eve of destruction,' it may well be that the return to the face-to-face
life in the small community unmediated by the electronic media is a very functional
response in terms of the perpetuation of the species." Viewed in this light, the rural
communes that sprang up in the late 1960s and early 1970s have a great deal to teach
us, even if most of them failed.

　　　　The "tragedy of the commons," in Hardin's phrase, ultimately extends to
population growth. Hardin sees that "individuals locked in logic of the commons are
free only to bring on universal ruin. . . . The most important aspect of necessity that
we now recognize, is the necessity of abandoning the commons in breeding. No technical solution can rescue us from the misery of overpopulation." Hardin believes we
should concentrate on persuading young women that they do not necessarily have to

pursue the career of motherhood. Paul Ehrlich, after discussing various tax incentive systems that he admits would probably be ineffective, discriminatory, or both, raises the specter of "an already inept, inefficient and sometimes corrupt federal establishment" making it a criminal offense for a couple to have a third child. Ehrlich hopes to see the United States attain zero population growth before the end of this century. It is a mathematical certainty that, except in the event of some disaster, this will not happen under the present voluntary system. When 50,000 wives aged 18 to 24 were asked by the U.S. Bureau of the Census in June, 1972, how many children they expected to have, the average number per wife came to 2.3. These results were particularly significant because this is the first generation of American women to accept "the pill" as the standard female contraceptive, and there is plenty of evidence that they are using it (nearly half of all younger women in 1970, according to one reliable estimate). But even with a fertility level as low as this, the U.S. population would not stop growing until "well into the next century," the bureau concluded. The main reason is that, because of the postwar baby boom, there are an exceptionally large number of women in this age group (figure 17.3). Moreover, the bureau's estimate was on the conservative side, since it assumed the women would have somewhat fewer children than they planned to have.

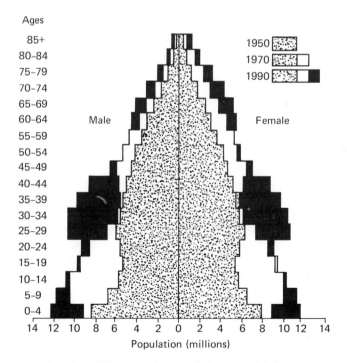

FIGURE 17.3.   Effects on U.S. population pyramid of postwar "baby boom," 1950–90. By 1970 the boom shows up in ages 5–29; by 1990, most of it will be in the peak reproductive ages of 25–49. (U.S. Bureau of the Census, *Current Population Reports*)

Perhaps Ehrlich is a little too ready to speak of compulsory methods. However, it is hard to escape the conclusion that family planning in the conventional sense is not likely to solve any country's population problems. Lyle Saunders, in a 1970 address before a Malaysian seminar on population growth, stated unambiguously that the "most effective and safest means of reducing fertility" was probably "any reasonably effective method of contraception backed up by legal abortion to handle the contraceptive failures." He added that the family planning approach, in addition to being an inadequate brake on fertility, was as unpredictable in its consequences as the individuals to whom such "planning" had been entrusted. Among the measures that go "beyond family planning" Saunders listed: stricter immigration laws (most immigrants tend to be males in their twenties and thirties); liberalization of abortion laws; compulsory abortion for unmarried mothers; higher taxes for married persons; later marriage; more education and jobs for women; better social security (so that parents need not depend on children in their old age); more and better information campaigns on methods of birth control; more effective contraceptives; removal of import duties on contraceptives; more sterilization; sex education in the public schools; more research into how the birth rate is affected by policies not directly related to birth control (military service, for instance); and more cooperation from nongovernmental institutions in "selling" birth control to the general public. We do not necessarily endorse any one of these methods as likely to prove effective in the United states; here, as elsewhere, acceptability is a prime factor. However, we do agree with Saunders on the desirability of a coordinated approach that creates a variety of social pressures unfavorable to population growth.

PLANNING

The general purpose of planning is to establish which resources are to serve which goals, and in what proportion. Unfortunately, the goal is usually growth—at all costs. But it does not have to be. The development of a plan provides nothing more or less than a central repository of objectives for proposed public action. In the realm of land use, as Israel Stollman has pointed out, a few simple principles are usually followed: (1) The plan is set up to cover the total geographic area in question. (2) Planning is applied simultaneously to all land use, circulation patterns, and economic interaction. (3) Logical and workable planning units are delineated. (4) Long-range consequences are examined and considered in the light of short-range needs.

A preliminary "general plan" is the best, though expensive, first step. In medium-size metropolitan areas this stage can cost between $200,000 and $500,000. Most U.S. cities are entitled to financial aid from the federal government, under certain conditions. Among these, very often, is a requirement for plans that involve the entire county, not just the city. Insofar as this reduces the kind of political fragmentation described in chapter 10, it is a step in the right direction. Preliminary planning utilizes such a wide range of inputs that it seems the logical point at which to introduce the goals of ecological balance and environmental quality. Some elements of systems analysis should also be introduced at this point.

The next step after preliminary planning is that of development planning. Here, situations are studied in greater detail. Participants in the plan, such as the various small cities and communities, are organized. The expertise of public and private interest groups is drawn upon. Planning commissions and departments give operational meaning to mathematical models. Alternative solutions are examined by means of computerized testing. This phase ends with submittal of the plan for acceptance, rejection, or modification by the citizens of the plan area.

Planning and Economic Efficiency

Public planning was for a long time considered to be inconsistent with economic efficiency. This doctrine is still with us to some degree, but no one has yet managed to prove that either planning or lack of planning is intrinsically superior. John Kenneth Galbraith feels that in many areas of resource utilization the free play of market resources provides a more satisfactory solution than planned development. Yet in many other sectors of the economy the opposite is true. "There is no natural presumption in favor of the market; given the growth of the industrial system the presumption is, if anything, the reverse. And to rely on the market where planning is required is to invite a nasty mess." (Galbraith 1967, pp. 361–362).

TACTICS

Once a plan is accepted the actual planning situation ends and is replaced by an administrative phase. Here, the management of community resources becomes the first task. It would be a relief if, at this point, we could begin to speak of a truly human ecology. But in the United States, it seems, we have not yet reached this point. For instance, Wolf von Eckardt feels that we should have high-rise housing in public parks. What could be more logical and, in the context of the private enterprise system, more impossible?

Zoning

The principal technique used in plan implementation is zoning. This technique was derived from police powers and was first used to isolate public dangers, such as gunpowder mills, from the population. A logical development from this was nuisance zoning, followed eventually by use districts. Comprehensive zoning ordinances

began appearing in the United States by the early 1920s. The principle underlying
these changes was upheld by the Supreme Court in 1926 and has been expanding ever
since.

Use regulation is most often applied in the form of exclusive zoning for
residential, agriculture, business, industrial, or related purposes. Other applications may
involve a zone in which land uses are mixed. Zoning is supposed to maintain consistent
and logical patterns of land use within a city or region. Of course, opinions may differ
as to what is "consistent." However, there is some agreement that zoning should maintain property values, both public and private.

The pitfalls of zoning are numerous. All too often it only reinforces the
status quo, which generally means the worst kind of unrestricted enterprise and random
land development. Thus zoning becomes a mere justification for existing land uses.
Meanwhile, vested interests seek to have the zoning laws changed wherever it would
be profitable for them to do so. The kind of rezoning they want is typically "down
zoning," that is, zoning for more inhabitants per acre. Such concentration may not be
bad itself, but it is often at the expense of open space or other irreplaceable features.
Communities that succumb to this kind of development may soon come down with a
bad case of urban sprawl, since the kinds of business that can survive in the rezoned
area may not be at all the kind they wanted to see there.

No doubt zoning will continue to be the chief tool at the disposal of planners, but it has little long-term effectiveness if applied piecemeal on a local basis.
For instance, according to a report prepared for the California Legislature Joint Committee on Open Space Lands, over half a million acres of *prime* California agricultural
land will probably have been converted to other uses by the end of the 1967–80
period—and this is only one-quarter of the total agricultural land to suffer such a fate.
California has about 7 million acres of agricultural land—not a huge amount for the
nation's leading agricultural producer and in any case not infinite. This urban encroachment on California's chief economic asset has come about because the state has been
too free in delegating its power over land use to local governments. California state law
now requires both cities and counties to develop zoning ordinances consistent with
"the interest of the public in . . . orderly growth." It also recognizes that open space
should be preserved for human enjoyment, not just economic use. Nevertheless,
despite the committee's valiant efforts to establish a state open space policy, the public
interest in "orderly growth" is still at the mercy of private developers.

Taxation

The problem of urban sprawl can be dealt with at least partly by proper
use of taxing powers—for instance, by reducing taxes on agricultural land and setting
very high rates for proposed urban uses—but it usually is not. It is a fact, however, that
developers are constantly nibbling at the urban fringe not only because land is cheaper
and available in larger parcels but because taxes are low. Land speculation at the urban
fringe, although usually very profitable to the speculator (it is, after all, a sure bet that
most cities will grow) is very wasteful from the community's point of view. Vacant

land bought up for speculation is held as it were in cold storage, while the city, which lacks the power of eminent domain (p. 16), has to make do with what is left. Short of granting the power of eminent domain to local governments (something that has been seriously recommended by many land use specialists) the only remedy would appear to be economic incentives through taxation, whether direct or indirect. Such incentives are not at all easy to devise.

Utility Extension Control

Since neither zoning nor taxing policies can assure the desired results, a city or region may try for further control through its jurisdiction over such utilities as water, power, and sewage. This is perhaps the most stringent measure that can be used to halt rapid suburban sprawl. Few developers are willing to risk investment in an area where they know that utilities will not be available. The day is probably near when utility control will be used to halt growth in many urban regions. Already many smaller cities and towns are opting for no-growth plans.

Metropolitan Government

As we pointed out in chapter 10, the government of metropolitan America is endlessly fragmented: the classic example is the existence within 50 miles of down-town New York City of 1,500 different political units having taxing authority. Trying to agree on a regional plan under such circumstances is a formidable if not impossible task. In one west coast metropolitan region a comprehensive planning organization had to coordinate the desires and needs of thirteen city councils, the board of supervisors, the unified port district, three major water districts, and the state government, to say nothing of pressure from private citizens, conservation groups, chambers of commerce, and tourist bureaus. No wonder that metropolitan government is more praised than practiced.

In spite of generally dismal prospects, a few places—notably Dade County, Florida, (greater Miami)—have made some progress in establishing metropolitan government. Northern California has its Association of Bay Area Governments (**A.B.A.G.**), and now a Southern California Area Government (**S.C.A.G.**) is being tried out. Both A.B.A.G. and S.C.A.G. have less power than Dade County, but they are attempting to coordinate local and regional planning. Unfortunately, this two-tiered approach is rather like trying to catch fish with blacksmith's tongs: the real problems keep getting away.

Review Functions

Neither planning nor metropolitan government will be effective unless the planning process includes a built-in review system. Policy and techniques should be reviewed at least every five years and perhaps annually if circumstances warrant. This is not to say that plans should be continually revised, since the general guidelines would remain quite constant. But neither should they be adhered to mechanically; no master plan should become master of the planners who created it. Changing birth rates, economic conditions, or legislative climate may all necessitate changes in planning goals and priorities, as indeed may a host of other factors. Although we may aim at the optimum, we can never be quite certain what it is or how to reach it.

SHAPING FUTURE GROWTH

If only planning could be done in the certainty that growth would stabilize and that each city or region would have fixed needs! However, this is not in the offing. The U.S. Department of Housing and Urban Development expects 272 new cities to be built between 1970 and 2000 in order to accommodate a population growth that could be as high as 100 million. If this growth is to be absorbed without major environmental deterioration there will have to be far more community planning. The 63 new communities started between 1947 and 1970 do not impress in this respect; let us hope that our next attempts will be better. There are a great many questions waiting to be answered. Do we scatter people as far and wide as modern communications will allow, or do we attempt to concentrate them in the traditional urban nodes? How large should an individual city be allowed to grow? If it is decided that a city is large enough, how is its growth to be stopped? Should we set up new towns to absorb excess growth? How long can we build such new towns and still have open countryside left for buffer zones? We also need to consider the relationship between community size and economic efficiency. Some authorities believe that the optimum size of a city, from both a private and a municipal point of view, is in the range of 200,000 to 300,000 people. The crucial factor, in a socioeconomic system like ours, is to achieve a workable balance between public and private costs (figure 17.4).

New Towns and Experimental Cities

The new town movement, as we saw in chapter 10, is well under way in both Britain and Scandinavia. The keynote appears to be decentralization. Thus Tapiola, in Finland, has a single town center surrounded by three independent neighborhoods of some 6,000 inhabitants each. Conceived as an economically and socially independent community, it offers a generous range of urban facilities. Parks and other recreational facilities extend away from the open ends of its central plaza, while pedestrian walks lead from the center into carefully landscaped residential areas. The industrial park that provides much of the economic balance is unobtrusively situated between two of the residential areas. Building designs are pleasant and unobtrusive; it is impossible to tell from the exterior of a building the income bracket of its occupants.

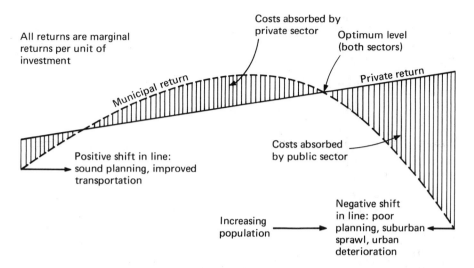

All returns are marginal
returns per unit of
investment

Costs absorbed by
private sector

Optimum level
(both sectors)

Municipal return

Private return

Positive shift in line:
sound planning, improved
transportation

Costs absorbed
by public sector

Increasing
population

Negative shift
in line: poor
planning, suburban
sprawl, urban
deterioration

FIGURE 17.4.   Public and private costs: Who will pay for sound planning? The relationship of
marginal returns in the public sector and private sector vary with size of city. In general increasing
city size makes return in the private sector more profitable, but in the public sector the city takes
in proportionately more than it pays out only in a certain *optimum* range. Outside that optimum
range the marginal returns fall off rapidly. (Lee E. Kapolski, "Toward a Survival Ethic: An
Economic Approach," unpublished paper, by permission of the author)

We have yet to achieve any comparable success in the United States.
Reston, Virginia, one of the oldest and best known of American new towns, has suffered from financial problems in recent years, and is in danger of becoming yet another
bedroom community for Washington. It is also very much a middle-class community;
Reston does not receive subsidy for low-cost housing. Closest, perhaps, to the model of
Tapiola is Jonathan, Minnesota, which will eventually have about 50,000 inhabitants
divided among several "villages." Only Village One is in operation so far, but the results
are at least architecturally impressive, and there is the same emphasis on pedestrian
traffic as in Tapiola (figure 17.5).
    The new town concept can be extended to include even larger, more com-
prehensive schemes. Athelstan Spilhaus calls his the "experimental city." Its comprehensive approach is for a system of dispersed cities, controlled in size and surrounded
by wide areas of open lands. A size limit of a quarter million has been suggested for
each city; it is hoped that this would drastically reduce the risks of pollution, congestion, and even social disorganization. Buckminster Fuller goes even farther: he thinks
that much of the industry of these future cities will be automated and located outside
the cities themselves, so that citizens will be able to concentrate more on nonmaterial
values. The present total population of the United States could be settled in only 800
such cities, constructed with minimum incursions on lands already tied up for urban
purposes. Little wonder that Spilhaus talks almost glibly about selectively dismantling
and dispersing the existing overgrown cities.

The Spilhaus design calls for a city with a self-sustaining economy; its independent status is reinforced by its situation, at least 100 miles from existing urban centers of any significance. A densely populated core is surrounded by open land of an area perhaps one hundred times as great as the core. This land is used for forestry, agriculture, recreation, nature preserves, or just open space. The city is constructed of the newest lightweight materials, following a modular plan. The idea here is to avoid absolute permanency of buildings—the opposite of the position we adopted in chapter 13, but nevertheless an idea worth considering. Waste collection and recycling is total. Spilhaus sees this as one of the major prerequisites. Although this is an admittedly futuristic concept, it is being taken seriously enough to warrant federal research grants (p. 202).

Whether we continue to concentrate our urbanization on a tiny portion of our land base or expand to something much larger, it is certain that we must consider all the alternatives as methodically as possible. Dispersal to new, planned cities is definitely one of the courses open to us. Where the ecological fabric has been worn thin, we may be forced to disperse. Hopefully, the building of new towns will be only a temporary phase, a prelude to a period of stability and zero population growth.

Renewal

Urban renewal has failed so badly in this country that almost any imaginative new approach is worthy of consideration. It has even been suggested that so-called urban platforms be constructed above blighted areas. Such platforms, made of steel and concrete, could be used as a base for new development. Entire communities could be relocated above the platform without major alteration in the existing spatial and social arrangements. The area below could then be renovated and put to some productive use. The additional space thus acquired would help pay for the cost of the operation. If such a scheme appears reminiscent of Fritz Lang's silent movie classic, *Metropolis,* this may well be a point in its favor: the metropolis in question was a great success technologically, and failed only because of social inequities we can hope to avoid.

NEEDED: A NATIONAL LAND USE POLICY

As we saw in chapter 10, the problem of the cities has many different aspects, from housing to taxation. But it can be summed up in a few words: poor use of centrally located lands. Poor use, in this case, as in so many others, means poor allocation of resources. We are taxed to rocket men to the moon, participate in foreign military adventures, and develop arsenals of biological and chemical weapons that only madmen would want to use. But although most of us live in cities, it seems that we cannot vote ourselves a decent urban environment or a sane pattern of urban development.

FIGURE 17.5.   An American "new town": Jonathan, Minnesota. Designed to house 50,000 inhabitants, Jonathan is organized into several village-like "neighborhoods," of which this is one. (Trumble, Spano, and Associates, Inc., Minneapolis)

On February 8, 1971, President Nixon sent Congress a message on the environment that included the outline of a national land use policy. The general aims of that policy have already been described (p. 368); it would be hard to find serious fault with them. How were these proposals translated into action?

In the first place, it is clear from the draft legislation subsequently transmitted to Congress by Secretary of the Interior Rogers Morton that what the president had in mind was primarily state land policy, not federal. The draft contained various incentives—chiefly, federal development grants—for the states to set up their own land use programs over a period of five years, and provided for federal land use in each state to be coordinated with such programs. However, the states were expressly forbidden to use their federal grants (which in any case were not large) to buy real estate, and it was not at all clear what the federal government could do about states that chose not to have land use programs at all. But perhaps the weakest point of the whole program was the fact that it was expressly limited to land use issues and decisions "of more than local interest." Damage to ecological processes in areas that were *not* of regional or statewide interest was not deemed to be "of critical environmental concern."

Even more controversial was the section of the bill—title IV—that dealt with the management of public lands. In the form in which it was reported out by the House Committee on Interior and Insular Affairs, the bill (H.R. 7211) was accused by conservationists of permitting the federal government to dispose of such public lands as national parks and national wildlife refuges for purely private and commercial purposes, of leaving such lands unprotected from mining and logging, and of leaving the door open to federal giveaways of natural resources in the form of grazing privileges, mineral rights, and so on. By contrast, the Senate version of the bill (S. 632) omitted mention of public land use (which was made the subject of separate Senate legislation) and concentrated on the president's program for encouraging better state land use. It was therefore supported by conservationists.

As of this writing, neither H.R. 7211 nor S. 632 had been brought to a floor vote, though many observers considered them the most important legislation of their type in half a century. Moreover, the fate of S. 632 was thought to be uncertain, and that of H.R. 7211 was complicated by personal political considerations and by jurisdictional squabbles between committees. It therefore seems appropriate to ask: Is our political system in its present form capable of producing and enforcing a national land use policy and if it is, will that policy make any real difference? If the answer is no, we should all ask ourselves very seriously if the reason is not our own laziness or indifference. How many of you who read this chapter had heard of either H.R. 7211 or S. 632, or would have written to your congressmen if you had heard of them?

REFERENCES

California Legislature Joint Committee on Open Space Lands, *State Open Space and Resource Conservation Program for California,* prepared by Eckbo, Dean, Austin & Williams (Sacramento: the Joint Committee, 1972).

Commission on Population Growth and the American Future, *Population and the American Future* (New York: Signet, 1972).

Crowe, Beryl L., "The Tragedy of the Commons Revisited," *Science,* November 28, 1969.

Eckhardt, Wolf von, *A Place to Live* (New York: Delacorte, 1967).

Ehrlich, Paul R., and Richard L. Harriman, *How To Be a Survivor: A Plan to Save Spaceship Earth* (New York: Ballantine, 1971).

Galbraith, John Kenneth, *The Affluent Society,* (Boston: Houghton Mifflin, 1958).

——, *The New Industrial State* (Boston: Houghton Mifflin, 1967).

Hardin, Garrett, "The Tragedy of the Commons," *Science,* December 13, 1968.

McHarg, Ian L., "Ecological Determinism," in F. Fraser Darling and John P. Milton (eds.), *Future Environments of North America* (Garden City: Natural History Press, 1966).

National Goals Research Staff, *Toward Balanced Growth: Quantity and Quality* (Washington, D.C.: U.S. Government Printing Office, 1970).

Saunders, Lyle, "Beyond Family Planning," A Ford Foundation Reprint (New York: the Foundation, 1970).

Spilhaus, Athelstan, "The Experimental City," *Science,* February 16, 1968.

Stollman, Israel, "Uses and Principles of Planning." in *A Place to Live: Yearbook of Agriculture, 1963* (Washington, D.C.: U.S. Government Printing Office, 1963).

U.S. Department of Health, Education and Welfare, *Strategy for a Livable Environment* (Washington, D.C.: U.S. Government Printing Office, 1967).

18 THE CHOICES BEFORE US

Although the main focus of this book is upon the United States, we have been at some pains to emphasize the global nature of the environmental problem. This problem, as it has become almost commonplace to remark, is not the same for the developing nations as for the developed ones. The United States, despite the hardships suffered by the one-fifth of the population who live below or just above the poverty level, is choking on its own affluence. In the developing nations, most of them far poorer than even the poorest areas of the United States, the enemies are still hunger and disease. Americans may worry about disappearing species of wildlife. But the most endangered species, as would be evident from a visit to Calcutta or Saigon, is man. Moreover it is possible to exaggerate the developing countries' freedom from pollution; for instance, some of the world's worst air pollution is found in Bilbao, Spain.

The developing countries, then, suffer from yet another handicap: they cannot afford to clean up the pollution generated by the level of industrial development they have managed to attain. From urbanization without industrialization they proceed—if they are lucky—to industrialization without environmental control. Following in the footsteps of affluent America, are they condemned to repeat America's mistakes?

THE END OF AFFLUENCE

If consumption of nonrenewable resources cannot long be sustained at present levels in this country, still less can it be sustained worldwide. The history of American-style mass affluence is therefore likely to be brief. Existing pressures upon land are likely to increase, and more advanced technology is just as likely to result in more pollution as in more efficient use of resources. The argument that larger populations will be able to solve their problems because they produce more geniuses ignores the fact that genius needs a suitable environment in which to unfold. This is not to deny the growth of knowledge. But we have at most a brief period in which we might be able to make use of that knowledge to free us from our dependence on nonrenewable resources. In the words of Kenneth Boulding, "it is not unreasonable to look upon the present era as a chance which man has (and probably a unique chance at that, which will never be repeated) of translating his natural capital into enough knowledge that will enable him to do without it."

How much knowledge will we need to accomplish this transition? Unfortunately, we do not know. Success may be almost within our grasp, or it may be so far removed that we will be unable to reach it soon enough. Certainly we are closer to it in the physical and natural sciences than in the social sciences. Perhaps this is just another

FIGURE 18.1.   This young woman is standing among marigolds growing in the four-acre student-community organic garden at the University of California, Santa Cruz. Garden is worked by "French intensive" method, which stresses mutual stimulation of certain species when planted closely together. (photo by Alexander Lowry, Santa Cruz, California)

way of saying that long-standing social arrangements are not easily changed, no matter what the current state of knowledge about them. But we cannot hope to survive with a set of social arrangements designed for use under economic and technological circumstances that no longer exist. Indeed, we seem headed for the worst of all possible worlds, since we persist in forms of social organization that are not only out of date on the human time scale but out of cycle with nonhuman ecological systems.

In so-called primitive societies, both the economic and the social system (insofar as they can be distinguished at all) are oriented to ecological realities. For societies preoccupied with mere physical survival, it could hardly be otherwise. But once survival is more or less assured, the means employed to this end become greatly elaborated, so that other ends can be pursued simultaneously. Despite the complexity of modern industrial civilization, survival remains the one overriding social and individual goal of which everyone is at least intermittently conscious. Nevertheless, the means of survival are not accurately perceived. Nature is still the enemy and scarcity the principal threat. In a society that has thoroughly subjugated nature and is stifling in its own abundance, these attitudes represent an example of what sociologists call cultural lag. It is time for us to accept nature as a friend and partner, while realizing that the greatest threat to survival is our own industrial way of life.

Man has reached the present dead end in his development by selectively upsetting the balance of natural systems. His success at this has been phenomenal. Simplification and streamlining of food chains has made it possible to increase human numbers as never before. Since human knowledge is cumulative, man has a potential for ecological disruption not given to any other species. The result has been a philosophy of economic growth as progress and economic stability as stagnation. This is true at present of both capitalist and socialist countries (whether the Chinese will prove the first major exception remains to be seen). Industrial societies are currently throwing away or wasting a greater volume of materials than they consume, thus adding to the already overloaded natural recycling processes that make life on earth possible. In many areas, human concentration is already approaching the level at which recycling systems, both natural and artificial, tend to break down completely. It is in fact quite possible to argue that the human race is more likely to perish from pollution than from lack of food.

Many of the best informed contemporary thinkers consider man a doomed species. S. R. Eyre, for instance, believes that man has reached the "swarming stage." The next stage, for most species, is rapid decline.

The Need for an Ethic

There is nothing new about materialism, but the dynamic materialism of contemporary America has a quality of its own. It is a materialism based on splendid certainties: economic goals are tangible, physical consumption is real, and growth rates are measurable. Under such a system the status quo involves not the preservation of a carefully developed ecological niche, but rather mass consumption of consumer goods, rapid resource turnover, and an unparalleled rate of obsolescence for virtually every kind of product. Any use of resources that results in lower profits or reduced individual consumption is ruled unacceptable by the system. Such conservation as is permitted generally means no more than conservation of the existing order.

It is becoming clearer every day that our highly competitive and wasteful economic system—the "cowboy economy," as one wit has dubbed it—is itself obsolete. By any reasonable standard, free enterprise is a failure. Victor Lebow, a businessman with a long and successful career, has aptly called it "the opium of the American people." The implicit comparison with medieval religion is a just one: propaganda in favor of the free enterprise system is so massive and continuous that most Americans are quite unconscious of how far it has pervaded their lives.

> *With its bait of free entertainment, television mesmerizes the consumer and shapes his wants, ambitions, opinions, prejudices. On that tube the "shows" are sandwiched between commercials for detergents, automobiles, deodorants, candidates for office, appeals to help victims of various diseases, calls to subsidize propaganda behind the Iron Curtain (actually to lend credibility to the supposedly uncontrolled "Radio Free Europe," a CIA operation), contests between competing rolls of toilet paper, nubile females offering themselves for mouthwashes and tooth pastes—a phantasmagoria of products and prejudices, of bodies yielding suggestively, of murder fictional and murder all too real from that day's battle fronts. It is the instant recording of a world gone quite mad. A Savonarola, were he on this scene, would liken it to Sodom and Gomorrah. And it is the world that business built, the world from which it profits. (Lebow 1972, p. 80)*

Clearly, we need a new ethic of resource use. But who is to say what it shall be? The concept of environmental quality is highly subjective; at least economic goals are clear-cut and tangible. It is hardly surprising that our environmental criteria are usually negative. Absence of severe air or water pollution, reasonable security from natural disasters such as floods, municipal services that, while not abundant, are adequate for the needs of most taxpayers—such are the amenities of modern living. What we call the good life is too often a matter of selfish acquisition and joyless consumption. The temptation, in a varied and rapidly changing society, is to opt for moral relativism, and throw all absolute standards overboard. Pursuing what we think is freedom we end up enslaving not only ourselves but future generations that will inherit the consequences of our mistakes. Surely, if we are ever going to survive, we should think less of freedom and more of justice. In the age-old words of Aristotle:

> *A social instinct is implanted in all men by nature, and yet he who first founded the state was the greatest of benefactors. For man, when perfected, is the best of animals, but, when separated from law and justice, he is the worst of all. . . . (Politics, 1.2)*

ALTERNATIVES

Let us assume that we want to survive. But mere survival is not a very elevated goal in this day and age. Survival that preserves the greatest flexibility of cyclic functions in the ecosphere is the most desirable alternative. Man-made systems and natural systems must coexist in a state of dynamic equilibrium. Once this is achieved, there will be maximum opportunity to restore altered and decayed habitats.

Population Problem or Technology Problem?

Some publicity has been given in recent years to the controversy over whether population growth or technology is "really" the main threat to our survival. Supporters of the latter view have tended to cite Barry Commoner, who has pointed out—quite correctly—that most of the industrial technology developed in the United States since World War II adds significantly to environmental pollution. The motive, of course, has been profit. Thus detergents, according to Commoner, are roughly twice as profitable as soap, and the continuous development and marketing of new synthetic organic chemicals, including the biocides, is the very basis of profitability in the chemical industry. Commoner sees modern technology as "the crucial link between pollution and profits," and points out that increased productivity might cease to be profitable if industry had to pay for effective control of the accompanying pollution.

The chief opponent of this viewpoint is, curiously enough, Paul R. Ehrlich, who has argued at length that there were man-made ecological disasters long before modern technology came on the scene, and that pollution is far from the only form of environmental deterioration. According to Ehrlich, the environmental impact of the new technology is likely to be far more severe in a population that is large, affluent, and growing. This description fits the United States:

> ... the vast majority of American babies are born into white, middle-class
> families. ... It is the affluent groups whose patterns of consumption are
> wasting the resources of our planet and destroying its environment. They
> buy the endless rounds of new cars, TV sets, appliances, and powered
> gadgets. ... Smog-producing coal fired plants and potentially deadly nu-
> clear power plants are not being built helter-skelter to meet the power
> demands of ghettos! (Ehrlich and Harriman 1971, pp. 21–22)

We suspect that the basic differences here are more ideological than scientific. Nevertheless, the fact that they have arisen is a good indication of how far we still have to go before arriving at a comprehensive science of the environment. For instance, Herbert Fox and Clarke Rees have pointed out that although the population of New York City has grown hardly at all over the last ten years, there have been average annual increases of 3 percent per capita in its solid waste disposal requirements and of

6 percent in its per capita energy consumption. They further calculate that only 20 percent of current increase in the GNP can be attributed solely to population; increased consumption and replacement account for the rest.

How are we to interpret such facts? Ronald G. Ridker, project director of the research team that supplied data to the Commission on Population Growth and the American Future, has systematically explored the relationship between pollution, resource consumption, population growth, and economic growth. He concludes that for the United States, at least between now and the turn of the century, a change in population growth would affect resource consumption less than a change in economic growth:"a one-percent reduction in population would reduce consumption of re- sources in the year 2000 by 0.2 to 0.7 percent, whereas the equivalent percentage reduction in per capita GNP would reduce consumption in that year 0.6 to 3.5 percent." Ridker also comes out strongly in favor of a direct attack on pollution as more likely to be effective, at least in the short run, than a reduction in either pop- ulation or economic growth. Such an attack need not cost more than 2 percent of what the nation's GNP is likely to be in the year 2000 (in 1970 the cost of fighting pollution was about 1 percent of GNP). After about 2000, however, simple control of pollution will start to bring in diminishing returns, and reductions in population and economic growth may offer the only hope of substantial further improvement.

Is There a Future?

Ridker and his associates succeeded in collecting a large quantity of infor- mation, but they actually considered a relatively small number of variables. Moreover (as they were commissioned to do) they focused almost entirely on the United States. The team that produced *The Limits to Growth* attempted to construct a world model that included a great many more variables and relationships (figure 18.2). Starting from what they called "the five basic quantities, or levels—population, capital, food, nonrenewable resources, and pollution," they went on to include as many other levels as possible, together with the rates determining their operation. Figure 18.2 is actually an earlier version of the model used in *The Limits of Growth,* but it was constructed along exactly the same principles. It will be seen that the model includes a great many feedback loops, or relationships that involve the mutual influence of two or more var- iables on each other. The great value of this exercise, as the authors would be the first to admit, is that it reveals our ignorance. For instance, we know almost nothing about how the various types of pollution affect average length of life. There are also a great many factors that the model omits completely—national boundaries, for instance, and world trade balances. Nevertheless, much is known about some of these relationships; the main problem is lack of information (anyone who doubts this is advised to read the table footnotes in any issue of the *U. N. Demographic Yearbook!*). The model has been severely criticized for oversimplifying a situation that is probably quite beyond the intellectual grasp of anyone. Nevertheless, we would do well to heed the projection

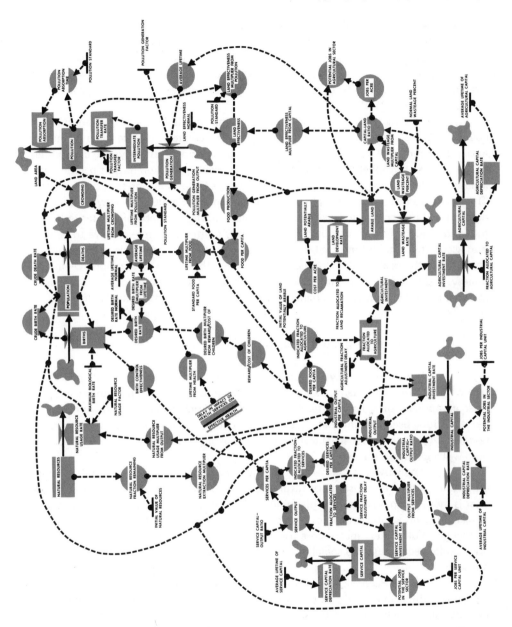

FIGURE 18.2.   World flow model based on data developed by Jay Forrester, Dennis Meadows, and their associates at the Massachusetts Institute of Technology. Rectangles stand for "levels" (see text), valves for "rates" (e.g., the birth rate), and circles for factors affecting rates. Clouds are unimportant factors. (reproduced by permission of the World Future Society, Washington, D.C., from *The Futurist,* August 1971, pp. 140–141)

based on the model. The computer showed that, after the depletion of nonrenewable resources, the amount of capital needed to obtain more resources became so huge that there was nothing left for investment. Since agriculture had become thoroughly industrialized, depreciation of capital stock meant the eventual collapse of food supplies and a rapid increase in deaths from starvation. Both economic and population growth were halted by the year 2100.

Once again it should be emphasized that this is only a projection. But it could easily become a reality if we do not move immediately to close some of the gaps in our environmental knowledge. For instance, to determine the recycling capabilities of the earth's atmosphere and then to set the allowable pollution output below that level is simple in theory. Its application, however, is beyond our present capabilities. The interaction between atmospheric oxygen and marine pollution, between energy demand and fuel conversion, between particulate matter and incoming solar radiation—to mention just a few of the obvious and primary control systems—all have to be taken into account in establishing a safety level. Consideration of man-made systems further complicates the issue. In the world of tomorrow—if there is to be a tomorrow—man, society, and nature must be linked into a system capable of supplying not only basic material needs but at least the chance of progress toward a better quality of life.

A Totally Planned Environment?

It will not be easy for Americans to give up the dream of mass consumption without limit. For many, perhaps most of us, the freedom to pollute is a cherished component of the good life. Surely a society as rich as ours can afford it. And yet it has long been evident that all is not well, and that drastic measures will have to be taken if our urban-industrial civilization is to avoid collapse. How much of our freedom will we have to surrender?

The answer is that we do not know, but that every day we put off facing up to the question diminishes our future store of freedom. The remedy for less freedom later is more planning now—not planning for its own sake, but planning that incorporates ecologically sound principles of design. Provided that population is stabilized, such planning can ultimately mean more freedom, not less. But first we have to get rid of our obsolete economic and social inventory, the embodiment of so many ecological mistakes.

Victor Papanek, one of the world's most creative industrial designers, has argued forcefully that nearly all present-day design serves only as a marketing aid; in fact, he calls industrial design the second phoniest profession after advertising. When designers are wholly at the service of advertisers, their products are likely to discriminate against the poor. In almost any product, according to Papanek, there are now five basic lines (in ascending order of price):

1. "Virtually a toy" (e.g., a cheap camera).
2. Junk (e.g., most small appliances).

FIGURE 18.3.   Demolition of Pruitt-Igoe public housing complex in St. Louis, 1972. Crime and vandalism so plagued this complex that authorities decided it was beyond rehabilitation. Same could be said of public housing policies that have created soul-destroying "vertical ghettoes" like one shown here. (St. Louis Post–Dispatch)

3. "An honest piece of equipment but vastly overpriced" (this should have been the first line).
4. So-called luxury (the third line, loaded down with extras).
5. Good design (sold on the same price scale as original works of art even if intended by the designer for mass production).

Besides the pressures of mass marketing, cultural blocks of various kinds discourage creative design and the research that goes into it. For instance, the whole topic of excretion and decomposition is taboo in our society. As a result, we tend not to take seriously the possible uses of decomposers as energy sources. Production of methane gas from animal wastes has already been discussed (p. 89); as Papanek says, it is practiced mainly by a few knowledgeable eccentrics who do not mind being laughed at. He goes on to recount a personal experience: a manufacturer of toilet bowls rejected his design for varying the amount of water used for flushing according to the type of waste to be flushed on the grounds that such a convenience would be in bad taste. In this connection it should be pointed out that in New York City during the water shortages of the late 1960s one of the most frequent official slogans was: Don't Flush for Everything! It seems that it takes a visible state of emergency to overcome inhibitions of this kind.

One of Papanek's main arguments is that, despite the alleged amenities of consumerism, designers are *not* producing what most people want.

> *Our townscape as well bears the stamp of irresponsible design. Look through the train window as you approach New York, Chicago, Detroit, Los Angeles. Observe the miles of anonymous tenements, the dingy, twisted streets full of cooped-up, unhappy children. Pick your way carefully through the filth and litter that mark our downtowns or walk past the monotonous ranch houses of suburbia where myriad picture windows grin their empty invitation, their tele-viscous promise. Breathe the cancer-inducing exhaust of factory and car, watch the strontium-90 enriched snow, listen to the idiot roar of the subway, the squealing brakes. And in the ghastly glare of the neon signs, under the spiky TV aerials, remember, this is our custom-designed environment. (Papanek 1971, p. 165)*

Under these circumstances, the best course is often to start again from scratch (figure 18.3).

Good design, as Papanek has emphasized, does not serve a merely cosmetic function; rather it is a whole way of life. It therefore involves a wholly new attitude toward resources. We are only just beginning to see how different this new attitude must be from the old one, and many people are unable to accept that so drastic a change is either necessary or desirable. Even the difference between the old concept of a resource as a commodity and the broader concept of the environment as the resource that contains all other resources is not yet firmly fixed in our minds. In time, however, people will adjust to the new attitudes. The main stumbling block will be not so much the attitudes themselves as the accompanying change in social patterns, which will be resisted to the end by economic vested interests and by all who find economics, or what currently passes for economics, an adequate guide to social policy. Probably the only answer in a society such as ours is to call in countervailing economic interests in the form of government subsidies for new programs. The corporate structure will undoubtedly respond to such pressure. It will also respond to heavier and swifter penalties for violations of environmental protection laws. What will *not* work is leaving the corporations to promote environmental and social reform at their own expense and in their own good time.

Some efforts have been made in recent years to prove that it is only a matter of time before corporations "get involved" in reform, and that when they do the burning issues of the day will all be resolved. Thus a collection of articles originally published in the *Wall Street Journal* (which itself takes a rather friendly attitude toward conservation and advocates moderate social reform) includes numerous examples of corporations that train the unemployed, go out of their way to hire members of minority groups, adopt nutritional or unit price labeling, and so on. A few of these programs sound quite impressive—until one measures them against the actual extent of the problem. But can we suppose that all corporations will ever act in the same way as the few socially motivated ones? The sad truth is that this is not at all likely to happen. Under existing law, corporations are allowed to deduct up to 5 percent of profits from their income for philanthropic purposes. The present average for all corporations is only 1 percent (*Getting Involved*, p. 8). No doubt many business executives—one would hope the majority—are men of good will. But the intentions of individuals can make practically no difference as long as the overriding purpose of the system to which they belong is to maximize commercial profit. There is rarely any money in programs of social reform—otherwise the reform would not be needed; there is certainly none at all in reducing and eventually eliminating pollution, because this will have to involve fewer products and less consumption. Corporations know this very well, and are quick to argue that it will also mean fewer jobs. This, of course, will be true only if we allow it to be true; it is only an extreme form of the dubious philosophy that the costs of corporate pollution and depredation have to be passed on to the consumer. But if the public cannot afford these costs and the corporations will not, then who will? Obviously, the only other power commensurate with the problem is that of the federal government.

It will be much harder to decide at what level government power should be applied. The sheer size of federal programs tends to make them unwieldy, and their impersonality generates alienation, which in turn generates corruption and inefficiency. Local programs, even if they can get adequate financing, are often too firmly in the hands of entrenched special interests, both political and economic, to effect any meaningful change. It is because of this situation—indeed, because of the political facts of life in the United States—that Joseph L. Sax, for instance, has argued in favor of a greater environmental role for the courts.

THE ETHICS OF SURVIVAL

The free enterprise system is based on the eighteenth-century idea that enlightened self-interest, if permitted to operate freely, will automatically bring about the common good. Although stated with more refinement by philosophers and economists, notably by Adam Smith (1723–90), the idea has been influential chiefly in its cruder form. Reinforced in the nineteenth century by the Darwinian idea of the survival of the fittest, it became the perfect rationale for unrestrained economic individualism.

Today, the majority of Americans have come to believe, however reluctantly, that the social sphere cannot just be left to take care of itself. If any evidence of this were still needed, the mounting welfare rolls would provide it. But few Americans indeed are in the habit of considering each economic act of theirs in the light of its social effects. It is therefore a most useful exercise to consider Walter Firey's fourfold typology of resource use (figure 18.4). Starting at the top with "gainful for self—gainful for others," we have a type of situation that, although superficially attractive, does not necessarily serve the ends of conservation. Such a use has sometimes been called "conservancy," because it is not harmful to societal needs insofar as it involves balancing the flow of goods and energy within the bounds of the resource base. But it is

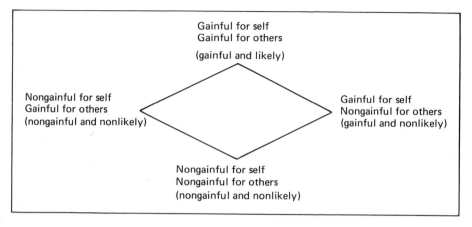

FIGURE 18.4.   Firey's typology of resource use: the choices are clear. (redrawn by permission of the Macmillan Company from Walter Firey, *Man, Mind and Land: A Theory of Resource Use,* Free Press, Glencoe, Illinois, 1960, p. 228)

deficient in long-term perspective. Firey himself feels that this pattern fits the situation that would exist in a freely competitive market economy.

Moving clockwise round figure 18.4 we come to "gainful for self—nongainful for others," which is resource use that takes no account of conservation at all. It is doubtful whether any major American corporation today is totally oblivious of environmental factors (one is tempted to add that it just looks that way!), but until about a generation ago such an attitude was the norm. It is still far too common; indeed, one may search in vain among the pronouncements of our industrial leaders for any indication of environmental conscience. They are, however, well aware that despoiling the environment carries more legal risks than it used to, in addition to being bad public relations.

The use that is "nongainful for self—nongainful for others" is not likely to occur in a modern industrial society except through ignorance and stupidity. However, there is plenty of both qualities still around. A good example is the common American practice of littering streams and lakes with beer cans. The results are not only unsightly but actually present a hazard to wildlife, particularly waterfowl.

In the end, it seems that the only safe good is Firey's fourth use: "nongainful for self—gainful for others." Of course, if the whole group gains so does the individual. Consciousness of this truth is found in virtually all so-called primitive societies, but we civilized people seem to have lost it somewhere along the way.

There is of course no question of returning to a more primitive form of society—or not unless we are forced to by the effects of man-made catastrophe. But a less materialistic way of life is not beyond our grasp. Its basis might properly be an enhanced consciousness of how fragile are the natural processes on which our survival depends. We cannot simply go on using the biosphere as a dumping ground for an ever-increasing volume of waste matter. Nor can we draw a boundary around the part of the biosphere that we inhabit and ignore the rest of it. For one thing, the other peoples of the world will not let us do this. The figures given in chapter 6 provide some indication of how much we depend on other nations for our mineral imports. What if we should come to depend on them for such basic resources as timber or even water?

But to state the problem in terms of our own national self-sufficiency is to miss the crucial point. The very survival of mankind as a species is at stake. Barbara Ward and René Dubos have pointed out that by the year 2000 there will probably be about 1.5 billion developed peoples and about 5 billion others. Since the 5 billion, thanks to modern communications, will be well aware of how badly off they are, we can expect worldwide unrest unless decisive moves are made in the direction of social justice. The present amount of aid going from the rich countries to the poorer ones is only about 50 percent more than the poorer countries are paying to the rich ones in interest. Ward and Dubos estimate that this amount, which is only a little over $6 billion a year, would have to be increased by a factor of more than 16 in order even to begin providing for the world's most urgent environmental needs.

Clearly, the only kind of environmental strategy worth considering is a global one. We should not be deterred by the fact that we do not yet have the political institutions to put such a strategy into operation. Despite the many disappointments of the historic 1972 Stockholm Conference, there is already enough consciousness of what Ward and Dubos call "our environmental interdependence" to begin implementing the first of their major proposals: a worldwide system for pollution monitoring and research. In the field of air pollution monitoring a good deal of international cooperation already exists. Their second proposal is a system for "progressive world sharing" by setting international standards for aid from rich countries to poor ones. Such a system, as they well realize, would need to be bolstered by international agreements for the nonviolent settlement of disputes, and by numerous international institutions of which the present United Nations Organization is only a shadow. The inspiration for this unprecedented international effort would be the hard scientific fact that there *is* only one earth, and that we are all inhabitants of it.

A MODEST PROPOSAL

Charity, it has been said, begins at home. If this country is ever to assume a position of world leadership in environmental affairs it will first have to set its own affairs in order. With all due respect to the individuals and agencies already in the field, we offer the following seven-point program. It should suffice for the next half-century or so.

1. Attack pollution by every available means, while subjecting all new technology to ecological review and regulation.
2. Apply pressure for corporate responsibility. In some areas, new laws

an up to the minute report:

YOUR TRANSIT SYSTEM ON THE MOVE!

Thanks to your overwhelming approval of the transit district, money will soon be available for planning and implementation of transportation solutions.

But time is short, We need your help to pick the system you want and need. Regional? Local (county only)? Buses or fixed rail? Or . . .?

Any system is complex and impossible to define satisfactorily but we must begin to think and question.

WHAT ARE THESE ALTERNATIVES?

- LIMITED BUS SYSTEM
- EXPANDED BUS SYSTEM
- REGIONAL RAPID TRANSIT with FEEDER BUSES
- REGIONAL TRANSIT with AUTOMATED FEEDER SYSTEM
- LIMITED PERSONAL TRANSIT
- COUNTYWIDE PERSONAL TRANSIT

HOW DOES EACH SYSTEM AFFECT PRESENT GROWTH PATTERNS AND LIFE STYLE?

Let's look at the bus systems (at this stage, any sketches are simply symbolic. Actual lines and vehicle types would be determined after much further study and public hearings.)

LIMITED OR EXPANDED BUS SERVICE

LIMITED PERSONAL TRANSIT

Emphasizes local County travel needs rather than full Bay Area regional links. Rather than use buses as feeders, we would have small or medium-sized electrically-powered trams running between small stations spaced at half-mile intervals. About 125 miles of two-way track and 200 station stops could provide several closed loops running throughout the existing urbanized area of the County. Development would occur along the transit corridors at mostly medium densities and would not tend to cluster in high-density activity areas. The auto would still be the dominant travel mode.

REGIONAL RAPID TRANSIT with FEEDER BUSES

This concept envisions about a 32 mile rail transit loop around the bay. Sixteen stations at major activity centers would be concentrated in the northern urbanized area of the County. Each of the stations would become high-density urban clusters. Because future development would be concentrated in the clusters, the remainder of the valley floor could remain low density and relatively decentralized.

LIMITED BUS SERVICE

This would involve only moderate changes in the present system. Most travel needs would still be met by auto. We would continue to develop and extend the present and planned roadway network. The dominant land use pattern would continue to be scattered low-density, residential development. This dispersal, however, is expected to require more roadway than presently planned for 1990.

EXPANDED BUS SERVICE

Assures purchase of the private local bus companies and establishment of a greatly expanded service area. About 300 to 400 new buses would be needed to cover about 70% of the County's urbanized area. All 15 cities would be covered. Again, the County's present form of dispersal would continue unless other growth policies are initiated.

This is Number 5 of 5 advertisements this month. If you missed any of the series, please phone 299-2367 for your copy.

COUNTYWIDE PERSONAL TRANSIT

This system would be the most competitive with the automobile. It is basically a grid system with 600 miles of one-way elevated guideways carrying small (12 to 20 passenger) automatic electric cars. Elevator type buttons would summon the cars and also permit discharge of passengers. There would normally be one transfer per trip. Each of the lines would not actually intersect but would pass over each other forming about 700 station stops. Development would continue to be scattered rather than concentrated. But parking and street needs would be much less. Local travel needs are emphasized rather than a regional Bay Area system. Speeds would be only medium range. Overhead structures would have to be designed to minimize noise and visual impact.

REGIONAL TRANSIT with AUTOMATED FEEDER SYSTEM

This has a regional rail line forming a Bay Area lap interconnected with a Countywide rail system of five or six closed loops. The regional line would be about 32 miles long with 16 stations whise the Countywide lines would be 100 miles long with about 150 stations. The development pattern would tend to be high-density around the 16 regional stations, medium density along the local transit corridors and low density in between.

LET'S HEAR FROM YOU!

HELP US DESIGN YOUR TRANSIT SYSTEM!

Contact:
DEPARTMENT OF PUBLIC WORKS
Santa Clara County, 20 West Hedding St.
San Jose, California 95110

The increase in population makes transit of great importance to us. Jot down your overall feelings. Take a few words. Take pages. But let us know your thoughts. Thank you.

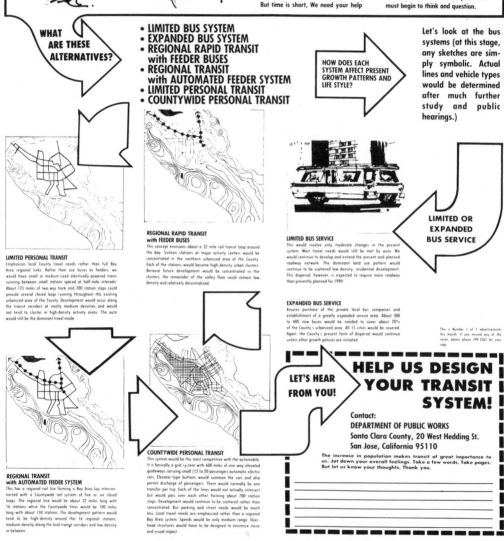

FIGURE 18.5. Newspaper advertisement issued by Santa Clara County following approval by voters of local proposition creating a mass transit district. Has your county ever offered you this kind of choice? Why not? (Department of Public Works, Santa Clara County, California)

may not be needed; in any case, strict enforcement of the present laws should be tried first.

3. Educate the public in the facts it needs to choose between alternative environments. Make environmental education a part of school curriculum at every level (figure 18.5).

4. Provide incentives for reducing material consumption. Decry at every opportunity the philosophy of endless economic growth. Encourage handicrafts and the do-it-yourself spirit.

5. Bring population into balance. If voluntary methods do not work, introduce selected compulsory measures, such as postponing the age of marriage. There should be no compromise on this issue; population simply cannot be allowed to grow indefinitely.

6. Propagate the philosophy of ecological wholeness. Man is no longer the measure of all things; rather, he is one species among many, and should cultivate his own ecological niche.

7. Develop a sense of the future—a sense of obligation to our children and our children's children. Recognize the "empire builder" for what he is: a successful criminal. Strive to close the gap between aesthetics and morality. Admit that without nature as our guide we shall all be lost.

REFERENCES

Commoner, Barry, and Paul Ehrlich, "Review: The Closing Cirlce," *Environment,* April 1972, pp. 23–26, 31–52. Not a joint article, but a review (by Ehrlich) and a reply (by Commoner) that should be considered together.

Commoner, Barry, *The Closing Circle: Nature, Man, and Technology* (New York: Knopf, 1971).

Ehrlich, Paul, and Richard L. Harriman, *How To Be a Survivor* (New York: Ballantine, 1971).

Eyre, S.F., "Man the Pest: The Dim Chance of Survival," *New York Review of Books,* November 18, 1971.

Firey, Walter, *Man, Mind and Land: A Theory of Resource Use* (Glencoe, Ill.: Free Press, 1960).

Fox, Herbert, and Clarke Rees, letter in *Saturday Review,* February 19, 1972.

Lebow, Victor, *"Free Enterprise"—The Opium of the American People* (New York: Oriole, 1972).

Meadows, Donella H., et al., *The Limits to Growth* (New York: Universe, 1972).

Papanek, Victor, *Design for the Real World: Human Ecology and Social Change* (New York: Pantheon, 1971).

Ridker, Ronald G., "Resource and Environmental Consequences of Population Growth in the United States: A Summary," in Ronald G. Ridker (ed.), *Research Reports of the Commission on Population Growth and the American Future, Vol. III, Population, Resources and the Environment* (Washington, D.C.: U.S. Government Printing Office).

Sax, Joseph L., *Defending the Environment: A Strategy for Citizen Action* (New York: Knopf, 1971).

Wall Street Journal, *Getting Involved,* edited by John Barnett (Princeton: Dow Jones, 1972).

Ward, Barbara, and René Dubos, *Only One Earth: The Care and Maintenance of a Small Planet* (New York: Norton, 1972).

APPENDIX

A. PROFESSIONAL JOURNALS

The impact of the environmental movement has been so far-reaching that almost any scientific journal nowadays is likely to contain at least one article of interest to environmentalists. However, a reasonably firm line can be drawn between scientific articles intended for other scientists and articles that, although written by scientists, aim at an audience beyond the scientific specialty in question. The latter type of article usually draws extensively on the professional literature of several disciplines, and it is on this literature that, in the final analysis, the environmentalist cause is based. The professional journals, then, should be consulted by anyone who is not simply content to take the experts' word for it. This, after all, is part of what the environmental movement is about: we cannot afford to leave our future in the hands of experts. It follows that we must learn the experts' language.

The following list of professional journals is highly selective, but will suffice as a sample of what is available. Serious environmentalists will find browsing through back issues of any one of these an extremely rewarding experience.

Agricultural Science Review, A.I.A. Journal (*the* architectural journal), *American Review of Respiratory Diseases, Annals of the American Academy of Political and Social Science, Annals of the Entomological Society of America, Architectural Forum,*

Archives of Environmental Health, Biological Reviews, BioScience, Botanical Review, Bulletin of the Ecological Society of America, Chemical Engineering News, Contamination Control, Compost Science, Demography, Design and Environment, Ecological Monographs, Ecology, Entomology, Environmental Science and Technology, Eugenics Review, Forest Industries, Health Aspects of Pesticides, Hilgardia (an entomological journal), *Journal of the Air Pollution Control Association, Journal of the American Institute of Planners, Journal of Biological Sciences, Journal of Economic Entomology, Journal of Geophysical Research, Journal of the Town Planning Institute* (British), *Landscape, Landscape Architecture Quarterly, Limnology and Oceanography, Nature* (British; the most prestigious general scientific magazine in English), *Nuclear Industry, Pesticides Monitoring Journal, Population Bulletin, Population Reference Bureau Selections, Population Review, Public Administration Review, Public Health Reports, Science* (U.S. counterpart of *Nature*), *Selected References on Environmental Quality as it Relates to Health, Studies in Family Planning, Toxicology and Applied Pharmacology, W.H.O. Chronicle, World Population Data Sheet.*

B. MAGAZINES AND NEWSPAPERS

The leading environmentalist journal of carefully researched articles that can nevertheless be read easily by the layman is *Environment,* official organ of the Scientists' Institute for Public Information and published by the Committee for Environmental Information. It has excellent illustrations.

Scientific American often contains first-rate articles of environmental interest, as do *American Scientist, Bulletin of the Atomic Scientists, Natural History,* and *New Scientist.*

On urban affairs, *City* is always worth reading; for the opposite side of the coin, read *The Living Wilderness* (journal of the Wilderness Society).

Of the very large number of conservationist magazines, *Audubon, International Wildlife* and *National Wildlife* are outstanding. The *Conservation News,* distributed free by the National Wildlife Federation, is a useful bulletin that covers much more than wildlife. *Cry California* is a first-rate magazine of interest to conservationists everywhere. On a more popular level, *Environmental Quality* (a magazine) and *Clear Creek* (a tabloid) often contain stimulating articles. Most of the conservation organizations listed in the *Conservation Directory* (see next section) issue a publication of some sort. Among nationally available newspapers, the *National Observer, New York Times,* and *Wall Street Journal* consistently feature excellent articles on the environment. Usually, clipping your local newspaper is one of the best ways of keeping up with environmental news, although some topics are systematically neglected by the wire services.

BIBLIOGRAPHY

This general bibliography does not contain works cited in the main text unless we want to make some comment about them. Nor does it attempt to be complete: all the works listed are worth reading, but many worthwhile and even classic works have been omitted. However, the student will find that, within each area of study as we have outlined it, the works listed, together with the ones cited in the main text, will furnish a good jumping-off point for more exhaustive reading. Especially worthy of note are the works that, like Charles F. Wurster's paper on aldrin and dieldrin, are major bibliographical achievements in themselves. Students who do not know what they want to read about should first consult the section on journals and magazines: most of those listed do a good job of reviewing current publications. Being firm believers in the value of owning books, we have cited paperback editions whenever we knew of them; these are denoted by an asterisk.

General

Some textbooks contain a list of organizations concerned with conservation. We prefer to recommend the comprehensive and low-priced *Conservation Directory** published by the National Wildlife Federation, 1412 16th Street, N.W. Washington, D.C. 20036. A good short list of organizations can be found in Appendix II of Richard Saltonstall, Jr., *Your Environment and What You Can Do About It**

(New York: Ace Books, 1972). For U.N. organizations, see Glossary under U.N.E.S.C.O.

An excellent list of ecological "dos and don'ts" entitled *71 Things You Can Do To Stop Pollution** can be had free from *Keep America Beautiful, Inc.,* 99 Park Avenue, New York, N.Y. 10016. Chapter 6 of Saltonstall, *op cit,* is also good on this.

For keeping up with federal legislation on the environment, the indispensable guide is the *Conservation Report,* a newsletter distributed free on request by the National Wildlife Federation. Pointed comments will also be found in "The Audubon Cause," a regular feature of *Audubon* (see Journals and Magazines, above). Some of the local organizations listed in the *Conservation Directory* put out newsletters on state legislation; check under your state.

Two works of reference will be found of particular value to the general reader or the specialist dealing with an unfamiliar discipline: Herbert C. Hanson, *Dictionary of Ecology* (New York: Philosophical Library, 1962), which deals with ecology in the strict sense; and Paul Sarnoff, *The New York Times Encyclopedic Dictionary of the Environment,* (New York: Quadrangle, 1971), which deals with nearly everything environmental. In addition, the *International Encyclopedia of the Social Sciences* (New York: Macmillan and Free Press, 1968) is especially strong in the area of population studies.

Among U.S. government publications, every user of this book should be aware of the President's Message on the Environment* (now an annual event) and the Annual Report of the Council on Environmental Quality* (which includes the president's message). A request to the Superintendent of Documents, Government Printing Office, Washington, D.C. 20402, will procure the free price list *Ecology,* a 37-page compilation of government publications on environmental topics from air pollution to wildlife preservation. Most of these publications are very cheap.

Many state governments publish reports and brochures of interest to environmentalists; some, like the San Francisco Bay Conservation and Development Commission's *San Francisco Bay Plan,** are classics. Write your state department of publications for a catalog.

An information retrieval service that should be available through most college libraries is *Environment Information ACCESS,* a semi-monthly compilation of abstracts published by Environment Information Center, Inc., 124 East 39th Street, New York, N.Y. 10016. Most of the papers, articles, and government documents listed in *ACCESS* are available on microfiche from Microfiche Systems Corporation, 305 East 46th Street, New York, N.Y. 10017.

Unique on the North American continent is the (free) Annual Report of *Resources for the Future, Inc.,* an independent arm of the Ford Foundation that finances every kind of environmental research, often with great distinction. Also of interest, especially in the field of population control, is the *Ford Foundation Letter* (free on request), which lists those of the foundation's publications that are available as free reprints.

Of the numerous collections of articles on environmental subjects, a few are so excellent that they can be called indispensable. In our opinion, these are: F.

Fraser Darling and John P. Milton (eds.), *Future Environments of North America: Transformation of a Continent** (Garden City, N.Y.: Natural History Press, 1966); Philip Handler (ed.), *Biology and the Future of Man** (New York: Oxford University Press, 1970); Sheldon Novick and Dorothy Cottrell (eds.), *Our World in Peril: An Environment Review** (New York: Fawcett, 1971); Paul Shepard and Daniel McKinley (eds.), *The Subversive Science: Essays Toward an Ecology of Man* (Boston: Houghton Mifflin, 1969); Study of Critical Environmental Problems (S.C.E.P.), *Man's Impact on the Global Environment: Assessment and Recommendations for Action** (Cambridge, Mass.: M.I.T. Press, 1970); and William L. Thomas Jr., (ed.), *Man's Role in Changing the Face of the Earth**, 2 vols. (University of Chicago Press, 1956). The May 1970 issue of *The Annals of the American Academy of Political and Social Science,* "Society and its Physical Environment," is also of interest. All these works are suitable for the general reader; more specialized collections are listed below under the appropriate section head.

PART ONE: MAN AND ENVIRONMENT— A CONFRONTATION

1. The Use of Land

Barnes, Carleton P., and F.J. Marschner, "Our Wealth of Land Resources," in *Land: The Yearbook of Agriculture, 1958.*

Chapman, John D., "Interaction Between Man and His Resources," in Preston E. Cloud, Jr., (ed.), *Resources and Man* (San Francisco: Freeman, 1969).

Land Tenure in the United States: Development and Status (Washington, D.C.: U.S. Government Printing Office, 1969). A useful short pamphlet.

Marsh, George P., *The Earth as Modified by Human Action* (New York: Charles Scribner's Sons, 1874). The classic work that influenced a whole generation of American conservationists and can still be read with profit.

Scofield, William H., "Values and Competition for Land," in *A Place to Live: The Yearbook of Agriculture, 1962.*

Sears, Paul B., "The Inexorable Problem of Space," *Science,* September 16, 1958.

2. Human Population

Appleman, Philip, *The Silent Explosion* (Boston: Beacon Press, 1965).

Hauser, Philip M., *The Population Dilemma* (Englewood Cliffs, N.J.: Prentice-Hall, 1963).

Hauser, Philip M., and Otis Dudley Duncan (eds.), *The Study of Population: An Inventory and Appraisal* (University of Chicago Press, 1964).

"Man Population Predicament," *Population Bulletin,* April 1971.

"Toward a U.S. Population Policy," *Population Bulletin,* June 1971.

Westoff, Charles F., Robert G. Potter, and Philip C. Sagi, *The Third Child: A Study in the Prediction of Fertility* (Princeton University Press, 1963).

Winsborough, Halliman H., "The Social Consequences of High Population Density," in Thomas R. Ford and Gordon F. DeJong (eds.), *Social Demography* (Englewood Cliffs, N.J.: Prentice-Hall, 1970).

Wrigley, E.A., *Population and History* (New York: McGraw-Hill, 1969).

3. The Ecological Basis

Allee, W.C., A.E. Emerson, O. Park, T. Park, and K.P. Schmidt, *Principles of Animal Ecology* (Philadelphia: Saunders, 1949).

Bates, Marston, "The Human Ecosystem," in Preston E. Cloud, Jr., (ed.), *Resources and Man* (San Francisco: Freeman, 1969).

Clarke, G.L., *Elements of Ecology* (New York: Wiley, 1965).

Cohen, Yehudi A., "Issues and Concepts in the Study of Adaptation," in Yehudi A. Cohen (ed.), *Man in Adaptation: The Biosocial Background* (Chicago: Aldine, 1968).

Dansereau, Pierre, *Biogeography, an Ecological Perspective* (New York: Ronald, 1957).

Gates, David M., "The Flow of Energy in the Biosphere," *Scientific American,* September 1971.

Hutchinson, G. Evelyn, "The Biosphere," *Scientific American,* September 1970.

Odum, Eugene P., *Fundamentals of Ecology* (Philadelphia: Saunders, 1959).

Woodwell, George M., "The Energy Cycle of the Biosphere," *Scientific American,* September 1970.

PART TWO: SUSTAINING THE BASIC PROCESSES

4. Energy

Alexander, Tom, "Some Burning Questions About Combustion," *Fortune,* February 1970.

Ayres, Robert U., and Richard P. McKanna, *Alternatives to the Internal Combustion Engine* (Johns Hopkins University Press, 1972).

Eastland, Bernard J., and William C. Gough, *The Fusion Torch: Closing the Cycle from Use to Reuse* (U.S. Atomic Energy Commission, 1969).

Ford, Daniel F., and Henry W. Kendall, "Nuclear Safety," *Environment,* September 1972.
Odum, Howard T., *Environment, Power, and Society* (New York: Wiley, 1971). Excellent general treatment.
Sternglass, Ernest J., *Low-Level Radiation* (New York: Ballantine, 1972). A scientist looks at so-called safe levels of radiation, as set by the Atomic Energy Commission, and does not like what he sees.
Williams, Robert H., "When the Well Runs Dry," *Environment,* June 1972. A study of U.S. natural gas resources.

5. Food

Borgstrom, Georg, *Too Many: A Story of Earth's Biological Limitations* (New York: Macmillan, 1969).
Brown, Lester R., "Human Food Production as a Process in the Biosphere," *Scientific American,* September 1970.
Grigg, David, *The Harsh Lands: A Study in Agricultural Development* (New York: Macmillan, 1970). Examines the reasons for the low agricultural productivity of tropical lands.
Hayami, Yujiro, and Vernon W. Ruttan (eds.), *Agricultural Development: An International Perspective* (Johns Hopkins University Press, 1971).
Pratt, Christopher J., "Chemical Fertilizers," *Scientific American,* June 1965.
Rockefeller Foundation, Progress Report: *Toward the Conquest of Hunger, 1965–1966.* Includes data on "miracle grains."

6. Materials

Davis, William E., "The Balloon Revisited," *Forest Industries,* November 1970. On logging by balloon.
Dickinson, Edward M., "Taking It Apart," *Environment,* July–August 1972. Difficulties of recycling automobiles.
Lackner, R.J., "Recovering Acid and Salable Ferrous Sulfate from Waste Pickle Liquor," *Metal Progress,* December 1970.
Sassaman, Robert W., and Schallan, Con H., "Can Log Rules, Intensified Forestry, Affect Falldown in Allowable Cuts?" *Forest Industries,* August 1970.
Study of Critical Environmental Problems (S.C.E.P.), *Paper Profits: Pollution in the Pulp and Paper Industries* (Cambridge, Mass.: M.I.T. Press, 1972).
U.S. Bureau of Mines, *Minerals Yearbook* (Washington, D.C.: U.S. Government Printing Office).

U.S. Senate, Committee on Public Works, *Problems and Issues of a National Materials Policy: Papers Delivered at an Engineering Foundation Research Conference on National Materials Policy* (Washington, D.C.: U.S. Government Printing Office, 1970).

Wenk, Edward, Jr., "The Physical Resources of the Ocean," *Scientific American,* September 1969. Deals with recovery of minerals from the ocean.

PART THREE: THE PHYSIOLOGICAL IMPACT

7. Air Pollution

Crenson, Matthew A., *The Un-Politics of Air Pollution: A Study of Non-Decision Making in the Cities* (Johns Hopkins University Press, 1971).

Englund, Harold M., (ed.), *The Clean Air Congress* (New York: Academic Press, 1972). Edited proceedings of an international conference on air pollution.

Ross, Richard R., *Air Pollution and Industry* (New York: Van Nostrand, 1972).

Steif, W., "Why the Birds Cough," *The Progressive,* April 1970.

Strauss, Werner (ed.), *Air Pollution Control* (New York: Wiley, 1971).

U.S. Department of Health, Education, and Welfare, *Air Quality Criteria for Carbon Monoxide* (1970).

——, *Air Quality Criteria for Hydrocarbons* (1970).

——, *Air Quality Criteria for Particulate Matter* (1969).

——, *Air Quality Criteria for Photochemical Oxidants* (1970).

——, *Air Quality Criteria for Sulfur Oxides* (1969).

All of the above were published by the U.S. Government Printing Office.

U.S. Environmental Protection Agency, *Air Quality Criteria for Nitrogen Oxides* (Washington, D.C.: U.S. Government Printing Office, 1971).

——, *The Economics of Clean Air* (Washington, D.C.: U.S. Government Printing Office, 1971). A report to Congress, as required by the (amended) 1963 Air Quality Act

U.S. Senate, *Air Pollution, 1970, Hearings Before the Subcommittee on Air and Water Pollution of the Committee on Public Works,* parts 1–5 (Washington, D.C.: U.S. Government Printing Office, 1970).

8. Water

Ciacco, L.L. (ed.), *Water and Water Pollution Handbook* (New York: Dekker, 1973). Four-volume set for use by engineers.

Dugan, Patrick R., *Biochemical Ecology of Water Pollution* (Ohio State University Press, 1972).

Environmental Protection Agency, *The Cost of Clean Water,* 2 vols. (Washington, D.C.: U.S. Government Printing Office, 1971). A report to Congress as required by the (amended) 1948 Water Pollution Control Act.

Federal Water Pollution Control Administration, *Lake Erie Report* (Washington, D.C.: U.S. Government Printing Office, 1968).

Hood, Donald W. (ed.), *Impingement of Man on the Oceans* (New York: Wiley, 1971).

Linsley, Ray K., and J.B. Franzini, *Water Resources Engineering,* 2nd edition (New York: McGraw-Hill, 1972).

Zajic, J.E., *Water Pollution: Disposal and Reuse,* 2 vols. (New York: Dekker, 1971).

9. Land Wastes

Caudill, Harry: *My Land is Dying* (New York: Dutton, 1971). Latest report by a national authority on the social and ecological effects of strip mining.

Council on Environmental Quality, *Ocean Dumping: A National Policy* (Washington, D.C.: U.S. Government Printing Office, 1970). Many of these recommendations were enacted into law by the 1972 Marine Protection, Research and Sanctuaries Act, a measure that unfortunately does not cover bays and estuaries but otherwise won the approval of most conservationists.

Environmental Protection Agency, *Santa Barbara Oil Spill: Short-term Analysis of Macroplankton and Fish* (Washington, D.C.: U.S. Government Printing Office).

Environmental Protection Agency, Office of Solid Waste Management Programs, *Annual Reports.* Formerly issued by the Bureau of Solid Waste Management (part of H.E.W. until converted to an office of the E.P.A. in 1970), these reports are the best single source of information on the problems of solid waste disposal. Also known as the annual *Solid Waste Report.*

Grinstead, Robert R., "Bottlenecks," *Environment,* April 1972.

——, "Machinery for Trash Mining," *Encounter,* May 1972. Two pioneering articles that probably represent the best available introduction, both economic and technological, to the problem of recycling solid wastes.

National Estuary Study, 7 vols. (Washington, D.C.: U.S. Government Printing Office, 1970). Volume 1 is the "Main Report." The study deals with every aspect of estuary resource use.

National Industrial Pollution Council, *Staff Reports.* The council has recently issued more than two dozen brief reports on industrial pollution sources of current concern, including detergents, junk cars, and noise pollution.

Pramer, David, "The Soil Transforms," *Environment,* May 1971. Study of how chlorinated aniline herbicides become still more toxic when subjected to microbial action in soil.

White-Stevens, R. (ed.), *Pesticides in the Environment* (New York: Dekker, 1971). Volume 4, part 2, of an ongoing series.

Wurster, Charles F., "Aldrin and Dieldrin," *Environment,* October 1971. Wurster, to the chagrin of the chemical industry, prepares his indictments of synthetic pesticides with the care of a lawyer preparing a brief for the Supreme Court (which is where they may go anyway). Anyone who thinks the pesticide issue is a lot of fuss over nothing should read Wurster's articles.

PART FOUR: INTENSIFICATION OF FUNCTIONS

10. Urbanization

Dickenson, Robert E., *The West European City: A Geographical Interpretation* (London: Routledge, 1962).

Fried, Joseph P., *Housing Crisis U.S.A.* (New York: Praeger, 1971).

Gordon, Mitchell, *Sick Cities** (Baltimore: Penguin, 1965).

Hawley, Amos H., *The Changing Shape of Metropolitan America: Deconcentration Since 1920* (Glencoe, III.: Free Press, 1956).

Jacobs, Jane, *The Death and Life of Great American Cities** (New York: Random House, 1965).

Mumford, Lewis, *The City in History* (New York: Harcourt, 1961).

Schnore, Leo F., "The Growth of Metropolitan Suburbs," *American Sociological Review,* vol. 22, pp. 165–173, 1957.

11. Transportation

Fisher, Franklin M., Zvi Griliches, and Carl Kaysen, "The Costs of Automobile Model Changes Since 1949," *Journal of Political Economy,* October, 1962.

Gilmore, Harlan, *Transportation and the Growth of Cities* (Glencoe, III.: Free Press, 1953).

Hamilton, William F., 2nd, and D.K. Nance, "Systems Analysis of Urban Transportation," *Scientific American,* July 1969.

Hellman, H., *Transportation in the World of the Future* (New York: Lippincott, 1968).

Lansing, John B., and Eva Mueller, *Residential Location and Urban Mobility* (Ann Arbor, Michigan: Institute for Social Research, 1964).

Nader, Ralph, *Unsafe at any Speed** (New York: Grossman, 1965). The classic exposé of unsafe auto design.

Owen, W., *The Metropolitan Transportation Problem* (Englewood Cliffs, N.J.: Spectrum).

Wingo, Lowdon, Jr., *Transportation and Urban Land* (Washington, D.C.: Resources for the Future, Inc., 1961).

12. Economic Pressures

Bookchin, Murray, *Post-Scarcity Anarchism* (Berkeley, California: Ramparts Press, 1971). What is to take the place of the consumer society? An interesting speculative essay.

Clawson, Marion, *Resources, Economic Development, and Environmental Quality* (University of Guelph, Canada: Center for Resources Development, 1971).

Gaffney, Mason, "Coordinating Tax Incentives and Public Policy: The Treatment of Land Income," in U.S. Congress, Joint Economic Committee, part 2 (Washington, D.C.: U.S. Government Printing Office, 1970).

Kneese, Allen V., and Blair T. Bower (eds.), *Environmental Quality Analysis: Theory and Method in the Social Sciences* (Johns Hopkins University Press, 1971).

Mintz, Morton, and Jerry S. Cohen, *America, Inc.: Who Owns and Operates the United States* * (New York: Dell, 1971). Very readable account, in the best muckraking tradition, of the role of big business in U.S. politics and social policy. Ralph Nader's introduction is a good summary of his philosophy.

Ridgeway, James, *The Politics of Ecology* * (New York: Dutton, 1971). Stimulating essay somewhat parallel to Mintz and Cohen, *op cit*, but more revolutionary in outlook. Ridgeway wonders if Nader goes far enough.

Theobald, Robert, *The Challenge of Abundance* * (New York: Mentor, 1962). Classic discussion of how American prosperity can be put to constructive social use.

PART FIVE: A HUMAN ENVIRONMENT?

13. Aesthetics and Open Space

Berland, Theodore, *The Fight for Quiet* (New York: Prism, 1971).

Burchard, John, and Albert Bush-Brown, *The Architecture of America: A Social and Cultural History* (London: Gollancz, 1967). The best short (450 pages) account of its subject, abridged and revised from a longer version first published in the United States in 1961.

Doxiadis, Constantinos, *Architecture in Transition* (New York: Oxford University Press, 1963). Seminal observations by one of today's great architectural thinkers.

Mumford, Lewis, *Sticks and Stones: A Study of American Architecture and Civilization* (New York: Dover, 1955). Revised edition of a work first published in 1924, but still very timely.

National Industrial Pollution Control Council, *Leisure Time Product Noise* (Washington, D.C.: U.S. Government Printing Office, 1971).

Rudofsky, B. *Streets for People: A Primer for Americans* (New York: Doubleday,

1969). If this lovely book were taken to heart, the United States could yet build great cities.

Zucker, Paul, *Town and Square from the Agora to the Village Green* (Columbia University Press, 1959),

14. Outdoor Recreation

Bronson, William, "It's About Too Late for Tahoe," *Audubon,* May 1971. How one of the world's most beautiful lakes was ruined by too many recreationists.

Cicchetti, Charles J., "Outdoor Recreation and Congestion in the United States," chapter 6 in Ronald G. Ridker (ed.), *Research Reports of the Commission on Population Growth and the American Future,* vol. 3 (Washington, D.C.: U.S. Government Printing Office, 1972).

Dasmann, Raymond F., "Wildlife and Outdoor Recreation," *Virginia Wildlife,* vol. 27, 1966.

Douglass, Paul F., and Robert W. Crawford, "Implementation of a Comprehensive Plan for a Wise Use of Leisure ," in *Leisure in America: Blessing or Curse?* (Philadelphia: American Academy of Political and Social Science, 1964).

Draper, W.H., "Parks or More People?" *National Parks,* vol. 40, 1966.

Ferriss, Abbott L., "The Social and Personality Correlates of Outdoor Recreation," in *The Annals: Society and Its Physical Environment* (Philadelphia: American Academy of Political and Social Science, 1970).

Krutilla, John V., and Jack L. Knetsch, "Outdoor Recreation Economics," in *The Annals: Society and Its Physical Environment* (Philadelphia: American Academy of Political and Social Science, 1970).

McPhee, John, *Encounters With the Archdruid: Narratives About a Conservationist and Three of His Natural Enemies* (New York: Farrar, Straus and Giroux, 1971). Perhaps this is as good a place as any to list this unclassifiable and perfectly marvelous book in which David Brower, the celebrated conservationist and publisher, is shown battling the forces of development, usually outdoors.

Meyersohn, Rolf, "The Charismatic and the Playful in Outdoor Recreation," in *The Annals: Society and Its Physical Environment* (Philadelphia: American Academy of Political and Social Science, 1970).

U.S. Department of Agriculture, *Outdoor Recreation in the National Forests* (Washington, D.C.: U.S. Department of Agriculture, 1965).

15. Wilderness and Wildlife

Allen D., *Our Wildlife Legacy* (New York: Funk and Wagnalls, 1954).

Crowe, P.K., *World Wildlife: The Last Stand* (New York: Scribner, 1970).

Douglas, William O., *A Wilderness Bill of Rights* (Boston: Little, Brown, 1965).

Gauvin, Aimé, "Rumblerattlebangclatterroar—You're on the Allagash Nonwilderness Waterway," *Audubon,* July 1972. What happens to a wilderness when it is opened up to logging companies, Boy Scouts, and much else.

Josephy, Alvin M., Jr., "The Murder of the Southwest," *Audubon,* July 1971. How the Four Corners power complex, described in chapter 4 of this book, is endangering six national parks, twenty-eight national monuments, two national recreation areas, numerous national historic landmarks and state parks, and, last but not least, thirty-nine Indian reservations.

Lack, D., *The Natural Regulation of Animal Numbers* (New York: Oxford University Press, 1954).

Lucas, R.C., "Wilderness Perception and Use: The Example of the Boundary Waters Canoe Area," *Natural Resources Journal,* vol. 3, 1964.

Platt, Rutherford, *Wilderness* (New York: Dodd, Mead, 1961).

Smith, Frank E., *The Politics of Conservation* (New York: Harper Colophon, 1971). Excellent study of U.S. conservation policies, from 1789 to 1964.

Udall, Stewart L., *The Quiet Crisis* (New York: Holt, Rinehart and Winston, 1963).

World Wildlife Guide, *A Complete Handbook Covering All the World's Outstanding National Parks, Reserves, and Sanctuaries* (New York: Viking, 1971).

PART SIX: ACHIEVING AN OPTIMUM

16. Population Limitation

Armijo, Rolando, and Tegualda Monreal, "Epidemiology of Provoked Abortion in Santiago, Chile," *Journal of Sex Research,* vol. 1, 1965. The suffering caused by legal restrictions on abortion.

Brackett, James W., "The Demographic Consequences of Legal Abortion," in Sidney H. Newman et al. (eds.), *Abortion: Obtained and Denied Research Approaches* (New York: Population Council, 1971).

Chamberlain, Neil W., *Beyond Malthus: Population and Power** (Englewood Cliffs, N.J.: Prentice-Hall, 1972). Takes over where Malthus left off.

Hardin, Garrett (ed.), *Population, Evolution, and Birth Control* (San Francisco: Freeman, 1969).

Lader, Lawrence, *The Margaret Sanger Story and the Fight for Birth Control* (New York: Doubleday, 1955).

Myrdal, Gunnar, *Asian Drama: An Inquiry into the Poverty of Nations** (New York: Pantheon, 1971). An abridgment of Myrdal's celebrated 3-volume work, the best single source of information about the Third World.

Rock, John, *The Time Has Come* (New York: Knopf, 1963). Historic declaration by the leading Roman Catholic advocate of population control.

Singer, S. Fred (ed.), *Is There an Optimum Level of Population?* (New York: McGraw-Hill, 1971).

Stycos, J. Mayne, *Ideology, Faith, and Family Planning in Latin America* (New York: McGraw-Hill, 1971). Why some Latin American Countries continue to have the world's highest rates of population growth.

Tien, H. Yuan, "Sterilization, Oral Contraception, and Population Control in China," *Population Studies,* vol. 18, 1965.

Vogt, William, "The Ethics of Parenthood," reprinted from his *People, Challenge to Survival* (1960) in Marian Maury (ed.), *Birth Rate and Birth Right** (New York: Macfadden, 1963). One of the most eloquent pleas for a lower birth rate.

17. Environmental Control

Citron, R., *National and International Environmental Monitoring Programs* (Cambridge, Mass.: M.I.T. Press, 1970).

Clawson, Marion, *America's Land and Its Uses** (Johns Hopkins University Press, 1971).

Executive Office of the President, Domestic Council, *The President's 1971 Environmental Program: Toward More Rational Use of the Land* *(Washington, D.C.: U.S. Government Printing Office, 1971).

Marcus, Norman, and Marilyn W. Graves (eds.), *The New Zoning* (New York: Praeger, 1970).

National Pesticide Monitoring Program, *Report of the Subcommittee on Pesticides of the Cabinet Committee on the Environment* (Washington D.C.: U.S. Government Printing Office, 1970).

Roueché, Berton, *What's Left: Report on a Diminishing America* (Boston: Little, Brown, 1969).

18. The Choices Before Us

Childs, Marquis W., and Douglass Cater, *Ethics in a Business Society** (New York: Mentor 1954). Old but good.

Commoner, Barry, *Science and Survival** (New York: Viking, 1967). It was Commoner who first suggested, in this little book, that science might be our enemy—an idea hard for Americans to swallow.

Derrick, Christopher, *The Delicate Creation: Toward a Theology of the Environment* (Old Greenwich, Conn.: Devin-Adair, 1972). Traces the environmental crisis to basic Judaeo-Christian attitudes.

Kolko, Gabriel, *Wealth and Power in America** (New York: Praeger, 1962). What they didn't teach you in high school about the American Dream.

Landau, Norman J., and Paul D. Rheingold, *The Environmental Law Handbook* * (New York: Ballantine, 1971). First-rate compilation, with index, glossary, and full instructions on how to sue the government.

Leiss, William, *The Domination of Nature* (New York: Braziller, 1972). Solid discussion of Western attitudes toward the natural world.

Rodale, Robert, *The Basic Book of Organic Gardening* * (New York: Ballantine, 1971). If we could all become organic gardeners, it would be some sort of a beginning. Rodale's manual is right on.

Tanzer, Michael, *The Sick Society: An Economic Examination* (New York: Holt, Rinehart, and Winston, 1971).

Udall, Stewart L., *Agenda for Tomorrow* (New York: Harcourt, Brace, and World, 1968).

GLOSSARY

A.B.A.G.   Association of Bay Area Governments, a largely consultative body in the San Francisco Bay area. A.B.A.G. hopes to expand its functions someday.

Abiotic.   Without life, consisting of inorganic materials.

Acre foot.   The amount of water needed to cover 1 acre to the depth of 1 foot.

Albedo.   A surface's reflectivity, as measured by the ratio of the light it reflects to the total amount of light falling upon it. Often used as the capacity of solids in the earth's atmosphere to reflect incoming solar radiation.

Aquifer.   Underground layer of soil or rock that absorbs and conducts water. See also **Groundwater table**.

ATP.   Adenosine triphosphate, a molecule created by green plants in the course of photosynthesis. ATP makes energy available for a wide range of chemical reactions. See also **PGA**.

Autotroph.   An organism capable of feeding itself by converting inorganic substances to organic ones. See also **Photosynthesis** and **Producers**.

B.A.R.T.   Bay Area Rapid Transit, the largely automated mass transit system by which it is planned to link the cities of the San Francisco Bay area, from San Jose in the south to Novato in the north. Part of the system is already in operation.

Biocide.   A substance deadly to life, whether by ingestion or on contact. For the major types, see essay 9.1.

Biodegradable.   Subject to biological degradation, that is, to the process of chemical breakdown by bacteria that is ordinarily known as decay.

Biological control.   Reduction of a pest population to acceptable levels by means of artificially introduced parasites, predators, or pathogens. See also **Sterile-male technique.**

Biosphere.   The narrow realm of life, existing at the interface of litho-sphere and atmosphere.

Biotic.   Living, consisting of organisms.

BOD.   Biochemical oxygen demand, essentially a measure of the amount of oxygen required for the biological degradation of a specific quantity of organic solids in a specific amount of water over a given period. In general, the cleaner the water the lower the BOD. See also **Tertiary treatment.**

Breeder reactor.   A reactor that produces more nuclear fuel than it con-sumes. It does this by converting U-238, which is nonfissionable, into fissionable plutonium. Breeder reactors have never been proved to be entirely safe, and plutonium is highly toxic.

BTU.   British thermal unit, one of which equals 252 calories or .0002931 of a kilowatt-hour. See also **Calorie, kwh.**

Calorie.   As used in this book, the amount of heat needed to raise the temperature of 1 kilogram of water from $15°$ to $16°$ C. Commonly used as measure of the energy "burned" by humans and animals in the form of food. See also **kcal.**

Carbohydrate.   Any one of several organic compounds, including sugar, cellulose, and starch, consisting of carbon, hydrogen, and oxygen. Carbohydrates are essential to human and animal metabolism, but in humans a diet consisting entirely of carbohydrates—e.g., in the form of starchy roots—causes the disease **kwashiorkor** (q.v.).

Charge.   As used in water management, a term that denotes the supply of water to the **aquifer** (q.v.). See also **Recharging.**

Chemical cycle.   A class of **life support system** (q.v.) by which chemical elements essential to life circulate through every level of the biosphere without being depleted. Often classified into *gaseous* and *sedimentary*, according to whether or not they have a gaseous stage. The chemical cycle of chief interest to ecologists are those of hydrogen, oxygen, nitrogen, carbon, phosphorus, and sulfur; the last two are generally classified as sedimentary.

Climax community.   The final state in **ecological succession** (q.v.), a biotic community with the highest degree of complexity available under prevailing conditions and with the capacity to reproduce itself.

Climax ecology.   The ecological study of climax associations or communities.

Commons.   Natural resources, especially land, reserved for the common use. Many experts in environmental law also treat rivers, lakes, oceans, and the atmo-sphere as commons, and believe that appropriation of the commons for private use is illegitimate.

Condemnation.   The legal process by which a government appropriates private property for public use. See also **Eminent domain.**

Consumers.   Organisms that live off other organisms. They are generally divided into *primary consumers* (herbivores) and *secondary consumers* (carnivores). See also **Decomposers** and **Producers.**

Contiguous United States.   The portion of the United States that is all contained within the same unbroken boundary, i.e., the United States excluding Hawaii, Alaska, and the outlying territories.

Council on Environmental Quality.   See **E.P.A.** and **N.E.P.A.**

Critical zone.   In the terminology of resource use, the range below which a decrease in the availability of a flow resource cannot be reversed. See also **Flow resource** and **Stock resource.**

Crude rate.   In demography, the rate per 1,000 of the general population per year, with no allowance made for age, sex, and other major demographic variables. See also **Gross reproduction rate** and **Net reproduction rate.**

DDT.   A chlorinated hydrocarbon, the most persistent of the biocides in general use (see essay 9.1). Although now largely banned in this country, it is still exported in large quantities.

Decomposers.   Organisms that assist in the chemical decomposition of dead plants and animals, thus making possible the various **chemical cycles** (q.v.). See also **Saprophytes.**

DNA.   Deoxyribonucleic acid, the molecule in the shape of a double helix that enables life to reproduce itself. See also **RNA.**

D.W.S.   Division of Wildlife Services, part of the Bureau of Sport Fisheries and Wildlife of the U.S. Department of the Interior. The D.W.S. used to be known as the Predator and Rodent Control Branch, which more accurately described its function. As of 1972–73, about 86 percent of the D.W.S.'s budget was earmarked for so-called animal damage control (for which see essay 15.1).

Ecological extinction.   When a species' numbers shrink to a point at which the ecosystem of which it forms part would be virtually unaffected by its total disappearance, it is said to be ecologically (as opposed to biologically) extinct. See also **Regional extinction.**

Ecological succession.   The tendency of less complex biotic communities to be succeeded by more complex ones. See also **Climax community** and **Sere.**

Ecology.   The science that deals with the reaction of plants and animals to their immediate environment and with their place in that environment. See also **Food chain, Human ecology,** and **Niche.**

Ecosphere.   A term coined in order to extend the idea of an ecosystem to the earth and all its support systems. Also used as a synonym for **biosphere** (q.v.). See also **Ecosystem.**

Ecosystem.   A self-sustaining and self-regulating community of organisms considered in relationship not only with each other but with their inorganic environment. See also **Habitat.**

Ecumene.   In geography, the part of the earth's surface suited to human habitation; also used as the part actually inhabited (nowadays, increasingly the same thing). See also **Restrictive environment.**

Eminent domain. The right of a government to declare that any land under its jurisdiction must be appropriated for the public use. Under U.S. law this right is generally held to reside in the state. See also **Condemnation.**

Energy. The capacity to do work. For the many forms of energy, see essay 3.1.

Energy flow. In ecology, the one-way flow of energy through an eco-system; more specifically, the way in which energy is converted and expended at each **trophic level** (q.v.).

Environment. The most abused word in the ecological dictionary. Anything that may affect an organism in any way is part of its environment. See also **Habitat.**

E.P.A. Environmental Protection Agency, the agency of the federal government now (1972) responsible for federal efforts in the control of air and water pollution, radiation and pesticide hazards, ecological research, and solid wastes disposal. It is subject to the directives of the Council on Environmental Quality, which are incorporated in the president's annual Message on the Environment. See also **N.E.P.A.**

External costs. When some part of the cost of an economic activity is borne by persons or organizations outside the economic unit or units engaged in that activity, it is known as an external cost. For instance, the cost of air pollution is to a great extent an external cost of automobile manufacture. External costs are also known as *negative externalities,* as opposed to *positive externalities,* which are external benefits.

F.A.O. The Food and Agriculture Organization, an agency of the United Nations that handles a larger number of U.N. technical assistance programs than any other. The F.A.O. has been criticized for neglecting social reforms in favor of technological ones that mainly benefit established commercial interests. This is probably just another way of saying that one should not expect too much of U.N. agencies.

Fee simple. In law, ownership of real estate without any restriction on who may inherit it or (within legal limits) on what use may be made of it. Generally contrasted with *fee tail,* which implies restriction in one or both of these categories.

Flow resource. A resource the future supply of which need not diminish because of present use, though the supply may fluctuate both in the present and in the future. Flow resources are often classified according to whether or not they can be increased or decreased by human intervention. See also **Stock resource.**

Food chain. The structure of an ecosystem depicted in terms of where each species gets its food; in general, the dependence of higher organisms on the nutrients provided by lower ones. Also called *food web* (a more accurate term in most cases). See also **Energy flow.**

General fertility rate. The number of births per 1,000 women of child-bearing age. See also **Total fertility.**

GNP. Gross national product, the nation's total output of goods and services in dollar terms. According to the *Statistical Abstract of the United States,* the goods and services included are largely those bought for final use in the market economy—except for illegal transactions. The GNP, then, excludes at least one major U.S. industry.

Gross reproduction rate. The number of girl babies that will ever be be born to all the women of childbearing age in a given population who are alive in a given year. Usually expressed per thousand women. This rate is calculated on the assumption that birth rates for each age group will not change and that none of the women will die before reaching menopause. See also **Net reproduction rate** and **Total fertility.**

Groundwater table. The highest level reached by the **groundwater** in a given area. See also **Aquifer.**

Habitat. The immediate natural environment of an organism or group of organisms. Sometimes used as a synonym for environment, in this book habitat denotes a subdivision of a *biome,* or major complex of ecosystems such as the tropical rain forest. See also **Niche.**

Heterotroph. Organisms that cannot produce their own food but live on other organisms, including **autotrophs** (q.v.). See also **Consumers.**

Human ecology. A branch of science that does not yet exist but that will have to be developed very soon if the human species is to survive.

Hydrologic cycle. The movement of water from the atmosphere to the earth and oceans, and back again. See also **Aquifer** and **Groundwater table.**

Hydroponics. The art and science of growing plants in a nutrient solution instead of soil. Already in commercial use for some of the more profitable and easily managed types of cash crop (e.g., tomatoes), hydroponics is not likely to have much effect on the world food situation for the time being because it requires a high level of investment and technological sophistication.

Hydrosphere. The parts of the earth's surface that are more or less permanently covered by water.

Internal costs. The part of the cost of an economic activity that is borne by the economic unit or units engaging in it. In U.S. society, this type of cost is generally kept as low as possible, as a result of which textbooks of this kind become necessary. See also **External costs.**

Inversion. In meteorology, the phenomenon that occurs when the layer of air nearest the earth's surface is cooler than the layer above, so that the pollutants in the lower layer are trapped there. Topographical features such as basins and river valleys intensify this phenomenon, which is also known as *temperature inversion.*

I.R.R.I. The International Rice Research Institute, located in the Philippines. It was the I.R.R.I. that developed IR-8, the so-called miracle rice (for which see essay 5.1).

kcal. Kilocalorie, the so-called large calorie, is here synonymous with **calorie** (q.v.). A small calorie is a unit denoting the amount of heat required to raise one gram of water one degree centigrade; it is used mainly in physics.

kg. Kilogram. One kilogram is equivalent to 2.205 pounds; it consists of 1,000 grams and 1,000,000 miligrams. See also **mg.**

Kwashiorkor. A disease caused by protein deficiency. The word, of

West African origin, denotes what happens to a baby when it is taken off mother's milk and put on a diet of starchy cereals.

kwh. Kilowatt hour. One kilowatt hour is equivalent to 3,412 **BTU** (q.v.).

Land franchise. Legal term denoting the authority that a person or corporation has over a piece of land. See also **Fee simple.**

Life support systems. Collective term for the various natural cycles, including **chemical cycles** (q.v.), that are essential to life. See also **Hydrologic cycle.**

Life table. A statistical table, based on a population's mortality rates, that is designed for the computation and display of life expectancy, usually by age and sex.

Limiting factor. In biology, any factor that prevents a species from realizing its full reproductive potential.

Lithosphere. The part of the earth consisting of rocks and metals, i.e., from the earth's crust (except for the soil, sometimes known as the *edaphosphere*) all the way to its core.

Luteolytic. Term applied to contraceptive chemical compounds that break up the *corpus luteum,* without which the fertilized ovum cannot grow. The compounds are still in the experimental stage.

Mediterranean pattern of settlement. In land use, locations of population centers predominantly on the marine fringes. Some geographers apply it to the growing pattern of fringe concentration in the United States and Canada.

Metric ton. One thousand kilograms, equivalent to 2,205 pounds (lb). Not to be confused with a *short-ton,* which is 2,000 pounds.

mg. Milligram (equivalent to .0154 of a grain); not to be confused with μg, for *microgram* (one-thousandth of a milligram).

N.E.P.A. The National Environmental Policy Act of 1969. The declared purposes of the act are: "To declare a national policy which will encourage productive and enjoyable harmony between man and his environment; to promote efforts which will prevent or eliminate damage to the environment and biosphere and stimulate the health and welfare of man; to enrich the understanding of the ecological systems and natural resources important to the Nation; and to establish a Council on Environmental Quality." The Environmental Protection Agency (E.P.A.) was created separately in 1970, by executive order of the president. See also **E.P.A.**

Net reproduction rate. The number of girl babies that will ever be born to all the women of childbearing age in a given population who are alive in a given year, provided that current life table mortality rates continue to apply until the last of the women has died. Usually expressed per thousand women. This rate is calculated on the assumption that birth rates for each age group will not change. See also **Gross reproduction rate, Life table,** and **Total fertility.**

Niche. The total role played by a species in an ecosystem, in relation to both the biotic and the abiotic environment. See also **Habitat.**

P.A.T.C.O. The Professional Air Traffic Controllers' Organization. Ask them if you want to know how bad air safety conditions are at our major airports.

PCBs. Polychlorinated biphenyls, chemical compounds containing chlorine, hydrogen, and carbon that have a wide variety of industrial uses, especially as plasticizers and adhesives. They are toxic, highly persistent, have an affinity for fatty tissue, and are not soluble in water. Organisms polluted by DDT usually contain PCBs as well.

PGA.   Phosphoglyceric acid, a compound formed in the course of photosynthesis from carbon dioxide and ribulose diphosphate; it may react to form amino acids, the constituent molecules of **protein** (q.v.). See also **ATP** and **Photosynthesis.**

Photosynthesis.   The process by which green plants are able to synthesize carbohydrates from carbon dioxide and water using energy from solar radiation. See also **ATP, Autotrophs, PGA,** and **Producers.**

Phytoplankton.   Minute floating plant organisms found in rivers, lakes, and oceans.

Pollution.   Wastes that, because of their abundance, their chemical composition, or both, cannot be disposed of by nature's own recycling mechanisms. Such wastes may be either treated or untreated and the problems they cause may be connected with either their accumulation (as with organic agricultural wastes) or their dispersion (as with DDT). In general, 60 tons of mud on the front lawn is less of a pollution problem than 6 ppm of DDT in one's gefilte fish, but it is hard to persuade the average homeowner of this. See also **Biodegradable.**

ppm.   Parts per million, a common measure of the occurrence of trace substances.

Producers.   An organism capable of **photosynthesis** (q.v.). Producers not only store energy in the form of food but also emit oxygen. See also **Autotrophs.**

Proteins.   A class of complex organic compounds, made up from amino acids, that are present in one form or another in all living things. In autotrophs, they are synthesized from inorganic substances; heterotrophs synthesize them from amino acids found in autotrophs or other heterotrophs. Protein deficiency is a common form of human malnutrition in the world's poorer countries. See also **DNA, Kwashiorkor, RNA.**

Radioactive tracers.   Radioistopes incorporated in some biologically active substance and then administered to an organism in such a manner that its movement can be followed by a scaler or other radiation-detecting instrument. See also **Radioisotope.**

Radioisotope.   A radioactive isotope. Atoms of the same element with different atomic weights are known as isotopes; thus U-235 and U-238 are both isotopes of uranium. When made radioactive, they can be used for a great variety of scientific purposes, from *radiation ecology* to medical diagnosis and therapy (especially cancer therapy).

Recharging.   In water management, the artificial replenishment of underground fresh water supplies, often undertaken to save the **aquifer** (q.v.) from contamination by salt water.

Regional extinction.   The disappearance of a species from a region; usually the prelude to **ecological extinction** (q.v.).

Restrictive environments.   In geography, lands that do not produce food.

RNA.   Ribonucleic acid, one of two classes of nucleic acids, the other being **DNA** (q.v.). The function of RNA seems to be to transmit the so-called genetic code, i.e., provide the structural factor in protein synthesis.

Runoff.   Precipitation that flows off the land into the **hydrosphere** (q.v.). either via the land surface or (as *groundwater runoff*) via the **aquifer** (q.v.).

Saprophytes.   Plants that live on decomposing organic matter. See also **Decomposers.**

S.C.A.G.   Southern California Area Government, a southerly version of **A.B.A.G.** (q.v.).

Scolytid.   An insect of the genus *Scolytus,* one of the ~~Xylophagi~~ or wood-eating insects that inspire the U.S. Forest Service and others to fling vast quantities of biocides from airplanes when a more sensible course would be to study the insect's habits. An even more sensible course would be to encourage birds, instead of poisoning them.

Secondary succession.   The type of **ecological succession** (q.v.) that takes place in a habitat that has already lost its original vegetation.

Sere.   A stage in **ecological succession** (q.v.).

Short ton.   Two thousand pounds (lb).

SST.   Supersonic transport, the name given to a faster-than-sound passenger plane for which the U.S. Senate, in a fit of sanity, refused to vote any funds in July, 1970.

Sterile-male technique.   A technique, used in the biological control of insect populations, by which large quantities of insects are sterilized through radiation and then set free to mate with unsterilized insects, hopefully causing their extinction. Despite the technique's name, both male and female insects are sterilized, since it is impractical to sort them by sex.

Stock resource.   A resource of which there is only a limited supply.

Systems analysis.   The analysis of any complex phenomenon in terms of the relations between the *subsystems* that form its constituent parts. The general idea is to predict the behavior of the whole from that of its parts rather than vice versa.

TACV.   Tracked air-cushion vehicle, a type of *hovercraft,* i.e., a vehicle that moves over sea or land supported on a cushion of air emitted by its own blowers. The tracked variety would move only along its own guideway. All air-cushion vehicles are still in the experimental stage, though one has been operated commercially—with varying success—across the English Channel.

Territoriality.   The tendency of some animal species to mark out and defend some portion of their habitat as their "own". Territoriality is not a universal instinct, as some popular sociologists claim, nor does it take the same form or serve the same function in the species that do display it. Still less does it resemble the human mania for owning property; many different species can coexist on the same piece of land provided each has a **niche** (q.v.).

Tertiary treatment.   In sewage treatment, additional filtration and chlorination of the liquid obtained by secondary treatment. A tertiary treatment plant (of which there are very few in the United States) is capable of making the water thus recycled fit for drinking—fitter, indeed, than it was to start with. Unfortunately, the U.S. public will not yet buy the idea of drinking artificially recycled water despite the fact that all water on earth is recycled one way or another (see **Hydrologic cycle**).

Total fertility. The number of babies, both girls and boys, that will ever be born to all the women of childbearing age in a given population who are alive in a given year. Usually expressed per thousand women. This rate is calculated on the same assumptions as the **gross reproduction rate** (q.v.).

Trophic level. The state in an ecosystem's **food chain** (q.v.) to which a class of organisms belong. Thus **producers** and **consumers** (qqv.) exist at different trophic levels. The term can also be applied to differences within major groups, e.g., between herbivores and carnivores, which are both consumers.

U.N.E.S.C.O. United Nations Educational, Scientific and Cultural Organization, a force for conservation ever since it was founded, and sponsor of much environmental research. You can find out what it and other branches of the United Nations do for the environment by writing for the U.N. pamphlet *The Human Environment: New Challenge for the United Nations* (New York, February 1971).

U.S.D.A. U.S. Department of Agriculture, a branch of the federal government maintained at vast expense by U.S. taxpayers largely for the benefit of rich agricultural corporations, or *agribusinesses.* It also includes the U.S. Forest Service, which is tough on people who like forests.

Usufruct. In law, the right to enjoy the use of property while maintaining it in good condition. The term, originally a Roman one, is beloved of modern conservationists because they see in it a pattern for man's use of the earth: by proper cultivation, not by using up.

Wet scrubber. A device that brings water into contact with an air-polluting gas stream in such a manner as to trap the particulates it carries and so prevent them from escaping into the atmosphere.

Zoning. In law, restriction by a municipality of the type of use (e.g., residential or commercial) to which a particular piece of land within its jurisdiction may be put. Zoning was originally an extension of police powers, designed to regulate public nuisances.

INDEX